UNDERSTANDING SOUTH CHINA SEA GEOPOLITICS

UNDERSTANDING SOUTH CHINA SEA GEOPOLITICS

Subhadeep Bhattacharya

MAULANA ABUL KALAM AZAD INSTITUTE OF ASIAN STUDIES
KOLKATA

PENTAGON PRESS

Understanding South China Sea Geopolitics

Subhadeep Bhattacharya

ISBN 978-81-8274-941-2

First Published in 2017

Published by
PENTAGON PRESS
206, Peacock Lane, Shahpur Jat
New Delhi-110049
Phones: 011-64706243, 26491568
Telefax: 011-26490600
email: rajan@pentagonpress.in
website: www.pentagonpress.in

Printed at Aegean Offset Printers, Greater Noida, U.P.

Contents

Acknowledgements

During the three long years of the research on this project at Maulana Abul Kalam Azad Institute of Asian Studies (MAKAIAS) I have received the support and guidance of numerous individuals. I am indebted to each of them but can thank only a few by name.

I am indebted to the Director of MAKAIAS Dr. Sreeradha Dutta for her continuous and valuable support throughout the project tenure. I am especially grateful to her for helping me interact with eminent scholars, both national and international, whom I got the scope to meet at seminars, both at the Institute and in other parts of the country where the Director was kind enough to send me to participate. I also extend my gratitude to her for approving my international field trips that I undertook during the project tenure which undoubtedly had been of immense help to my research.

I also take the opportunity to extend my gratitude to the professors of University of Calcutta who helped me with their valuable suggestions. I extend my thanks to Dr. Hari S. Vasudevan and Dr. Kingshuk Chatterjee who have been very kind to deliver pertinent comments and suggestions regarding my research and help me clear queries which had occurred to me regarding issues related to the research.

I also extend my thanks to the Vietnam Institute of Social Sciences (VASS), Hanoi, where I got the scope to visit as part of the project research. The eminent scholars whom I met at Institute were tremendously helpful in enlightening my knowledge. And I specially wish to thankfully remember Dr. Lee Hang Nga who had been my host and guide during my stay at Hanoi.

I also extend my thanks to the scholars, professors and the librarians of Institute of South East Asian Studies (ISEAS), Singapore, Rajaratnam

School of International Studies and National University of Singapore who were of immense help to me.

I take the scope to extend my heartiest thanks to the librarians of MAKAIAS who have been very cooperative in helping me consult the valuable collections of the library. I take the opportunity to thank Mr. Sandip Sarkar (librarian) who got me the books time to time which I requested him to collect for me which were of immense help for my research. I also thank Tarak da, Godhuli di, Jayanta da and Bapi for their kind assistance with the library affairs. Here I like to mention the invaluable Vivekanada Mukherjee Collection in possession of the library. This is the collection of rare books related to international relations which are of immense help to anyone working on international relations. This collection has been of massive help to me and I sincerely extend my thanks to the librarians of MAKAIAS for giving me the scope to consult them.

I must also extend my gratitude to my colleagues of MAKAIAS who also had been of valuable help. I thank the fellows of the Institute, Dr. Anita Sengupta, Dr. Suchandana Chatterjee, Ms. Priya Singh, Dr. Arpita Basu Roy and Dr. Sayantani Sen Majumdar, to name a few, who had been very helpful in guiding me in my project format.

I thank Sushanto da, Dhiman da, Amarnath da and Debasish da who were very helpful in conducting my successful field trips. I also thank Ashish da, Manoj da, Pradyut da and also Priyanka di for their kind cooperation in helping me abide by the Institute's rules and regulations. I also extend thanks to Tanmoy (Das) who had been a valuable and consistent help in managing my computer related hiccups which occurred at times.

I also take the chance to extend my thanks to my friends Anwesha Ghosh, Rajat Kanti Sur Sagnik Roy Choudhury and Saikat Ray for their support and encouragement.

Last but not the least I extend my gratitude to Maulana Abul Kalam Azad Institute of Asian Studies for giving me the opportunity to do the research on a topic which has also intrigued me.

Subhadeep Bhattacharya

Introduction

Geopolitics are played by the major powers where the smaller states are pawns in the game. However, the current South China Sea dispute is making the smaller states of the region major factors in the shaping of the local geopolitics of the current century while the big players, China and USA, are emerging as the main directors of the game. The sovereignty dispute over the territorial jurisdiction of the South China Sea and its geographical features is fast becoming the latest source of geopolitical conflict in East Asia. Whether such conflict will trigger war is still questionable but many suggest that it has such potentials. The Economist opines, "armed conflict in the South China Sea is a long way from being inevitable. But it is far from unthinkable".[1] China and other rapidly developing economies of Southeast Asia along with their complicated relations with China, the intriguing and challenging role of ASEAN and the growing engagement of the extra regional powers, especially USA, in the evolving maritime affairs of South China Sea are shaping the twenty first century geopolitics of East Asia. At this point of time it is necessary to analyze the geopolitics of the South China Sea in order to know why the apparently local affairs of Southeast Asia involving the littoral states of the Sea are impacting, or rather directing, the larger East Asian international relations concerning the extra regional powers as major contributors in the regional geopolitics. Today the South China Sea territorial sovereignty row is not limited to mere disagreement over who owns how much possession in the maritime zone of Southeast Asia, but is taking the shape of a major and serious issue which transcends the boundary of intra-regional territorial spat. The dispute has already become the fodder for military preparedness of the disputants and also a pretext for the extra regional powers to engage further in the geopolitics evolving around the dispute. And in this context it is necessary to study this current geopolitics of South China Sea with reference to its history which narrates the story of eternal activities of the extra-regional powers in shaping the international relations of the South China Sea region. The reference is important since "*....the present cannot be understood and the future cannot be envisaged without recognition of what happened in the past.*"[2]

The South China Sea has always been the zone of activities of the powers outside its 'territory' marking its economic as well as geostrategic significance where the local players have been in supporting role. South China Sea geopolitics is marked by its disputes since the region being the bridge between the Indian Ocean and the Pacific Ocean world, as the sole maritime communication channel, has been the zone of interests (and conflicts) of the world players and therefore any development in the waters of South China Sea is sure to send ripples all over. Looking back to the history of its commercial and geopolitical vibrancy, we find the eternal role of the big powers in the South China Sea region, who sometimes used the locals as tools of their strategic games while sometimes mingled with them as 'security guarantee' intertwining their larger strategic goals with the local fear factors.

The twenty-first century Asia is looking to the sea to seek her destiny. This is all the more evident in East Asia since, to quote Robert Kaplan, "Europe is a landscape; East Asia is a seascape."[3] The life of East Asia lies in her vast maritime world. And it is this East Asia which has been the centre of glamorous economic prosperity since the second half of the last century. The economic boom of East Asia was seen as the sign of an emerging vibrant Asia with huge potentiality to replace the dominant European world system directed from both sides of the Atlantic for the last five hundred years. As Kishore Mahbubani argues, "...we have reached the end of the era of Western domination.....we will see an enormous renaissance of Asian societies."[4] There is strong opinion that the twenty-first century will be the century of Asia and in this shift of seat of power from the West to the East, Eastern Asia, including Southeast Asia, is going to play a major role. From the time of the rise four Asian Tigers-South Korea, Taiwan, Hong Kong and Singapore- in the second half of the twentieth century, East Asia gradually emerged as the economic powerhouse of the new century, especially with the emergence of China in the post Mao era. Today China is the largest economy of Asia and second in the world, after USA. This rise of China is all the more important in the historical context of Asia which is seen as the 'revival' of the old Asian economic order of the pre-colonial as well as colonial period where

China was the prime trading destination of the East Asia bound traders, Asians and outsiders. The introduction of the *One Belt One Road* (OBOR) project by the Chinese government also confirms this where it attempts to revive the old trading network, the Silk Road, with which ancient China maintained her commercial and other relations with the world outside. By this project China wants to bind Europe and Central Asia by land while East and Southeast Asia and beyond by sea. The Maritime Silk Route project proposes to bind Southeast Asia and the Indian Ocean world into a single zone of activity involving all the major littoral states of the two regions. And in this way the maritime Southeast Asia, or the South China Sea region, is coming up as a vital tool of the twenty-first century Asian economic success story, ensuring the further shift of the global power to the East. But the geo-economics of South China Sea is currently overtaken by the geopolitics, the eternal aspect of the international relations of this maritime region.

Defining geopolitics

Geography has always been the determinant of the power relations among its participants. Whether the state is to become a formidable land or sea power depends on its geographical location, with the condition of its capacity to utilize its gifted position. If Britain rose to the zenith of her naval prowess in the colonial period it was because she well utilized the sea around her overcoming the handicap of her island-location and if USSR failed to be major naval power even being a super power it was because of the lack of any naval culture in the Russian history. The geography decides the history of the state and thereby the character of its international political activity. Geopolitics is thus 'the relation of international political power to geographical setting'.[5] In the state-centric international relations study of the colonial period, up to the first half of the twentieth century, the geography played vital role in framing the role of the state beyond its territory. Friedrich Ratzel (1844-1904), who considered the state as 'a fragment of humanity on a piece of soil', viewed the state through the prism of organic theory in which the state, like living organism, will expand since growth of state is represented by its expansion. Ratzel emphasized on the space as state cannot live without territory or space. Ratzel is remembered for the development of political geography.[6] The growing importance of geography as part of the international politics was evident from the *Heartland theory* of Halford Mackinder (which was published in 1904) where Mackinder divided the world into islands where there is the Eurasian Heartland which is inaccessible by the sea power and therefore he argued that if the Heartland could be united into a single great political authority, it could dominate the World Island, and thereby the whole world.[7] Later Swedish political thinker Rudolf J. Kjellen argued that the state should seek to preserve the conditions for healthy living and space for growth.[8] Thus territorial expansion, hunting for *space,* was the main emphasis of the geopolitical study of the colonial period. The territorial expansion of the Axis powers in Asia and Europe can be viewed in this context. During this time the 'state organism' was growing and expanding in shape and size. When European landmass was swallowed by the mighty German forces, Japan was expanding over East Asia, both on land and in sea. She could create the vast 'East Asian Co-prosperity Sphere' throughout Northeast and Southeast Asia only after enhancing her naval strength.

The sea has had played important role behind the rise of world powers. The domination of the maritime world made the British a global player till the first half of the last century followed by the Americans. And it is because they achieved excellence in maritime prowess they could rule the Asian waters and the territories adjacent to them. This is best evident in East Asia. East Asia, as mentioned earlier, is a seascape according to Robert Kaplan. Thus the Europeans could establish their domination in the region only after achieving maritime as well as naval prowess. Prior to them, the East Asian waters were ruled by the Asians. The Chinese admiral Zheng He conducted expeditions to the Indian Ocean, up to the shores of Africa, in the early fifteenth century. This he could do with the patronage of the Ming Dynasty who later scrapped any further funding in naval empowerment in order to deal with the continental threat emanating from the north. Even a century prior to this the Hindu rulers of India forbade the sailing to the sea in order to halt the outflow of the human capital. And it was at this point of time when Europe looked seaward, 'as Asia renounced the sea.'[9] Now in the twenty-first century the Asian maritime world is again coming up as the playground of the Asians when the ancient powers like India and China are attempting to revive their naval strength. The case of China is even serious in the context of East Asia. The growing emphasis on the naval power among the East Asian countries, to whom the maritime world is the lifeline, is well depicted by Paul Kennedy making a comparative study of the changing assumption about the power of the sea by Asia and Europe. In his article *The rise and fall of navies* he argues that when naval budget is dwindling in European countries, East Asian countries, from

South Korea in the north to Vietnam in the south, are emphasizing on achieving naval strength.[10] There are two reasons working behind this attitude of the fast growing economies of East Asia. One is undoubtedly the economic security since these countries are heavily dependent on sea lanes of communication of the neighbouring maritime areas (which also contain natural resources underneath which are beneficial for their energy requirement) for their economic survival. The other reason is geopolitical. East Asia is marred with territorial tension. The countries do not consider their territorial maps complete since many portions 'are left out', in possession of the neighbours. Moreover the gradual economic growth of these countries, when in one hand are making them more dependent on the seas and their geographical features, is also helping them to invest in their navy to enhance their assertive claims in the disputed areas. This is making the case all the more complicated. Moreover the dependence of the extra regional powers on the maritime world of East Asia for both economic as well as strategic reasons are dragging them into the 'local affairs', as reason of delight for some while displeasure of others. In this way the maritime world of East Asia is fast becoming a major geopolitical affair of the twenty-first century Asia, where the global power is shifting. And here the South China Sea maritime zone is coming up as a crucial factor. This is so because China, with territorial claims in this maritime zone, is emerging as a powerful naval strength which is ruffling the feathers of the weaker counter-claimant littoral states of the South China Sea region who are not only focusing on their own naval build up as counter measures, but are also involving the extra regional powers to counter the Chinese 'menace'. And in this way the consistency is maintained in the geopolitics of South China Sea region.

South China Sea region has had experienced the predominance of the extra regional powers since the early colonial period when the Portuguese and the Dutch arrived on the scene followed by the *Pax Britannica* and then the Americans during the Vietnam War.[11] Throughout the long colonial and the post colonial Cold War period the activities of the extra regional powers while shaped the geopolitics of the region, they also established the integrity of the region with the global geopolitics. Prior to the advent of the colonial era however, the local powers were the rulers of the South China Sea.

Chapter 1 thus discusses the situation in the South China Sea region before and after the coming of the Europeans. It attempts to depict a picture of South China Sea world in pre-colonial as well as early colonial days. It is seen that the region was *the* important hub of commercial activities of the East Asian world involving the local traders before the coming of the European traders and the entire South China Sea region became a vibrant centre of economic as well as political activities later with the beginning of the European colonial period. The trade in the South China Sea brought Southeast Asia at the centre of the East Asian commercial zone in the pre-colonial period and also boosted the economy of its littoral states. There is no doubt that the major maritime powers of pre-colonial Southeast Asia, *Funan, Champa* and *Sri Vijaya,* were the creations of the South China Sea trade who prospered on it. These maritime kingdoms acted as the economic centres in the east-west trade between the Indian and the Pacific Ocean region. So in a way they were the nerve centres of the *ancient Indo-Pacific or trans-Pacific commercial network*. And in this network China was the major trading destination. It is seen that the traders' ships from the Indian Ocean region were China-bound. On the other hand China was equally dependent on the sea lines of the south to reach out to the world beyond her vicinity. The *Nanhai* trade was thus so important for the Chinese dynasties. The importance of the South China Sea region increased further with the coming of the Europeans who founded the colonial network throughout the region. In this way the South and East Asian trading highways were now dominated by the extra regional powers where the South China Sea played a vital role as the bridge between the Indian and the Pacific world. The commercial activities in the South China Sea region therefore shaped the history of the Southeast Asian maritime region where both the regional as well as the extra regional powers took part and the sea route was never dominated by any single power until the mid twentieth century with the rise of Japan.

This is to be noted here that the historical aspect of the South China Sea trade certainly deserves a separate and detailed discussion which is not done here. The reference to the pre-colonial and early colonial history of the South China Sea here can be treated as an introduction to the understanding of the character of the South China Sea maritime geopolitics which is made in order to put the issue of the economic and geopolitical vibrancy of the maritime zone in the historical context in order to understand the significance of its current affairs.

Chapter 2, while initially focusing on the colonial root of the current territorial disputes eventually takes up the geostrategic importance of the South China Sea region. As discussed in the chapter, the extra regional power France was the main actor in the South China Sea affairs as the colonial master of Indochina, especially Vietnam, from the late nineteenth century. Although the French did not officially claim the Spratly and the Paracels before the 1930s, they were active in the islands from the late nineteenth century and it was their activities in the region which made the Chinese gradually assertive in the South China Sea the way the US activities today are making the Chinese insecure in the region. It also mentions Japan's significance in the regional geopolitical affairs who started appearing in the scene by the beginning of the twentieth century. It was well understood during the World War II when Japan seized entire East Asia blocking the main sea lane of communication passing through the South China Sea occupying the littoral colonies of the French, Dutch and the English. In this way Japan not only cut the communication link between the Indian Ocean and the Pacific Ocean world (which was the first such incident in history when the Asian sea lanes came under the control of a single power) she also delinked the European industrial states from their sources of raw materials available in their respective colonies. The discussion of Japanese occupation of East Asia is significant since it shaped the geopolitics of the entire East Asian region in the context of its sea lanes communication network, especially South China Sea. The Japanese episode is also noteworthy since it established the role of the extra regional powers, mainly USA, permanently in the South China Sea affairs, which was to be prominent further in the subsequent Cold War period.

Chapter 3 thus discusses the shape of the Cold War geopolitics with the rise of two contending powers, US and USSR, in the South China Sea region. It is seen here how the inter-state relations of the region got intertwined with the larger Cold War geopolitics and what role South China Sea played in it. What is noteworthy here is the rising significance of the naval policies with emphasis on naval strength of the parties involved in the Cold War affairs of Southeast Asia. The importance of the South China Sea lane of communication, especially for the outsiders which was realized during the Japanese occupation, increased further with the Soviet Navy sailing in the region. Another important aspect of the Cold War geopolitics of the South China Sea was the gradual increase in the Chinese role in the affairs, but only as part of the larger Sino-Soviet duel. The chapter analyzes how the extra regional power politics shaped the geopolitics of the South China Sea region while the local inter-state tensions also moulded themselves into the overall Cold War geopolitics.

However what is noteworthy about the Cold War geopolitics of the South China Sea region was that it was although directed by the larger geopolitics of the big powers but at the same time established the integrity of the extra regional affairs with the local affairs of the region. This is the reminiscent of the concluding phase of the colonial period when the Allies-Axis duel of Europe got extended to the Asian waters when Japan, a partner of the Axis group, undertook territorial expansion mission. The Soviet-US duel, as the chapter shows, was a similar situation in maritime Southeast Asia, or the South China Sea region to be precise, where the larger Sino-Soviet-America strategic calculation shaped the geopolitics of the region where the local players also played their part. Such a situation continued until the collapse of the Soviet Union and the beginning of the post Cold War era in the 1990s. Another important aspect of the Cold War geopolitics of South China Sea was the emergence of communist China, ostracized for long, as a major factor. It also discusses how the geopolitics of the Sea impacted the naval policies of its littorals.

Chapter 4 picks up the issue of the post Cold War geopolitics of South China Sea reflecting in the changing geopolitical set up after the demise of Soviet Union. This was a significant development since inter-state relations of the region which so far remained latent under the Cold War feud started influencing the South China Sea geopolitics of the post Cold War period. And the core to this change was the rise of China, a dissatisfied power which now was preparing to regain her 'rightful place' in the world. On the other hand the US withdrawal from the South China Sea region following the withdrawal of the Soviet bases also catered scope to the Chinese to get active in the region. China's economic missions also impacted her South China Sea policy. On the other hand the weak contenders of China attempted to thwart 'Chinese aggression' through balancing act involving extra regional powers like US through ASEAN which catered the scope to the Association to act as the arbiter raising its significance in the Southeast Asian geopolitics. However, the continued economic prosperity of China reflecting in her investment in the military kept on sending ripples all around the neighbourhood while the clashes in the disputed water between China and other claimants added to the tension. The South China Sea region entered the new millennium with these two simultaneous developments.

Chapter 5 discusses the emerging twenty-first century geopolitics of the South China Sea in the context of emerging Cold War between China and the US. The East Asian maritime world is the neighbourhood of

China, which she considers as her zone of influence where the Americans are intruding. Moreover, China's perceived 'incomplete territorial map' includes portions of this maritime zone with Taiwan and the geographical features in the East and South China Seas which are yet to be annexed. Moreover, the region is becoming important for China both for economic and strategic reasons. Meanwhile, the other claimants of the South China Sea disputes are also spending on their military, especially navy, following their economic growth, as mark of preparations to encounter any adverse situation in future. The Stockholm International Peace Research Institute (SIPRI) has informed that military spending in Asia and Oceania has grown 5.4% in 2015 under Chinese influence contributing substantial increase in defence spending by Indonesia, the Philippines and Vietnam.[12] In this situation the role of the extra regional powers is becoming important who also have vested interests in ensuring the unhindered navigation in the South China Sea region. Besides, these 'outsiders' are essential for the small China-wary states of the region. And in this complicated situation, the ASEAN is playing vital role in maintaining balance in the emerging geopolitics of South China Sea, however it does not speak in one voice over the alleged Chinese expansionism since the sovereignty dispute of the South China Sea does not impact all the member countries of the Association equally which is diminishing the confidence of the main disputants on the Association as a reliable factor and thus forcing them to look elsewhere, especially the extra regional powers like US. In this way the Cold War situation is again created where the role of the extra regional powers are becoming important. However this time the small and medium powers of Asia are also active in the South China Sea affairs since they have their economic gains attached with the region. One such country is India.

Chapter 6 analyzes the growing role of India in the South China Sea region as part of her Act East Policy which is both economic as well as strategic in character. India is not a South China Sea littoral and has no territorial claims in the region but the stability and freedom of navigation are the two important factors which India emphasizes in South China Sea region. Southeast Asia is important from the strategic view point, apart from her economic significance to India. India shares both land and maritime border with the region. The Nicobar Islands of the Andaman and Nicobar archipelago are few nautical miles away from Indonesian island of Sumatra. Moreover, these islands are most strategically situated at the gate of the Malacca Straits, gateway to South China Sea and beyond. As India's trade relations with the east grew, this maritime region gained strategic significance for India. However from the strategic and geopolitical viewpoint China is a major factor in India's East Asia policy which is becoming all the more important in the twenty-first century as India entangles herself further in the regional affairs there in collaboration with other China-wary countries of the region, especially in the South China Sea region. India is fast engaging with the South China Sea littorals, especially Vietnam, to handle the growing influence of China in the region. South China Sea is fast becoming an integral part of India's Act East Policy which is a 'proactive' stance of India's East Asia/Asia Pacific policy.

Chapter 7 concludes that South China Sea geopolitics has been an integral part of East Asian geopolitics from the colonial period. And the most important feature of it is the role of the extra regional powers in it. South China Sea has never been dominated by any single power, except by Japan for short duration. However, that occupation when established the benefit of control of the sea lane also exposed its vulnerability to the threat of seizure by any major power, local or outsider, if left unattended. Also the importance of the sea lanes to all the states, both regional as well as extra regional, for their economic prosperity is well known. From the pre-colonial time the region attracted outsiders whose activities shaped the regional politics of South China Sea. When the trade with China shaped the destiny of the local maritime powers in the pre-colonial Southeast Asia, the advent of the Europeans and their introduction of territorial sovereignty concept gave a new shape to the South China Sea international relations in the colonial period which continues even today. The World War II signified the strategic importance of the sea. Throughout the Cold War period, the South China Sea geopolitics was shaped by the super power global rivalry while today the region is subject to local rivalry fast taking global shape. Contrary to the Cold War period when the outsiders' policies shaped the South China Sea geopolitics involving the local players, today the policy of the local players is attracting the outsiders. The disputes over the Sea are now integral to the larger geopolitics of the entire East Asian region where the extra regional powers like US and India intend to play deciding role. Although US has been a great power in the region since the World War II, India's growing involvement in the region commensurate her growing economic and strategic interest of her twenty-first century East Asia policy. On the other hand the growing role of the disputants are featuring fast in the emerging South China Sea geopolitics, firstly, because the claimants of the disputes also have their economic stake in the Sea and its geographical features which are important for their current economic growth and secondly their policies vis-à-vis South China Sea are also influenced by their internal political compulsions, nationalistic zeal based on historical animosity, all of which shape their military modernization programmes adding to the geopolitical tension of the region.

The book narrates the evolution of the geopolitics of South China Sea. Here it attempts to analyze the geopolitical aspect of the South China Sea region in the historical context. It excludes any detailed discussion of the disputes but attempts to examine the South China Sea geopolitics in the larger global geopolitical context with reference to the territorial disputes of the maritime zone. It studies, in one hand, the consistent role of the extra regional powers in shaping the local geopolitics while on the other hand also tries to observe how the geopolitics, once directed by the outsiders, is now operating under the direction of the policies adopted by the local players.

END NOTES

1. Cited in Jean Pierre Lehmann, 'The South China Sea Dispute And China's Peaceful Rise', *Forbes/Asia*, April 10, 2016, http://www.forbes.com/sites/jplehmann/2016/04/10/the-south-china-sea-dispute-and-chinas-peaceful-rise/#3adbf2e148b7 (accessed on 12.04.2016)
2. Ibid
3. Robert D. Kaplan, *Asia's Cauldron: The South China Sea and the End of a Stable Pacific*, New York, Random House, 2014, p.5
4. Kishore Mahbubani, *The New Asian Hemisphere: The Irresistible Shift of Global Power to the East*, New York, Public Affairs, 2008, p.9
5. Mackubin Thomas Owen, 'In Defense of Classical Geopolitics', *Orbis*, Volume 59, Issue 4,2015, p.463
6. Charles B. Hagan, 'Geopolitics', *The Journal of Politics*, Vol.4, No.4, Nov, 1942, p.479
7. Ibid, p.481
8. Ibid, p.482
9. James R. Holmes, Andrew C. Winner, Toshi Yoshihara, *Indian Naval Strategy in the Twenty-first Century*, London and New York, Routledge, 2009, p.1
10. Paul Kennedy, 'The rise and fall of navies', *The New York Times*, April 5, 2007, http://www.nytimes.com/2007/04/05/opinion/05iht-edkennedy.1.5158064.html?_r=0 (accessed on 31.03.2016)
11. Lim Joo Jock, *Geostrategy and the South China Sea Basin: Regional Balance , Maritime Issues, Future Patterns*, Singapore, Singapore University Press, 1979, p.1
12. 'World military spending resumes upward course, says SIPRI', *Stockholm International Peace Research institute*, 5 Apr., 2016, http://www.sipri.org/media/pressreleases/2016/milex-apr-2016 (accessed on 18.4.2016)

1

South China Sea and Her Littorals in History

The history of maritime world has generated interest among the scholars for a long period of time and produced scholarly writings. Sea has been a vital and integral part of human civilization. The unknown world became known through maritime linkages. The voyages unveiled one side of the world to the other. If there was no thirst for explorations of the other side via sea, Americas would have remained obscured for a long time, land route would have been the only option for Europe to reach India and China while Southeast Asian history would have been different. The voyages by sea in the last five centuries have written and re written the history of the world.

Southeast Asia's history is primarily maritime in character. The ancient kingdoms of Southeast Asia flourished on the sea borne trade while this maritime connection gave new shape to the Southeast Asian culture, taking elements from the neighbours, India and China. And the medium of these activities between Indian, Chinese and the Southeast Asians was the South China Sea. The separate identification of Indian Ocean and the South China Sea was not known to the early modern sea farers visiting this region. It is argued that the areas of the Indonesian archipelago falling within the ambit of today's Indian Ocean region were considered as part of South China Sea because to the early modern Asian merchants South China Sea and Indian Ocean formed one single stretch of water body with series of seas, islands and bays extending from east coast of Africa to west coast of Malaya and Sumatra and from the Chinese coast to west coast of Malaya including the Philippines, Taiwan and the Indonesian archipelago.[1] This whole region formed a heart of trade network in South, Southeast and East Asian region.

The maritime history of Southeast Asia cannot be discussed keeping South China Sea out. South China Sea is at the heart of the sea trade of Southeast and East Asia. It has been the bridge between Indian Ocean and the Pacific world. From time immemorial, ships carrying people and goods have traversed this water body. To the north of the Sea lies China, to the south Malaysia and Indonesia, to the east the islands of the Philippines and to the west, Vietnam. The academia world over has extensively discussed the early trade between Southeast Asia, China and India and the later advent of the Europeans in the scene with the same motive. Anthony Reid's *Southeast Asia in the Age of Commerce* (1988-93), Nicholas Tarling's *Cambridge History of Southeast Asia* (Vol. I & II, 1992), D.G.E. Hall's *A History of Southeast Asia* (1981), all discuss the commercial history of Southeast Asia in the pre-colonial and colonial period. Here we find the maritime trade link Southeast Asia had with China and India and see how the maritime Southeast Asia became the commercial hubof the east in the pre-colonial period. However, these books do not single out the South China Sea to study its contribution in the then economic prosperity of its littorals. The Arab merchants reached the shores of China via this Sea. Apart from that Buddhism and Islam also crossed the South China Sea to reach the east. Sugata Bose's *A Hundred Horizons: The Indian Ocean in the Age of Global Empires* (2006) extensively discusses the human interactions in the Indian Ocean region, including trade, does not however, exclusively discuss the South China Sea region. *The Indian Ocean: A History of People and Sea* (1993), written by Kenneth McPherson, also narrates the story of trade in the Indian Ocean region with reference to Southeast Asia but mainly talks about its interaction with the world via Indian Ocean in its west. Satish Chandra and Himanshu Prabha Ray edited *The Sea, Identity and History: From Bay of Bengal to South China Sea* (2013), however, makes an attempt to draw a picture of the human interactions in the South and Southeast Asian maritime world but does not mention the distinct contribution South China Sea holds in shaping the history and identity of East Asia. The history of South China Sea is yet to be written. The chapter here makes a humble attempt to curve out South China Sea and place it in the sphere of much discussed history of trade in Southeast and East Asia on the basis of the theses produced so far on the subject.

The South China Sea has been a connecting body among the zones around it. From the early period of human history, the human progress in one part of the zone has reached and influenced the other part across the Sea. The archaeological sites in Taiwan and northern Philippines belonging to the third and second millennia BC establish the ancient connection between the two islands where red slipped pottery found in the Philippines resembles the Yuanshan culture of eastern Taiwan. The discovery of postholes of two ground level houses in Luzon, shell bracelets and baked clay in Arku Cave in Cagayan valley suggest the human settlements in Luzon from Taiwan in the Neolithic period.[2] The people from Taiwan, it can be supposed, crossed the South China Sea to land in Luzon in northern Philippines at the dawn of human history. There are archaeological evidences that the people on both sides of the Sea did influence each other. The system of jar burial practised in southern Vietnam's Lang Thanh site in Nghia Binh in first century millennium had its traces found in Tabon Caves in the Philippines which confirm cultural linkages across South China Sea.[3] The South China Sea has retained its significance in the field of trade and commerce of Southeast and East Asia. The Sea is the bridge between the east and the west. The sailors from both sides have had traversed the water body in ships hunting for both commodities and markets of the other side.

Although the written sources about early maritime trade in South China are limited and mostly written in Chinese, the archaeological evidences do narrate the early history of trade in the region. These evidences confirm the trade moving beyond South China Sea and reaching up to India and Arabia.[4] The main parties of trades were the Chinese kingdoms and peoples from the west. Since the commodities produced in Southeast Asia did not have any market in India and China, Southeast Asian ports acted as a hub of passing ships and gradually became important ports.[5]

Early Maritime trade in South China Sea

Southeast Asia has traditionally been an important centre in the (eastern) maritime trade route. This centre was a vital point in the Chinese concept of *Nanyang* or southern seas which stretched from coast of China and the South China Sea to the Indian Ocean and coast of Africa.[6] Commerce has always been vital to Southeast Asia. Situated at the centre of the maritime trade routes between China in one end and India, the Middle East and Europe on the other, Southeast Asia very quickly became an important trade hub.[7] The economic development of Southeast Asia began long before the Christian era when Southeast Asia had skilled farmers, musicians, metallurgists and mariners. The Southeast Asian people developed expertise in three areas, cultivation, metallurgical techniques and sailing. The people of Southeast Asia were the early introducers of watercrafts in the adjacent oceans. From the very early period, they were expert riders in the monsoons, the seasonal winds.[8] They sailed thousands of kilometres from their homes, navigating by means of swell and wave patterns, cloud formations, winds, birds and sea life. Although it is difficult to mention the exact time of this far reaching maritime activity, the Chinese were acquainted with the Malay sailors (*Kunlun*) since the third century BC.[9] Thus, we may presume that the Malayan traders navigated the South China Sea route to visit Chinese ports since the early days of their maritime activities. Products like cinnamon reached the shores of India with these Malay sailors. Even they reached the markets of Southwest Asia and the Mediterranean with their commodities via Malay trading stations in East Africa.[10] Pre modern maritime exchange in Southeast Asia was transacted in five commercial zones—the northern Malay Peninsula and southern coast of Vietnam, Java Sea region, the Strait of Malacca, the Philippines and north Borneo and Bay of Bengal.[11] Except the Bay of Bengal zone, all other zones fall within the ambit of South China Sea littorals. The foreign sea fearers, in the last millennium BC, regarded Southeast Asia as an intermediary between India and China which was an unknown area for them.[12] Passage through Southeast Asia by international traders became important in the second century AD as the central Asian caravan routes, the previously preferred connecting link between East and West commercial networks were disrupted by internal strife.

In the early period in the third and fourth centuries, the trade route used to cross the Isthmus of *Kra*. The traders used to disembark on the east side of the Kra at *Takaupa* and then crossed the Kra to reach Bay of Bandon (Gulf of Siam) from where they travelled for the Funanese port of Oc Eo. This route came under the control of the Malayans by the fifth century AD. Now the route went through the Malacca Strait to reach Sumatra and then Java Sea.[13] The sailors did not travel from West Asia to China and vice versa directly since the monsoon winds were important for navigation which was not available throughout the year. One group would travel from West Asia to India, the other travelled from India to Isthmus of Kra via Bay of Bengal. After reaching the isthmus their goods were transported to lower Vietnam in Funan via Gulf of Thailand where they were exchanged with the goods of the East which were then taken by another group of sailors to China.[14] Thus it was the sailors from Funan who travelled to south China via South China Sea. The sailors from the west did not travel to south China directly. They assembled at Funan where they exchanged goods for those which were brought from the east. In Oliver Walters' opinion, the Malay sailors were doing most of the sailing between India and Malay coast and between Funan and China during this era.[15]

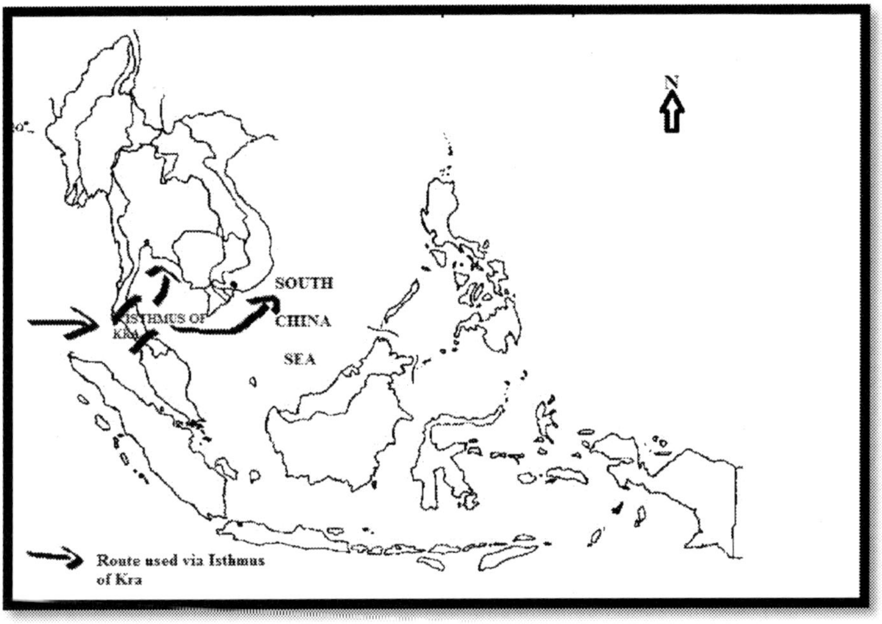

Map 1.1: Isthmus of Kra

It was not until the late fourth and early fifth century AD that Malacca Strait and South China Sea were being used as a maritime route by the international traders.[16]

The countries around the South China Sea started having contacts with the major countries of Indian Ocean around 3rd to 6th centuries AD, when the trade became more frequent.[17] During the thirteenth and fourteenth centuries, Southeast Asia earned fame by producing spices. Ships from the neighbourhood gathered on the shores of Southeast Asian islands to collect the renowned spices. According to Chinese geographer Wang Ta-yuan Chinese vessels regularly visited Maluku (in Indonesia) in the 1340s to collect small amounts of clove.[18] Many important trade centres emerged in the neighbourhood of South China Sea centring the maritime trade in the water body. These trade centres eventually arose as strong empires like the Srivijaya, Sailendra, Singhasari and Majapahit dynasties of Indonesia-Malaysia archipelago. Also, Funan and Champa of Indochina (present day Vietnam and Cambodia) contacted with China and Southeast Asia via the South China Sea.

Funan and South China Sea trade

The important political centre in Southeast Asia known to the Chinese was *Fun-nan* (first-seventh century AD) located on the lower reaches of the Mekong River in the delta area. Its sea port, called *Oc-Eo*, was originally located in Mekong River delta in what is now Vietnam, very near the Cambodian border, the point where the Gulf of Thailand recedes closest to the river. Funan was a network of coastal trading port cities with one having hegemony over the others. It was the first Southeast Asian state to be accorded the status as a kingdom by the Chinese envoys that travelled to the region as early as 3rd century AD. According to the Chinese account, the ambitious king of Funan constructed a large fleet and attacked more than ten foreign kingdoms around the Gulf of Thailand. Vyadhapura, "The City of Hunters", was the capital of Funan located about 200 km from the sea.[19] The three kingdoms (Wu, Wei and Shu) of China were behind the rise of Funan. Wu, the kingdom in the south of China which did not have any access to silk route to India, controlled by the northern kingdom of Wei, used the alternative maritime routes. The demand for foreign products in the wealthy kingdom of Wu (221-263 AD) generated a trade boom in the South China Sea and Funan's ports were strategically located to ensure control over the Chinese supply routes. The ports also provided natural harbours and a supply of fresh water to vessels traversing between the Malay Peninsula and China. In this way Funan exerted a trade monopoly.[20] Till fourth and fifth century AD, Funan remained as a privilege partner of the Chinese in Southeast Asia. The Chinese sources suggest that the ruler of Funan, during the third century, approached the Malaya peninsula bringing most of east coast city-states into its sphere of influence. The Funanese ports were the centre of Chinese mercantile activities in Southeast Asian waters.[21] Thus, we see that Funan became an important trading centre during the fourth and fifth century AD. Although there is no reference to the maritime route the Chinese merchants used to reach the Funanese ports, it can be inferred that it was South China Sea since there are no other sea routes they could have navigated through to reach Funan. In these harbours, the Chinese merchants procured both the trade goods from India and Western Asia which were assembled at these ports by the sailors coming from the west. The Chinese merchants also acquired products of insular Southeast Asia gathered at these centres, to which they still had no direct access.[22]

As mentioned earlier, *Oc Eo* was a major port of Funan. In 1940s, French archaeologist Louis Malleret said that O Eo was one major settlement of the polity then known from Chinese sources as Funan. Malleret carried out one single but extensive excavation in 1944.[23] Kang Tai and Zhu Ying, the two emissaries of the Wu emperor visited Southeast Asia in the third century AD and recorded their visit in writing, including that of Oc Eo. Malleret discovered archaeological evidence for many of the activities described by Kang Tai eighteen centuries earlier like bricks, tiles, glass beads, pottery vessels, fragments of gold, copper, bivalve moulds for casting tin ornaments.[24] The information collected by Louis Malleret for the origin and distribution of artefacts, mostly from Oc Eo area, confirm that Oc Eo thrived on maritime trade. The rich archaeological evidence of locally manufactured variety of artefacts (gold, tin and bronze ornaments, beads, pottery etc.) suggest that urban centre at Oc Eo was gradually transformed into a kind of 'industrial' site for production and exportation, inland and overseas, of wonderfully crafted objects.[25]

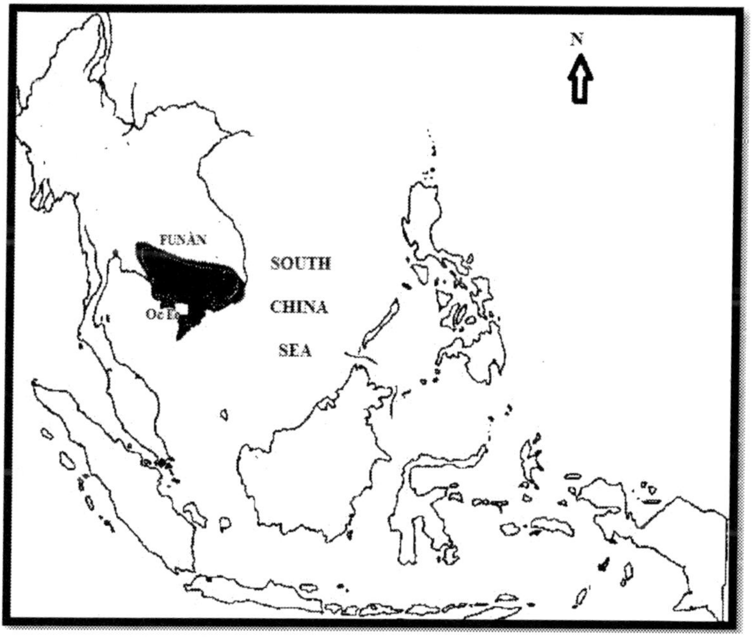

Map 1.2: Oc Eo port in the kingdom of Funan

It can hardly be doubted that Oc Eo's maritime trade had been through the waters of South China Sea. Given the location of harbour and its maritime visitors, particularly from China, it can be argued that the South China Sea was the vital maritime trade route between Funan and the world outside. For example, Funan imported goods which the Malaya sailors brought from other Southeast Asian ports.[26] These sailors could not reach the shores of Funan bypassing South China Sea. The traders in Funan sailed to China to collect Chinese silk in exchange of Mediterranean, Indian, West Asian and African goods such as frankincense and myrrh, other plant resins and other substances used to manufacture perfumes and incense.[27] Such trading was certainly done via South China Sea.

During the early third century, *Fan Shih-man* became the ruler of Funan. At the time Fan Shi-man embarked on his sea expedition voyaging from Malay Peninsula to China via South China Sea along the coastline. Ships navigated along the coast instead of sailing directly across the Gulf of Thailand to Funan's ports. Since the ships seldom ventured into the open sea before fifth century, Funan dominated the coastal route between the Malay Peninsula and China at this time.[28] Therefore Funan's rise and prosperity depended on the trade between the west and China via Southeast Asia. And here the South China Sea did play a critical role since the Funanese ports were at the shoreline of the South China Sea. The maritime trade to and from China had to navigate through the Sea. For this reason the Funanese ruler Fan Shi-man employed the Malayan sea population who provided him with a naval force to protect the sea lanes between Malay Peninsula and south China.[29] In that way it can be said that the Funanese had governed the coasts in the east of the South China Sea.

Champa and South China Sea trade

The rise of *Lin-yi* in the fifth century AD from the Funanese suzerainty, was due to the expansion of the Chinese maritime trade in the South China Sea under Chin dynasty when the ships bound for China had to visit the Cham ports.[30] When, in 605 AD, a Chinese general forcibly opened the southern trade, *Champa* (from which is derived the name of the Chams) responded favourably and soon became a major international trading hub for the maritime commercial activities between Malay and Canton.[31] What is noteworthy here is that Champa's hey days began with the trade shifting to the maritime domain of Southeast Asia following the expansion of the South China Sea trade. In that way, Champa's prosperity was caused by the South China Sea.

The name Champa is used to describe a series of small coastal kingdoms which developed in central Vietnam during the first millennium AD. The economy of the Champa states largely depended on the coastal trade with China and north Vietnam. China imported many luxury items like ivory, rhinoceros horn and aromatic woods from Champa while ports such as Hoi An and Nha Trang provided shelter and supplied fresh water for ships coming from Cambodia, Malay peninsula, South India, Persia and Oman. Champa was the only recorded trading partner of China in Southeast Asia in the first millennium AD from where Chinese goods were distributed in mainland Southeast Asia.[32] However, the land route through mountain passes linking central coastline of modern day Vietnam to Mekong valley in Cambodia and Laos and northeast Thailand were used for trading silk, iron and later porcelain.[33]

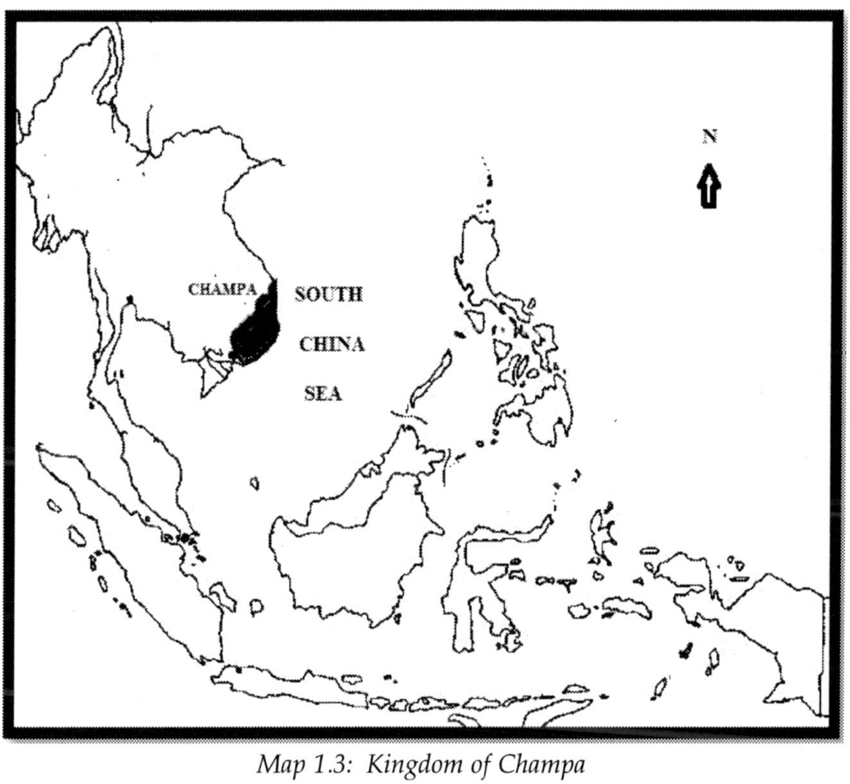

Map 1.3: Kingdom of Champa

Many archaeological discoveries in the coastal region of Vietnam have hinted the early trade conducted between Champa and the neighbouring region. The discovery of large quantities of glass and semi-precious carnelian agate beads, belonging to the pre-historic Sa Huynh Culture (of the south-central coastal Vietnam in vogue between 500 BC and 100 AD) were manufactured in India, or reproduced in Southeast Asia using Indian techniques and raw materials, according to mineralogical analysis. The discovery of Chinese sword with possible traces of silk at Phu Hoa in the east of Ho Chi Minh City, of Chinese coins from the reign of Wang Mang (9-23AD), at Hua Xa, west of Hoi An in Quang Nam province, corroborates the assumption of early trade between Champa and China. Similar discoveries of Han mirrors of the first century BC in Sa Huynh burial jars and the Han Chinese sealings, roofing tiles and bronze arrowheads and personal ornaments at Go Cam near Tra Kieu in Vietnam are also made which are evidences of growing trade between Champa and China from the end of second century BC onwards.[34]All these trades were maritime in character and given the location of the Champa, the only maritime trade route can be through the South China Sea. The port of *Thi Nai* (modern Quy Nho'n in central Vietnam) which emerged in the mid twelfth century in Vijaya prospered on the trade between Java and China.[35] It served as the principal port on the coast of Champa. Thi Nai was not only a contact point between the sea and land but also an entrepot of regional sea trade. The merchant ships used to visit Thi Nai on their regional routes. The port became a strategic connecting point between China and the south eastern and south western regions of Asia.[36] The port was located on the shore of South China Sea and a meeting point for the ships traversing the South China Sea water both from and to China and Southeast Asia. The traders outside the region, like the Arab and the Persian Muslims, also participated in the Cham trade since the tenth century AD. The cham envoys in the Song Court of China sometimes represented the Arab lands, *Da-shi.* A northern Song source from that century notes: '*Many people of Champa and Da-shi come annually from across the seas and trade in China*'.[37] These 'seas' cannot exclude South China Sea since to reach the coast of China from Champa, one has to pass through the South China Sea. Champa also practised long range trade networks even with West Asia (Middle East).[38] Such trade link has to pass through the South China Sea which was the ultimate connection between Champa and the outside world.

Srivijaya Empire and South China Sea trade

After the fall of Funan, China looked for alternative trading entrepots in Southeast Asia to sustain the east-west trade. On the other hand, various Southeast Asian centres were at that time attempting to emerge as dominant trading centre in the region. One such state was *Srivijaya*.[39] The southeast coast of Sumatra became important as the maritime link with China developed in the beginning of the fifth century AD. It was the "favoured coast" of the early Indonesian commerce, according to Dr. (Oliver) Walters. The South China Sea voyage was spearheaded from this coast. In as early as 441 AD, the Sumatran coast of *Kan-t'o-li* used to send tributes to China.[40] Although there is no evidence of the exact location of *Kan-t'o-li*, Dr. Wolter is of the view that this port was the predecessor of Srivijaya where the Malaya shippers used to visit. This port sustained the maritime trade with China.[41] Thus we see that prior to the emergence of the Srivijaya Empire, the Sumatran sailors did have close connection with South China Sea. It was, like today, the only maritime route of Sumatra to connect with China.

The rise of Srivijaya depended on the Chinese demands for West Asian products. The Chinese did not have naval and ship building capacities and therefore had to rely on Southeast Asian kingdoms for keeping the *Nanhai* (South China Sea) trade active. With the Malaya shipping developing from the fourth to seventh century AD along with increase in Chinese trade of West Asian products, the Malayan ships started playing even bigger role in the trade between China and the Indian Ocean. And this helped Srivijaya to rise as a prime entrepot with the support of the Arab traders who found it profitable to break journey at Srivijaya and take on board Southeast Asian goods than to undertake direct voyages to China. In this way, the Malayan kings used to protect the Chinese commercial interests in *Nan-yang* or maritime Asia from seventh to eleventh centuries.[42]

As Map 1.4 suggests, the Srivijayan jurisdiction extended to the adjacent sea which is none other than the South China Sea. Moreover, the prosperity of the Srivijayan kingdom depended heavily on the Chinese trade with the Malaya Peninsula which depended on the Srivijayan ports. This Chinese trade with Malay Peninsula, it can be presumed, was done via South China Sea, as we know that the trade shifted to the sea in the fifth century A.D and Srivijaya controlled the maritime commerce passing through Southeast Asia during this time. Thus, it can be said that South

China Sea was the main driving force behind the prosperity and dominance of Srivijayan kingdom.

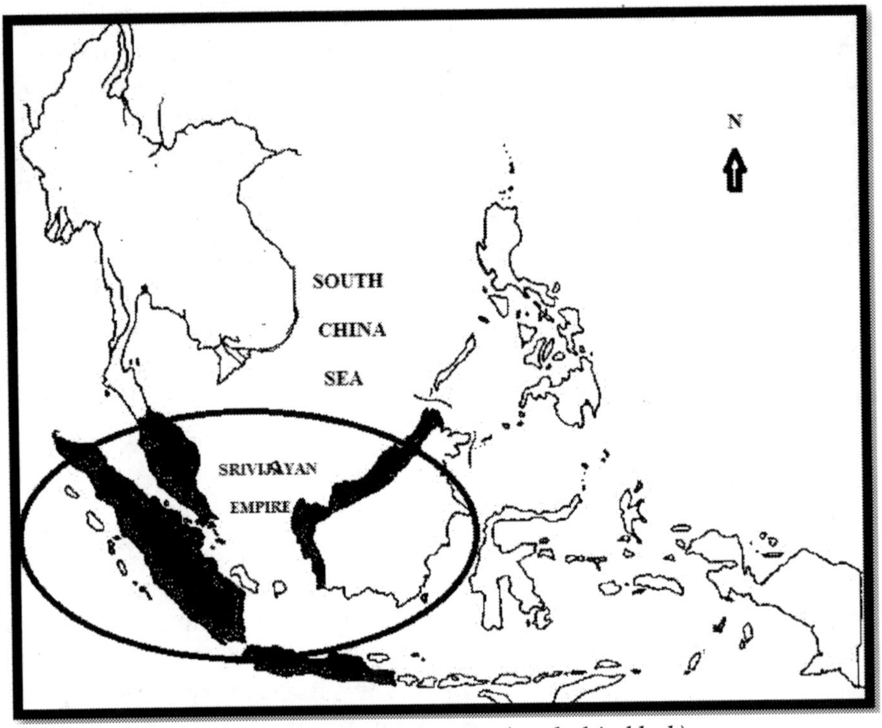

Map 1.4: Srivijayan Empire (marked in black)

Srivijaya was commercially very dynamic whose extensive trade relations with China are evident from the Chinese coins unearthed in the region. Derek Heng notes that archaeological expeditions in Jambi (Malayu) and Palembang, the capitals of Srivijaya[43], reveal few Chinese copper coins.[44] The nine Srivijayan missions to the Song (dynasty of China) in the last decades of the eleventh century supplied Straits of Malacca with copper coins.[45] The only way of such maritime trade and missions was South China Sea, no doubt. The capital city of Palembang, which still exists, was the political, religious and economic centre of Srivijaya between seventh and eleventh centuries AD. The centres were situated either on the banks of river Musi or within reach of the river or sea, downstream from Palembang. The discoveries here suggest long distance trade networks and the role of the merchants and ship masters in the voyages.[46] Given the location of Palembang, such 'long distance' trade had to wade through the South China Sea. It can be said that maritime trade was the lifeline of the Srivijaya kingdom. Geoff Wade writes that it was likely the booming trade of the Srivijayan entrepôt which induced the attack on the polity by Javanese forces in 992 AD and the later attacks by the contending Chola Empire (of India) in the early eleventh century.[47] He continues saying that the Javanese and Chola polities were attempting to control the commercial trade which Srivijaya enjoyed both regionally and with China.[48] Such power, it can be presumed, the Srivijaya rulers acquired by controlling the trade through the South China Sea since it was the South China Sea which was the major maritime opening the kingdom had towards outside, especially China. The attacks themselves substantiate the argument that Srivijaya controlled the maritime trade in South China Sea and the Malacca Straits which connects South China Sea with Indian Ocean.

The Philippines and South China Sea trade

The Philippines archipelago is made up of seven thousand islands scattered over three lakhs square kilometre area. The archipelago is bound on the east by the Pacific Ocean and on the west by the South China Sea. The only connection the Philippines has with the world is via sea around her and South China Sea is between her and rest of Asia. So, it is obvious that Philippines' trade with Asia, particularly China, has been via South China Sea. Although the Philippine community had trade relations with Southeast Asia since the later centuries BC, China's appearance in first millennium AD boosted the trade between the two sides. With the expansion of the maritime trade under the Tang Dynasty (960-1279 AD), due to closure of overland silk route, China developed commercial relations with the Philippines and rest of South China Sea littorals. The archaeological discoveries of Tang and Song glazed trade wares-porcelains and stoneware vessels in the Filipino archipelago sites are the proofs of early trade between China and the Philippines.[49]

The early trade of the Philippines further developed until the end of the sixteenth century (when the Spaniards came) as the various lowland areas of the archipelago started taking part in the commercial activities, both directly and indirectly. During the Ming Dynasty, the trade was boosted with the Chinese producing ceramics for overseas trade.[50] Unfortunately, the lack of resources due to the destruction of the native creations during the Spanish rule make the writing of pre-colonial Filipino history very difficult. As in case of the Latin America, the fanaticism characterized the native writings of the Philippines as 'devil' which were callously destroyed. However, arriving in the Philippines archipelago in 1521, Spanish explorer Ferdinand Magellan found, instead of a land occupied by ignorant wild savages, one of the epicentres of the international trade industry which extended from the Atlantic to the Pacific.[51] William Henry Scott in his book the *Pre-Hispanic Source Materials* itinerates *"When the pre-Hispanic epoch was brought to a close by Ferdinand Magellan's arrival in 1521, Luzon traders were sailing to Timor, Malacca and Canton, had a colony in Minjam on the Malay Peninsula, a Portuguese appointed magistrate in Malacca and marriage relations with the Sultan of Brunei, and the Manila bourgeoisie were learning to speak Malay"*.[52]

Therefore we see that the Filipinos were seafarers and established traders who practised international trade well before the advent of the Spaniards. And following the quotation of William Henry Scott, it is evident that they navigated through the South China Sea waters to reach Malacca and Canton. They maintained trade relations over the South China Sea with the traders of the west and China.

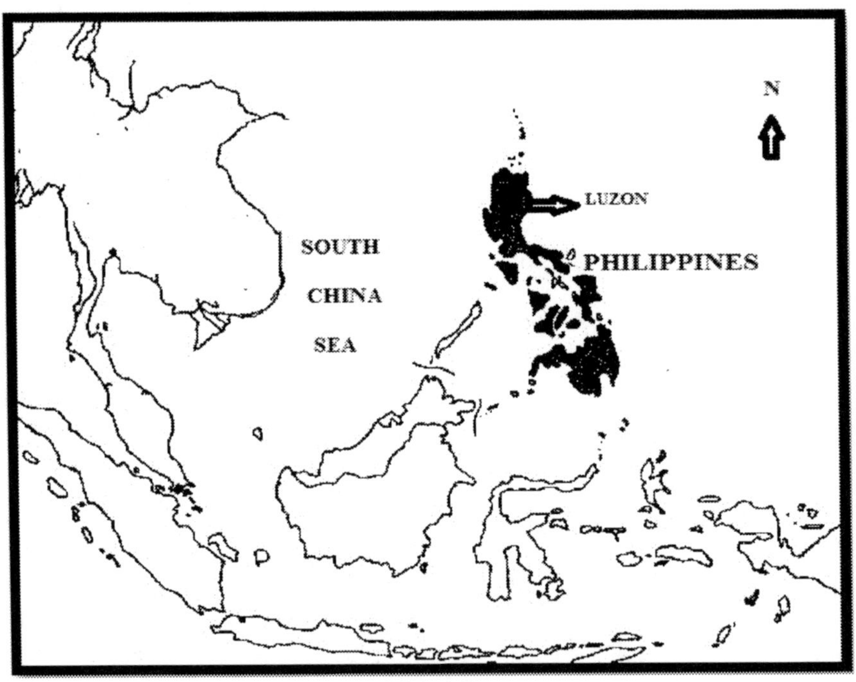

Map 1.5

The Sung history of China have the first mention of the Philippines referring to the visit of traders from *Ma-i* (present day Mindoro) bringing valuable merchandise to Canton in 982 AD. As early as the tenth century Philippine vessels were crossing the oceans to China and Champa for exportable trade goods[53] Here the 'oceans' refer to has to be South China Sea since this is the only route from Philippines to the destinations mentioned. The Philippine trading centres are mentioned in several Chinese documents of Sung and Yuan period where ports in Sulu are described having a well-developed organized network for exportable forest and maritime products (sandalwood, laka-wood, ebony, animal hides and pearls). The trade relations between the two sides became stronger in the fourteenth century while in 1406, a Filipino chieftain visited the Imperial Court at Nanking followed by other trips.[54]

The early Spanish documents narrate the visit of large trade ships (apart from China), from Borneo, Thailand and Japan at some of the larger Philippine coastal ports: Manila, Mindoro, Pangasinan, Cebu, Jolo (Sulu), and Cotabato. The Filipino traders were acquainted with the trading ports of Melaka, Borneo, Ternate (Moluccas) and Myanmar.[55] Therefore the Filipinos and the outside world practised trade among themselves in the pre-colonial period in the Philippines. Although these documents do not mention the trade route the sailors followed, but from the visited ports, it can be deciphered that sailors coming from Thailand and Borneo to Manila and particularly Pangasinan which is in Luzon in north Philippines, must have paddled through the South China Sea. Similarly, the Filipino traders visiting Melaka (Malacca), Borneo and even Myanmar had to follow similar maritime route. Therefore we see how South China Sea acted as a link between Philippines and the international market.

The traces of the mortuary remains and settlements in Butuan in the Mindanao province of southern Philippines confirm maritime commercial activities in the region in pre and post eleventh century. The Chinese *Song-Shih* might have referred to Butuan as *P'u-tuan* sending tributes to the imperial court in the early eleventh century and which had contacts with Champa.[56] This shows that a southern Philippines polity maintained connections with both China and Champa via maritime trade which undoubtedly passed through the South China Sea.

China and South China Sea trade

China is an integral part of South China Sea trade. China has been the prime destination of the traders traversing the South China Sea since the onset of trade through its waters. The study of South China Sea remains incomplete or soulless, to be precise, without discussing its relations with China. It is noteworthy that South China Sea is the only maritime route that opens the gate of Southeast Asia, India and far west to the Chinese. It is the bridge between the west and China and the Chinese have used this maritime route to maintain connection with the world far beyond through South China Sea. During the Song dynasty, between eleventh and thirteenth century, the Chinese engaged in long distance trade with Southeast Asia, promoting the regional commercial relations.[57] However, we will see in the following paragraphs that China's trade relations with Southeast Asia dates back to much earlier period of history.

Chinese traveller Faxian took the old silk route from China to reach northern India between 309 and 414 AD, passing through Central Asia. He spent twelve years in India and Sri Lanka to study Buddhism. He took the maritime route via the Bay of Bengal and the South China Sea to return home. On his way home he saw the route 'busy with large boats full of people and cargo'. These ships were filled with pilgrims travelling to and from the Buddhist centres in Sri Lanka and Indonesia and also the cargos were containing cloves, nutmeg, cinnamon and silk for trade.[58] Thus one gets an idea from the writings of Faxian about the picture of the maritime trade in South China Sea which was *'busy with large boats full of people and cargo'*. The records of the first maritime trade across the South China Sea are found in the archaeological findings (mostly in Chinese) according to which the trade happened in the ancient Chinese kingdom of Nanyue or Southern Yue which continued from 203 BC till the collapse of the Qin dynasty in 111 BC.[59]

Initially, the Chinese considered the "southern ocean" and the Indian Ocean to be single stretch of water body. They started getting acquainted with the southern ocean after conquering the Tonkin region towards the end of the third century BC. They gradually became familiar with the vast ocean having widespread maritime activities stretching from southern China to the Mediterranean when some "barbarian" ships were sent to India via Southeast Asia during the rule of Han emperor Wu Ti (141-87 BC).[60] The reference to the 'southern ocean' must be South China Sea which the Chinese got acquainted with after the annexation of Gulf of Tonkin. Now, as mentioned earlier, it is assumed that during the Nanyue kingdom's rule trade via South China Sea was started by the Chinese. During the early period of maritime activities in this region, the Nanyue vessels waded through the coastal waters rather than undertaking transoceanic voyages, sailing along the coasts of southern

China, India and the west beyond.[61] So it can be said that the Chinese maritime trade initially was confined to the coastal areas of the South China Sea and did not voyage beyond the boundary of the Sea. When the traditional inland "silk road" via Central Asia was abandoned in the second century AD, the maritime route through Southeast Asia came up as an alternative to the international traders which helped the rising of sea ports along the South China Sea coasts.[62] Thus, South China Sea did not emerge as a vital economic route for China before the collapse of inland Silk Road in the second century AD.

Nevertheless, China's earliest contacts with Nan-yang or maritime Asia were intimately tied to the southward expansion of the Chinese culture zone and the gradual and largely peaceful assimilation of peoples south of North China plain. China's relations with Southeast Asia in the ancient period was 'non-threatening' in character, compared to that with Inner Asia, which might have encouraged China to foster trade ties with the region. The first account of *Nanhai* trade with the south dates back to the Eastern Chou period (770-221 BC) when the non-Chinese kingdoms of Wu and Yueh, located in present Kiangsu and Chekiang regions of modern China, practised commercial activities extending along the coasts of China and mainland Southeast Asia. The archaeological evidence tells that this trade was 'well established'.[63]

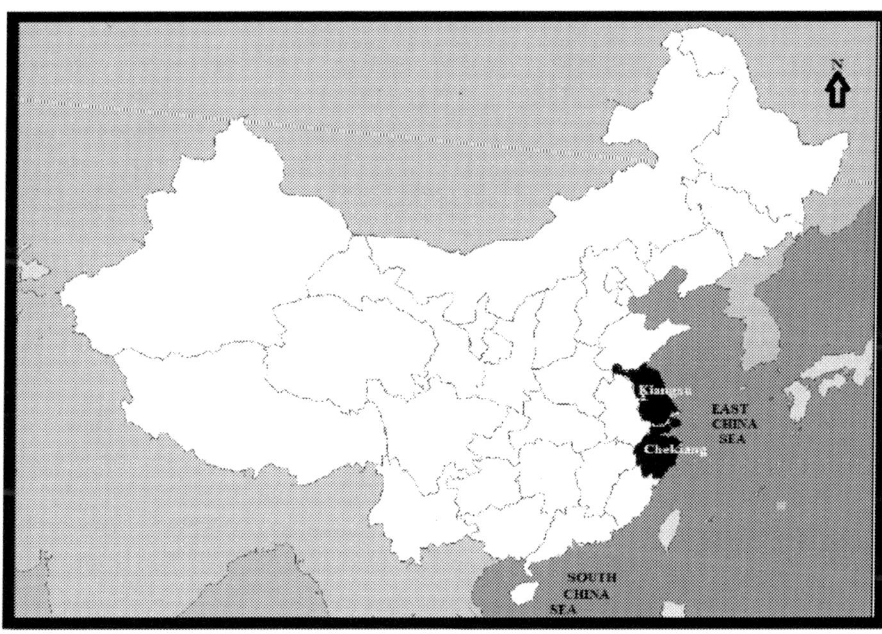

Map 1.6: Kiangsu (Jiangsu) and Chekiang

As we can see from the Map 1.6 both Kiangsu (Jiangsu) and Chekiang are located on the shores of East China Sea. Therefore it is evident that the sailors of ancient non-Chinese kingdoms of Wu and Yueh navigated down through the South China Sea extending the trade along the coasts of mainland Southeast Asia from that of China. As mentioned earlier, the early Chinese maritime trade used to take place along the coasts since the transoceanic trade was yet to start. This trade, which continued till the end the nineteenth century, transacted items like ivory, pearls, tortoise shells, kingfisher and peacock feathers, rhinoceros horns, cinnamon and scented woods. These commodities were collected in the southern China, as far as Tonkin. The Yueh kingdom gradually developed an administrative set up in the southern coastal region thereby establishing trade ties with maritime Southeast Asia. The popular demands of the 'Nanhai exotica' led to the expansion of Chinese contacts with Indian Ocean during its three kingdoms period (220-279 AD), particularly under the Wu kingdom of the southern coastal region.[64] Therefore we see that the ancient traders from China traversed the South China Sea route to reach the south eastern Asia and beyond and in that way developed a flourishing trading hub along the coasts of South China Sea. The Yuan dynasty (1271-1368), set up centre at Shanghai, Hangzhou, Ningbo, and Quanzhao to supervise and encourage maritime trade of China and the centre at Quanzhao dealt with China's trade in South China Sea.[65] The growing importance of the South China Sea trade route had a reason behind it. After the Silk Route collapsed (by the second millennium AD), which brought West Asian goods to northern China via Central Asia, the Wu Kingdom of China looked for the alternative maritime route to sustain the supply of luxury wares, including a small supply of products from India and the Roman Orient. New items like woods, scents, coral, dye, gemstones, medicines and sandalwood statues of Buddha (as Buddhism spread later) etc. were also imported via this Nanhai trade. In this way coastal Nanhai trade expanded from localised commercial network to become an important part of maritime Asian trade which extended to the Indian Ocean region.[66]

Receiving tributes from the neighbouring 'vassal' states was the soul of ancient China's international relations. From the time of the Han dynasty, Chinese regimes have organized their relationships with foreign states through two mechanisms: tribute and trade. The tribute system required foreign rulers to send embassies to China bearing tribute in the form of local exotica. The emperor in turn presented these emissaries with gifts of equal or greater value, which they took back to their rulers.

John King Fairbank and his collaborators in their 1968 book *The Chinese World Order* said that the ancient Chinese considered the world to be 'All under Heaven' and their emperor as the governor of all human beings and the mediator between them and the universe, he being the 'son of the heaven'. They considered China as the Middle Kingdom (*Zhongguo*) and the people around it as 'barbarians'.[67] These vassal states acknowledged their subordinate status by sending annual tribute to the Chinese court. These tributes were sent with the purpose of acquiring trading prerogative from China along with Chinese goods. This mission also meant for gaining recognition from China which became important token of political legitimacy for the Asian trading kingdoms. Between third and sixth century, several missions from Southeast Asia, India, West Asia and even the Roman Orient visited China.[68] During the time of the Hongwu emperor who founded the Ming dynasty (1368-1644), tributes from Champa, Annam and Korea visited China. In 1370, tributes from Java and the Coromandel coast of India reached the Chinese shore followed by Srivijaya, Siam, Japan and Cambodia next year.[69] It can easily be assumed that these missions were maritime and they reached the Chinese coasts via South China Sea (except the one from Korea which could have used either the land route or East China Sea route) since the kingdoms of Southeast Asia were South China Sea littorals and the kingdoms of South India and Ceylon (today's Sri Lanka) were sea faring no doubt whose only communication bridge with China was South China Sea. Thus, we see that South China Sea was the source of political legitimacy for the Chinese emperors. Eventually, a commercial network developed among the traders of South China Sea trading with the kingdoms who sent tributes to the Ming emperor and in that way the Chinese products became part of the local trade of the South China Sea.[70] This shows how important South China Sea was (as it is now) for China, both economically and politico-strategically. In a word, South China Sea was the lifeline for the ancient Chinese empires who opened the door to maritime Southeast Asia for China. China has traditionally used South China Sea to meet her economic and politico-strategic objectives.

Arab traders in South China Sea trade

So far we have discussed the activities of the neighbours of South China Sea in the region. Now, let us see the activities of the 'external' people, that is the traders from the region outside Southeast Asia who traversed the South China Sea maritime route to do business in the region. The date of the arrival of the Arabs in Southeast Asia is unknown but their contact with the region is very old undoubtedly. Being prominent sailors, the Arabs were acquainted with the oceans of East Asia and visited the Indian Ocean and the South China Sea on which they wrote travel books and navigational guides for the future sailors.[71] The role of early Arab navigators and their commercial activities in this part of the world, and their pioneering work in showing its importance in the history of international trade are noteworthy.

According to Andre Wink, the Arab and Persian merchants spread out their trading network in the Indian Ocean region during eighth and eleventh century turning it into an 'Arab Mediterranean' and said that it was strictly commercial. After settling on the west coast of India, in Konkan and Gujarat, the Arabs expanded to the south in Sri Lanka and Coromandel between eighth and ninth century, moving further to Guangzhou in southern China. The commercial relations between West Asia and Southeast Asia developed in the tenth century when the Persians, Jews and the Arabs traded with Southeast Asia via the ports in the Indian sub-continent.[72] The Chinese records of the tenth century says that missions from *Da-shi* (the Arab land) had arrived at the Song court (at Kai-feng), apart from *Zabaj=Zabag* (likely Srivijaya), Chola empire and Champa with names which were interpreted as Islamic. Such missions prove the extensive maritime trade existing between the Arabs and the Chinese about which Claudine Salmon provides the details saying that the trade was done via the ports in India and Southeast Asia.[73] So from the eighth to the eleventh centuries, the West Asian traders, the Arabs and the Persians, did trade with East Asia, particularly China via Southeast Asian ports. These traders visited the ports of Champa and Srivijaya while sailing to southern China wading through the South China Sea.

The Arabs, after reaching India, sailed further east and established trading link with China. Eventually, they set up a vast commercial network from China to West Asia and even Europe. Maritime Southeast Asia and the Malabar Coast of India played a very important role in this network. Several trading centres developed in these places which boosted the trade providing transport facilities and commodities like spices.[74] The Arab travel documents have the mention of these commercial linkages. One such document, *Akhbar al-Sin wa'l-Hind*, the earliest Arabic source of the mid ninth century, depicts the journey from Muscat to Southeast Asia and then China via Quilon (Kollam) in the Malabar Coast.[75] According to Sulayman Tajir (who wrote *Akhbar al-Sin wa'l-Hind*), the traders from the Persian Gulf first reached Kolan Mali in the Malabar Coast from Suhar and Muscat from where they sailed for Sarandip and on the way anchored at Langabalus (Nicobar) to collect fresh water. They reached Straits of Malacca, Taimon Islands and Kadarang from Kolan Mali in ten days and took another ten days to reach Sanf Fulaw in Champa. From Champa the traders sailed to Khanfu (Canton) in China navigating through South China Sea.[76]

Abu'l Qasim 'Ubayd Alah Ibn Khuradbhih, in his document '*Kitab al-Masalik wal-Malamlik*' said that the traders, while sailing from India to China reached Langabalus in ten to fifteen days and then Kalah (Kedah), famous for tin mines and bamboo plantations, in six days. After sailing by Jaba (Java) islands, Salahit (Singapore Strait) and Harang, they reached the Spice Islands (Moluccas). The sailors from Mait (on of Riau Islands) sailed for Tiyoma (Tioman in Malysia) anchoring at Qamar and then journeyed for Sanf, then arriving at Luqin in three days which was 'gateway to China'.[77] The route depicted here however is slightly confusing. It is unclear whether the sailors got divided into two sections, one passing through the Strait of Malacca, sailed via the Salahit (Singapore Strait)and Tiamon in Malaysia and reached Luqin, while the other passed by Java reached the Moluccas Islands finally sailing for China. The former sailors no doubt sailed through South China Sea to reach China.

The Muslim traders of Champa were called '*Pu*' in the Chinese records. These traders migrated to Hai-nan, Guangdong and Fujian in the late tenth to twelfth century.[78] Hai-nan is an island on the South China Sea off the Chinese shore in south and that of modern day north Vietnam, while Guangdong and Fujian are the coastal provinces in southern China on the shore of South China Sea. From the above narrative it seems that the Muslim traders, who were based in Champa, sailed to the Hai-nan island of China through the South China Sea and settled there. Some others also used the same route to reach the shores of Fujian and Guangdong provinces of southern China, on the shores of South China Sea. Evidences suggest that the Muslim community of Hai-nan, including that of the Pu clan, were, according to Geoff Wade, "tied by kinship and trade to both Champa and China and located on the maritime route linking southern China with Southeast Asia."[79] Such a trade was done, no doubt, through the South China Sea, since we have seen earlier, Champa's maritime trade link was based on South China Sea. After the Chola raid of Srivijaya in early eleventh century AD, the Arab trade in the Straits got affected. It resumed in the second half of the eleventh century via the maritime route of Southeast Asia. During this time the Fujian port of Quan-zhou replaced Guangzhou as the new trading hub. By the late twelfth century, the Muslim traders were controlling the 'southern sea trade'.[80]

Japan and South China Sea trade

Japan's early trade with Southeast Asia thrived in the sixteenth and the early seventeenth century promoted by *Shogunate* or the military government of old Japan when the Japanese ships were forbidden in Chinese ports. This trade was termed as 'vermilion seal ship trade'. The Japanese exported silver, copper, iron while imported silk, medicine and spices. The Japanese traders travelled to the Philippines, Thailand, Vietnam, Cambodia, Taiwan, Indonesia and Macao. This vermilion seal ship trade continued till 1639 when Japan adopted the national seclusion policy closing the trade network with Southeast Asia.[81] Thus we see that the Japanese trade with Southeast Asia was very active in the 16th and mid 17th century. And to do this trade, the Japanese ships did traverse the water of South China Sea, especially to reach the shores of Thailand, Vietnam, Cambodia and Indonesia. Although the record suggests that the Japanese were late comers in the South China Sea trade, in contrast to the Chinese and the Indians, they were regular visitors in the region until the mid 17th century. During the Ryukyu Kingdom's rule in southern Japan (1429-1879), Japanese missions visited Southeast Asia to collect products like pepper and sapanwood to send to China as tributes since these products were not produced in Japan.[82] The *Rekitai hoan*, the collection of official records of tributary trade of Japan, suggests that during the Ming rule in China, Japan maintained commercial relations with Southeast Asian kingdoms of Siam, Srivijaya, Java, Malacca, Sumatra, Annan and Patani. These trade relations were based on the tribute trade with China since the Japanese collected products like sappanwood and pepper from Southeast Asia to send as tribute to Chinese court.[83]

There were two maritime trade routes followed by the Ryukyu Kingdom. One would pass along the east of South China Sea, from Luzon to Sulu while the other would run along the west coast of mainland Southeast Asia, from Siam to Malacca, in the west of South China Sea.[84] The maritime routes depicted here help us to construe the fact that the Japanese traders chose to travel along the shores of both sides of the sea. This route is similar to what the traders coming from Funan, Champa had used, following the coastal routes of South China Sea. The maritime route from Kuangchou (or Guangzhaou in southern China) followed the coastal routes to reach various parts of Southeast Asia like Siam, Malacca and Sumatra and thus rice, spices and marine products were the main trade items in this route.[85] This route passed through South China Sea. What is noteworthy here is that in both directions, the traders started their voyage from southern China. So it can be deciphered that the Japanese merchants did not directly traverse the Southeast Asian waters but chose south China as their base.

The advent of the Europeans and the South China Sea trade

The competition for the control over South China Sea started with the advent of the Iberian forces, the Spaniards and the Portuguese, in the region in the sixteenth century. Eventually, the area became zone of competition among the Western colonial powers with the Dutch occupying Malacca, Java and Taiwan, the British occupying Malaya, Borneo and Hong Kong, the French in Indochina and the Americans in the Philippines by the nineteenth century. In this way, Chinese movement in the zone got seriously challenged.[86] With the coming of the Europeans, the Bay of Bengal and the South China Sea commercial zone transcended their limited space between India and China and got connected with the wider maritime zone connecting with the distant parts of the globe. The Moluccan spices attracted the Iberian traders to undertake the long maritime route to come to the new world.[87]

From the early era of the modern age, Europe came up as an 'oceanic power' undertaking voyages at every corner of the world, from Americas to Asia and the Portuguese spearheaded this age of exploration. Such explorations had both economic and religious missions. Apart from profiting from the spice trade of South and Southeast Asia, proselytization was the other part of the Portuguese exploration of new lands in Asia and Americas. The Portuguese were seen as 'ruthless foreigner' in the East who implemented uniform policies, methods and means throughout colonial period.[88] The visit of Marco Polo to China was a major event in connecting the East with the West. In 1271, young Marco Polo joined his father and brother on their third journey to Kublai Khan's court in China. Medieval Europe had no recorded of contacts with Southeast Asia until late thirteenth century, when Polos, returning from the court of Kublai Khan by sea route, passed down the coast of Champa, rounded the southern extremity of Malay Peninsula, and were held up for five months by monsoon conditions in northern Sumatra before passing on their way across the Indian Ocean. The Polos travelled to China overland crossing the caravan route.[89] Marco's homeward voyage, which began in 1292, contains interesting materials on Southeast Asia. They took the sea route to return to Europe crossing the South China Sea. There is no detailed documentation of Marco Polo's return voyage from China which took two years. However, there is information available about the death of six hundred passengers and crews on way home although Marco Polo did not clarify the reason of their death. Some suggest scurvy, cholera or drowning while others blame hostile natives and pirate attacks for the death. Marco Polo reached Sumatra wading through South China Sea and from there to Hormuz via Indian Ocean.[90] This visit of Marco Polo to China connected Europe with Asia and also opened the sea route to reach the continent which so far was only reached via land. The South China Sea, which was so far the bridge among the Asians to reach China, was now open to the outsiders.

Marco Polo had travelled to various places of Southeast Asia on his way home via sea. He said that 'Chamba' that is Champa was very rich and its ruler paid annual tributes of elephants to the Chinese emperor Kublai Khan. He also documented the victory of the Mongol ruler over Champa in 1291 AD. He, while discussing about the 'Great Island of Java', named Sumatra as 'Java the Less'. However, it is difficult to identify the other islands he named like Pulo condore, opposite to Mekong Delta and Bitang at the east end of Straits of Malacca.[91] Pulo Candore, today known as Côn Sõn Island, lies off the mouth of Mekong River in the South China Sea.[92] Thus we see that Marco Polo visited the littoral states of South China Sea on his way home from China and spent some time there.

Before Marco Polo started for home, John of Monte Corvino started for Peking to convert Kublai Khan to Christianity. Passing by Ormuz (Hormuz) and Persian Gulf, Corvino, along with his companions, reached the Coromandel Coast of India where they stayed for over a year before moving further via the maritime route through the (Indonesian) archipelago to reach China.[93] Although it is not clear whether they used the South China Sea route to reach China, but it is improbable for them to take any other route since that is the most popular, easy and commonly used route to reach the Chinese shore. Another European explorer, Francisian Odoric of Pordenone, visited China in the early fourteenth century (between 1316 and 1330). Like Corveno, he also reached the

Coromandel Coast of India and sailed further to Sumatra, Java, Borneo and Champa and finally reached Canton.[94] This route no doubt crossed South China Sea. Like Marco Polo, this traveller also wrote an account on his visits to Southeast Asian kingdoms, including Champa, which no doubt he travelled via the sea.

The Portuguese

The main demand for the spices of the East in Europe in the medieval period emanated from urge to prepare flavour salted and pickled meat which was very important part of the European diet that time. The demand for spices like pepper, cinnamon, clove, nutmeg and mace propelled the trade between Europe and Asia in the early days and it was the Muslims and the Venetians who were in charge of the spice trade between Indonesia and Europe in late Middle Ages.[95] Gradually, the Portuguese planned to do direct trade with Asia to give up dependence on the Muslim traders which inspired them to explore sea route to Asia. Portuguese' coming to Asia (with Vasco da Gama) was the mission mixed of religious motive, national zeal and economic gain.[96]

At the end of the Middle Ages the Portuguese were well fitted for the leadership of the European effort to exploit the trade of the Indian Ocean. Their position on the Atlantic made them a race of mariners able to cope with the risks of the sea. The Portuguese mission in Asia was meant to meet the demands for spices among the then European elites. Vasco da Gama bypassed Africa and reached Calicut in India in 1498.[97] The Portuguese wanted to control the maritime trade between East and West. Although by the onset of the sixteenth century, they had set forts along the routes from Red Sea to west coast of India in Goa and Daman and Diu, Hugli in eastern India and in Ceylon, they could not control the Arab shipping to Malacca in the Malay Peninsula and Macau in China. That means the maritime route of South China Sea was still outside the Portuguese control. To meet this objective, the Portuguese seized Malacca in 1511.The Portuguese arrived at Vietnam in 1516 on their way to China from Malacca. Later, in 1523, Portuguese envoy Duarte Coelho went to Vietnam to initiate trade relations, but in vain. It was Antonia da Faria, another Portuguese envoy who finally initiated the trade in 1535 by visiting south Vietnam and identifying *Faifo* (also known as HÙi Ansea port) as Portuguese trading hub. The Portuguese started operating at Faifo in 1540. They did trade from southern Vietnam (till seventeenth century) since they were in good terms with the southern rulers.[98] Thus we see that the Portuguese settled themselves on the shore of South China Sea to do trade with Macao in China which was also under their control. The prospering Macao-Vietnam trade since the early seventeenth century can be held responsible for the gradual decline of Portuguese bastion in India and the Far East notwithstanding their effort to sustain it. Frenchmen Pierre Poivre on Cochin-China (1742-1743), reported that "They [the Portuguese] bring tutenag, tea, porcelain and other goods from China for use by the Çochin Chinese. The main return cargo consists of sugar, which was sent to India, eaglewood and raw silk which was sold to the Dutch".[99] During this time, the Vietnamese commodities were important part of Portuguese trade which strengthened their trade in Far East.[100] So, until the advent of the Dutch, the Portuguese were major European traders in Southeast Asia doing trade with China mainly and also Vietnam via South China Sea. It was the Portuguese who first named the waters east of Malacca as *Mare da China* (emphasis added) or Sea of China. Later, as they moved towards Japan, they distinguished the 'South Sea of China' from other seas off the long Chinese coast, which to the Chinese was just the 'southern sea' or *Nanhai*.[101]

The Portuguese introduced an alien European society, coming by sea and in return got acquainted with a society rich in culture and material splendour. The success or failure of the Portuguese depended on how they could use their resources to sustain the trade in the South China Sea region.[102] The Portuguese enlarged and sustained their trade in South China Sea throughout the sixteenth and seventeenth century. At the same time, the neighbouring Chinese, Buddhist and Malay world started taking shape while the new European competitors like the Dutch emerged in the scene challenging first the Portuguese and then the local state system.[103] The Portuguese expanded their trading tentacles all over South China Sea in the following years. By the early seventeenth century, South China Sea zone emerged as a vital market zone due to rivalry between the Portuguese and the Spaniards and the supply of silver from the New World (the Americas). As the flow of silver from both Japan and the New World to China increased and East Asia experienced the movement of silver bullion, with Chinese raw silk and piece goods getting market in Europe, Asia and the New World, the Portuguese engaged more with the inter-Asian trade where the Indian goods like cotton textiles were exchanged in the South China Sea trade for spices from Moluccas.[104]

Thus we see that the Portuguese had ruled the South China Sea regional market at the dawn of the European explorations in the Asian waters. They settled themselves in certain pockets in Asia, starting with Goa in India, moving further east in Malacca and at Macao in China which is located at the extreme south of China in the north of South China Sea. From Macao they governed their trade in the South China Sea market through *Esto da India*, the Portuguese East India Company. The Portuguese traders in Macao initially did trade mainly with India, Japan and Manila although they took part in the South China Sea trade.[105] Thus, the South China Sea, which so far was the medium of trade for the Indians, Chinese and the Arabs, now started catering to the European traders also.

The Spaniards

Unlike the other European travellers, the Spaniards took the Pacific route to reach Asia. They first conquered the West Indies and South America and then sailed off for Asia via the Pacific. By the time, the Spaniards reached the Philippine shore there existed a very dynamic trading centre operated by the Chinese, mainly in Laguna and Mindoro. The archaeologists suggest that the Philippines had an extensive and comprehensive regional trade network of both imports and the exports, mainly forest products which were of high demand among the Chinese.[106] The Spaniards found Cebu to be the most vibrant trading hub where the Southeast Asian products were exchanged for the Chinese articles.[107] The Spaniards had an eye over the lucrative spice trade, apart from their other missions of setting contacts with Japan and China and converting the Filipinos to Christianity.[108] But they were successful only in their third objective that is to convert the Filipinos to Christianity. The Portuguese presence in Southeast Asia hindered the Spanish trade mission. The Spanish encountered strong resistance from the Portuguese in their mission of doing trade in East Asia. However, as a counter measure, they converted Manila into a major trade destination of the Asian traders of China, Japan, Siam, Cambodia and the Spice Islands. Eventually, as the Chinese trade with the Philippines expanded, the Spaniards started transacting with them in exchange of the silver dollars and bullion supplied to Manila from the Mexican port of Acapulco.[109] When the Spanish government was shifted from Cebu to Manila in 1571, the trade between the Chinese and the Spaniards grew with the Chinese silk replacing the spice trade mission of the Spaniards. This started the 'galleon trade' where the Chinese traders from Macao came to Manila with Canton silk and exchanged them with silver brought from the American colonies of Spain. This trade is termed as 'Macao-Manila-

Acapulco trade'.[110] This trade undoubtedly followed the South China Sea route from Macao to Manila. Moreover, the Spanish trade with Siam and Cambodia was also done through the South China Sea route which was not unknown to the locals who were involved in intra-Asian trade of the region before the advent of the Europeans.

The Dutch

The Dutch-Portuguese competition for the Asian trade, which was by the fifteenth-sixteenth century under the control of the Iberian kingdom, compelled the Dutch to look East. The Dutch came to the East Indies with the object of trade and commerce, not with any crusading or missionary zeal. The first Dutch fleet to reach Indonesia was in 1596. The Dutch founded the United Netherlands Chartered East India Company (*Veerinigde Geoctroyeerde Oost-Indische Compagnie* or V.O.C.) in 1602, an amalgamation of several Dutch companies and sailed for East Indies. The Dutch selected the island of Java to settle with the objective of controlling the maritime trade of both Indian Ocean and the South China Sea. They found Java as the transit point for the ships coming from the Indian Ocean bound for both the Maluku islands and China via South China Sea. They also wanted to take part in the trade between China and Japan conducted by the Portuguese settled in Macao who were supplying the Japanese with Chinese silk thread and gaining formidable profit of Japanese silver.[111] After occupying Jakarta in 1619 and renaming it as Batavia, the V.O.C. attempted to control the trade with Moluku and China. They tried to found their trade centre in Fujian but when failed due to Portuguese opposition, they turned to Japan for trade.[112] Gradually the V.O.C. got involved more in the East Asian trade including the arms trade. The Wokou were the Chinese traders who smuggled Japanese silver in the Chinese south eastern provinces of Zhejiang, Fujian, and Guangdong· which converted them into powerful armed group in the southern seas. The V.O.C. also started participating in this illegal trade with their base in Hirado, Japan. In exchange of the Japanese silver, the V.O.C factory in Hirado imported Chinese silk thread and textiles from Patani in Malay Peninsula and sapanwood from Ayuthia kingdom of Siam. Later, the Dutch sent arms and even Japanese warriors to assist its missions in Maluku against the English and the Spaniards and sent ships against the Portuguese and Spanish settlements in Macao and Manila and to seize the Chinese junks. The 'Dutch rule' in the southern seas continued till 1621 when the Japanese Shogunate asked them to rein in under Spanish and Portuguese pressure.[113] These piratical arms trade no doubt was carried via the South China Sea. The import of silk trade and textiles from Patani factory on the Malay Peninsula and sapanwood and deerskins from the Siamese kingdom of Ayutthaya to Japan was also done via South China Sea. Also, it is seen that the Dutch were involved in fierce competition with the English, Portuguese and the Spaniards in the South China Sea region during first half of the seventeenth century.

However, the Dutch were not comfortable with their base in Hirado. Firstly, the base was distant from the Chinese coast and secondly, the Ming rulers of China had imposed ban on foreign trade with Japan. Also, the Dutch attempt to occupy either Macao or Penghu Islands of Taiwan was unsuccessful due to opposition from the Portuguese and the Chinese force. Later in 1624, they built a fortress, Fort Zeelandia, in Taiowan (present-day Tainan) in southwest Taiwan and eventually had trade monopoly over Taiwan.[114] Therefore the Dutch were shaping their trading network around the South China Sea and their main target was to do trade with south China and Japan which was possible only through the South China Sea route.

The English

The British involvement in Southeast Asia had two objectives, ensuring security to the British Empire and its trade with China both of which were important for the English. Keeping Southeast Asian maritime trade network under the British control was important to ensure the British economic interest in the region. The British control of Penang (in today's Malaysia) in 1786 was driven by this objective since the French naval presence in the Bay of Bengal in the late seventeenth century threatened the British hold of India's south eastern coast. They considered Penang, a week sail from Madras, as a vital defence base against the French.[115] Till the mid-19th century, the British commercial interests in the East were centred around India and under conducive circumstances, with China. When the other European traders like the Portuguese, Dutch and the French had limited trade relations with the Chinese, the English traders were in an advantageous position after the Industrial Revolution who wanted access to the vast Chinese market offering lucrative commercial gains. To meet this objective, the British got interested in exploiting the land and the maritime routes to China and in the first half of the 19th century, they started acquiring dominance over the sea route to China with bases along the Malacca Strait and South China Sea.[116] Therefore, we see that in the first half of the 19th century, that is, at the initial stage of the English trade in Southeast Asia, South China Sea provided the only trade route to the English to China.

The main thrust of the English trade in Southeast Asia was to do trade with China. Their main rivals there were the French and the Dutch. The English captured the western Sumatra in order to ensure smooth trade via Strait of Malacca and South China Sea amidst the French obstruction and the English navy built bases in Penang and Bencoolen during the Revolutionary War with France to conduct naval operations. The British trade in Southeast Asia was boosted with the concurrent expansion and strengthening of the British Empire in the Indian sub-continent with domination of India's southern ports. With the Dutch trade monopoly waning, the Indian trading vessels took their place in the Southeast Asian waters carrying cotton textiles from Bombay and opium from Calcutta bound for Canton which was the main British trade destination in China. In post 1783 period, the British gradually gained trade dominance in Southeast Asia and acquired Penang in 1786 and Malacca in 1795 to ensure easy transport via the straits.[117] All these were done to ensure the English maritime trade with China through the South China Sea and their strategic interests in the region.

Due to restrictions imposed on the import of Indian textile goods by the British Parliament in the post Industrial Revolution period till eighteenth century, the English East India Company, who had to limit trade with India, found China as an alternative market which boosted the English trade with China and the English import of Chinese goods including tea.[118] At the same time, the English wanted to export items to China. However, the British could not find suitable items to market in China because the Chinese hardly depended on imported items since they considered themselves self sufficient. Therefore, they chose the Malayan tin to export in Chinese market.[119] However, with the growing demand of tin back home in England from the early nineteenth century, the East India Company tried to balance the Anglo-Chinese trade by selling commodities mainly of South and Southeast Asia. For this they promoted the 'country trade', which included Indian raw cotton and opium which were of great demand in China, carried on by the Company's officials and some Indian subjects outside the Company's official transactions. The volume of such trade had grown phenomenally from the last decade of the eighteenth century.[120] This country trade was no doubt maritime in character. As mentioned earlier, until the first half of the nineteenth century, the English trade with China was carried through the sea route via Malacca Straits and South China Sea. This is more evident from the statement of D.R. Sardesai who opined that "All in all, the strategic significance of Southeast Asian water passages, through which the extensive 'country trade' and the East India Company's vessels passed was obvious in the first half of the 19th century".[121] He substantiates his point by referring to C. Northcote Parkinson's description of the maritime route the English used to avail in Southeast Asia *en route* China. Parkinson said,

> "These opium ships...from Bengal... (touched) Junk Ceylon, Penang, Selangore, Malacca, Lingin, Pelambang and...Batavia....At all these ports of call the ship would get rid of some of her cargo, taking tin, ivory and (Mexican) dollars in exchange. Any cargo left over was then disposed on the west coast of Borneo, for gold, and the ship would then collect more tin and pepper and proceed to the Strait of Banca to meet the Company's China ships... These would take on board much of the tin and pepper on payment of freight.... Paying in specie, the ship was then to buy more tin, pepper, rattans, wax and betel nuts, and then follow the China ships towards the end of September. It was necessary to discharge and load the return cargo with extraordinary speed in order to sail again in November and reach Calcutta in the following month, ready to begin the voyage again".[122]

This entire voyage of the English ships to and from China was done via South China Sea, undoubtedly. They used the same maritime route what their predecessors, Indians and Arabs, did in the earlier times. The English settlement in the Malay Peninsula was meant to secure this maritime trade route. The foundation of British trading spot at Singapore was also meant to counter the then growing Dutch challenge to the British trading interests around South China Sea.The location of Singapore was well suited to facilitate the English trading activities with China. It offered the shortest passage for the European ships bound for China, particularly the English ships coming from India and Ceylon.[123] The ships passed through the Strait of Malacca and then touching the Singapore harbour which was located at the southern part of the South China Sea and wading through the sea, moved towards China. However, D R Sardesai writes that Thomas Stamford Raffles, the Lieutenant Governor of Java from 1811-1816, who practically founded the British base in Singapore, expected Singapore to develop a trade with Sumatra and Borneo and to divert Malacca's trade with South and East, as Malacca has obstructed Penang's.[124] With the foundation of Singapore, Thomas Raffles initiated the mission of establishing British control over the Malacca trade routes and of Malaya Peninsula.[125] It can also be said that Singapore's gradual prosperity depended on the South China Sea. In the 18th-19th century period, other English firms were prohibited from doing direct trade with China since the English East India Company had the monopoly over trade with China. Thus, the traders, with foundation of Singapore, contemplated of treating it as an entrepot port for transhipment of goods from China bound for England. This had bolstered Singapore's prosperity. The expansion of the Sino-British trade helped in the development of Singapore's shipping and other facilities. By early twentieth century, there were 35000 tons of shipping done at the Singapore port while the population of the port city increased with the people coming from all over Southeast Asia and coastal China.[126] Thus the Sino-British trade via South China Sea was the backbone of the opulence of Singapore. The location of the port on the mouth of the Malacca Straits had an immense contribution behind the growth of the port in its initial days.

The French

Another prime European country to involve in the Southeast Asia and China trade was France. The French started taking interest in Asia from the early seventeenth century with the foundation of French East India Company in 1604. In 1611, the French ships sailed for the East and by mid seventeenth century, they founded many Oriental establishments. They regarded Madagascar in Africa as a suitable spot to further trade with Southeast Asia and the French priests came to coastal Burma, Siam and Cambodia by 1663.[127] It should be remembered however, that the French trade with China, mainly Yunnan, was done via land route. The French occupation of Indochina (present day Vietnam, Cambodia and Laos) had helped them in this case while the British occupation of upper Burma was also meant to thwart the French connection with both the Burmese Kingdom and France's trade with Yunnan.[128] The French mainly depended on the Indochinese rivers like the Irrawaddy, the Salween, the Menam, or the Mekong for 'an economical entrance to China'. Indochina became the epicentre of French activity in the Far East during the late 19th and early 20th centuries. To the west of French settlement was Laos and Cambodia, and to the east, the country's 2,025 mile coastline bordering the South China Sea and the Gulf of Tonkin. Between China in the north and the Gulf of Thailand and the South China Sea in the south, the French dominated 1,025 miles of land. Presumably the French were not involved much in the maritime trade with China via South China Sea since they had discovered the alternative route via the land to reach China. Therefore, it can be construed that France was not involved in the early South China Sea trade. However, in the subsequent chapter we will see how France took interest in the South China Sea territorial affairs in the later period although did not contribute much in the maritime trade of the region.

South China Sea is the lifeline of Southeast Asia. It is the bridge between China, Southeast Asia and the rest of the world. It is this sea which has shaped the history of the region. The ancient kingdoms of Southeast Asia, in the South China Sea neighbourhood, were the products of this Sea. The trade activities in the South China Sea maritime zone not only boosted the economy of its littoral states, it brought Southeast Asia at the centre of the East Asian commercial zone. No East Asian commercial activities could take place bypassing South China Sea. And that flourished the maritime kingdoms of Southeast Asia. On the basis of their role in the South China Sea commerce, Funan, Champa and Sri Vijaya emerged as the powerful kingdoms. South China Sea was a vital commercial link between China, Japan and the rest of the world. For China, it was (and is) the only maritime opening to the world outside. Thus the *Nanhai* trade was so important for the Chinese dynasties. Similarly, for the ships from the west, of the Arabs, Indians and the Europeans, South China Sea was (and is) the only route to reach the Chinese shores. Since this connectivity is in existence from the early period of human interactions, the littorals of the South China Sea became the point of confluence of trade and culture. South China Sea is intertwined with the East Asian life. And all these happened due the freedom of navigation in the Sea. What Ganga is to the Indians, Nile to the Egyptians, South China Sea is to East Asians, especially Southeast Asians. The chapter here gives the readers a brief idea of the importance of the South China Sea, in its historical context, to not only its littorals but also to the outsiders who have jointly shaped its history. The following chapters will discuss the South China Sea international relations in details which will show how the players, both regional and the extra-regional, have contributed (and are still contributing) in the framing of its geopolitics on the basis of the historical factors discussed in the chapter. This started with the onset of the colonial geopolitical game initiated by the Europeans and subsequently taken over by Japan leaving an indelible mark on the East Asian maritime geopolitics.

END NOTES

1. George Bryan Souza, *The Survival of Empire: Portuguese Trade and Society in China and the Trade in South China Sea, 1630-1754,* Cambridge University Press, New York, 1986, p.1
2. Nicholas Tarling (ed), *Cambridge History of Southeast Asia, From Early Times to c.1500,* Vol. 1, part 1, Cambridge University Press, 1999, pp.104-105
3. Ibid p.130
4. Hye jin Lee, *Maritime History: The South China Sea until the 19th Century,* term paper, AP World History Class, June 2012, www.zum.de/whkmla/sp/1314/hyejin/lhj.1.html#ii (accessed on 29.7.2013)
5. Ibid
6. Kenneth R. Hall and John K. Whitemore, 'Southeast Asian Trade and the Isthmian Struggle, 1000-1200 AD', Kenneth R. Hall and John K. Whitemore (eds), *Explorations in Early South East Asian Statecraft,* Ann Arbor Centre for South and South East Asian Studies, the University of Michigan, Michigan Papers on South and South East Asia, 1976, p.303
7. Anthony Reid, *Southeast Asia in the Age of Commerce, 1450-1680: Expansion and Crisis,* Vol 2, Yale University Press, New Haven and London, 1993, p.1
8. Nicholas Tarling (ed), op cit, p.185
9. Ibid, p.186
10. Ibid
11. For details see Kenneth Hall's *Maritime Trade and State Development in Southeast Asia,* University of Hawaii Press, Honolulu, 1985, pp.20-24
12. Ibid, p.20
13. Kenneth R. Hall and John K. Whitmore, op cit, p.305
14. Kenneth Hall, *A History of Early Southeast Asia: Maritime Trade and Societal Development, 100-1500,* Plymouth, UK, Roman and Littlefield Publishers Inc, 2011, p.31
15. Cited in Kenneth Hall, op cit (see chapter 1, reference no.45, p.267)
16. Ibid, p.26
17. Li Qingxin, *British Maritime Silk Road,* China Intercontinental Press, 2006, p.26
18. Anthony Reid, op cit, p.4
19. *Vietnam: Form Myth to Modernity,* Asian Civilizations Forum, Education Resource Pack, 21-30 May, 2008, http://www.acm.org.sg/resource_docs/147_Vietnam_Exhibition_Funan_ERP.pdf (accessed on 1.8.2013)
20. Ibid
21. Pierre-Yves Maguin, 'The Archaeology of Early Maritime Polities of Southeast Asia', in Ian Glover, Peter Bellwood (eds), *Southeast Asia: From prehistory to history,* London and New York, Routledge Curzon, 2004, p.297
22. Ibid
23. Ibid p.290
24. Charles Higham, *The Civilization of Angkor,* University of California Press, Berkley and Los Angeles, 2001, p.26
25. Pierre-Yves Maguin, op cit, p.300
26. Nicholas Tarling (ed), op cit, p.194
27. Ibid p.195

28. Kenneth Hall, op cit, p.65
29. Ibid, p.67
30. Kenneth Hall, op cit, p.178
31. Ibid, p.179
32. William A. Southworth, 'The Coastal States of Champa', in Ian Glover, Peter Bellwood (ed), op cit, p.209
33. Ibid
34. Ibid pp. 212-213
35. Geoff Wade, 'An Early Age of Commerce in Southeast Asia,900–1300 CE',*Journal of Southeast Asian Studies*, 40(2), June 2009, pp. 221–265
36. *The Port of Thi Nai (in Nagara Vijaya, from 12th to 15th Centuries CE)*, The Vietnam Maritime Archaeological Centre, http://www.themua.org/vietnam/prt.php?content=prt4 (accessed on 6.8.2013)
37. Cited in Geoff Wade, op cit, p.243
38. Ibid, p.244
39. Kenneth Hall, op cit, p.78
40. D.G.E. Hall, *A History of Southeast Asia*, Palgrave McMillan, 1981, p.47
41. Ibid
42. Jane Kate Leonard, *Wei Yuan and China's Rediscovery of the Maritime World*, Harvard East Asian Monographs, Council on East Asian Studies, 1984, p.42
43. Kenneth Hall writes that by 1079-1082 A.D, Srivijayan kingdom's capital was shifted from Palembang to central Sumatra port of Jambi. See Kenneth Hall, op cit, p102. It seems after Srivijayan power declined following the Chola invasion, the capital was shifted.
44. Geoff Wade, op cit, p.253
45. Ibid p.254
46. Pierre-Yves Maguin, op cit, p.307
47. Geoff Wade, op cit, p.254
48. Ibid
49. Elizabeth A. Bacus, *The Archaeology of the Philippine Archipelago*, in Ian Glover, Peter Bellwood (ed), op cit, pp.266-267
50. Ibid, p.267
51. Charity Beyer-Bagatsing (From the notes of Dr. H. Otley Beyer), *The Philippines Before Magellan*, www.sdsanantonians.com/...magellan/the%20philippines%20before%20... (accessed on 14.8.2013)
52. Cited in ibid
53. Ibid
54. Ibid
55. Ibid
56. Elizabeth A. Bacus, op cit, p.269
57. William T. Rowe, *China's Last Empire: The Great Qing*, The Belknap Press of Harvard University Press, 2009, p.122
58. David W. Del Testa (ed), *Global History: Cultural Encounters from Antiquity to the Present*, Volume 1, Sharpe Reference, New York, 2004, p.107
59. Hye jin Lee, op cit
60. O.W. Wolters, *Early Southeast Asia: Selected Essays*, Southeast Asia Program

Publications, Cornwall University, New York, 2008, p. 66

61. Hye jin Lee, op cit
62. Ibid
63. Jane Kate Leonard, op cit, p.36
64. Ibid, pp.36-37
65. Timothy Brook, *The Troubled Empire,: China in the Yuan and Ming Dynasties*, The Belknap Press of Harvard University Press, 2010, p.219
66. Jane Kate Leonard, op cit, p.37
67. William T. Rowe, op cit, p.133
68. Jane Kate Leonard, op cit, p.39
69. Timothy Brook, op cit, p.226
70. Ibid
71. Dr. Arshad Islam, 'Arab Navigation in the Indian Ocean Before European Dominance in South And Southeast Asia: A Historical Study', *Journal of the Pakistan Historical Society*, 58 (2), http://irep.iium.edu.my/3462/, p.8
72. Geoff Wade, op cit, pp.231-232
73. Ibid, pp.232-233
74. Sebastian R. Prange, 'Like banners on the Sea: Muslim Trade Networks and Islamization in Malabar and Maritime Southeast Asia', R. Michael Feener, Terenjit Seuea (ed), *Islamic Connections: Muslim Societies in South and Southeast Asia*, Singapore, Institute of Southeast Asian Studies, 2009, p.26
75. Ibid, p.29
76. Dr. Arshad Islam, op cit, p.15
77. Ibid, p.16
78. Geoff Wade, op cit p.233
79. Ibid
80. Ibid, pp.233-234
81. William E Deal, *Handbook to Life in Medieval and Early Modern Japan*, Oxford University Press, Oxford, 2006, pp.128-129
82. Takeshi Hamashita, *A History of Maritime Asia and East Asian Regional Dynamism 1600-1900: Maritime Asia from the Ryukyu-Okinawa to the Hong Kong Networks*, Institute of Oriental Culture, the University of Tokyo, http://www.oslo2000.uio.no/program/papers/m1b/m1b-hamashita.pdf, (accessed on 5.11.2013), p.3
83. Ibid, p.6
84. Ibid, p.7
85. Ibid
86. Marwyn Samuels, *Contest for South China Sea*, Methuen, New York, London, 1982, p.42
87. Charles A. Fisher, *Southeast Asia: A Social, Economic and Political Geography*, Methuen & Co. Ltd, London, 1964, p.126
88. Kailash K. Beri, *History and Culture of Southeast Asia: Modern*, Sterling Publishers Pvt Ltd, 1994, p.19
89. D.G.E. Hall, op cit, p.252
90. *Marco Polo and His Travels*, http://www.silk-road.com/artl/marcopolo.shtml (accessed on 12.7.2013)
91. Ibid, pp.253-254

92. Diana Preston and Michael Preston, *A Pirate of Exquisite Mind: The Life of William Dampier, Explorer, Naturalist and Buccaneer*, UK, Doubleday, 2004, p.228
93. D.G.E. Hall, op cit, p.254
94. Ibid
95. Charles A. Fisher, op cit, pp.127-128
96. Nicholas Tarling (ed), op cit, p.354
97. Kailash K. Beri, op cit, p.20
98. Ngyuen Thi Ha Thanh, *European Trade on the Far East and the Mercantile Relationship with Vietnam from the 16th to 19th Century*, http://www.icis.kansai-u.ac.jp/data/journal02-v1/24_nguen.pdf (accessed on 14.11.2013), pp.357-358
99. Quoted in Ngyuen Thi Ha Thanh, op cit, p.358
100. Ibid
101. Bill Hayton, *The South China Sea: The Struggle for Power in Asia*, New Haven and London, Yale University Press, 2014, p.33
102. George Bryan Souza, op cit, p.11
103. Ibid, p.15
104. Ibid, p.63
105. Ibid, p.18
106. Kenneth R. Hall, op cit, p.319
107. Ibid, pp.319-320
108. D.G.E. Hall, op cit, pp. 272,273
109. Ibid, p.274
110. Nicholas Tarling, op cit, pp.356-357
111. Ota Atsushi, *The Dutch East India Company and the Rise of Intra Asian Commerce*, http://www.nippon.com/en/features/c00105/ (accessed on 19.6.2014)
112. Ibid
113. Ibid
114. Ibid
115. D.R. Sardesai, *British Trade & Expansion in Southeast Asia, 1830-1914*, Bombay, Allied Publishers Pvt. Ltd, 1977, pp.30-31
116. Ibid, p.23
117. Kailash K. Beri, op cit, p.47
118. D.R. Sardesai, p.24
119. Ibid, p.25
120. Ibid, pp.26, 27
121. Ibid, pp.29-30
122. Quoted in ibid, p.30
123. Ibid, pp.35-36
124. Ibid, p.36
125. Ibid, p.39
126. Ibid, p.41
127. John L. Christian, 'Anglo-French Rivalry in Southeast Asia: Its Historical Geography and Diplomatic Climate',*Geographical Review*, Vol. 31, No. 2 (Apr., 1941), http://www.jstor.org/stable/210208 (accessed on 23.12.2013), pp.272-273
128. For details refer to ibid

2

South China Sea in Colonial Period: Sea of Conflict

The previous chapter highlighted the significance of the South China Sea trade in shaping the history of Southeast Asia, from the pre-colonial to the onset of the colonial era. The freedom of navigation in the Sea promoted the emergence of Southeast Asia as an economic hub around South China Sea. However, the modern South China Sea can be called the 'Sea of disputes' and the dispute revolves around the question of territorial sovereignty over its geographical features and the adjoining waters as well as the strategic significance of the Sea amidst the emerging East Asian geopolitics with power shift to the East. The dispute centres mainly around two archipelagos, the Spratly and the Paracel (Map 2.1). The Spratly archipelago is comprised of more than hundred islets, coral reefs and seamounts which are scattered over some 410,000 square kilometres in the central South China Sea, in the north of Borneo, east of Vietnam and west of southern Philippines. The Paracel islands, located in the north of South China Sea and equidistant from Vietnam and Chinese island of Hainan, are made of two groups, the Crescent Group and Amphitrite Group together containing thirty islets, sandbanks or reefs and they are spread around 15000 square kilometres of ocean.[1] Today, this sea is the zone of conflict and coercion among its littoral states. China, Vietnam, the Philippines, Malaysia, Indonesia- all are the claimants of the territorial sovereignty over the Sea and its features. These claims are based both on historical as well as legal grounds. On the other hand the extra-regional powers like India and USA insist on the freedom of navigation in the waters connecting the Pacific and the Indian Ocean world. Thus the South China Sea dispute revolves round the question of eternal freedom of navigation and the colonial concept of territorial sovereignty, introduced by the European colonisers. All these have made the region most disputed with high conflict potentials. And these potentials are not only based on the claims of the respective disputants, or the interests of the extra-regional forces only, but also on the strong sense of nationalism and national aspirations of these countries. Such zeal is natural for the countries which were subject to colonial oppression and exploitation under the European colonisers. On the other hand, the appearance of the European traders-turned-rulers in the Asian scene had injected the notion of 'territorial sovereignty' extended to the geographical features, inhabited or uninhabited, habitable or uninhabitable. The South China Sea, as we have seen in the previous chapter, became the playground of the European colonisers by the nineteenth century where the outsiders fought for their dominance, extending their European feuds to the Asian waters, to preserve their economic and strategic interests in the region. This European duel in the form of territorial sovereignty got injected in the later nation-states of South China Sea region giving birth to the unending international dispute. However, as we shall see here the Sea rose to the other level of geopolitical significance, independent of its territorial disputes, during the war time which ultimately (and perhaps permanently) mingled the local sovereignty affairs with the larger geopolitical calculations of the extra regional powers with interests in the region.

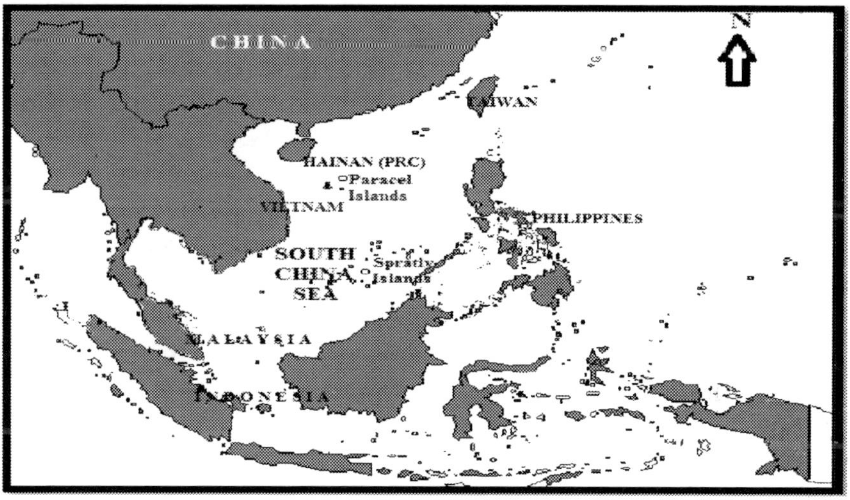

Map 2.1

Colonialism and territorial disputes in South China Sea

The Westphalian notion of sovereignty, which propagates the concept of immunity of states from external interference, is sometimes held responsible for the inter-state territorial disputes. In Asia, the territorial disputes among the states have their roots in the colonial period when the extra-regional rulers from Europe divided the Asian territories under their possession among themselves or settled the disputes over borders with the neighbours in a way to sow the seed of future squabble. Sometimes, the concerned parties of disputes refuse to consider them as dispute at all thus blocking the chance of negotiations with other disputants. The anxiety further rises with one disputant being powerful than others and getting assertive day-by-day triggering a sense of insecurity among others thereby encouraging them for preparations for counter measures. All these factors fit in the South China Sea case. The dispute seems to be a colonial legacy. This legacy of Western colonialism still influences the inter-state relations of Asia and with the West.[2] The scholars are unanimous that the territorial disputes in the erstwhile colonies are rooted in the colonial era. Referring to the territorial disputes between China and her neighbours, the Global Times wrote, *"In the past, Western suzerains usually controlled colonies by demarcating controversial border lines and raising internal ethnic tensions...This is the root cause for the territorial disputes between China and some of its neighbors."*[3] The South China Sea dispute also bears this colonial legacy. It is most evident from the question of sovereignty that fuels the dispute.

The coming of the Europeans in Asia brought in the Westphalian notion of territorial sovereignty. The Westphalian sovereignty concept, based on the Treaty of Westphalia signed in 1648 among the European Powers, established the supreme authority of the State over its territory, independent of any external interference. This was meant to settle the disputes among the European powers, who were fighting for thirty long years, to ensure stability and tranquillity in Europe and recognize the equality among the states, big or small. When these Europeans came to Asia as traders, later to become rulers, they started exercising their version of territorial sovereignty over the regions possessed by them. The prime concern of these European traders-cum-rulers was the control of the trade and trade route. The rivalry among them for this control fuelled the exercise of sovereign rights over territories even further. In a way, the Europeans brought their 'in-house' feud to the world outside, especially in Asia. As we have seen in chapter I, the Europeans started coming in

Asia, especially Southeast Asia, in the late fifteenth century, starting with the Iberian kingdoms of Spain and Portugal, followed by French, British and Dutch. Eventually, the South China Sea became zone of competition among the Western colonial powers with the Dutch occupying Malacca, Java and Taiwan, the British occupying Malaya, Borneo and Hong Kong, the French in Indochina and the Americans in the Philippines by the nineteenth century. We have also seen how one European trading power, in the initial days of exploration of the region, deposed the previous one who already established itself as a major trading entity. Ultimately the Europeans divided the South China Sea littoral states among themselves as a mark of permanent settlement of the territorial boundaries as seen in Map 2.2.

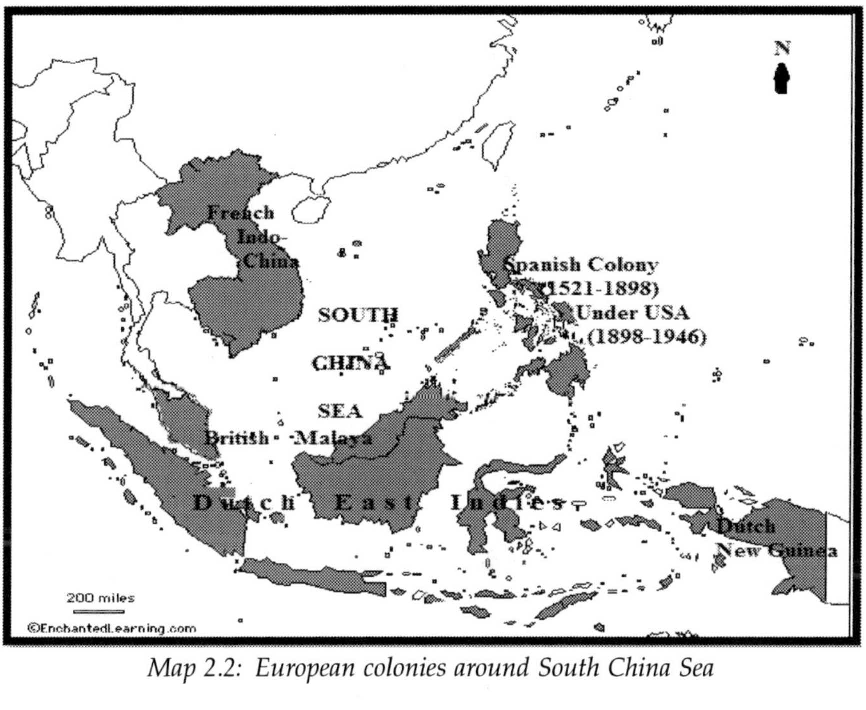

Map 2.2: European colonies around South China Sea

The main target of the European trade in East Asia, as already mentioned, was China. The Chinese market and products retained their value even in colonial time, especially in the early years of European colonialism, as was the case during the hey days of pre-colonial commercial activities in Asia, governed by the Chinese, Arabs and Indians. But with European colonialism anchoring in the South China Sea region, the control over the trade and the trade route passed to the

Europeans. Between the seventeenth and nineteenth century, many port towns around South China Sea fell to the Europeans who were keen to dominate the trade and the trade route there. The port towns of Batavia, Riau, Benkulen, Makassar, Ambon, Manila and Timor came under the European control and in this way many commercial centres along the Indian Ocean-South China Sea were taken over by the Europeans.[4] The Malacca Strait, connecting Indian Ocean with South China Sea and beyond, has traditionally been an important passage of commercial activities in Asia. Therefore whoever controlled this Strait became the lord of South China Sea trade and paved the way for domination. The Europeans, by the virtue of their command over the South China Sea trade, eventually appeared as the rulers of the littoral States of the region. And with them came the concept of territorial sovereignty. Sovereignty is a modern notion which is exercised within the demarcated border of the state. The pre-modern states had frontiers as defensive space within their core territory while the frontiers did not require control so long as the rivals were kept at bay.[5] The current South China Sea dispute is the dispute over sovereignty issue and the disputants were European colonies, either semi (China) or full (Southeast Asian disputants, see Map 2.2). The European colonisers, apart from introducing the notion of territorial sovereignty, also distinguished between the land and sea. When the land is divided along the territorial boundaries, the sea should be free of all except the territorial waters along the coasts.[6]

Root of the dispute: European activities in the South China Sea in the nineteenth century

The European trading companies had ventured in the South China Sea waters since the early sixteenth century. By the nineteenth century the British (East India Company) and the Dutch (V.O.C.—*Vereenigde Oostindische Compagnie* or United East India Company) 'had become governments in their own right'.[7] Both the companies' rules over their Asian colonies were eventually taken over by their respective home governments, the English in 1858 and the Dutch, much earlier, in 1800. By the end of the nineteenth century, the South China Sea region was colonised by the European powers. This colonisation laid the foundation of current boundaries around the South China Sea. The colonisers introduced the concept of the state system, based on the Westphalian model with specified territorial boundaries. The foundation of states with borders initiated the measurement of maritime frontiers.[8] The Iberian states of Spain and Portugal had divided the non-European (or non-Christian to be precise) world among themselves under two treaties, Treaty of Tordesillas (1493) and Treaty of Zaragoza (1529). Prior to this, Pope Nicholas V had authorized the King of Portugal to conquer the non-Christian world prohibiting other Christians from interfering in Portuguese possessions.[9] Later on this duopoly of the Iberian kingdoms collapsed with the emergence of other European powers expanding their naval strength and spreading to different corners of the globe.

In South China Sea region, the British, French and the Dutch possessed more territories than Spain (limited to the Filipino islands) and Portugal (first European traders in the region subsequently ousted by the three mighty powers). In 1877, the British colony of Labuan (located off the coast of Borneo) allowed an American named Graham and two Britons, Simpson and James, to claim the Spratly Island and Ambona Cay on behalf of the British Crown in order to extract guano (from the islands). It was announced in the *Government Gazette*.[10] Similarly, Britain named the Spratly Islands after Richard Spratly in 1881 in the Royal Navy's Hydrographic Office charts where it is named 'Spratly Islands' since then. The islands, which Captain Richard Spratly identified as 'sandy isle' in 1843, were seen by many navigators before him like East India Company's surveyor James Horsburgh.[11] The French, like the British, were also very active to assert their maritime possession in the South China Sea region since the late nineteenth century. The Sino-French war of 1884-85 resulted in the delimitation of the frontier between China and Tonkin (present day northern Vietnam). This delimitation, China has argued, recognized the Paracel and the Spratly islands as parts of China by France.[12] However, notwithstanding this 1887 convention, France kept on seeking hegemony over the Paracels. There were reports of French plans of naval patrols in the islands and also about French plan to construct lighthouse in one of them. The Kuangtung Province (or Guangdong province of China), after being reported about the French plans, sought permission to exercise administrative control over the Paracels.[13] The Germans also started taking interest in the South China Sea trade by the late nineteenth century. Its navy conducted series of surveys in the Paracel Islands between 1881 and 1884 but never took permission from either China or France for that. The respective governments also did not notice the German activities and so did not protest against it. In 1885, the Germans published their survey which was used as reference by both the British and the French, but not the Chinese.[14] In a way, the European activities in the South China Sea had already started spreading the ripples of contention. Also, the appearance of the new European forces, the latest being the Germans, added to the complications with their surveying activities in the Paracel Islands which got unnoticed by both China and France. It should be noted here however, that the German surveys were conducted between 1881 and 1884 and they were published in 1885, the period when the Sino-French conflict was going on, which was to settle the boundary between the two powers not before 1887. Therefore, it can be said that the South China Sea territorial dispute did not arise before 1887 and the Europeans got the time to carry on with their maritime objectives in the sea without much hindrance. China's later definite claims, as we will see in the following paragraphs, in the post 1887 period can therefore be taken as the beginning of the South China Sea dispute.

China and the South China Sea territorial conflict during the nineteenth century

The dispute regarding claims over the South China Sea islands did not arise with the Chinese until the late nineteenth century. China's first ambassador to Britain, Ku Sung-tao, had claimed the Paracel Islands in 1886-87 for China. He had also put forward an implicit claim over the Spratly Islands in 1883.[15] However, as we have mentioned earlier, the British Royal Navy's Hydrographic Office had already named the Spratly Islands after Captain Richard Spratly in 1881. Yet, these two claims were no unequivocal claim of Chinese sovereignty over the islands.[16] Nevertheless, some evidences are put forward to establish that the Chinese history books refer to the Chinese knowledge and the use of South China Sea throughout history. In *Yi Zhou Shu* (Scattered Books of Zhou Dynasties) there are mentions of tributes coming from South China Sea to the Zhou Dynasty (21st-16th Century BC) which continued through the Shang Dynasty as well (16th-11th Century BC).[17] Attempts are also made to prove that China is first to name the Paracel and Spratly Islands as *Xisha* and *Nansha* respectively. There is an argument that the Chinese were less acquainted with the Spratly or Nansha Islands since there is little historical evidence of Chinese interest in the Spratlys.[18] Yet, some evidences tell the contrary. It is said that one Yang Fu of the East Han Dynasty referred to the Nansha Islands in his book *Yiwu Zhi* (Records of Rarities). General kang Tai, the famous navigator of the East Wu State also mentioned about Nansha Islands in his book *Funan Zhuan* (journey to and from Phnom that is ancient Cambodia). There are also mentions of Nansha and Xisha Islands in various history books of Tang and Song dynasties which are named differently like Jiuruluo Islands, Shitang, Changsa (etc). The geographical locations and descriptions of the Nansha Islands and even specific positions of the various islands were mentioned in the book named *Abridged Records of Islands and Barbarians*, written by Wang Dayuan, a Chinese navigator of the Yuan Dynasty. Similarly, *The Road Map of Qing Dynasty* also mentions the Nansha in details.[19] However, mere historical knowledge about the islands and the sea do not gain sovereignty right. Regarding the Chinese exercise of jurisdiction over the Nansha Islands, it is said that Emperor Zhenyuan of Tang Dynasty (785-805 AD) included the Islands in the administrative map. The local history books and officials maps have recorded the exercise of this jurisdiction by the subsequent governments of China. There is mention of South China Sea and the 'territories beyond the Sea' as part of Ming China in the inscription gauged on the memorial tablet of the tomb of General Qian Shichai. Under Qing Dynasty, the Nansha Islands were marked in the Chinese maps including the 1724 *Map of Provinces of Qing Dynasty*, 1755 *Map of Provinces of Imperial Qing Dynasty*, 1767 *Map of Unified China of the Great Qing for Ten Thousand Years*, 1810 *Topographical Map of Unified China of the Great Qing for Ten Thousand Years* and the 1817 *Map of Unified China of the Great Qing for Ten Thousand Years*.[20] What is noteworthy here is the consistency in the mentioning of the Nansha Islands as part of Imperial China throughout the eighteenth and early nineteenth century. The Chinese history books also mention about the naval patrolling in the South China Sea waters during the Han Dynasty rule. Admiral Ma Yuan, in his book *Hou Han Shu* (Books of Latter Han Dynasty) mentioned that one Chen Mao of the East Han Dynasty and Zhou Chang undertook naval inspection and patrolling cruise to the islands in the South China Sea.[21] Similarly, the *Guide to South China Sea* of 1868 mentions about the activities of the Chinese fishermen in the Nansha Islands saying,

> "fishermen from Hainan Island went Zhenhe Isles and reefs and lived on sea cucumbers and shells they got there. The footmarks of fishermen could be found in every isle of the Nansha Islands and some of the fishermen would even live there for a long period of time. Every year there were small boats departing from Hainan Island for the Nansha Islands for sea cucumbers and shells from the fishermen there. The ships used to leave Hainan Island in December or January every year and return when the south-westerly monsoon started."[22]

The above quotation proves that the Chinese not only had knowledge about the Nansha or Paracel Islands but they did visit the Islands on a regular basis. The *Road Map* produced during the Ming Dynasty and updated subsequently was the navigational guideline to Nansha and Xisha (Spratly) Islands which mention about the developmental activities done there by the Chinese. The map showed the navigational routes to the Spratly and Paracel Islands from Qinglan, Wenchang county, Hainan island and Tanmen Port of Qionghai County.[23] Thus these evidences show that the Chinese were in constant connection with the Islands in the South China Sea where they lived 'for long time' (in Paracel) and were engaged in developmental activities.

Everything said and done, however, the Chinese did not put forward their claims over the South China Sea Islands formally before 1887 that is late nineteenth century, when the European activities, as already mentioned, increased in the waters there. It is said that the prohibition on Chinese maritime trade imposed by the Ming rulers, between fourteenth and seventeenth century, and also the lack of maritime governance by them actually facilitated the opening of the sea to the Europeans.[24] Thus, China did not claim her sovereign rights over the islands or even the Sea in the pre-colonial period since the very concept of Westphalian territorial sovereignty did not arise in the Asian context before the advent of the Europeans. It is true that the Chinese were acquainted with the islands of the Sea and, as has already been mentioned before, used the Sea for trade and communication before the advent of the Europeans, and according to the Road Map were engaged in developmental activities in the Islands, yet, whether that automatically makes South China Sea, along with its geographical features, part of Chinese territory is difficult to conclude due to the absence of the concept of exclusive territorial sovereignty before the coming of the Europeans. The South China Sea is an indeterminate area, away from the mainland and therefore was never part of Chinese empire. The Chinese woke up with their claims only when the Europeans started splish-splashing in the waters of *Nanhai* in the late nineteenth century. The British had been navigating through the waters of South China Sea since the late eighteenth century with Captain Richard Spratly visiting the area in 1843 and discovering the islands and named after him subsequently. They already claimed Spratly Islands and Ambona Cay by 1877. The Germans on the other hand undertook surveys in the islands of the Sea between 1881 and 1884 without the knowledge of China or France who were busy in their mutual conflicts during that time. Also, the French even after concluding the frontier between Tonkin and China did not give up their claims over the South China Sea islands. So, the European powers were already exercising their freedom of navigation in the South China Sea along with the right of exploration (or exploitation?) of the islands without seeking any permission from any state authority, which was never strongly challenged by anybody, let alone China, which established the non-existence of any sovereignty claim over the South China Sea and its islands by any state during the nineteenth century. Another claimant of the current South China Sea dispute is Vietnam who also refers to her historical association with the Sea.

Vietnam and the South China Sea territorial conflict during the nineteenth century

The Vietnamese, like the Chinese, have been sailing in the waters of South China Sea, which they call *East Sea*, since the early period of their history. As already discussed in chapter 1, the ancient kingdoms of Funan and Champa, which were parts of modern day Vietnam, had flourished because of the South China Sea trade. The archaeological discoveries along the coasts of Vietnam have established the commercial activities of these kingdoms in the pre-colonial era which were part and parcel of the South China Sea trade. Similarly, the Red River Delta region in the north of Vietnam emerged as a major Buddhist centre *en route* China since the pilgrims, using maritime route, used to sail along the coastal line of the South China Sea to reach Red River Delta region from where they embarked on a fresh journey to China. Therefore, it can be said that like the Chinese, the Vietnamese were also active in the South China Sea. Today, the Vietnamese also claim both the Spratly Islands (*Truong Sa* Islands in Vietnamese) and the Paracel Islands (*Hoang Sa* Islands in Vietnamese) as part of its territory backed by the historical evidences. The Ministry of Foreign Affairs of the Govt. of Vietnam, in its report in 1988, has affirmed strongly the Vietnamese case in the following words:

> "Vietnam's case is that it has maintained effective occupation of the two archipelagoes at least since the 17th century when they were not under the sovereignty of any country and the Vietnamese State has exercised effectively, continuously and peacefully its sovereignty over the two archipelagoes until the time when they were invaded by the Chinese armed forces."[25]

The White Paper on the Hoang Sa and Truong Sa Islands published by erstwhile South Vietnam in 1975 attempted to establish the Vietnamese claims over the Hoang Sa Islands with historical evidences. It read,

> "The Vietnamese have had knowledge of the Hoang Sa Islands long before the arrival to the South China Sea of Westerners who publicized internationally the name of "Paracels" for this part of their territory.... Evidence showing Vietnamese sovereignty over the Hoang Sa Islands extends back over three hundred years. The oldest Vietnamese document on this part of the national heritage is the work done sometime between 1630 and 1653 by a scholar named Do Ba and also known under the penname of Dao Phu. It is a series of maps of Viet Nam which constitutes the third part of the "Hong Duc Atlas" (1): the Atlas started under the reign of Emperor Le Thanh Tong alias Hong Duc (1460-1497). Notes accompanying the maps clearly indicate that as far back as the early 17th century, Vietnamese authorities had been sending, on a regular basis, ships and men to these islands, which at that time were named "Cat Vang" (both "Cat Vang" and "Hoang Sa" mean "yellow sand"). These are the islands now known internationally by the name "Paracels".[26]

Therefore, it is seen that Vietnam, bifurcated as well as unified, kept on insisting on ancient Vietnam's 'sovereignty' over the South China Sea archipelagos. What is noteworthy in the 1988 report is the affirmation that during the seventeenth century, the archipelagos of Spratly and Paracel were not under the sovereign control of any country. The official report of South Vietnam on the Paracel or Hoang Sa archipelago actually establish the pre colonial Vietnam's activities extended far north near the Chinese coast. Like the Chinese, the Vietnamese also cite the maps including the disputed islands as part of their kingdom. However, the early Vietnamese did exercise some kind of sovereignty over the islands via occupation. This is clear from the1988 report of Vietnam which says that:

> "It was recorded in *Toan Tap Thien Nam Tu Chi Lo Do Thu* (Route Maps from the Capital to the Four Directions) by Do Ba Cong Dao in the 17th century that at least by that century the map of Vietnam had designated the two archipelagoes by a single name Bai Cat Vang and placed them within the administrative confines of Binh Son district.. Vietnam consolidated its occupation and established its sovereignty by organizing Hoang Sa brigades for the purposes of exploitation in a State capacity...".[27]

Thus it is seen that the Vietnamese had been exercising some sort of sovereignty over the Spratly and the Paracel Islands even before the advent of the Europeans. The court documents of King Le Thanh Tong of fifteenth century (1460-1497) mentions the archipelagos as part of Vietnamese territory. Similarly, the Journal of Batavia confirmed Vietnamese sovereignty over the Paracels in 1630s after Dutch merchant boats were assisted by the Vietnamese when it went stranded.[28] The 1975 South Vietnam report also mentions about the incident to justify Vietnam's historical claim over the Paracel Islands. The report read that according to the Journal, published between 1634-36 period, the three Dutch ships named Veenhuizen, Schagen (7) and Grootebroek left Touron (present-day Da Nang) on their way to Formosa (present day Taiwan), coming from Batavia, (Jakarta, Indonesia) on July 20, 1634. These ships got stuck in a tempest and lost contact with each other. Later when Veenhuizen, Schagen managed to reach Formosa, Grootebroek capsized near Paracel Islands. The captain of the ship, after storing remains of the cargo on the islands under the guidance of 50 sailors, had sailed to Vietnam coast, with 12 sailors, to seek help from the Nguyen Lords. The report argues that the sailors chose Vietnam instead of China, which was nearer, because they assumed that Paracel were under Vietnamese jurisdiction.[29] Thus, the Vietnamese claims of sovereignty were established, before the advent of the French, not only by the Vietnamese but endorsed by the externals as well. So, from these documents the Vietnamese' historical claims of sovereignty over the Spratly and the Paracel seemed to have some ground. The report of 1988 gave more historical evidences to establish Vietnam's sovereign right over the two archipelagos in the pre colonial period. It said that Emperor Gia Long (of the early nineteenth century), the founder of the Nguyen dynasty, and his successors like Minh Mang, Thieu Tri and Tu Duc attempted to ensure national sovereignty overthe two archipelagoes. Between 1815 and 1835 the Vietnamese emperors had exercised their sovereignty over the archipelagos by conducting exploration of the islands, undertaking sea route and cartographical surveys.[30] Therefore, we see, following the government reports of 1975 and 1988, that the Vietnamese rulers had been exercising their sovereignty over the islands. Such exercise was not challenged by anybody, let alone China whose protests surfaced not before late nineteenth century. In that case the perception of the Europeans introducing the notion of sovereignty in Asia can be questioned since the mention of the Spratly and the Paracels within 'Vietnamese administrative confines' in the old Vietnamese record substantiates this viewpoint. However, whether such 'sovereignty' exercise matches the current character of state sovereignty notion of European system is subject to detailed analysis.

French and the South China Sea dispute

Vietnam became a protectorate of France in 1884 after southern part of Vietnam, called Cochinchina, went to French possession in 1867. Thus, the responsibility to protect and defend the Vietnamese territory passed into the hands of the French. And from now on, France began to assert its claims over Paracel and Spratly Islands. However, the French claims over the islands did not become prominent before 1930s. So, initially, the French did not officially claim the sovereignty over the archipelagos but did act in that manner. The French undertook the project of construction of light house in the Paracel islands and carried out naval patrols in the South China Sea to ensure protection and combat smuggling.[31] They concluded the frontier delimitation agreement in 1887 with China on 26th June 1887 called *Convention relative a la delimitation de la frontiere entre la Chinee tl e Tonkin.* This agreement was about delimiting common frontier between China and French Indochina in Tonkin. Notwithstanding this agreement, the French kept on seeking hegemony over the Paracels. This was because the agreement did not specify, beyond the islands adjacent to the Sino-Vietnamese coast, the delimitation of the maritime frontier farther south in the Gulf of Tonkin.[32] The French proposal to construct light house in the Paracel archipelago in 1899 shook the Chinese. The Kuangtong (Guangdong) province, as mentioned earlier, sought permission to induct Paracel Islands within their administrative network. The Chinese undertook an inspection of the islands, first of its kind, in 1902. According to Marwyn Samuels, this was the first attempt on the part of the Chinese to implement the convention of 1887 (concluded with the French) to assert China's effective authority over the Paracel.[33] So, by the turn of the new century we see that the dispute over the South China Sea archipelagos is taking shape with the Chinese and the French becoming active with their claims.

South China Sea Dispute in the early Twentieth Century

The South China Sea dispute started gathering momentum at the dawn of the new century. The colonial era in Southeast Asia was at its zenith. The region was divided among the four Western colonisers, British,

French, Dutch and the Americans, each exercising its own economic interests and acting as the boss of the region. In the mean time, the assertive stance over the South China Sea archipelagos was initiated by China. China undertook expeditions to the Paracel Islands in 1902 and 1908 and issued sovereignty notice over these islands and inducted Paracel within her administrative ambit.[34] The appearance of the Japanese in the scene was sudden and unexpected when a Japanese entrepreneur and adventurer Nishizawa Yoshiji occupied Pratas Island in the Paracel archipelagos in 1907 and named it after him. Perturbed Chinese sent Admiral Li Chun and Vice-General Wu Ching-yung first to establish Chinese sovereignty (over the island) and also to negotiate a settlement with the occupiers.[35] Before that, when the Chinese team reached Pratas and challenged Nishizawa and his team, Nishizawa told them that he discovered the Island. When the news reached Guangzhou, demand arose for the government to do something. The nationalists gathered evidences to prove Pratas belonged to China. With pressure mounting, Chinese government wanted to resolve the dispute once and for all even against monetary settlement.[36] The negotiation was done in 1908 after paying Nishizawa an indemnity of 1,30,000 silver dollars after which Japan formally recognized Chinese sovereignty over the Pratas Island.[37] Returning to Canton, after conducting one-month survey in 1909, Admiral Chun (Zhun) proposed to the Qing administration to develop the Paracel Islands. The Qing court approved the proposal. In 1909, the Paracel Islands were absorbed as part of a county which was part of Hainan Island.

In this way, Chinese central government asserted the authority over the islands of 'Southern Sea' with the Guangdong provincial administration's role to defend the territorial rights of China.[38] There was reason of Imperial China becoming so assertive with her sovereignty claim over the South China Sea Islands during this time. The dawn of the twentieth century brought bad fate for Qing rulers of China. By the late nineteenth century Japan emerged as a major Asian power. She occupied Korean Peninsula and Taiwan, located at the fringe of South China Sea in the north. Meanwhile pressure was mounting on Qing Emperor of China for being incapable of upholding the territorial integrity of China. So, the Chinese government felt the urgent need to turn the country's issue of sovereign rights over its maritime territories as a national pride.[39] The current dispute over the South China Sea, as we will see later, also has the sprinkle of this 'national pride' issue over it. Presumably the Qing Dynasty's assertive posture over the maritime dispute at the dawn of the twentieth century was mainly to save its image as the defender of the territorial integrity and thereby the torchbearer of national pride. Its decision to develop the Paracel Islands can be seen in this context where its urge to establish China's territorial sovereignty over the disputed Islands is easily understood. Also, China's measure to end the Japanese control over the Pratas, even through financial bargain, and gain recognition by them of China's sovereignty over the Island are significant. The recognition by the Japanese was all the more important for the Qing Dynasty, beleaguered by the strong sentiment within China against its inability to safeguard the Chinese territorial integrity and dignity. During the negotiations with Nishizawa under Qing Dynasty, the Guangdong Governor Zhang Yen Chun sent a survey mission to the Paracel Islands in 1909 in the aftermath of which a map was published by Guangdong which showed the Paracel as the part of the province, for the first time shown in any Chinese map. This was the last act of the Qing Dynasty.[40] This was also an attempt of the dying Qing Dynasty to prove its seriousness about China's territorial integrity.

The Qing Dynasty however could not continue the approved plan of developing the Paracel Islands which was abandoned by it later (and this was how Imperial China's policy towards South China Sea ended). Subsequently, the Republic of China (established in 1911) gave permission to its citizens to exploit natural marine resources in the Paracel Islands. In this way the new Republic of China attempted to control the matters related to the islands of that area. However, the real power of approving such permits remained with the Guangdong province which was a loophole in the central-provincial coordination. This showed that the provincial authority of Guangdong had its own policy of dealing with its littorals, independent of any central guidance.[41] We will see later that such lack of parity between central and provincial policies towards South China Sea dispute is in vogue even today. This shows that the Chinese coastal provinces traditionally enjoyed an upper hand in formulating policies towards South China Sea policy of the central government. That the Guangdong authority was the main decision making body regarding South China Sea islands affairs was clear when some Chinese sought permission from the provincial government to exploit natural resources in the Paracel Islands.[42] The new Republic of China published a map in its *Alamanac* in 1912 where there was no mention of borders. However, the new constitution of Republic of China declared that the *sovereign territory* of new China would be the continuation of the *domain* of the previous Chinese Empire. Meanwhile, a guide of China's historic territory which got published in December 1914 as *New Geographical Atlas of the Republic of China*, prepared by a private Chinese cartographer Hu Jinlie, contained a map of China with a line drawn across South China Sea mentioning which islands belonged rightfully to mainland China. The lines in the map demonstrated the Chinese state 'control' (over the Sea) before 1736 which included the islands of Pratas and the Paracels. The Chinese government showed the line up to the 1930s in its maps.[43] So the map was suggesting that the Chinese state control over the South China Sea in the eighteenth century was extended up to the Paracel Islands and that the new Chinese government of the twentieth century accepted that Chinese 'sovereignty' over the South China Sea which was extended up to the Paracels. Interestingly, the map published by the Central Cartographic Society in Shanghai in 1916, as a protest against the Republic of China's surrender of territory and other rights to the Japanese in 1915, did not show the islands of South China Sea while showing Hong Kong, Taiwan and Tonkin.[44]

In 1928, a conference was held in Canton (Guangdong) to determine the priority of developing the Islands in future. Later, a commission was set up to investigate the islands. This commission, after undertaking an inspection of the islands, advised that China should reaffirm her sovereignty over the archipelago.[45] Thus we see that China, under the new Republican government, was becoming more assertive with her claims of sovereignty over the South China Sea archipelago and also they were now concentrating more on the Paracel Islands which are nearer to the Chinese coast. We can assume that such emphasis was the product of the French activity in the Islands since late nineteenth century. As mentioned earlier, the Guangdong province attempted to absorb Paracel Islands as part of its administration immediately after the French attempt to construct light house in the islands in 1899. Admitting the traditional Chinese ignorance about the Islands, She Peng-fi, the head of the commission set up in 1928, said, "The Paracel archipelago is our nation's southern most territory. However, our people have paid little attention and natural resources of the area have been coveted by the foreigners...".[46] The Chinese interest in the Paracel islands was not mere urge to establish sovereignty but to extract the economic benefit from it also. The Chinese were mainly interested in the Woody Islands (*Lin-tao*) of the archipelago, where the Paracel Archipelago Industries Company's activities were concentrated, since it is large in size with dense vegetation and mainly because of its large phosphate reserves. The investigating commission found that this phosphate reserve was exploited by the Japanese since

1919 where the Osaka based Southern Prosperity Industries, with branches in Taiwan (under Japanese possession since 1895) initiated the phosphate mining.[47] The Chinese were not only focusing on the economic aspect of the Islands but also on the strategic benefits of the Paracel and the entire South China Sea. This is clear from the report of the commission which dealt with the strategic question of the Paracel Islands. The military contingent of the commission expressed its view while conducting the strategic assessment of the Paracel Islands saying, "Besides the mining resources, the Islands (Paracel) occupy highly strategic position for the naval defence of the Pacific.... In the event of the war breaking out suddenly, these islands could be used to severe the shipping lines between Singapore and Hong Kong...".[48] The Paracel Islands (marked in circle in Map 2.3) is nearer to Hong Kong than to Singapore but the strategy to 'severe the shipping lines between Singapore and Hong Kong' means the control of the entire South China Sea region (as can be construed from Map 2.3) by China. The choice of the target ports of Singapore and Hong Kong is also interesting since both were, at that point of time, British territory, and Hong Kong is more important since it was a Chinese territory ceded to the British by the Qing ruler, something very difficult for China to forget.

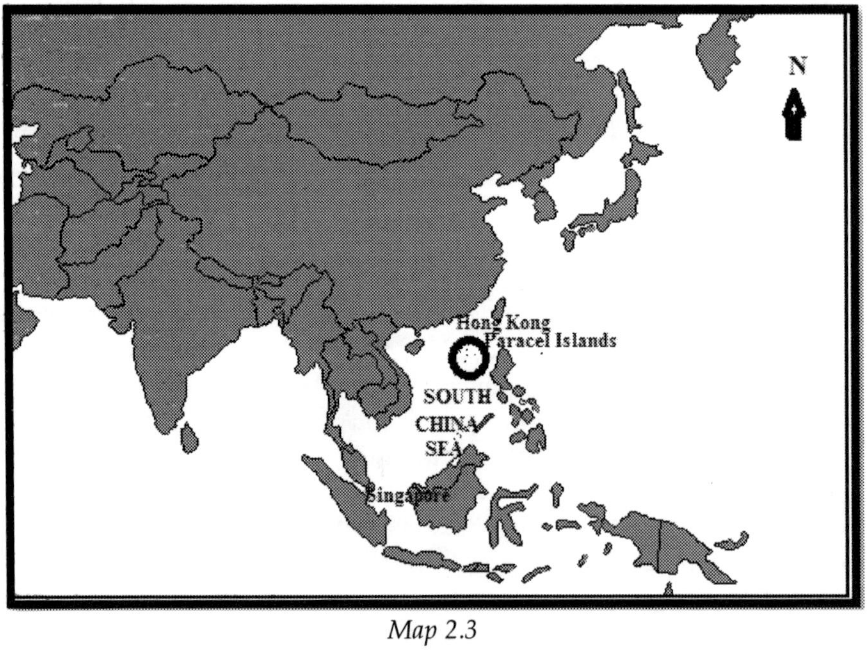

Map 2.3

However, the commission report was an indication regarding the Chinese strategic viewpoint towards South China Sea and its Islands, especially after the Japanese seizure of the Pratas Island. The Japanese occupation of the Island had undoubtedly galvanized the Chinese establishment since by then Japan emerged as a major imperial power with Korean Peninsula and Taiwan under her possession. It can also be said that the new Republic of China wanted to overcome the weakness of the previous Qing Dynasty who succumbed to the foreign powers and surrendered Chinese territories to them. Nevertheless, China lacked the physical strength to defend her claim on the disputed islands of the South China Sea. In the inter-war period (1919-1939) the French and the Japanese were very active in the South China Sea. The Chinese opted for diplomatic challenge to counter this. The provincial government in Guangdong issued Provisional Regulation to Attract Investment to Undertake Marine Production in 1929 and set up an office for marine production control in 1935. In the same year, the government of Guangdong set up a circuit to survey the mineral resources of the Pratas group. But these initiatives failed to deter the French and Japanese from continuing with their fishing activities in the disputed waters.[49]

As it is already mentioned that the French were active in the South China Sea region since the latter half of the nineteenth century. In fact one of the reasons the Chinese got active in the region was the French activities. Although the French were active in the Paracel Islands since the late nineteenth century, it was not before the early twentieth century that they made concerted efforts *'to absorb the islands into French Indochina'*, writes Marwyn Samuels.[50] Thus the French effort to seize the Paracel islands started only in the twentieth century. Yet, the 1988 report of Vietnamese government on South China Sea suggests that after officially converting Vietnam to a French Protectorate in 1884, France started administering the Hoang Sa and Truong Sa archipelago on behalf of Vietnam. It even says that the French allowed the Japanese to collect Guano from the Hoang Sa Islands.[51] However, the French got active in the region only after the World War I which is confirmed by the 1988 report also. It says that between 1930 and 1932, *Inconstant*, *Alerte* and *La Malicieuse* warships and also SS *De Lanessan* made several voyages to Hoang Sa (Spratly Islands).[52] The sending of the warship *Malicieuse* on 13th April 1930 by the Governor of Cochinchina was in response to the report of possible Japanese takeover of the island which was 500 km away from the French coast. The French officially annexed Spratly into the Vietnam Protectorate in 1933. The Chinese when failed to notice the occupation of the Spratly by the French in 1930 did however lodge their protest against its annexation in 1933.[53] Prior to this annexation of Spratly, the French sent an inspection team to the Paracel Islands in 1925 which included scientists of the Oceanographic Institution of Na Trang. This team reported about the presence of large guano/phosphate deposits in the islands.[54] Marwyn Samuels suggests that the French did not officially claim the Paracel Islands before 4th December, 1931. This was in protest to the Chinese attempt to open a guano mining in the islands when the French filed an official protest with the Chinese legation in Paris. Samuels also says that the French claim was based on history citing the incorporation of the islands by King Gia Long in 1816 and the construction of a Pagoda and Stone tablet on one of the islands of the Paracel by King Ming Mang in 1835.[55] The 1988 report of Vietnamese government says that between 1930 and 1933 "French naval units were stationed on the main islands of the Truong Sa archipelago: Truong Sa, An Bang, Ba Binh (Itu Aba), the Song Tu cluster, Loai Ta and Thi Tu".[56]

The Japanese expansion in East Asia between the two World Wars sent ripples all around the region. By then Japan had emerged as a major industrial power. Thus Japan required minerals and markets. On the other hand, the changed equation of the geopolitics of the post WW I turned the older allies like Britain and Japan against each other. At the same time, the big powers of the time were fighting for the control of Manchuria in China. Meanwhile the global economic crisis of the 1920s, also known as *Great Depression*, forced Japan to undertake assertive posture. The result was the Sino-Japanese war in 1938. As Japan got more and more entangled in the ensuing WW II in the East Asian scene, the French became cautious about defending their territories in Asia. Thus in 1938, France founded a permanent base in the Paracels, alongside the Japanese.[57] The 1975 report of South Vietnam read that in his report to the Minister of Colonies in Paris on 20th March 1930, the then French Governor of Indochina said that he asked the Japanese Consul in Hanoi in 1927 to enquire with the French Indochina Government regarding the status of some islands in South China Sea. The Japanese Consul Mr. Kurosawa, following his Government's instruction, did not discuss the Paracel islands' sovereignty status with France since they were disputing French ownership of the Spratly islands that time.[58] Meanwhile France incorporated the Paracel islands through a decree of incorporation on July 27, 1932. The Chinese protest against this action was ignored by France. When the Chinese asked the French to respect the 1887 Sino-French Convention, France refused saying that the Convention was not applicable to Paracels but only Macay area of northern Vietnam. They even cited the Vietnamese historical record which said that the islands were claimed by Vietnam in 1816 and said that the Chinese purported incorporation did not take place before 1909 (as already mentioned).[59] Therefore, it can be construed that the rising Japanese activities in East Asia along with the Republic of China's proactive stand forced the French Indochinese government to get into action to safeguard the territorial integrity of Vietnam in the maritime zone. What is noteworthy here is the Chinese mode of action. As already mentioned, China was not a powerful entity during this time. Therefore, she opted for diplomatic channel of protest since she could not meet the challenge by military means (exactly what the less powerful disputants of the South China Sea are doing today). What China was doing was that she was registering her protest consistently in case of every development. Thus, in response to the French incorporation of the Paracels, China forwarded a note on March 1934 reiterating her claim on the islands based on 1887 Convention. Also, responding to the Vietnamese record of 1816 that France put forward in support of her claim, China negated it saying that Vietnam was a tributary state of China during that time. After years of silence in 1937 France offered a settlement of the dispute via international arbitration which China turned down reiterating her sovereignty claim over the islands. Thus, the government in Paris formally declared Paracel archipelago as owned and occupied by France on 3rd July, 1938. The Chinese were busy fighting the Japanese during this time so could not resist the French action.[60] So, the French could easily turn the wave in their favour in absence of any strong resistance from China. It can be said that this was first defeat of China. China was weak and beleaguered by rivals all around of which the Japanese were the major one. Republic of China miserably failed to establish China's claim or at least thwart the actions of the others in the South China Sea islands for the rest of its tenure. The French took the advantage and between 1931 and 1940, they expanded their presence in the Paracels. However the South China Sea geopolitics took a new shape with the rise of Imperial Japan.

Japan's Maritime Policy between 1901 and 1945 and the South China Sea geopolitics

The geopolitics of the South China Sea during the interwar period will be incomplete without the mention of Japan. Japan's emergence as a major sea power started in the second half of the nineteenth century after the Meiji Restoration in 1868 and the subsequent development of military industry in the country which benefitted the navy.[61] The Japanese Navy previously was operating only to defend her coastal areas. By the dawn of the twentieth century the Imperial Japanese Navy (IJN) eyed on the command of the 'Far East' (that is entire region termed as East Asia today) maritime zone after defeating Russia in the Russo-Japanese War (1904-05). The main objective behind such move was firstly to ensure unhindered supply lines for the Imperial Japanese Army (IJA) units in Eurasian continent and secondly to secure the maritime trade routes to sustain the economy of Japan.[62] Thus it is seen that Japan's urge to strengthen her navy was motivated by the urge to sustain her economy by controlling the sea lanes of communication in her vicinity (and as we shall see in the following chapters, the current dispute centring South China Sea is also guided by the same objective). During the World War I the IJN acted as a helping hand to the Allied forces, especially the British. In 1917, the Japanese Navy's special squadrons protected the sea lanes of communication in the Mediterranean Sea and waters around Australia and New Zealand, as requested by the British. It was done in response to the German submarine warfare and the Japanese Navy hunted for the German raiders like SMS *Emden* in the Indian Ocean and patrolled the sea lanes along the North American west coast.[63] So we see that during the WWI, the IJN had spread its tentacles from the Mediterranean to the American coast and down to the Indian Ocean. Things started turning critical in the post war period after the Washington Naval Conference (1921) forced Japan to roll back her shipbuilding aspirations. In the first half of the twentieth century, Japan planned to possess large big-gun capital ships. In 1920, Japan proposed eight-eight fleet project, which, initially turned down by the Diet (Japanese Legislature), was approved in 1920. But Japan had to reduce the project to only nine vessels after the Conference.[64] In a way, the Washington Naval Conference restricted the Japanese naval aspirations. However Japan denounced the Washington and London (naval) treaties and refused to sign the Second London Naval Treaty and embarked on massive shipbuilding programme of heavy ships, carriers, destroyers, submarines and auxiliary vessels.[65] Also, Japan's Imperial Defence Policy (*teikoku kokubō hōshin*) or IDP had been identifying USA as a prime threat to Japan since 1907 and read that the basic policy for deploying the IJN was to 'wipe out the enemy's primary Far East naval forces in order to take command of the Western Pacific and thereby protect Japanese sea lanes...'.[66] Thus it is seen that since the dawn of the twentieth century Japan, as mentioned earlier, was getting ready to expand her naval strength to control the East Asian maritime zone and we will see in the following lines how Japan turned South China Sea into Japanese 'New South Archipelago', a major strategic zone during the next world war.

The Japanese were eyeing southwards since the late nineteenth century after taking possession of Taiwan in 1895 following the victory over China in the Sino-Japanese War of 1894-95. The occupation of Taiwan initiated the era of southward expansion of Japan towards South China Sea for commercial, political and military interests. The Russo-Japanese War of 1904-05, in which Japan emerged victorious, was almost a milestone event for the Japanese, and also for the world in the era of colonialism. The war proved that the 'whites' (that is the Europeans), who were ruling half of the world at that time, were not invincible. Japan's victory over the 'white' Russians (who were however not colonial power *per se* since they had no colonies anywhere) proved the established perception of 'might of the white' a myth and released the wave of Pan-Asianism further.[67] In the post war period, the Japanese strategists increased their emphasis on the maritime power of Japan. One of the thinkers of the IJN, Satô, referring to Alfred Mahan's theory of sea power in his work *On the History of Imperial Defence* (1908), emphasized on the importance of Japanese navy which played decisive role in the victories over both the Russian and the Chinese navy. He endorsed Mahan's opinion about importance of communications for the great maritime power which can be assured with battle-fleet capability to clear the enemy from vital waterways.[68] The southward expansion of Japan into the wider maritime zone of Asia can be viewed in this context. The seizure of Taiwan in 1895 was an important strategic move. Taiwan is located at the northern part of South China Sea. In a way, Taiwan can be considered as a gateway to maritime Southeast Asia, via South China Sea, and beyond from the north of Asia. Therefore, occupation of Taiwan, in the eye of Tokyo, was essential as a base for further expansion towards Southeast Asia and also for defending Japanese islands from the possible threat originating from there (from the European colonizers of Southeast Asia).[69] Thus, the Japanese were ensuring maritime security of Southeast Asia against the European powers, present in the South China Sea region, by bringing Taiwan under their control. This is clear from the statement of Inoue Tsuyoshi, advisor to the then Japanese Prime Minister Ito Hirobumi, who said, "Taiwan...can control maritime rights in the Yellow Sea, the North China Sea and the Sea of Japan. It is the door to Japanese defense. If we lose this good opportunity, the island of Taiwan will be taken by other powerful countries within two or three years."[70] Thus, it is seen that Taiwan was considered as a defence unit of Japan. Located at the northern tip of the South China Sea, with the mighty European powers dominating the Sea from their colonies in the region, it was logical for the Japanese strategic thinkers to be wary and prepared. Also, control of Taiwan helped the Japanese to control the northeast Asian maritime zone. And to expand further south, Taiwan was to play the role of vital naval base. As Robert Kaplan identifies, *"Taiwan is the cork in the bottle of the South China Sea, controlling access between Southeast Asia and Northeast Asia..."*.[71] Thus control of Taiwan was essential for the control of entire East Asian waters by the Japanese, exactly what was to happen during the World War II. There was an economic aspect to this strategy also. By the beginning of the twentieth century Japanese economy was soaring and so did her population. The newly Industrialized Japan was hungry for raw materials and also food for her exploding population. Also, Taiwan was attractive market for the Japanese products.[72] So Taiwan was important, both as strategic as well as economic benefactor, for Japan. However, here we are concerned about Taiwan's seizure by Japan as a base to expand further south, into the South China Sea zone.

As already mentioned, the Japanese entry in the South China Sea zone in the twentieth century happened through a private initiative. Japanese businessman Nishizawa Yoshiji occupied the Pratas Island of the Paracel archipelago in 1907. He handed it over to the Chinese only in return of the payment of 1,30,000 silver dollars to Japan. Meanwhile the Japanese phosphate companies were operating in the Spratly islands from Taiwan. The Japanese confronted with the French over the territorial dispute for the first time in the 1930s.[73] Also, the French formally claimed the South China Sea islands not before 1930s. The Japanese protested against the French occupation of the Spratly Islands which Japan termed as 'infringement upon the rights of Japanese commercial interests in the islands as Spratlys had been occupied and mined by the Japanese phosphate companies for years'.[74] Thus, the Japanese were active, although only verbally, to lodge their protest against any 'external meddling' in the South China Sea waters. However, it was not until 1939, they acted to defend their 'territory' in the South China Sea. By early 1939, Japan had occupied the entire coast of China. On 9th April, 1939, Japan declared that she completely occupied Pratas, Paracel and Spratly Islands putting them under Governor General of Taiwan and few days later named the three islands as 'New South Archipelago'. This occupation, according to Marwyn Samuels, was in response to the French naval and air power operating in the South China Sea zone during that time.[75] Thus the Japanese assertiveness in the South China Sea was in response to that of an extra regional power, as we see today in the context of the Chinese and American activities in the region. However, the apprehension about the French was not the only cause behind Japan's strategy in the South China Sea region, on the eve of the World War II.

Kinoaki Matsuo, the Japanese Navy Admiralty and navy strategist, in his wartime book *How Japan Plans to Win* (published in 1942) made a detailed analysis about the impending hostilities with USA just before the war began and how Japan can win the war. In this book he has discussed about the US strategy in the waters of East Asia to launch an attack on Japan. It is to be remembered that not only USA by then had her bases in Guam and Hawaii in the Pacific Ocean but also colony in the Philippines. The book of Matsuo mainly focuses on the US naval strength on the eve of the world war and one gets the sense that Japan's war preparation in East Asia was done in view of US naval strength. He wrote,

> "As soon as she (USA) declares war against Japan, it is thought she will resort to tactics of attacking the Japanese fleet...the United States expeditionary fleet will meanwhile advance to the Philippines, while armaments on the islands of Guam, the United States base of operations for the occupation of all the Japanese islands in the South Seas, will be strengthened all the more strongly. As soon as it finds an opportune time, the United States Fleet will occupy Formosa (Taiwan) and Ogasawara Islands (Bonin Islands) while Japanese islands will be bombed from the air by the United States air force, thus creating epoc of great terror. As a result, Chinese coasts and South Seas will be probably blockaded by the United States Flee, and thereby Japan's foreign trade as well as her naval activities will be in jeopardy."[76]

The interesting part of the above prophesy is that it implies the immense strategic and economic importance of the South China Sea zone. Taiwan is located at the northern point of South China Sea. The occupation of the island by USA would undoubtedly have given the Americans an upper hand against the Japanese. The occupation of Taiwan would mean a challenge to the Japanese position in the Chinese coastal area and also the main islands of Japan in the north. Not only this, the presence of the American fleet in Taiwan meant the control of the sea lanes in the adjacent maritime zone via both East and South China Sea, connecting the Indian

Ocean world and East Asia which, as rightly mentioned by Matsuo, would have jeopardized Japan's wartime economy. Thus, the analysis shows how much significance the maritime zone around Taiwan, including South China Sea, held for Japan. The author thus advises his country's war time naval policy makers to resist the expansion of the US naval presence in the region, and to eventually 'annihilate' it. To do this Matsuo advised that, "*....Japan should hold sea supremacy in the South China Sea and Sea of Japan, thus guaranteeing the safety of communications between Japan and the Asiatic continent.*"[77] He insisted that this would sustain smooth operation of Japan's foreign trade while would also promote her sea supremacy 'extending to the eastern apart of India by conquering Singapore Naval Base' thereby challenging England.[78] The author, thus, insists on both economic as well as strategic importance of South China Sea to Japan during the war. His opinion reflects Japan's dependence on the maritime route on which his country depended so much. Moreover, the emphasis on 'sea supremacy' of Japan implies Mahan's prescription of naval supremacy to 'rule the world' by ruling the sea.[79] Thus, it can be construed that wartime Japan (or Imperial Japan) eyed on the East Asian maritime world as the base to establish her 'East Asian Co-prosperity Sphere'. The dominance of the seas of Asia, especially South China Sea and Sea of Japan, was important for Japan to establish her supremacy in Asia. Such importance was acknowledged by USA also. When Japan was planning to occupy Indochina in 1941, the US Secretary of State Cordell Hull instructed Acting Secretary of State Sumer Welles to see the Japanese Ambassador and, "*Make clear the fact that the occupation of Indochina by Japan possibly means one further important step to seizing control of the South Sea area, including trade routes of supreme importance to the United Sates controlling such products as tin and other commodities. This was of vital concern for the United States...*"[80] The 'South Sea' mentioned here cannot be anything but the South China Sea which was the vital supply route for the United States. Thus the occupation of Indochina by Japan had threatened the US who feared about the loss of South China Sea. The Americans viewed the Indochina strategy of Japan as means to occupy the 'South Sea' was clear from the viewpoint of the Secretary of State Hull who negated the theory of occupation of Indochina defending Japan and said, "The only alternative is that this venture into Indochina has a close relation to the South Sea area and its value for offense against that area."[81] This statement acknowledges the strategic significance of the South (China) Sea in controlling the Southeast Asian region.

Apart from protecting sea lanes of communication, Japan's aim was also to oust the European powers from the vicinity of the South China Sea. The three European colonisers, Dutch, British and the French, were ruling the East Indies (today's Indonesia), Malaya Peninsula (today's Malaysia and Singapore) and Indochina (today's Vietnam, Cambodia and Laos) respectively. They were exploiting the natural resources of these colonies and were also controlling the adjacent maritime trade routes. These colonies were the economic power houses for the Europeans in Asia. The Japanese aim to oust them from the region would not only establish their pre-eminence in the South China Sea region (since all the colonies mentioned were littorals of the Sea) but would also let the Japanese have access to the resources there which the Europeans were exploiting since the eighteenth century and prospering themselves. The prosperity of Japan by wresting the Southeast Asian colonies from the 'whites' was well depicted by Ian Morrison, an Australian journalist, during the war in his book, *The War Against Japan,* in the following lines:

> "Economically Japan now controls plentiful resources of raw materials. Since 1941 alone, she has gained more than 88 per cent of the world's rubber, 54 per cent of tin, 28 per cent of the rice, 19 per cent of tungsten, 4.5 per cent of the oil. In the Indies she has richest single colonial area in the whole world. Burma, Malaya, the Philippines, Thailand, Indo-China, are all rich in raw materials....Japan at present is the richest *have-nation* in the world. And in the millions of inhabitants of these occupied areas, in addition to China market, which is the greatest single undeveloped market in the world, Japan has monopoly market whose potentialities are simply unlimited."[82]

It is noteworthy here that the advent of the Europeans in the region was also inspired by the desire to access to the big Chinese market and the resources of the region. Even before the advent of the Europeans, the Arabs and the Indians were also doing business in the region. The world war of the 1940s gave new dimension to the South China Sea, both strategic and military. The strategic importance of South China Sea and the adjacent area was well depicted by Matsuo, mentioned before in the chapter. Indochina, after the fall of the French in June 1940, provided the Japanese a base from where they could launch attack both on mainland (Burma and Malayan peninsula via Siam or Thailand) and maritime Southeast Asia (the Philippines and Borneo). Also, the Japanese could control the air and sea routes of the South China Seas.[83] Thus South

China Sea region gained immense strategic significance during the war of 1940s with the Japanese colonies in the region and the British and American presence in its outer rim. Japan could control Southeast Asia during the war till 1945 since she could control the South China Sea region. She controlled the lifeline of East Asia, the East and South China Seas. The main reason for European prosperity in Southeast Asia was the trade via South China Sea. The economic policies of the Western imperialists during the 1930s in a way impacted the Japanese imperialism, following the footsteps of the Europeans. The British Indian government imposed prohibitive tariff on import of Japanese cotton goods, to boost their cotton industry. When Japan was experiencing shortage of iron, steel, oil and other important industrial materials, supplies were in abundance in the colonies of the Netherlands and Britain in Asia. The Americans, who were in control of the Philippines, had imposed 100 per cent tariff on Japanese items.[84] These were deliberate attempts, no doubt, to squeeze the growing economy of an Asian 'non-white' power in the era of 'white colonialism'. Japan, being an island country needed the unhindered supply of raw materials from outside as well as access to the regional markets to sustain her economic growth which, unfortunately, were in the hands of the Europeans who were challenged by the emerging Japanese competition. That is why Noam Chomsky says that *"liberalism was all very well when Britannia ruled the waves, but not when Lancashire industry was grinding to a halt, unable to meet Japanese competition."*[85] He says that Japan could hardly withstand such economic pressure, especially with her textile industry suffering the most due to high tariff barriers imposed on Japanese goods in India, Malaya, Indochina and the Philippines.[86] He goes to the extent saying, "It (Japan) was, in fact, being suffocated by the American and British and other Western imperial systems, which quickly abandoned their lofty liberal rhetoric as soon as the shoe began to pinch."[87]

Geography played an important role in the Imperial Japan's policy in East Asia. Japan possessed insufficient resources to reduce her dependency on great power rivals. She opted for expansionism and regional hegemony in the interwar period was because she was aspiring for economic autonomy.[88] Japanese imperialist policies during the 1940-45 era can be seen from this angle also, without, however, overlooking the heinous atrocities committed by the Japanese forces in the East Asian region which are still alive in the memories of the people there. The European powers who branded Japan as imperialist during the war had also established their colonies in Asia, and also in Africa, with the same motto of economic survival and prosperity.

Map 2.4: Japanese Empire of East Asia during WW II

As the war was approaching its conclusion in 1945, with the imminent defeat of Japan, the geographical sovereignty dispute of the South China Sea resurfaced. Japan so far was the master of East Asia with almost all of maritime zone, from Taiwan to Sumatra, under her occupation. With the Allied Powers, US, UK and Soviet Union along with their allies, gradually gaining upper hand in the war, by 1945 they started intruding in the Japanese-occupied features of South China Sea. On 4th February 1945, two Australian commandoes sailed to the Woody Island in the Paracel (archipelago), from an American submarine USS *Cargo,* where the Americans found the French flag flying a week ago. The commandoes however, not only found the French but also the Japanese. The Americans dropped their newly invented *Napalm* bombs on the Japanese occupied island of Itu Aba on 1st May, 1945. Likewise, the Americans raided Woody and Pattle islands in March-April 1945. However, it is not clear exactly when the Japanese abandoned these islands.[89] Thus by the 1945, the US started ending the dominance of the Japanese in the South China Sea region. Now the fate of South China Sea and its islands was to be decided by the victors. The Allied Powers did not mention the islands of the South China Sea in any of their agreements, Cairo Declaration (1943, of no territorial expansion) or even the Atlantic Charter. The principles of the agreements cannot be applied in the case of South China Sea islands since these islands were already in dispute (over territorial sovereignty). Moreover, although the Cairo Declaration mentioned about returning Taiwan to Republic of China, however, did not clear whether the South China Sea islands, governed from Taiwan since 1939, would automatically be handed over to China.[90] Meanwhile the Americans did not clear their position regarding sovereignty issue over the disputed South China Sea islands in the US document T-324 which was meant to discuss the fate of the islands since they carried no interest to any single country or territory. The later documents of USA continued with the same argument of non-existence of any claim over the islands.[91]

So it is seen that the territorial dispute over the islands of the South China Sea only surfacing again after the war. This was a very obvious situation. Prior to the advent of the Japanese, China and the colonial powers, mainly France, were fighting over the sovereignty rights of the islands. When the Japanese occupied them, the issue was not settled at all. The arrangement of governing Spratly, Paracel and Pratas archipelago from Taiwan was a Japanese arrangement which was unacceptable to the Allied Powers. It can be presumed that the silence of the Cairo Declaration regarding the handing over the islands' administration to China along with Taiwan was a deliberate attempt to keep the dispute alive. This can be because the partners of the Allied Powers were colonial masters of Asia who were determined to return to the colonies after the conclusion of the war. So the signatories of the Cairo Declaration deliberately skipped the South China Sea islands dispute issue to let the colonisers handle it in their way. USA was, however, more inclined to hand over the issue to the newly founded United Nations. In her Document CAC-301, prepared on 19th December 1944, before the Yalta Conference, she recommended that Spratly islands dispute be handed over to the United Nations but mentioned that such can be done only after acquiring approval from France.[92] Clearly, USA could hardly upset her wartime fellow who is also partner to the dispute. Such 'fellow-feeling' would continue, as we know, in the anti-colonial liberation war in Indochina starting after the conclusion of the World War II. On the question of Paracel, the US document CAC-308 offered three proposals: international trusteeship, deal between France and China and supporting China until France gives proof of handing over of Paracel to Annam by China in 1816. However, after the war, USA abandoned her position of placing the islands under the United Nations' supervision finding its improbability demanding too much flexibility from France.[93] The Yalta Conference also remained silent over the settlement of the sovereignty dispute of the South China Sea islands. The Instrument of Surrender signed by Japan on September 2, 1945 did not have any specific mention of handing over of the occupied territories of Japan (including islands) in east and Southeast Asia to any particular country or organization.[94] So Japan left the dispute over the possession of the islands of South China Sea unresolved and alive. The agreements compiled under General Order No.1 for the surrender of Japan also made no discussion about the Pacific Islands to the south of Japan which Tokyo governed during the war. However, it was decided that they were to remain in the hands of the Americans or be handed over to the Australians if US decides so.[95]

The end World War II not only ended the five years Japanese occupation of Southeast Asia but it initiated the beginning of the end of two centuries old European domination of Asia also. At the dawn of the colonial era the European powers fought among themselves for domination and influence. Their main target was trade which lured them to Asia. To facilitate the objective they first attempted coercive methods, then resolved for cohesion. And the method of exercising cohesion was the 'territorial sovereignty' concept, a pure Westphalian notion. This was mainly meant to demarcate the boundaries of the colonised areas, both land and maritime zones rich in resources, to preserve exclusive rights of exploitation, unhindered by the 'outsiders'. Subsequently, the colonial powers of Southeast Asia, especially French Indochina, gradually absorbed in the local power China into this dispute related purely to the Western arrangement of 'territorial sovereignty' question. In a way, the colonial era, especially of the late nineteenth century, unveiled a new dimension in the geopolitics of the South China Sea region. The maritime zone which remained a mere bridge between two parts of Asia, west and east, and an economic hub eventually emerged as a conflict zone among the littoral states. It is true that in the pre-colonial period also the power centre in the South China Sea zone shifted from one point to the other, from *Funan* to *Champa* to *Srivijaya*, but such shifting happened with the course of time and it never turned the region into a definite conflict zone. This was the gift of colonial era when the concept of territorial sovereignty was articulated in a most aggressive fashion with reference to historical data. The South China Sea itself was important to the local powers which they all 'exploited' together. Thus the dispute centring the islands of the Sea can be termed as the gift of colonial epoch, introduction of geopolitics, a European territorial competition. Also, the world wars, especially World War II, gave a new aspect to the Sea, the significance of its geopolitical advantages. The Japanese were invincible in the initial days of the war since they could dominate the South China Sea. This sea lane was their lifeline. Their trade as well as their supply route of raw materials passed through this lane. Also, they could cut off the European imperialists of the Allied Forces from their Asian colonies as well as China only by their presence in the South China Sea. China could also be suppressed if South China Sea is controlled with the coastal area of China under Japanese seizure. So the World War II showed how important the South China Sea lane of communication is, both economically as well as strategically, for any East Asian power. Even the Japanese occupation of the South China Sea region is relevant in the context of freedom of navigation argument significant today, which will be discussed in subsequent chapters in details. It can be said that the significance of the South China Sea in the context of communication lane was well established to the extra regional powers by the World War II who were virtually delinked from the region by Japanese occupation. The occupation can be seen as the starting point of the argument of freedom of navigation and most importantly the ill-effect of the domination of the maritime zone by any single power. This geopolitical argument of the South China Sea will become prominent further in the Cold War period with a new ambience of post-war international relations.

END NOTES

1. Robert C. Beckman, 'ASEAN and the South China Sea Dispute', in Pavin Chachavalpongpun (ed), *Entering Uncharted Waters: ASEAN and the South China Sea*, Singapore, Institute of South East Asian Studies, 2014, p.15
2. David Kang, 'Getting Asia Wrong: The Need for New Analytical Frameworks', *International Security*, Vol.27, No.4, MIT Press, p.85
3. Ding Gang, 'Colonial legacy buried seeds of territorial row', *Global Times*, 6.3.2015, http://www.globaltimes.cn/content/925267.shtml (accessed on 31.08.2015)
4. Nordin Hussin, *Trade and Society in the Straits of Maleka: Dutch Maleka and English Penang 1780-1830*, Singapore, NUS Press, 2007, p.8
5. Leszek Buszynski, 'The origins and development of South China Sea maritime dispute', Leszek Buszynski, Christopher B. Roberts (eds), *The South China Sea Maritime Dispute: political, legal and regional perspectives*, London and New York, Routledge, 2015, p.2
6. Stein Tønnesson, 'The History of the Dispute', Tomo Kivimäki (ed), *War or Peace in the South China Sea*, Copenhagen, Nias Press, 2002, p.8
7. Bill Hayton, *The South China Sea: The Struggle for Power in Asia*, New Haven and London, Yale University Press, 2014, p.47
8. Ibid, p.49
9. Ibid, p.92
10. Ibid, p.93

11. Ibid, p.91
12. Marwyn S. Samuels, *Contest for the South China Sea,* London, Methwin, 1982, pp.52-53
13. Ibid, p.53
14. Bill Hayton, op cit, pp.48-49
15. Marwyn S. Samuels, op cit, p.52
16. Ibid
17. Jianming Shen, 'China's Sovereignty over South China Sea Islands: A Historical Perspective', *ChineseJournal of International Law* (CJI) 1 (1), 2002, http://chinesejil.oxfordjournals.org/content/1/1/94.full.pdf (accessed on 03.09.2015), p.102
18. Leszek Buszynski, op cit, p.3
19. Wang Hanling, 'China's Stance on Some Major Issues of the South China Sea', Pavin Chachavalpongpun (ed), op cit, p.116, 117
20. Ibid, pp.118, 119
21. Jianming Shen, op cit, p.122
22. Cited in Wang Hanling, op cit, p.117
23. Ibid, pp.117-118
24. Jing Huang and Sharinee Jagtiani, 'Introduction: Unknotting Tangled lines in the South China Sea Dispute', Jing Huang, Andrew Billo (eds), *Territorial Disputes in the South China Sea: Navigating Rough Waters,* New York, Palgrave McMillan, 2015, p.2
25. 'The Hoang Sa (Paracel) and Truong Sa (Spratly) Archipelagoes and International law', Hanoi, Ministry of Foreign Affairs, Socialist Republic of Vietnam, April, 1988, file:///C:/Users/User%20Account/Downloads/42905-bngvietnam88.pdf (accessed on 07.09.2015), p.4
26. 'White Paper on the Hoang Sa (Paracel) and Truong Sa (Spratly) Islands', Saigon, Ministry of Foreign Affairs, Republic of Vietnam, 1975file:///C:/Users/User%20Account/Downloads/lpbcta_1975_vietnam%20claims%20of%20spratlys%20part%201_002.pdf (accessed on 07.09.2015)
27. April 1988, op cit, p.5, emphasis added
28. Mark J. Valencia, Jon M. Van Dyke, Noel A. Ludwig, *Sharing the Resources of the South China Sea,* Honolulu, University of Hawaii Press, 1999, p.30
29. Saigon, 1975, op cit
30. April 1988, pp.5,6
31. Ibid, p.6
32. Ulises Granados, 'As China Meets the Southern Sea Frontier: Ocean Identity in the Making, 1902-1937,'*Pacific Affairs, Vol.78,* University of British Columbia, 2005, www.jstor.org/stable/40023725, p.445
33. Marwyn S. Samuels, op cit, p.53
34. Ibid, p.54
35. Ibid
36. Bill Hayton, op cit, p.51
37. Marwyn S. Samuels, op cit, p.54
38. Ulises Granados, op cit, p.448
39. Bill Hayton, op cit, pp.50-51
40. Ibid, p.52

41. Ulises Granados, op cit
42. Ibid
43. Bill Hayton, op cit, pp.52-53
44. Ibid, p.53
45. Marwyn S. Samuels, op cit, p. 57
46. Cited in ibid
47. Ibid, p.59
48. Ibid
49. Ulises Granados, op cit, p.450
50. Marwyn S. Samuels, op cit, p.60 (emphasis added)
51. April 1988, op cit, p.6
52. Ibid
53. Bill Hayton, op cit, p.53
54. Marwyn S. Samuels, op cit
55. Ibid, p.61
56. April 1988, op cit
57. Stein Tønnesson, 'An International History of the Dispute of the South China Sea', *EAI Working Paper No. 71*, 2001, p.8
58. Saigon, 1975, op cit
59. Marwyn S. Samuels, op cit, p.62
60. Ibid
61. Japanese strategists were insisting on the investment in the navy after the country embarked on military buildup in the late nineteenth century. One such strategist was Sato Tetsutaro who concluded that the navy, and not the army, stood as Japan's first line of defence. Japanese naval strength reached such a height by the dawn of the twentieth century that the 1921 Naval Conference resolved to restrain the strength of the Imperial Japanese Navy. See Vijay Sakhuja, *Asian Maritime Power in the 21st Century: Strategic Transactions, China, India and Southeast Asia*, Singapore, Institute of Southeast Asian Studies, 2011, p.13
62. Naoko Sajima and Kyoichi Tachikawa, *Japanese Sea Power: A Maritime Nation's Struggle for Identity*, Australia, Sea Power center, Govt. of Australia, 2009, (http://www.navy.gov.au/sites/default/files/documents/IntSP_2_JapaneseSP.pdf), p.35 (accessed on 07.12.2015)
63. Ibid, p.38
64. Ibid, p.41
65. Vijay Sakhuja, op cit
66. Naoko Sajima and Kyoichi Tachikawa, op cit, p.42
67. The doctrine of Pan-Asianism was formulated by the Asian intellectuals in the late nineteenth century. It was the concept of Asian Unity against Western domination. This concept became the base of Japan's wartime policy. For details read Eri Hotta, *Pan-Asianism and Japan's War: 1931-1945*, New York (USA) and Hampshire (England), Palgrave Macmillan, 2007
68. James R. Holmes, 'Japanese Maritime Thought: If Not Mahan, Who?', Toshi Yoshihara and James R. Holmes (eds), *Asia Looks Seaward: Power and Maritime Strategy*, Westport, Connecticut, Praeger Security International, 2008, p.152
69. Denny Roy, *Taiwan: A Political History*, Ithaca, New York, Cornell University

Press, 2003, p.132

70. Cited in ibid

71. Robert D. Kaplan, *Asia's Cauldron: The South China Sea and the End of a Stable Pacific*, New York, Random House, 2014, p.143

72. Denny Roy, op cit, p.132

73. Marwyn S. Samuels, op cit, p.63

74. Ibid, p.64

75. Ibid

76. Kinoaki Matsuo, *How Japan Plans to Win* (translated by Kilsoo K. Haan), London, George Harrap & Co. Ltd., 1942, p.142

77. Ibid, p.143 (emphasis added)

78. Ibid

79. Alfred Thayer Mahan, the renowned American naval admiral and strategist of the nineteenth century, emphasized on the importance of the sea power as a vital means for the countries to have greater worldwide impact. The concept had an enormous influence in shaping the strategic thought of navies across the world, including Japan.

80. Cited in 'Vietnam and the United Sates: 1940-1950', *United States-Vietnam Relations, 1945-1967*, Vietnam Task Force, Office of the Secretary of Defense, I, (Pentagon papers, declassified), https://www.archives.gov/research/pentagon-papers/ (accessed on 07.12.2015),p.A-11

81. Ibid, A-12

82. Ian Morrison, *The War Against Japan: Thoughts on the Present Conflict in the Far East*, London, Faber And Faber Ltd., 1943, p.80

83. Sir John Hammerston and Major General Sir Charles Gwynn (eds), *The Second World War: A Standard History*, London, The Amalgamated Press Ltd, 1946, p.2309

84. Noam Chomsky, *American Power & the New Mandarins*, Gurgaon (Haryana, India), Penguin Books, 2002, pp.190,191

85. Ibid

86. Ibid, p.191

87. Ibid, p.192

88. Robert Ross, 'The Geography of Peace: East Asia in the twenty-first century', in Leszek Buszynski (ed), *Asia Pacific Security*, Volume 1, London and New York, Routledge, 2014, p.59

89. Bill Hayton, *Calm and Storm: The South China Sea after the Second World War*, Asia Maritime Transparency Initiative, August 13, 2015, http://amti.csis.org/calm-and-storm-the-south-china-sea-after-the-second-world-war/ (accessed on 11.11.2015)

90. Kimie Hara, *Cold War Frontier in the Asia-Pacific: Divided Territories in the San Francisco System*, Oxon, Routledge, 2007, p.144

91. Bill Hayton (2014), op cit, p.57

92. Ibid

93. Ibid

94. Please refer to Walter Consuelo Langsam, *Historic Document of World War II*, New York, D Van Nostrand Company Inc, 1958, pp.151-152

95. Herbert Feis, *Japan Subdued: The Atomic Bomb and the End of the War in the Pacific*, New Jersey, Princeton University Press, 1961, pp.138, 139

3

South China Sea Geopolitics during Cold War Period

The World War II (WWII) opened a new geopolitical stage in the pacific water. The end of the war in the Pacific resulted the emergence of the USA as the dominant figure in the East Asian post World War scene. To quote Peter Calvocorassi and Guy Wint, *"In the course of the war, the United States developed amazingly. It grew the alarming speed of Alice when she swallowed the potion in the bottle marked 'Drink me'.*[1] Undoubtedly, during the war, USA prepared herself militarily, especially enhancing her naval power, following the advice of Alfred Mahan who, citing the British example in his famous work *The Influence of Sea Power Upon History 1660-1783*, strongly advised, in as early as the late nineteenth century, for powerful navy for an aspiring global power. The Japanese, as discussed in the previous chapter, followed the advice and rose with a strong Imperial Navy and captured entire East Asia, ousting the mighty European colonisers during the war. The Americans finally managed to do the same with them bringing an end to the world war in Asia. Although the war in the Pacific was fought by the UK, Australia and New Zealand also, it was basically an American show. The British handed over Australia to General Douglas McArthur of the US South West Pacific Command and Gen. McArthur used Australia as a base to launch counter attack on Japan. It is to be noted here that while Japanese were successful in occupying entire East Asia, from Taiwan in the north to Dutch East Indies in the south, they failed to capture Australia. Thus the Americans could use the island-cum-country as their base of operation. The Pacific

War in a way established the strategic importance of the Pacific Ocean in the world affairs. It was recognized, during the five years Japanese occupation, that the East Asian waters are strategically very important to maintain dominance over the entire geopolitical as well as economic landscape of the region. And this became all the more important with the new phase of international politics started taking shape in the post WWII era—the Cold War—which, a duel between capitalist USA and communist USSR, spread its tentacles all over the world, on both sides of the equator. Smaller and weaker countries of Asia, Latin America and Africa fast became the victims of this super power contest for strategic dividend. The littorals of the South China Sea region were no exception. This region was all the more important since the European imperialists were now attempting to regain their colonies after the ouster of Japan and they were facing tough resistance from the local freedom fighters. And subsequently this region would become the hot bed of Cold War spar.

Cold War in Southeast Asia

The Cold War had originated in Europe. It was mainly Europe's claim for continued attention of the two super powers (which she was having since the First World War, 1914-19) which also promoted United States' involvement in the post-war international affairs.[2] The US-USSR brief honeymoon period was over with the conclusion of the war after the defeat of the Axis. The capitalist-communist duel, which was brushed under the carpet for the sake of 'unity against Nazism' and ending Third Reich's occupation of Europe, revived again in the post war Europe. Soon the European continent got bifurcated into East under Soviet influence and West tagging around USA. The NATO (North Atlantic Treaty Organization) founded in 1949 under US leadership was a security guarantee against 'communist expansionism' to the Western Europe while Warsaw Treaty Organization, commonly called Warsaw Pact, was concluded in 1955 as a Soviet countermeasure to unite the communist states of Eastern Europe against the 'US-led Western imperialism'. It can be concluded that the capitalist-communist conflict in Europe was a question of survival for both Soviet Union as a communist country and the capitalist-cum-imperialist West European countries since they shared the same landmass and were neighbours of each other. For this West Europe needed US assistance since the WWII had exhausted them of any material or even mental strength to withstand Soviet threat. However, in the world outside Europe, the Cold War was more a duel between USA and USSR since both were fighting for strategic gains in the 'non-white world' with Europe's colonial heydays coming to an end. Actually, the USA, who emerged almost unscathed of the ravages of the world war unlike Europe, was not fighting for the survival. She fought the war against the Nazis apparently to restore and safeguard values like freedom and justice which the Nazis and the fascists had mauled in Europe. The risk was it coming back with the communist government. Thus the United States' war spirit did not end with the war.[3] This can be seen as the root of Cold War.

The Cold War in East Asia should be seen in this context. The end of the World War II unfolded many events in short intervals in this part of the world which were to decide the fate of East Asia for the next four decades and impact the international policies of the two super powers of the post colonial twentieth century. Soon after the war, the communist triumph in China in October 1949 was a jolt to the anti-communist West and a jubilant moment for the communist camp. It was even a bigger blow to the Americans who established their dominance in the East Asian waters by the end of the war. In a position to influence the strategic environment of Asia, the 'loss' of China and the subsequent conclusion of Sino-Soviet alliance in 1950 and the Chinese intervention in the Korean War were viewed by USA as part of Soviet objective of world domination. When America viewed Soviet Union as the principal enemy, she treated China, believed to be under Soviet control, as a threat to Asia.[4] These were the major developments in East Asian geopolitical scene in short intervals after the end of the war. It was also important since the WWII established the strategic as well as economic significance of maritime East Asia to the Allied forces of which both USA and USSR were partners. East Asia was preparing for new form of geopolitics.

East Asia, from north to south, fast became the hot bed of Cold War. The triumph of the communist forces in China and the Korean War had enthused the communist factions spread all over, especially Southeast Asia. Actually, between 1937 and 1947, the Chinese Communist Party, under Mao Tse-tung, emerged as the ideological leader of communist movements of East and Southeast Asia.[5] With the conclusion of the war and the end of Japanese occupation of East Asia, the anti-Japanese war got converted to anti-imperialist struggle against the European domination of Southeast Asia. On the other hand, the imperialist Allies' decision to take the region back to the pre-world war state bringing back the old exploitative, sometimes racist, European colonisers in their former colonies of Southeast Asia triggered strong resistance in the colonies. It is to be remembered that although the Japanese had occupied Southeast Asia, they never projected their rule as colonization, in conventional sense, but as the liberation of Asia from the bondage of 'White Western rule'. Japan termed the Anglo-Saxon colonialism as guided by profit motive which weakened the traditional Asian values of cooperation and public welfare. Japan projected herself as a force whose ideological objective was to revive the values of Asian civilization putting cooperation over individual profit.[6] In a way this was the first ever promulgation of the concept 'Asia for the Asians'. Japan's rise in the early twentieth century, as discussed in the previous chapter, had generated an era of *Pan-Asianism* focusing on the emerging Asian power amidst European colonial glory. Also, the rise of Japan undoubtedly established the might of the Asians in the era of 'white colonialism'. Once liberated from the European bondage during the war, the Southeast Asians were in no mood to welcome it back. On the other hand, imperial European victors of the war were determined to restore the colonial system in Southeast Asia. However, the anti-imperialist war in Southeast Asia subsequently turned into a branch of global Cold War with communist and anti-communist factions emerging in the scene especially in the aftermath of the communist adventure in China and Korea.

The communist doctrine started penetrating in Southeast Asia long before in the 1920s after the foundation of Comintern (Communist International, a Soviet mission to turn the world to communist rule).[7] As the colonial powers ultimately agreed to hand over power to the local 'responsible' hands, differences arose on the line of means of achieving liberation. The communist factions accused the nationalists of compromising with the imperialist powers and decided to adhere to the Marxist philosophy of armed revolution, following the Chinese example. In this way, Cold War crept into the post-war Southeast Asian geopolitical scene. The Southeast Asian geopolitics was an integral part of this Cold War tussle where the South China Sea played its part. The geopolitical tussle between the two super powers in the post-war world was well articulated in the waters of Southeast Asia. However, the geopolitics of South China Sea region, that is maritime Southeast Asia, was exclusively guided by the developments of the global Cold War where China played a major role when the ripples reached the Southeast Asian shore.

The leaders of the Cold War, USA and USSR, were initially not interested in the Southeast Asian affairs of the post-war era. The Cold

War, like all other previous wars, actually was getting staged in Europe. The United States was never interested in entangling in the Asian affairs after the war. She treated post-war Asia, in the light of the spread of Russian sponsored communism, the responsibility of Europe for whom USA revived the colonies in the region during the war. This was all the more specific in Southeast Asia where the spirit of communism got blended with the liberation movement. The policy of USA in the region between 1949 and 1950 was of negligence. She was not ready to take responsibility of Southeast Asia during that period.[8] It was just the reverse of the policy that Washington pursued during the war. During the war, USA was wholeheartedly concentrating on reviving her position in East Asia where she lost a major colony-cum-base in the Philippines. Also, being the partner of the Allied force, it was the responsibility of USA to assist her other partners of the alliance to regain their lost control over the Southeast Asian region. However, USA did not have any post-war strategy for the region. The American journalist Ian Morrison lamented, during the war, that *"The Allies have no programme, as have the Japanese, for the future re-organization of the East."*[9] Obviously, the prime objective of USA entangling in the Pacific War was to defeat Japan and revive the region for the Allied powers. It can be assumed that the Americans fought the war in Southeast Asia more to restore the British and other Allied Powers' occupation rather than serving her own interests since she already decided to liberate the Philippines. The Japanese, on the other hand, were concerned more about the American dominance on the maritime zone between Japan and Southeast Asia at the outset of the war. This is evident from the wartime literature of Kinaoki Matsuo who opined at the beginning of the war that, *"The worst period for Japan to open war with the United States would be when the powerful United States Fleets are stationed at the Philippines and Singapore....the sea routes south of the East China Sea will be cut, and thus maritime communication routes connecting Japan to South Seas, Australia, India and Europe, will no longer be of any use to her."*[10] So, the American interest and emphasis in the Southeast Asian waters during the war, especially in the 'south of East China Sea' which cannot be anything but South China Sea, is understandable. The American war-time strategy in East Asia was to lure the Japanese 'into the open water' in order to annihilate them. For this, they framed a strategy which was asserted by one American Commander-in-Chief of the US Fleet in the Senate where he said, *"The United States Western Pacific Strategy is divided into three steps; the first is to advance to the Philippines, the second to organize a fleet at Manila and third is to attack the Japanese mainland."*[11] Thus

Southeast Asia was the stage for Western Pacific strategy of the Americans during the war. After the completion of the war with the defeat of Japan and loss of the Philippines (the only colony they had in Asia), Washington did not have any reason to heed to the emerging challenges in the region in the initial days of the Cold War. The bitter experience that USA encountered in China (in the form of the triumph of communists and defeat of the nationalists) also discouraged the Americans from involving in the Southeast Asian affairs.[12]

The Russians, like the Americans, were also not interested in Southeast Asia after the war. Even when undertaking the 'responsibility of communizing the world', the Soviet Union did not pay attention to Southeast Asia. They expected the region to adhere to communism following the communization of Europe. This policy they maintained for several years after the war.[13] However, Lenin, in his speech to the Moscow cadres on Dec 6, 1920, prophesied the nature of the future conflict between the colonial powers and their colonies and advised that 'Soviet Union should stand as a defender of the world's oppressed peoples'.[14] The Soviet Union, however, did influence the Southeast Asian anti-imperialist thinking since the 1920s. Between 1920s and 1930s, the communist revolutionary organizations were coming up one after another in Southeast Asia. The *Partai Kommunis Indonesia* (PKI) was founded in 1921 (the same year Communist party was founded in China) and the Indochina Communist Party (ICP) and Malayan Communist Party (MCP) were founded in 1930. They were inspired by the crucial position that Soviet Union held between the capitalist and colonized worlds and the foundation of the communist parties in Asia (inspired by Soviet Union) was a combined revolutionary camp of the working class of developed world and 'masses' of the colonies.[15] The foundation of the communist camp in Asia was undoubtedly, as mentioned earlier, the handwork of Cominturn. Also, the Bolshevik success in Russia in 1917 (which founded the Soviet state) did influence the Asian thinkers. However, the Russians were never physically involved in Asian affairs. It should be noted here that another reason for the Soviet reluctance to engage with Southeast Asia, far away from her 'zone of influence', is that the region did not matter to them even during the war. There was no Soviet presence in the Pacific War in the Far Eastern maritime zone. However, we can attribute the 'discredit' of Russia's absence in Southeast Asia to the lack of naval power of Moscow. The most active and geopolitically significant region of Southeast Asia is her maritime zone that is South China Sea region. The Japanese occupied the region to block the sea lanes of the South China

Sea, from Taiwan to Sumatra, in order to delink the European imperial connection with Southeast Asia and also secure the lane for their unhindered supply of resources from region. Practically, this was a major development in the twentieth century geopolitics of South China Sea region which established the vitality as well as vulnerability of the 'life-lane' of East Asia. It was realized that to dominate Southeast and larger East Asian scene, control of South China Sea region is *sine qua non*. The European colonisers showed the way which the Japanese followed later. And both could do it since they had strong navies. The British were masters of the sea for more than three hundred years while the Japanese rose since the late nineteenth century. The Russians seriously lacked this potential. But then they had no reason to invest in navy until the Cold War began.

Soviet naval policy and the South China Sea

Russia had never been considered a sea power. Unlike other European powers, Russia never ventured to colonize distant lands. Nonetheless, Russia did exercise her naval power but in her locality. She used her navy to capture the Baltic Sea and Black Sea coasts and sailed in the Mediterranean Sea between 1768 and 1827. Also, she was challenged by the British Navy in the Black Sea during the Turkish War (1853-56) and lost her fleet in the East during the Russo-Japanese War (at the dawn of the last century).Therefore, Russia faced challenges from the dominant maritime sea powers in her neighbourhood from the beginning which forced her to formulate defensive naval policy.[16] However, Russia has been predominantly a land power and her naval policy was mainly directed towards security of the Russian territory from the maritime threats.[17] This inward and continental outlook of the *Czars* continued later with the Soviet leaders. Stalin was never interested in involving Russia beyond her immediate vicinity. He limited his 'communization' policy to the areas lying immediately outside the Soviet periphery and disliked engaging Soviet Union with global obligations.[18] However, it would be wrong to construe that the Soviet leadership was ignorant or reluctant about developing considerable naval strength. They did nurture ambitious naval plans even before the war which included construction of aircraft carriers. The war however impeded the proceedings on the plan while Russia under Stalin became too engaged with Europe and Northeast Asia.[19] It is also noteworthy here that naval build up requires formidable monetary investment. A country emerging from revolution with poor economic background lacking any immediate maritime threat or even requirement would certainly consider the naval expenses a luxury. Thus initial reluctance of the Soviet leadership about naval ambition is understandable. It was the Khrushchev era, after the death of Stalin in 1953, which marked the beginning of the strategic shift in Soviet global policy. This was aimed mainly to counter the US' global dominance. Till the 1960s, the Soviet naval capacity was limited to defending the Soviet coasts and nearby areas. After 1960, especially after the Cuban missile crisis in 1962, as agreed by many scholars, the Soviet strategists started delving into the plans of turning the Soviet navy from land-based fleet to ocean-based fleet. This was also needed to respond to the growing naval might of the Americans. It is said that the Cuban crisis proved the incapacity of the Soviet Union to keep her missiles on the islands, amidst pressure, due to lack of any powerful ocean fleet as a support. This was the time when strategy shifted from sea denial to sea control.[20] The main driving force, hence we see, behind the shift of Soviet naval strategy was the growing power of US Navy. The US Navy was already a major power by the end of the World War II and since the Korean War in early 1950s its engagement with the Pacific increased for which USA undertook mission of achieving further naval superiority in the region.

The Soviet Union was mainly concerned about the strategic nuclear forces of the United States. In the post war period, the Soviet leadership concentrated in constructing vessels to counter the formidable sea-based nuclear weapon systems of the Western navies, especially USA. The Soviet Naval Commander-in-Chief Admiral Sergei G. Gorshkov, the father of the post-war Soviet naval expansion policy, emphasized on the importance of naval vessels carrying nuclear arms for both land-based as well as sea-based targets. He also focused on the significance of the sea as the supply routes of food and raw materials which the Soviet Union can utilize to strengthen her military and political links with the foreign countries.[21] The post-war naval strategy of the Soviet Union was to secure the sea routes of the world. Her priority was firstly to secure the maritime zones in her neighbourhood, the Northern, Baltic and the Black Sea and then the Pacific. The emphasis on strengthening the Pacific Fleet followed the Soviet entrance in the Indian Ocean region in the late 1960s, apart from the Soviet interest in regional and security objectives in the Pacific region.[22] It should be noted here that the northern Pacific region is of importance to the Russians, adjacent to their Asian territory of the 'Far East' of Soviet Union, especially after the Korean War which ushered in the post-war permanent military entanglement of USA in the region. As part of her growing involvement in the Pacific, the Soviets started the patrolling of the *Yankee* nuclear-powered submarines in 1971, followed by the deployment of the *Delta* submarines in the region. All these deployments brought the major American cities like Seattle, Portland, San Francisco, Los Angles a well as Hawaii and Alaska within the range of the Soviet missiles. Also, with these the Soviets secured their eastern coasts along the Pacific and even established control over a portion of Sea of Japan.[23] Subsequent Soviet control was ensured in the vicinity of the Marshall Islands and from 1970s off the US coasts and coasts of China.[24] In this way, by the 1970s it is seen that the Soviet Pacific Fleet was patrolling a larger portion of the Pacific Ocean, from the north to the vicinity of the South China Sea in south. They even conducted Pacific Fleet exercise, named *Okean-75*, in April 1975 in the east of Japan, in the Philippine and East China Seas and east of Kamchatka Peninsula. In this exercise, they rehearsed in interdicting the sea lanes of communication of the Philippine and the East China Seas.[25] In this way, the Pacific Ocean was fast becoming the Asian stage of Cold War tussle. What is noteworthy here is that the Soviet activities in the Pacific region were being conducted so far at the rim of the South China Sea region, notably in the Philippine and East China Seas. Does it mean they were avoiding the South China Sea region, that is maritime Southeast Asia?

USSR's engagement with post-war Southeast Asia, especially maritime Southeast Asia, dates back to the Khrushchev era and it should be noted here that such engagement was the product of Cold War. Prior to that, during the Stalin era, as already mentioned, the Soviet Union gave less importance to faraway lands of Southeast Asia. Stalin's priority was the immediate neighbourhood of USSR, and in Asia, his prime objective was mainly to contain the Japanese influence and also expanding the Soviet influence in her neighbourhood.[26] It was after the death of Stalin in 1953 that Soviet Union under Nikita Khrushchev paid attention to the 'Third World' of South and Southeast Asia. Soviet entanglement with Southeast Asia was initially to boost the anti-imperialist/anti-colonial struggle against the West in this region which subsequently turned to an anti-China policy. Among the littorals of South China Sea Moscow's engagement with Indonesia is noteworthy. It was not limited to mere diplomatic rendezvous but the seriousness of Soviet's commitment was understandable from her supply of sophisticated weapons to Indonesia including submarines and surface ships in the 1950s and 1960s.[27] However, USSR's major engagement in the Southeast Asian affairs was best articulated during the Vietnam-China crisis in the 1970s when the South China Sea became the stage of conflict amidst the growing Soviet naval power.

The Vietnam War, popularly known as the Indochina War, started with the end of the World War in 1945 and turned into a protracted show of blood bath subject to the Cold War tussle. However, as the war approached its conclusion in the 1970s with the unification of two Vietnams, the shadow of the Cold War cast larger and larger over the geopolitics of Southeast Asia. Socialist Republic of Vietnam, as united Vietnam was named, is a littoral of South China Sea which emerged as the prime challenger to the growing Chinese influence in Southeast Asia. Meanwhile, after the Sino-Soviet rift over apparently ideological differences during the Khrushchev period, Moscow undertook policy to contain and counter China in Asia, especially Southeast Asia. In this region, it found Hanoi as its partner to corner China in her own backyard. It is to be noted here that Sino-Vietnam relations already started experiencing strains over the South China Sea island disputes even before the unification of Vietnam. And, as we will see later in the chapter, unified Vietnam became assertive with her claims over the islands which added to such strains. Soviet Union wanted to capitalize the situation against China. Apart from that, Hanoi's Cambodia policy against the notorious Pol Pot regime in Phnom Penh (1975-79) also isolated Vietnam from her neighbours, including China, who viewed the policy as expansionist strategy of Vietnam. They all were more upset since USSR was supporting Hanoi.

On the other hand, this complicated and boiling situation in Southeast Asia catered to Moscow with an opportunity to encircle China and also paved the way for bigger role for the Soviet Navy. In the 1970s, the Soviet naval policy was not only about promoting political purpose and projecting naval might but also deployment of the navy to project strategic power ashore. During that time Vietnam could only find USSR as the sole source of supply of sophisticated weapons to counter any possible Chinese moves against Vietnam. The Soviet anti-ship *Shaldock* missile with a range of 300 miles was enough as a strategic weapon for Vietnam to put her in equal terms with China in the South China Sea.[28] Soviet Union was offered with the golden opportunity to sail in the South China Sea with the possibility of war between China and Vietnam arising. Here, we should also keep in mind the normalization of Sino-US relations in 1971 altered the geostrategic picture of East Asia. As the Americans made up their mind to withdraw from the costly and exhausting Vietnam War, they initiated the process of normalizing relations with People's Republic of China, at the cost of Taiwan based Republic of China whom so far they considered as 'actual Chinese government'. This was also the time when Washington was paying attention to the growing Soviet Navy and wanted to take advantage of the Sino-Soviet spat. Also, both the US Seventh Fleet and Soviet Pacific Fleet were sailing in the Pacific during this time. So, the Sino-Vietnamese conflict was shadowed by the overall Cold War geopolitics between Moscow and Washington which was to have its reflection in the South China Sea waters.

As the possibility of the war arose, USSR, apart from stationing her troops along the China-USSR border, stationed the naval forces in the East and South China Seas.[29] This strategy of using the navy was in accordance with the advice of Admiral Gorshkhov who said: 'naval power should be stationed close to a crisis area to influence the conflict through its potential rather than by initiating hostilities'.[30] As the war finally broke out in 1979, the Soviet commissioned her intelligence collectors, naval ships operating along Chinese and Vietnamese coasts, long-range TU-95 Bear D reconnaissance aircraft and other surveillance systems to receive updated information about the war back in Moscow. During, and even after the war, USSR assisted Vietnam with efficient airlift and sealift of supplies with Soviet ships supplying with arms to Haiphong. Also, the Soviet Naval Fleet patrolled the East and South China Seas, the route that was used by those ships.[31]

The Soviet involvement in the South China Sea region escalated after the Sino-Vietnam war. There happened surge in port visits of the Soviet ships to Vietnam and by the end of 1980 Vietnam became the second most visited country by the Soviet Navy in the Pacific, after Singapore. The Soviet Fleet *Misnk* visited Cam Ranh Bay in September 1980. The Soviet submarines visited both Cam Ranh Bay and Haiphong almost throughout the year. The ships returning from the Indian Ocean Squadron or from repairs in Singapore were sent to the Vietnam and Chinese coasts. The other units patrolling in the Pacific Ocean were also sent to the South China Sea.[32] The role the Soviet Navy in the Sino-Vietnam war in 1979 was very significant in two ways. Firstly, the very presence of the Navy had limited the scope of the conflict. On the other hand in return of this friendly gesture, Moscow acquired the permit to use the naval base at Cam Ranh Bay in Vietnam. This was undoubtedly a major gain for USSR, since in this way, Moscow could now influence the geostrategic ambience of the entire Indo-Pacific world, from South Pacific to Indian Ocean, that is both South and Southeast Asia. With bases in the Cam Ranh Bay, the Soviets could now respond quickly to the developments in the Indian Ocean. Also, the Soviet ships now could avoid sailing hundreds of miles to reach Vladivostok in Soviet Far East passing by the restricted straits under Japanese and Korean watch. Apart from that, from the Cam Ranh Bay, the Soviets could easily disrupt the Japanese commerce through the sea lanes passing by the Bay to the Indian Ocean.[33] Thus the naval base in the Cam Ranh Bay in the South China Sea was a vital strategic gain for the Soviets. Their presence in the Sea had served them with the purposes of firstly, controlling the major sea lane of communication, secondly, bringing the entire South China Sea region including the hostile competitor China under the watchful eye of Moscow, and thirdly, monitoring the activities of the Americans in Southeast Asia. Also, they could now squeeze the Japanese economy by controlling Tokyo's sea lanes of communication via the South China Sea route. This is very significant since here we can see the reflection of Imperial Japan's similar strategy when they, by occupying the entire Southeast Asia, had chocked the supply routes of the European colonisers during the World War II by delinking them with their Southeast Asian colonies. This time it was Japan's turn to face similar fate as an ally of USA.

The Soviet naval presence in the South China Sea after 1979 had sent ripples all around. There were apprehensions that Soviet presence, both naval as well as air force, could disrupt the economic and military traffic in the South China Sea. There were serious concerns about the security of the shipping lanes of Southeast and Northeast Asia and Taiwan. Also the fate of the Indonesian and Malaysian straits was discussed through which 50 per cent of the oil imports of the West and 80 per cent of its strategic materials passed (during that time).[34] This shows to what extent the South China Sea mattered both as strategic and economic zone to the Soviet-wary West. This was also seen as a 'strategic encirclement' of China and an attempt to 'linking the Soviet Northeast Asian strategic military complex with Afghan, Yemeni and Ethiopian bases'.[35] This is very intriguing. Such an apprehension points to the fact that with bases in Cam Ranh Bay in the South China Sea, any state can have its zone of influence stretched from nearby Northeast Asia to far away Africa. Such an assumption may be an exaggeration since during a war, no matter how 'cold' it is, one side has to blow up the panic irrespective of the logical possibility in order to substantiate the reason to fear the enemy as a pretext to strengthen oneself. However, encircling China sounds logical.

The Cold War in Southeast Asia was more between USSR and China, especially in the later period, rather than USSR and USA. Moscow sided with Hanoi in its war with China because of the Sino-Soviet tussle and also by then US-China relations became normal. To Moscow, Vietnam was a 'strategic stick' against US-China rapprochement.[36] China has traditionally seen Southeast Asia as her zone of influence. The reason for Soviet naval visit to the Vietnamese ports of Cam Ranh Bay, Haiphong, Da Nang and Ho Chi Minh was to restrain the Chinese from attacking these ports where the Chinese could launch both air and naval attacks.[37] The Chinese were also uncomfortable with the presence of the Soviet Navy in the South China Sea. They accused USSR of an expansionist and aggressive policy in South Asia and Indian Ocean route which, they asserted, got exposed with Moscow's support of Vietnam during the war. The Chinese press reported the visit of the Soviet carrier *Minsk* in the Pacific Ocean via Malacca Straits and its exercise in the East China Sea and alleged Soviet expansionist strategy in South Asia and coasts of East Asia.[38] Such a report undoubtedly hinted at the creation of Soviet influence zone in and around South China Sea. In a way, this was Soviet's 'string of pearls' in South China Sea against China. The naval facilities in the Cam Ranh Bay had intelligence gathering equipments to monitor the US as well as Chinese military movements communication traffic while there were satellite communication facilities to contact with Moscow.[39] Prior to 1979, Soviet Navy's presence in the South China Sea was occasional with five to eight ships while after the war the number increased to 25 to 30 which routinely patrolled the Sea.[40]

From the above narration it is evident that the geopolitics of South China Sea region got inseparably intertwined with the larger Cold War politics. The activities of the Soviet Navy in the region were the reflection of the growing ambitions, with rising confidence, of USSR to dominate the global affairs far away from her neighbourhood. However, it will be wrong to brand Southeast Asia, or South China Sea to be precise, as a region far away from Russian mainland since, it is an extended neighbourhood of 'Asian Russia'. The Soviet Navy was ruling the South China Sea since the Sino-Vietnam war in 1979. However, friendship is hardly ever lasting, especially in politics.

The advent of the Gorbachev era in March 1985 initiated the beginning of the end of Soviet-Vietnam closeness. Even before that, Gorbachev's criticism of Vietnamese leadership's incapacity to implement the Soviet aid programme, while attending the Fifth Congress of the Vietnamese

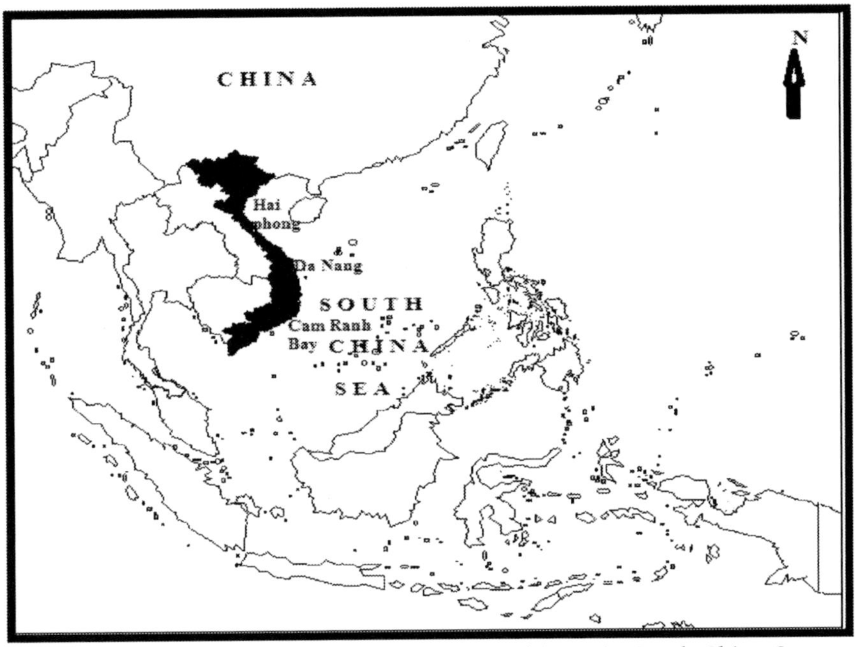

Map 3.1: Vietnamese ports with Soviet naval bases in South China Sea

Communist Party in 1982 where he represented CPSU, had given the idea about the future of the relation between the two communist states.[41] It is to be remembered here that the over-enthusiastic Soviet leadership had already damaged its reputation, not to mention economic debacle, by invading Afghanistan the same year they involved in the Sino-Vietnam War, 1979. This earned them criticism worldwide, especially from Southeast Asia. ASEAN (Association of Southeast Asian Nations), the club of non-communist countries of Southeast Asia, was very uneasy with the Soviet naval presence in Cam Ranh Bay which they viewed as proof of Moscow's diabolical scheme to dominate their region. Gorbachev had to allay these fears. With this objective, Mikhail Gorbachev delivered his famous speech at Vladivostok on June 28, 1986. In this speech he outlined the Soviet government's wish to normalize relation with both USA and China through concessions and compromises. Apart from announcing Soviet withdrawal from Afghanistan, he insisted that Soviet Union 'stand for peaceful, good neighbourly relations and beneficial cooperation' extending to Far East and Pacific.[42] He even spoke warmly about ASEAN which his predecessors had characterized as an anti-Soviet organization tied with US plot in Southeast Asia.[43] The impact of Gorbachev's East

Asia policy started showing effect with Moscow warming up relation with China, in contrast to its earlier anti-China posture and also settlement of the Cambodian crisis. So, with Moscow-Beijing relations improving and Hanoi-Moscow rapport waning, the bases in Cam Ranh Bay and Da Nang were losing significance to USSR. The Soviets started withdrawing from the Cam Ranh Bay in December 1989 while their Foreign Minister Eduard Shevardnadze assured US Congressmen touring Moscow about Soviet withdrawal of forces from Asia 'outside its own border'.[44] In 1990 January *The New York Times* reported that the Soviets have withdrawn their MIG-23 fighter planes and about half of its TU-16 bombers from its base at Cam Ranh Bay.[45] Pentagon, in its 1988 report had mentioned that Cam Rahn Bay "extends the Soviet wartime reach over East Asia's sea lines of communication in the South China Sea and poses a challenge as well to the U.S. military presence in the Philippines".[46] Thus, the Soviet withdrawal relieved Pentagon of major geopolitical challenge in the South China Sea region. However, the Americans were not sure about the total Soviet withdrawal since Pentagon voiced suspicion about Moscow's intention saying that, 'The ships have not left,.... The people have not left. Strategically, it is still pretty important to their deployments in the Indian Ocean. There is no sign that they intend to leave."[47] Nevertheless, the State Department in Washington welcomed the news saying that "We anticipate that less Soviet military involvement in southeast Asia would contribute to regional stability and to efforts to achieve a comprehensive political settlement in the Cambodia conflict".[48]

USA and the South China Sea geopolitics

Already mentioned before, the United States was not keen to involve militarily in the Southeast Asian affairs immediately after the conclusion of the war in 1945. The main reason for this disinterest can be traced in the American focus on Europe to contain the Soviet threat which was non-existent in far away Southeast Asia due to Stalin's emphasis on the immediate Russian neighbourhood, which included Europe. However, the British, who were keen to involve US in containing communist spread in Southeast Asia, identified the American defeat in China as the reason behind American reluctance. As H.A. Graves, Councillor to the British Embassy in Washington had opined in 1949, 'they (the Americans) have burnt their fingers so badly in China that they are at present in very cautious mood'.[49] However, it would be wrong to conclude that the Americans washed their hands of East Asia with the conclusion of the war. Until the fall of China to the communists (in 1949), USA provided large financial subsidies to her and through Economic Cooperation Administration or ECA aided Korea, Formosa, Burma, Thailand, Indochina and Indonesia.[50] Moreover, USA even took up the responsibility of reconstructing the war-ravaged Japanese economy through aids and assistance. But the Anglo-American military alliance to thwart communist spread in Southeast Asia was still a matter of apathy for Washington. R.C. Blackham of the British Foreign Office had observed in March 1949 that the Americans were not ready for any proposal offering Anglo-American military assistance to the Indochina War since they were not in favour to do anything to combat communism in Southeast Asia.[51] However, by December, 1949, the Americans were changing their mind, after the communist victory in China in October the same year. The Americans were cautious about the impact of this victory on the areas with 'considerable Chinese settlements'. To counter this, US Secretary of State, Dean Acheson dispersed 75 million dollars to Indonesia, Indochina and possibly Siam (Thailand) to strengthen the (anti-communist) regimes of these countries. The Secretary was even contemplating of dividing Southeast Asia, with the (British-led) Commonwealth, on the line of responsibility to counter the communist challenge, keeping the Philippines, Indochina and Siam while Commonwealth would look after the Indian Ocean countries and Burma.[52] Thus US was taking up the responsibility of the South China Sea region, from the coasts of Vietnam to the coasts of the Philippines. US was also supporting the revival of the old imperialist regimes by the European colonisers, British, Dutch and the French in the region. As a result the British could sail through the South China Sea to recapture Hong Kong, (only to return it to China, after fifty years, in 1997). They also recaptured Singapore, North Borneo and Malaya and assisted the Dutch to seize Indonesia and French to regain Indochina again. The US allowed such re-colonization efforts, often assisting with weapons.[53] It is noteworthy here that the European colonisers first eyed on the littorals of the South China Sea, immediately after the Japanese withdrawal, where they had their vital economic stake. Also, the region is the prime sea lane of communication between the East and the West and it was easier for them to re conquer the region due to the presence of the American Seventh Fleet in the vicinity. These colonizers earnestly sought for American assistance not only to revive their colonies in Asia but also to contain the growing communist influence in the region, which was compounded by the communist victory in China. They knew they could not do it alone since their might, and with that their glory, got evaporated with the end of the last war. The war had exhausted their strength and confidence to undertake any mission in the distant lands. But they could hardly quench their hunger for colonies, both for power and prestige. This they could do only with the American help. On the other hand, the US was not incognizant about the strategic importance of Southeast Asia. The Secretary of State, John Foster Dulles while narrating the significance of the region to US had said,

> "...The most direct developed sea and air communication between the Pacific Ocean and South Asia pass through South East Asia. The most important naval and air force bases are situated in this area."[54]

Undoubtedly he was referring to South China Sea while mentioning the air and sea communication between Pacific Ocean and South Asia. Prior to the occupation by the Japanese, South China Sea housed major Imperial naval and economic bases in its region, Singapore and Hong Kong. However, as mentioned previously, USA was not ready to take up responsibility of Southeast Asia, until the communist takeover of China and more precisely until Korean War took place in 1950-52. The war had impacted in revising the US naval policy in the Far East with reversing of the naval reduction. It is to be remembered that the Korean War was the first major outbreak of the US-USSR feud. Discussing the war in 1954, the US Navy noted the rapid expansion of the Soviet Navy rising from the rank of seventh most powerful during the WW II to third. It also noted that the new Soviet ships were 'versatile and rugged'.[55] However, such evaluation was based on incomplete information and about a navy with outdated construction concepts and the note was prepared at the time of budget cuts in the US Navy.[56] The American policy makers were haunted by the 'Domino Theory' which they prepared to analyze the communist threat to Asia which started with the fall of China to the communists. Such thinking was boosted by the Korean War. Thus, containing communism, which they viewed as tantamount to expansion of the Soviet influence, from further expansion in Asia became the cornerstone of post-war US' Asia policy. US' Indochina War should be viewed from this angle. The National Security Council paper of 1949 read, *"The USSR is now an Asiatic power of the first magnitude with expanding influence and interest throughout the continental Asia and into the Pacific...."*.[57] Referring to the colonial-nationalist war going on in Southeast Asia at that point of time, the paper read, "In any event, colonial-nationalist conflict provides a fertile field for subversive communist activities, and it is now clear that Southeast Asia is the target of a coordinated offensive directed by the Kremlin. In seeking to gain control of Southeast Asia, Kremlin is motivated in part by a desire to acquire Southeast Asia's resources and communication lines, and to deny them to us..."[58] This is very important in the sense that US was quite concerned of losing the resources as well as the communication lines if Southeast Asia falls to the communist hands. Thus it is clear that the Americans were viewing the nationalist struggle in Southeast Asia, including Indochina, as an extension of the 'war against communism 'or Soviet Union, to be precise. The 'contain communist' policy had guided the US in the war siding with the imperialist French. US Secretary of State Dulles was determined not to 'lose' Indochina, unlike the 'loss' of China.[59] In its memorandum to the Secretary of Defence in 1950, the Joint Chiefs of Stuff opined that,

> "The fall of Indochina (to the communists) would undoubtedly lead to fall of the other mainland Southeast Asia ... (Which) would result in the virtually complete denial to the United States of the Pacific Littorals of Asia..."[60]

Therefore, the US involvement in the Indochina War was in accordance with her broader 'war against communism' by siding with the French, who, the US admitted, was 'fighting more a colonial than anti-communist war'.[61] Thus, the South China Sea region was emerging as a stage for the US-Soviet geopolitical duel, an extension of their European feud. However, it should be remembered that the physical presence of the Soviets in the waters of South China Sea was a remote possibility at that point of time. But the Americans were haunted by the possible Soviet expansion in Asia via the fall of the continent to the communists, especially after the Korean War with the northern half of the Korean peninsula 'occupied' by the communists and the rise of communist China which played crucial role in the war. The triumph of the communists in China was a jolt to US post-war plans in Asia. After the emergence of 'Red' China the Americans were extremely wary about the future of Asia. The National Security Council report (dated 7th February, 1950), following the communist victories in China and the movement of the Chinese troops along the Indochina border, said that the US was relieved of her dilemma, regarding which side to support, France or Vietminh, in the war after communist China and USSR recognized the Ho Chi Minh regime, with her support to Bao Dai regime (of South Vietnam).[62] This was in accordance with the broad containment strategy of communism called Domino Theory. The Joint Chiefs of Stuff in its 1950 report to the Secretary of Defence said, "Southeast Asia is a vital segment in the line of containment of Communism stretching from Japan southward and around to the Indian peninsula..."[63] This 'southward expansion' from Japan included the South China Sea region where liberation struggle, inspired by communist ideology, was going on, from Indonesia, to Malaya and Indochina, all littoral states of South China Sea. Thus the South China Sea was all set to embrace the Cold War geopolitical conflict long before the appearance of the Soviets in the scene.

In compliance with the strategy to 'save' Indochina from the communist menace, President Harry Truman released $15 million to newly independent states of Vietnam, Laos and Cambodia in 1950. He also dispatched *USS Stickell* and *USS Anderson* for a port visit to Saigon (modern day Ho Chi Minh City and capital of the then South Vietnam). When the communists were taking over North Vietnam and many were trying to come southward, US Navy conducted Operation *'Passage to Freedom'* (in 1954) which was a ferry service from north to Saigon and other cities. The evacuation involved 113 ships which evacuated 3, 04740 refugees and tons of cargo and vehicles.[64] This was the major US non-combatant naval operation in the South China Sea. The US conducted this humanitarian assistance on the request of the South Vietnamese President Ngo Dinh Diem and the French military stationed in Indochina. The evacuation with naval assistance was conducted by Admiral Sabin who sought assistance of the Seventh Fleet.[65] As the Indochina War entered its second phase with the bifurcation of Vietnam into communist ruled North Vietnam and anti-communist South Vietnam after 1954, the US commitment to smash the communists in region became more prominent. The capabilities of the US Navy to project power ashore, meet the overseas commitment of the US armed forces and also the capacity to control the sea absorbed it in the Indochina War further. The long coastline of Vietnam with thousands of islands and many miles of inland waterway had provided the US Navy with suitable naval activities.[66]

Thus, it is seen that the South China Sea suited the US naval operations. It is to be remembered that the Sea presents an open stage for action in the mainland Southeast Asia for any naval power. US already had a formidable presence with her Seventh Fleet in the Pacific and also naval bases around the South China Sea. With this naval presence in the South China Sea vicinity, the US conducted the Tonkin Gulf raids in August 1964. The US provided South Vietnam with small patrol boats which were stationed in small base in Danang (in South Vietnam). In covert operation named 34*A* the US used these boats to shell radar stations along the coasts of North Vietnam and landed saboteurs to destroy bridges and other military targets in North Vietnam.[67] This was major US offensive on the communist-run North Vietnam. It was termed as a crucial event which fostered the American involvement in the Southeast Asian affairs which opened a new direction in the American policy towards North Vietnam.[68] Even before this, the US was snooping into the water of South China Sea, off the North Vietnamese coasts. In December 1962, the American destroyer, USS *Agerholm*, surveyed the South China Sea and the Gulf of Tonkin around the Hainan Island. In April 1963, USS *Edward* revolved round the Hainan Island and then moved downwards the North Vietnamese coasts. These patrols were part of the DESOTO patrol which the Americans had planned in 1961 to initiate off the Chinese coasts.[69] The DESOTO patrol was intelligence-gathering missions outside the territorial waters off the coasts of communist countries like China, Soviet Union and North Korea. In the early August 1964, USS *Maddox* conducted surveillance patrol along the North Vietnamese littoral in the Gulf of Tonkin.[70] The main purpose of this patrol was to obtain the navigational and hydrographic data and intelligence about the North Vietnamese Navy, apart from observing the junk fleet suspected of transferring the guerrillas to South Vietnam. The intelligence collection about the North Vietnamese Navy was important given the restriction imposed on North Vietnam by the Geneva Accord 1954 against maintaining any naval force. The SIGINT (or Signal Intelligence) had a major role to identify the naval activity of North Vietnam. The SIGNIT identified 30 vessels of the Vietnamese naval communication in late 1957 and also modern Vietnamese fleet in 1959.[71] Long before the Tonkin Gulf raid in August 1964, the US conducted the Operation Plan 34A or OPLAN 34A. This operation was undertaken following a proposal of Secretary of Defence Robert McNamara which he sent to the President (Lyndon) Johnson in December 1963 where he advised to undertake 'wide variety of sabotage and psychological operations against North Vietnam'. OPLAN 34A was a clandestine naval and air operations to pressure Hanoi to give up its support to the insurgency in the south. By the end of July, the OPLAN 34A MAROPS (maritime operations) were launched daily from Danang and the South Vietnamese naval commandos raided North Vietnamese islands of Hon Me and Hon Nieu in the Gulf of Tonkin on July 30 when the USS *Maddox* was 120-130 miles away.[72] Thus USS *Maddox* was providing support to the Vietnamese commandos from the mid-

South China Sea while the latter were conducting their amphibious raids on North Vietnamese islands. Meanwhile on August 2, North Vietnam dispatched Soviet-built P-4 motor torpedo to attack USS *Maddox* which however missed the target.[73] Thus we see that the South China Sea became the major stage of maritime conflict between US and North Vietnam with South Vietnam playing the supporting role under US protection.

This war, as discussed earlier, was the extension of the geopolitical tussle between the Soviet camp and the American camp. The Americans were well aware that the South Vietnam regime was the unpopular continuation of the French colonial set up which they left as a responsibility on the US shoulder (or taken up by US herself) before retreating in 1954. However, the US was not prepared to see the war as a simple struggle for just and logical unification of a bifurcated country but an extension of Soviet plot for dominance of Indochina at the cost of US interests. Thus the coastal state of Vietnam became the zone of US-Soviet Cold War (in physical absence of the Soviets) with South China Sea as the base of naval operations. The presence of the American fleet in the Gulf of Tonkin (northwest of South China Sea) could not be warded off by North Vietnam who could only challenge it on fewer occasions. Also, because of the US sea power, the Chinese could not interfere in the naval operations. The *Operation Market Time* of the US Navy, Vietnam Navy and US Coast Guard (initiated in 1965) had thwarted the infiltration (into the South Vietnam) by North Vietnam via sea which they started in the early 1960s. The US, by virtue of the capacity to deny the enemy free use of sea, could maintain her forces in the Pacific Ocean.[74] Thus, the presence in and control over the South China Sea helped the US with naval advantages.

The US-'introduced'[75] Cold War in Southeast Asia, with the fall of China and especially the Indochina War which eventually termed as Vietnam War, had unnerved the non-communist countries of the South China Sea region who increasingly depended on US protection. Countries like Singapore and Malaysia insisted US military presence in the region as a shield against North Vietnam's expansive posture. While visiting Bangkok in 1973, Singaporean Prime Minister Lee Kuan Yew appealed for the presence of American military forces in Southeast Asia for at least next four years. The Malayan leaders in Kuala Lumpur, capital of Malaysia, were suspicious of the military protection of UK, Australia and New Zealand, and proposed for US military presence in Thailand. Similar tacit request also came from Indonesia. Even Japan also, privately, insisted the US military presence in Southeast Asia for her unhindered imports of 90 per cent of oil from the Middle East and transport of fuel via Straits of Malacca and South China Sea.[76] Thus, it is seen that during the Vietnam War, the US military protection was vital for the littorals of the South China as well as Japan (as we will see in the subsequent chapters such vitality continues even today). The Americans were also prepared with the considerable naval force in the vicinity of the South China Sea and in the Pacific. As a major countermeasure of the perceived Soviet expansion, US founded the South East Asia Treaty Organization or SEATO in 1954 with her allies, mostly outside Southeast Asian region, including Pakistan, with only Thailand and the Philippines representing the region. It was decided at the first session of SEATO in Bangkok in February 1955 that the US Pacific forces would be the power of SEATO. In September 1960, Seventh Fleet was patrolling the shores of Indochina to assist anti-communist forces in Laos while in April 1963, it was in the Bay of Siam (or Thailand). The strategy of the SEATO was to operate from the Asian countries including South Vietnamese bases of Nga Tran Nge, Phu Bai and Tan San-Nghe.[77] All these ports are located on the South China Sea. So South China Sea was used by SEATO as the operation ground to keep mainland Southeast Asia under surveillance.

As the 1960s drew to a close, the US started contemplating of abandoning the military responsibility of Vietnam War. After the new Nixon administration took charge in White House, it initiated the process of 'disentanglement of Asia' mission. In his Guam Doctrine, or Nixon Doctrine as it was called later, delivered on July 25, 1969, US President Richard Nixon said, "Defense of freedom is everybody's business-not just America's business."[78] Thus he was implying on 'sharing' the responsibility of security provision rather than keeping his country bear the burden of it alone. This was a shift from the previous policy of Washington towards securing Asia. Thus he said, "In the previous administration, we *Americanized* the war in Vietnam. In this administration, we are *Vietnamizing* the search for peace."[79] This *Vietnamization* plan, he clarified, was to 'enable the South Vietnamese forces to assume the full responsibility for the security of South Vietnam'.[80] The plan was complete withdrawal of the US combat forces and their replacement by South Vietnamese forces. Another major event that happened by the 1970s was the normalization of the Sino-US relations. We can say that these two developments were complementary to each other. In this way, the new Carter Administration was buying the Chinese support for its 'shared responsibility' challenges in Southeast Asia along with the promotion of the ASEAN forum.[81] The striking feature of the US strategy in the region after the conclusion of the Vietnam War was her reluctance of any military engagement in the Southeast Asian region after the war. This continued even during the Sino-Vietnam War which promoted Soviet naval deployment in the South China Sea region, as discussed earlier. The lack of interest in Washington in continued engagement in the Indochinese affairs can be traced in the US defeat in the Indochina War. The American policy makers, even if interested to 'prevent the conflict (between China and Vietnam) from becoming crisis', were restrained due to strong public opinion at home against any involvement in Indochina affair.[82] This was evident from the fast decrease in the amount of intelligence assessments on the Indochina region between 1975 and 1977. During this time the intelligence assessments of the US intelligence community fell from 58 in 1975 to 17 in 1976 to 7 in 1977 and just a little high 10 in 1978.[83] On the contrary, Washington was now keen on utilizing its relations with China to counter the Soviet threat in the region (the way she is now utilizing her allies in East Asia to counter China). However, there were differences regarding this policy within the US government. When Secretary of State Cyrus Vance was against using 'China card' against Soviet Union, the national security adviser Zbigniew Brizezinski opined that the Southeast Asia policy of the US was 'subsumed under global strategy of aligning Untied States with China against Soviet Union'.[84] When Hanoi, although keen to normalize relations with US, ultimately aligned USSR in November 1978 to counter China, Brizezinski's opinion prevailed.

The growing might of the Pacific Fleet was a matter of concern of USA. The US considered the Soviet Union as the most difficult national security problem. So the US strategic thinking emphasized on maintaining the Seventh Fleet as an important deterrent against the growing Soviet naval strength although the strategic emphasis was more on Northeast Asia, including Japan, rather than South China Sea or Southeast Asia.[85] However, it was assumed that the US would limit herself to promoting the anti-Soviet powers of the region, like Indonesia and the Philippines with military aid, in order to form a strategic arc stretching from Japan to Southeast Asia with an American base in Diego Garcia in Indian Ocean.[86] The successful military intervention in the maritime region depends on advanced technology, particularly in naval and air power which was in possession of USA which actually made the Chinese feel necessary of US presence in the South China Sea region at that time as a sole security guarantee against Soviet naval involvement, even at the expense of Chinese interests. The non-communist countries of the region, like Singapore, also wanted the continued presence of the US naval vessels in the vicinity of the South China Sea as a security shield against the Soviet naval presence.[87] The presence of Soviet fleet in the Cam Ranh Bay in Vietnam was seen by the Chinese as significant saying that in the event of war the air and naval units of the Soviets of the Bay could collaborate with the Soviet forces based at home could launch a two-pronged attack on the US Seventh Fleet and the military installations in the Western Pacific. It could also delink the US fleets stationed in the Indian and Pacific Ocean by capturing the Malacca Straits from the Cam Ranh Bay.[88] Thus the US' concern in the South China Sea region was logically analyzed by the Chinese. The US on the other hand was in dilemma regarding how to handle the growing might of the Soviets in the South China Sea region, especially after the defeat in the Vietnam affairs when the policy makers back home were reluctant to involve US further in the affairs of the region. Thus, they opted for utilizing the anti-Soviet sentiments and fear growing in the region with the presence of the Soviets in the South China Sea. The Americans were pushing for a game of balance between the Soviet and anti-Soviet camp, Vietnam vs. the rest, including China. The small states and China wanted the American naval prowess to be utilized as a security shield (or rather balancing tactic) against the Soviet naval fleet in the South China Sea region (the way the small South China Sea littoral states are now opting for engagement with US to counter China). The Chinese here were most interested in order to contain the Soviet influence in their backyard. And this was fast bringing the US and China closer, promoting the strategic understanding between the two on one hand and deliberation of modernizing the Chinese naval strength on the other.

China in South China Sea geopolitics

As we have seen, the Soviet involvement in the South China Sea geopolitics during the Cold War period was mainly to restrain the growing Chinese activities in the region. It can be said that the Sino-Soviet rift played a major role in promoting the Soviet naval expeditions in the Southeast Asian waters which was very prominent during the Sino-Vietnam war of 1979. Moscow considered Hanoi an important 'strategic stick' against the growing Sino-US engagement.[89] Since the US withdrawal after the Vietnam War and until the Gorbachev era, the South China Sea geopolitics reflected the Sino-Soviet tension. China saw the

Soviet involvement in the Southeast Asian affairs as an 'intrusion' in what China considered as her zone of influence. The Chinese apprehended Soviet encirclement of China, with the help of the American and the Japanese, economically, politically as well as militarily.[90] China's Southeast Asia policy in the 1960s and throughout 1970s was revolving round the Soviet strategy in the region. This was all the more significant to Beijing in the context of the Nixon Doctrine of USA and the East of Suez policy of UK.[91] Such a situation did ruffle Southeast Asian non-communist countries who were dependent on the Western protection. The Chinese found the proposal of Soviet leader Leonard Brezhnev for worker-peasant alliance in Southeast Asia in this context as the means of establishing Soviet military and economic strength in Afro-Asian region.[92] So, we see that the Chinese were wary of the Soviet expansionist strategy in their vicinity in the 1960s and 70s, especially in the context of US-UK proposed withdrawal.

This was the reason why the Chinese were not in favour of American military withdrawal from the Philippines which they saw as a counterpoise to Soviet ambition in the region. Beijing considered the continued US presence in the Philippines more important than its dispute with Manila over the Spratly Islands' sovereignty. To China the mutual defence treaty between US and the Philippines was very important in the context of the Soviet threat and growing Soviet-Vietnam rapport amidst the Hanoi-Beijing tension.[93] Therefore, emerging geopolitics of South China Sea region was taking a new form with growing Chinese favour of US military presence in the region to counter the Soviet threat. The Americans were also favouring the Chinese support in the East Asian geopolitical scene. The US Defence Secretary Harold Brown opined that the continued US-Chinese relations would bolster the Chinese stake in regional stability while the Assistant Secretary Richard Holbrooke emphasized on US support for Chinese role in maintaining peace and stability in Asia and the Pacific.[94] These opinions can be construed as the American strategy of involving the Chinese more and more in the East Asian geopolitics, including the South China Sea region, since Washington could not leave the region to the rival's mercy after its withdrawal. On the other hand, the Chinese were not confident about their capability to thwart the growing Soviet influence single-handedly which forced them to favour the continued US presence in the Southeast Asian region. This was mainly because Beijing lacked the superior technology required for naval and the air power which the Americans had. Hence it considered the US naval presence the sole guarantee against the Soviet naval prowess and means to maintain status quo in the region until it acquires long-range air and naval support capability.[95] However, China was in a dilemma with her policy in the South China Sea region regarding her support for armed revolution in the Southeast Asian countries. The growing Soviet threat was the prime concern for Beijing at that time. Thus, its total disavowal of communist insurgencies in the Southeast Asian countries was to promote the Soviet involvement in the region encroaching upon the Chinese sphere of influence in the region. Hence, during his tour of Bangkok, Kuala Lumpur and Singapore in November 1978, the Chinese leader Deng Xiao-ping refused to discontinue China's support to the armed struggle in the region which, in long term would create unrest in the non-communist countries of Southeast Asia, according to many scholars of the time. However, in the light of growing Soviet influence reflected in the Sino-Vietnam Friendship Treaty, signed in November 1978, China's natural option was not to confront the (non-communist) littoral states (of South China Sea) which might encourage Soviet involvement. So, it was natural for China to opt for status quo, for some time, which would not allow any power, including herself, to establish influence in the region which would make China a stabilizing factor in the South China Sea region.[96]

In a way, a balance of power was exercised in the South China Sea geopolitics with the appearance of the Soviets in the scene when the region was simmering with the Sino-Vietnam tension. There was a clear balancing tactic going on among the Chinese, the non-communist Southeast Asian states with US as the fulcrum against the Soviets. This geopolitical game in the South China Sea region was more a result of the Sino-Soviet 'Cold War' with US in a supporting role. Chinese activities in the sea were limited subject to her lack of blue water naval capability, apart from her hesitance of arousing US or Soviet hostility (something she could not handle at that point of time) and the risk of turning the regional states, brimming with strong nationalist zeal, against her by supporting extreme revolutionary movements (in those countries).[97] So, China was little confused with her policy but her Soviet wariness was beyond doubt.

Lim Joo-Jock opines that the sea (the South China Sea) did offer China strategic advantage in cornering Vietnam during the war. According to the author, China could open 'an avenue (in the Sea) for distraction of Vietnamese on an additional front. Keeping Chinese claims (on the disputed islands of the South China Sea) alive serves to keep Vietnamlicensed off-shore oil exploration outside of disputed waters, thereby inhibiting Vietnamese oil development and retarding the long-term use of Vietnamese oil instrument in interstate diplomacy'.[98] Thus we see how the dispute can be used in promoting strategic gains during tension. China, however, was expanding her naval forces since 1960. Initially it started with the 21 Soviet W-class submarines in 1956, while from 1964 she started building her own design of destroyer escorts which were larger, faster and more heavily armed than the Soviet Riga-type and very large numbers of fast missile, gun and torpedo boats. Nonetheless, Chinese naval forces were, at that point of time, designed for coastal defence.[99] Apart from strategic concern, the South China Sea bothered Beijing for the economic reasons as well. Although, the Chinese trade with the South China Sea littorals did not count much, since the late 1970s the government-to-government deals pushed the volume upward. Under the agreement with the Philippines, Manila was to export sugar and other products like copper concentrates and timber to China and import Chinese crude oil mainly, besides some manufactured products. Also, China was a consistent exporter of rice each year to some Southeast Asian countries. Also, the rubber of the littoral countries (of the South China Sea) like Malaysia was important for China.[100] The Chinese were interested in an open sea route to these South China Sea littorals. An article of Peking Review wrote in 1975 that, *"...the South China Sea is an important junction for navigation and an important maritime gateway from China's mainland, and nearby islands."*[101] The Paracel Islands were strategically most important to the Chinese in terms of surveillance and potential control of the main north-south shipping route which passes between Singapore and Hong Kong.[102]

The Chinese policy towards South China Sea during the Cold War emphasised on the open and free navigation across the Sea. This was more evident in her support to the Malaysia-Indonesia claim for joint jurisdiction over the Malacca Straits while insisting on South China Sea remaining open for international shipping. This was a strategy of Beijing not to antagonize either US or Japan (who also have interest in open South China Sea) and to thwart any super power domination of the Malacca Straits by approving the Malaysia-Indonesia joint jurisdiction claim over the Malacca Straits.[103] It can also be construed as the Chinese strategy to leave the Malacca Straits to the weaker states' hands who can be manipulated with eventual increase in Chinese strength while keeping them as the guard against the super powers for the time being. So, in a way, the Chinese were trying to keep the South China Sea region hazard

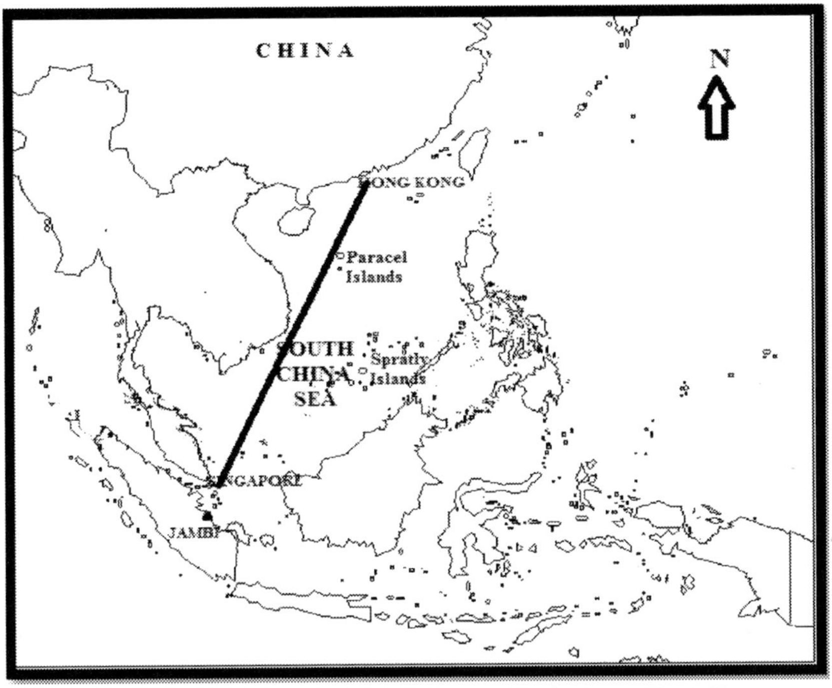

Map 3.2: Chinese north-south shipping route between Hong Kong and Singapore

free, especially from the Soviet Union. For this, Beijing was depending mainly on US naval strength, given her own lack of naval strength, while courting the anti-Soviet (and anti-Vietnam) non-communist and pro-US South China Sea littorals. On the other hand it was also championing the freedom of navigation in the South China Sea, not only to ensure its own economic interests but also as an appeasement tactic of US and her allies. This is interesting in present day context when the countries like India, Japan and USA are insisting on such freedom in the South China Sea amidst the growing Chinese assertiveness (to be discussed in details in the subsequent chapters). During the Sino-Vietnam tension, China turned the South China Sea geopolitics as her own Cold War with Moscow.

Southeast Asian navies and the South China Sea geopolitics

So far we have discussed the big and medium power tussle in the South China Sea during the Cold War which has used the Southeast Asian countries as the launch pad. However, it is important to see how the Cold

War tussles had impacted the Southeast Asian naval policies during that time although it is to be remembered that the naval prowess of the countries there were comparatively insignificant during the Cold War. The reason behind this is that the naval strength, which is required primarily for far off missions with vested economic as well as strategic interest, firstly demands huge capital investment expected only from a strong economy and also from a state aspiring to become major power globally. The post-war Southeast Asian countries satisfied neither of the conditions. Moreover, they were engrossed in fighting internal challenges like insurgency and had no time (or even reason) to ponder on naval ambition. Nevertheless, the Cold War somehow absorbed them in the neighbouring South China Sea geopolitics and directed their respective naval policy.

Vietnam, immediately after the end of the Second World War, was dependent on the French naval protection. The French, during the war, paid much emphasis on the reverine operations since the inland waters were very important in Vietnam which was the landward extension of the sea power.[104] The Vietnamese Navy was founded following the Franco-Vietnamese Agreement of 30th December, 1949 and it came into being with an Imperial Ordinance No.2 by Bao Dai, the head of the Vietnamese State, issued on March 6, 1952. The agreement ensured French assistance to the Vietnamese with cadre and training.[105] It is to be remembered here that the Vietnamese did not require any naval assets directed to the sea missions since the land was protected by the French Navy, along with the British and US fleets, during that time. The Vietnamese Navy was meant to operate in the rivers inland. Thus, the first Vietnamese Navy unit, composed on 10th April, 1953, was a *dinassaut* (river assault group), with five machine gun-armed landing craft which were operative in the Mekong Delta and based at the junction of two rivers, Bassac and Can Tho.[106] With the bifurcation of Vietnam after the Geneva Conference in 1954 into Viet Minh controlled North Vietnam and Bao Dai controlled South Vietnam, the naval policy of the two Vietnams was directed by the Cold War rules since now the Americans appeared in the scene. Meanwhile, after the transfer of the naval command to the South Vietnam government by the French in 1955, the South Vietnam government undertook the policy of reorganizing the navy emphasizing on making it a sea-going force of patrol vessels and mine-sweepers with expanded riverine capabilities. As a result, the South Vietnamese Navy soon had three operational divisions—River Force, Sea Force and Marine Force.[107]

The Americans replaced the French as the assistance to the South Vietnamese Navy after the handover of 1955 when the French training school was shut down and the Vietnamese were sent to US Navy establishments for training since 1956. In early 1956 the South Vietnamese Navy founded five sea zones with eight flotillas operating in Da Nang, Nha Trang, Vung Táu, Con Son Island and later Qui Nhon. Meanwhile, the US was helping the Vietnam Navy to maintain security in the coastal waters of South Vietnam including the offshore islands there.[108] Thus, it is seen that the South Vietnam Navy was taking small steps forward with the US assistance. Soon it was to emerge from the confinement of the riverine activities to concentrate on wider sea-oriented activities. It widened its zone of actions by visiting to Manila, Singapore and Bangkok. Its patrol crafts visited the Paracel Islands and Spratly Islands in July and August, 1956 respectively. During both these visits, South Vietnam established her claims on the disputed islands by landing a Territorial Company in the Paracels and unfurled her flag taking down the Taiwanese flag in the Spratlys. The US Seventh Fleet and the South Vietnamese Navy conducted joint patrols from the 17th parallel from the coast east to the Paracel Islands in December 1961 which mainly meant to train the Vietnamese Navy about the open sea operations and survey theextension of waterborne infiltration from the North (Vietnam).[109]

Thus, as the geopolitical feud between the communist and anti-communist factions (assisted by the US) grew in Vietnam War, the Americans took the South Vietnamese Navy's potentials to a new height by training them in the open waters of South China Sea. Also, the disputed sovereignty over the islands was touched upon with the joint patrolling near the disputed islands. This was a significant activity in the light of the Chinese claims in the dispute who was in the opposite camp. In January 1974, the South Vietnamese Navy clashed with the Chinese in the Paracel Islands which apparently took the advantage of the growing weakness of the South Vietnamese Navy (as the Vietnam War was approaching conclusion). According to some scholars, Beijing is expert in 'capitalising on the right moments to make a move' when its opponent is either too weak to respond or distracted.[110] 1974 was the time when the Americans were unravelling Southeast Asian engagements following the Nixon Doctrine which was weakening South Vietnam and making it vulnerable to both Chinese and North Vietnamese invasion while on the other hand, by then Sino-US rapport had developed where the US needed China to counter the Soviet threat in Asia. It is noteworthy here that during the clash, US remained absolutely neutral ordering the Seventh Fleet to 'keep out of the vicinity'.[111] Thus, countering South Vietnam over the South China Sea island dispute was beneficial for Beijing at that point of time. It is assumed that the Chinese leadership under Mao undertook the operation as a pre-emptive measure to thwart the Russians using the islands after the war.[112] So, the 1974 clash over territorial disputes in the Paracels can be seen as the result of the changing Cold War geopolitical landscape of South China Sea region, in favour of China vis-à-vis the weak South China Sea littorals states, rather than a result of mere territorial tension between China and Vietnam.

Like the South Vietnamese Navy, the North Vietnamese Navy or the Socialist Republic of Vietnam Navy also grew with time. Initially, the North Vietnamese leadership of Viet Minh were reluctant to use the sea as the stage of combat operation and preferred ambush operations on the *dinassaut* with mortar fire from ashore. However, North Vietnam used the sea as a supply route to the Viet Cong (the communist guerrilla faction in South Vietnam) with the North Vietnamese Naval Transportation Group 125 composed of steel-hulled 100 t trawlers and sea-going junks, regularly confiscated by the US Navy.[113] With the reunification of Vietnam, its navy was facilitated with the acquisition of the bases in the South developed by the Americans. One such base was the Cam Ranh Bay. This became a major issue with the development of the Moscow-Hanoi rapport following the deterioration of the Sino-Vietnam relations and Sino-US normalization of relations, as already discussed. Hanoi not only allowed Soviet Union to use the Cam Ranh Bay but also permitted Moscow to exploit oil deposits off the southern coast of Vietnam, following the signing of Treaty of Friendship and Cooperation in 1978. By 1985, the Soviets stationed 20 surface ships and three or four submarines along with Tu-95 and Tu-16 (Badger) bombers.[114]

This Hanoi-Moscow friendship had its impact on the South China Sea territorial dispute which is evident from the Vietnamese Navy's amphibious manoeuvres, assisted by Soviet Navy, around the Spratly Islands occupied by Vietnam.[115] This can be seen as a part of the then existing geopolitical ambience of South China Sea when China, assured of US naval presence at the height of the US-Soviet Cold War tension in East Asia, was poking the Soviet ally Vietnam in the disputed islands and Hanoi was responding under the Soviet protection. It is interesting to know whether both China and Vietnam would have acted the same way in the absence of the respective Super Powers' protection during that time. As we have already seen the Chinese were in favour of the presence of the US navy even after the US plan to give up military responsibility in Southeast Asia following the Vietnam fiasco. However, the Sino-Vietnam clash in the Spratlys in March 1988 can be viewed as a result of the changed geopolitical situation. As we have discussed before, the advent of the Gorbachev era in Moscow in 1985 worked against Vietnam-Soviet strategic friendship. On the other hand, in mid-1985 the Chinese military emphasized on the local and limited wars around China's periphery in which the territorial dispute of South China Sea was considered as a focal point.[116] This can be seen again as the opportunistic strategy of China capitalizing the gradual withdrawal of the Soviet protection guarantee to Hanoi. It is to be remembered that Gorbachev also attempted to normalize relation with Beijing. This was the repetition of the US-South Vietnam situation following the Nixon Doctrine and Sino-US friendship in 1970s which the Chinese took the advantage of. China began to make physical presence in the Spratlys in 1987 when People's Liberation Army Navy or PLAN carried out large scale patrol of the Spratlys.The clash finally took place in March 1988. The skirmishes did not gain China anything significant except some reefs and also failed to expel Vietnam or the Philippines from there.[117] However, the clash can be seen as a result of the changing geopolitical landscape in the South China Sea region following the new policy of withdrawal by Soviet Union in the concluding phase of the Cold War era.

The Philippines, a former US colony and a staunch American ally in the latter's war against communism in Asia, did not heed much to naval strength after the conclusion of the World War II in spite of being subdued by the Japanese forces during the war. The reason behind this aloofness was the US protection guarantee. This was further ensured with the continuation of the US base at the Subic Bay, until the conclusion of the Cold War in 1990. Also, Manila's over engagement with the internal challenges of insurgency in the southern parts of the country diverted the country's military budget to the land forces depriving the navy although the country is composed of islands. Manila sensed the heat of the Cold War for the first time with the conclusion of Vietnam War and the appearance of the Soviet Navy in South China Sea. This was compounded by the Nixon Doctrine or Guam Doctrine since now, apart from dealing with the challenge of Soviet ally united Vietnam, Manila had to handle its any assertive move in the disputed Spratlys archipelago without the US support.[118] It is to be remembered here that on 10th July 1971 the Ferdinand Marcos government in Manila iterated that Spratlys were under *defacto* trusteeship of allied powers and no one can deploy troops in the islands there without the consent of the powers. This was in reference to the Taiwanese seizure of Itu Aba Island.[119] President Marcos declared Spratlys as part Filipino territory in 1978. Manila's interest in the archipelago grew from 1970s with the prospect of the discovery of oil in the area which became a major factor in the sovereignty claims over the islands at the height of the Vietnam War between 1969-73. In 1971 the Philippines declared *Kalayaan* (east of the Spratlys) as her territory and in 1974 permitted a consortium of oil companies to explore the Reed Bank area after occupying it.[120]

Indonesia, although possessing a maritime state like condition and a major littoral of the South China Sea, never got the scope to exploit her naval potentials. This was mainly because of the non-cooperation of her Dutch colonisers after independence (which the Netherlands was forced to grant to Indonesia). The Dutch had been reluctant to include the native Indonesians in their RNLN (Royal Netherlands Navy) and thus the newly liberated Indonesian state lacked well-trained naval personnel to start her navy with. Also, the Dutch was ready to supply materials to the Indonesian Navy with a reduced valuation of 20 per cent which was too much for a weak economy like Indonesia to afford and the former were very 'moderate' in their supply.[121] Thus Indonesian effort to build up naval strength was paralysed at the outset.

However, unlike the Indochinese states and the Philippines, Indonesia was not embroiled too much in the Cold War geopolitics of Southeast Asia with the presence of either of the contending Super Powers in the country for 'assistance'. The *Konfrontasi* policy or the Confrontation Policy (1963-66) of Sukarno against the British foundation of Malaysian Federation in 1963 was apparently attached to the overall Cold War geopolitics where Sukarno took an anti-imperialist stand. The policy involved armed incursions, bomb attacks and other subversive acts that were aimed at destabilising the former British colonies that were to be included in the federation, namely, Singapore, Malaya, Sarawak, Brunei and North Borneo (Sabah). However, the Indonesian Navy was reluctant to be too much involved in it. Firstly it was unable to face the naval might of the British and their allies. On the other hand, the policy threatened the suspension of Western aids and loans which was to impact the naval build up of Indonesia. Also, this 'Crush Malaysia' mission was seemed to be strengthening the communist party of Indonesia, the PKI.[122] It is to be remembered here that the military of Indonesia was anti-communist and suspected the Chinese hand in the communist activities in the country.

Thus, the enthronement of General Suharto to power in 1966 by ousting President Sukarno turned Indonesia an anti-China and pro-West country. Nevertheless, the Nixon Doctrine, followed by US-China rapprochement, did upset Jakarta with China becoming more active in South China Sea forcing Indonesia to package of measures to improve her security position.[123]

Malaysia's naval build up took place, unlike Indonesia, with the help of her colonial master. The Royal Malayan Navy (RMN) was founded in the Straits Settlement Royal Naval Volunteer Reserve (SSRNVR) in 1934 to assist the Royal Navy of Britain to defend Singapore. After the war, the Malayan Naval Force (MNF) and Malayan Royal Naval Volunteer Reserve (MRNVR) were constituted where the recruiting began in 1949 with two Malayan officers and from 1954 the cadets were trained in Britain. The MNF was renamed as RMN by that time which assisted the British and the Commonwealth naval forces during the anti-communist Emergency operations in the Malayan Peninsula after the war.[124] The British concluded a security pact called Anglo-Malayan Defence Agreement in 1957. The Malayan communist rebellion was the major challenge that the British encountered which forced them to unveil the anti-communist Emergency operations. However, while granting independence to the Malayans, the British inked the defence treaty with them in order to ensure them British defence and the latter's continued presence in the region. Under articles 1 and 2, Britain was to assist Federation of Malaya for external defence and training and developing armed forces in Malaya. Article 3 says that Federation of Malaya agreed to afford to the British government, the "right to maintain in the Federation such naval land and air forces including a Commonwealth Strategic Reserve as agreed between the two governments as necessary (for the purpose of article 1 of the agreement) and for fulfilment of Commonwealth and international obligations."[125] In this way the British arranged for their stay back in the Southeast Asian waters after the liberation of Malaya. The Malayan government requested the British to stay back after 1957 to help 'complete the Emergency job' which was declared to have ended in 1960.[126]

Meanwhile as the Vietnam War concluded with the unification of the country, assisting the southward flow of the refugees from Indochina and thwarting the 'pirates of opportunity' sneaking in the guise of refugees put a heavy pressure on the RMN. On the other hand the rise of Chinese threat of assertion after the war in the disputed islands in

South China Sea worried Malaysia which was now determined to protect her claims on the Spratlys. Such fear was compounded by Vietnam's operation in Cambodia and the Soviet activities in South Asia (that is her friendship treaty with India). Such developments triggered the revival of the FPDA (Five Powers Defence Arrangement),[127] by Australia mainly, with the *Starfish* series of naval exercises in 1981.[128] That Malaysia was now concentrating on naval activities was apparent from the statement of Chief of her Navy, Admiral Mohammed Zain bin Mohammed Saleh who said in 1980 that, "the Navy must change its present operational concept of coastal patrolling to...ocean surveillance."[129] Thus by the 1980s the Malaysian Navy was contemplating on operating in the adjacent larger oceanic platform of South China Sea. It was in 1980 when Malaysia declared formally a 200 mile EEZ (Exclusive Economic Zone) encompassing much of the Spratlys.[130] This was the time when China was also getting assertive with her claims in the Sea resulting to the Sino-Vietnam clash of 1988.

As discussed earlier, Sino-Soviet closeness developed since 1985 after Gorbachev came to power in Moscow which encouraged China to be further assertive in South China Sea. This was a major geopolitical development in the region. Thus Malaysian Navy Chief, Admiral Abdul Wahab bin Haji Nawi, emphasized in 1986 for a 'forward defence' in the South China Sea to meet any emergency situation there. Kuala Lumpur started garrisoning the Layang Layang Reef of the Spratlys in 1983 while more units were stationed in Ubi and Mantanani Reefs in 1986. Malaysia was very upset with the growing Sino-Soviet friendship anticipating Chinese effort to divert resources to her navy directed towards the southern waters. Malaysia announced to increase patrolling in the South China Sea following the Sino-Vietnam clash in 1988 and later engaged in disputes with Manila over fishing rights. These developments were happening amidst the shadow of proposed US withdrawal.[131]

The Cold War had a deep impact on the South China Sea littorals' naval policies. However, such an impact should be viewed as the result of the Cold War geopolitics itself among the big powers. The global developments of the Soviet-US duel had its repercussions in the waters of South China Sea. When the colonial period established the geographical importance of the Sea, the World War II added the geopolitical significance to it especially with the defeat of the European powers at the hands of Asian challenger Japan who turned the entire East Asian waters into a Japanese lake. The fear about Sino-Soviet dominance of the waters of

Southeast Asia thus was a frightening issue for the Western liberal states remembering the Imperial Japanese nightmare. The US-Soviet-China trilateral activities marked the geopolitical character of the South China Sea during the Cold War period. The developments centring the traditional territorial disputes were also part of the overall developments of the Cold War geopolitics of South China Sea. Thus the Cold War strengthened the link of the local affair of South China Sea with the larger geopolitics of the big powers. However the gradual appearance of China as a distinct local player in the South China Sea affairs was a major development during the Cold War period. Such development continued in the post Cold War era even with one super power remaining in the scene.

END NOTES

1. Peter Calvocoressi and Guy Wint, *Total War, Volume II: The War in Asia*, New York, Ballantine Books, 1972,p.371 (emphasis added)
2. Peter Calvocoressi and Guy Wint, *Total War, Volume I: The War in the West*, New York, Ballantine Books, 1972,p.628
3. Ibid, p.622
4. Muthiah Alagappa, 'International Politics in Asia: The Historical Context', Muthiah Alagappa (ed) *Asian Security Practice*, Stanford, Stanford University Press, 1998, p.88
5. Clive Christie, *Ideology and Revolution in Southeast Asia, 1900-1980*, Richmond, Curzon, 2001, pp.89-90
6. Ibid, pp.78,79
7. For details see ibid
8. For details see Richie Ovendale, 'Britain, United States and the Cold War in South-East Asia, 1949-1950', Royal Institute of *International Affairs*, Vol.53, No.8 (summer 1982)
9. Ian Morrison, *The War Against Japan: Thoughts on the present conflict in the Far East*, London, Faber And Faber Ltd., 1943, p.99, also quoted in Maj. Gen. J.F.C. Fuller, *The Second World War, 1939-45: A Strategical and Tactical History*, London, Eyre and Spottiswoode, 1968, p.402, emphasis added
10. Kinoaki Matsuo, *How Japan Plans to Win* (translated by Kilsoo K. Haan), London, George Harrap & Co. Ltd., 1942, p.160, emphasis added
11. Cited in ibid, p.144, emphasis added
12. Richie Ovendale, op cit, p.456
13. Warner Levi, The Future of Southeast Asia, *Asian Survey*, Vol.10, No.4, 1970, p.348
14. Cited in Bruce W. Watson, *Red Navy at Sea: Soviet naval Operations on the High Seas, 1956-1980*, Colorado, Westview Press, 1982, p.2
15. Clive Christie, op cit, p.37
16. Michael MccGwire, 'Naval power and Soviet Global Strategy', *International Security*, Vol. 3, No. 4, Spring 1979, MIT Press, p.135

17. Ibid, p.136
18. Thomas W. Wolfe, *The Soviet Quest for More Globally Mobile Military Power,* Memorandum RM5554-PR, December, 1967, Santa Monica, California, The Rand Corporation, http://www.rand.org/content/dam/rand/pubs/research_memoranda/2009/RM5554.pdf (accessed on 27.11.2015), p.2
19. Bruce W. Watson, op cit, p.3
20. K.R. Singh, *The Indian Ocean: Big Power presence and Local Response,* New Delhi, South Asia Books, 1978, pp.58, 59
21. Peter Polomka, *Ocean Politics in South East Asia,* Singapore, Institute of South East Asian Studies, 1978, p.30
22. Bruce W. Watson, op cit, p.133
23. Ibid, 134
24. Ibid, p.136
25. Ibid
26. For details read Sergey Radchenko, 'Soviet Union and Asia, 1940s - 1960s', Uyama Tomohiko (ed), *Empire and After: Essays in Comparative Imperial and Decolonization Studies,* Hokkaido, Slavic Research Centre, Hokkaido University, 2012
27. Ibid, p.109
28. Lim Joo-Jock, *Geostrategy and South China Sea Basin: Regional balance, Maritime Issues, Future Patterns,* Singapore, Singapore University Press, 1979, p.73
29. Bruce W. Watson, op cit, P.139
30. Cited in ibid
31. Ibid
32. Ibid, p.138
33. Ibid, p.140
34. Richard D. Fisher, 'Moscow's Growing Muscle in Southeast Asia',*Asian Backgrounder,* Asian Studies Center, April 4, 1984, http://www.heritage.org/research/reports/1984/04/moscows-growing-muscle-in-southeast-asia (accessed on 30.11.2015), pp.1,2
35. Ibid, p.2
36. Richard D. Fisher, op cit, p.7
37. Bruce W. Watson, op cit, pp.139, 140
38. Ibid, p.141
39. Richard D. Fisher, op cit, p.3
40. David Winterford, 'Assessing the Soviet Naval Build-up in Southeast Asia: Threats to Regional Security', Naval Postgraduate School, Monterey, California, Report for the period Oct 1987-January 1988, September, 1988, http://calhoun.nps.edu/bitstream/handle/10945/28864/assessingsovietn00wint.pdf?sequence=1, p.10
41. Michael C. Williams,' New Soviet Policy Toward Southeast Asia: Reorientation and Change', *Asian Survey,* Vol.31, No.4, University of California Press, April 1991, www.jstor.org/stable/2645390 p.367 (accessed on 04.12.2015)
42. Excerpts from Gorbachev's Speech, *The New York Times,*29th June 1986, http://www.nytimes.com/1986/07/29/world/excerpts-from-gorbachev-s-speech.html (accessed on 04.12.2015)

43. Michael C. Williams, op cit, p.369
44. Ibid, p.375
45. Soviets said to Withdraw Fighters and Bombers from Vietnam Base, *The New York Times*, 19th January, 1990, http://www.nytimes.com/1990/01/19/world/soviets-said-to-withdraw-fighters-and-bombers-from-vietnam-base.html (accessed on 04.12.2015)
46. Cited in ibid
47. Cited in ibid
48. Cited in ibid
49. Cited in Richie Ovendale, op cit, p.454
50. Kenneth Scott Latourette, *The American Record in the Far East, 1945-1951*, New York, The Macmillan Company, 1952, p.43
51. Richie Ovendale, op cit, pp.450-451
52. Ibid, p.460
53. Stein Tønnesson, 'The South China Sea in the Age of European Decline', *Modern Asian Studies*, Vol.40, No.1, Cambridge University Press, Feb, 2006, p.20
54. Cited in Ram Tirath, *US Octopus in Asia*, New Delhi, National Publications, 1964, pp6,7
55. Bruce W. Watson, *The Changing Face of the World's Navies: 1945 to the Present*, London, Arms and Armor Press, 1991, p.70
56. Ibid
57. Cited in 'Aid for France in Indo-China 1950-54', in *United States-Vietnam Relations, 1945-1967*, Vietnam Task Force, Office of the Secretary of Defense, Pentagon Papers (Declassified), IV.A.2 https://www.archives.gov/research/pentagon-papers/ (accessed on 07.12.2015), P.2
58. Cited in ibid, p.3
59. Cited in 'US Involvement in Franco-Viet Minh War: 1950-54' in *United States-Vietnam Relations, 1945-1967*, Vietnam Task Force, Office of the Secretary of Defense, Pentagon Papers (declassified), p.A-3, https://www.archives.gov/research/pentagon-papers/ (accessed on 07.12.2015),
60. Cited in 'Aid for France in Indochina', Pentagon Papers (declassified) in op cit, p,4
61. US Involvement in Franco-Viet Minh War: 1950-54', op cit, p.A-2
62. Cited in'Aid for France in Indochina' in op cit, p.3
63. Cited in ibid, p.4
64. Bruce W. Watson, op cit (1991), p.68
65. For details see Ronald Bruce Frankam, *Operation Passage to Freedom: United States Navy in Vietnam, 1954-1955*, Lubbock, Texas, Texas Tech University Press, 2007
66. Edward J. Marolda, 'The US Navy in the Cold War Era, 1945-1991', *Naval History and Heritage Command*, http://www.history.navy.mil/research/library/online-reading-room/title-list-alphabetically/n/the-navy-in-the-cold-war-era-1945-1991.html (accessed on 07,12,2015), p.6
67. Ibid,
68. 'Gulf of Tonkin Incident: The Desoto Patrols and OPLAN 34*A*', Declassified National Security Agency report, https://www.nsa.gov/public_info/_files/

gulf_of_tonkin/articles/rel2_gulf_tonkin_incident_desoto.pdf (accessed on 08.12.2015) p.43

69. Ibid
70. Edward J. Marolda, op cit
71. 'Gulf of Tonkin Incident: The Desoto Patrols and OPLAN 34*A*', op cit, p.43
72. Ibid, p.44
73. Edward J. Marolda, op cit
74. Ibid, p.8
75. I call the Cold War 'introduced' by the US since the Americans were haunted by the 'presence' of Soviets, if not physically but ideologically, long before the actual appearance of the Red Navy in the South China Sea region and the fall of next door China in 1949 to the communists were seen in Washington as Moscow's route to Southeast Asia.
76. Frank C. Darling, 'United States Policy in Southeast Asia: Permanency and Change', *Asian Survey,* Vol.14, No.7 (July, 1974), University of California Press, pp.611-612
77. Ram Tirath, op cit, pp.15,16,18
78. Address to the Nation on the War in Vietnam, November 3, 1969, p-691101, 11/3/1969 www.nixonlibrary.gov/forkids/speechesforkids/silentmajority/silentmajority_transcript.pdf (accessed on 11.12.2015)
79. Ibid, emphasis added
80. Ibid
81. Association of South East Asian Nations or ASEAN was founded on Aug, 8, 1967 by the anti-communist countries of the region, who were mostly US allies, to cope with the challenges of the Cold War geopolitics in the region amidst the Vietnam War.
82. Gareth Porter, 'The Decline of U.S. Diplomacy in Southeast Asia', *SAIAS Review,* Number 1, Winter 1981, John Hopkins University Press, pp.151,152
83. Declassified secret report titled 'Forecasting the Sino-Vietnamese Split', author name concealed as (b)(3)(c), Studies in Intelligence, Central Intelligence Agency, Volume 30, 1986, www.foia.cia.gov/sites/default/files/DOC_0000620600.pdf. (accessed on 11.12.2015), p.68
84. Gareth Porter, op cit, p.152
85. Lim Joo-Jock, op cit, p.74
86. Ibid, p.76
87. Ibid, p.77
88. David Winterford, op cit, p.22
89. Richard D. Fisher, op cit, p.7
90. Melvin Gurtov, Sino-Soviet Relations and Southeast Asia: Recent Developments and Future Possibilities, *Pacific Affairs*, Vol.43, No.4, Winter, 1970-1971, p.499
91. Like the US, UK was also planning to disentangle from the Southeast Asian scene (along with Persian Gulf) in the 1960s which was considered a major turn in the British foreign, especially military, policy which promoted the British refusal to bear the defence burden of distant areas any more.
92. Melvin Gurtov, op cit
93. Lim Joo-Jock, op cit, p.75

94. Ibid, p.76
95. Ibid, p.77
96. Ibid, pp.78,79,80, the analysis follows the opinions of this author
97. Ibid, p.81
98. Ibid
99. Peter Polomka, op cit, p.33
100. Lim Joo-Jock, op cit, pp.16,17
101. Cited in ibid, p.18
102. Ibid
103. Ibid, pp.18,19
104. James Goldrick and Jack McCaffrie, *Navies of South-East Asia: A Comparative Study*, London and New York, Routledge, 2013, p.177
105. Ibid, p.178
106. Ibid
107. Ibid, p.182
108. Ibid, p.183
109. Ibid, p.183, 186, It is to be remembered here that during this time Taiwan's Republic of China government, and not the communist regime in Beijing, was recognized by the US as the lawful government of China.
110. Read Ang Cheng Guan, 'The South China Sea Dispute Re-visited', *Institute of Defence and Strategic Studies (IDSS)*, Singapore, Rajaratnam School of International Studies, August, 1999, pp.2,3
111. Tridib Chakrabarti, 'The Territorial Claims in South China Sea: Probing Persistent Uncertainties', in Arun Kumar Banerji and Purushottam Bhattacharya (eds), *People's Republic of China at Fifty: Politics, Economy and Foreign Relations*, New Delhi, Lancer Books, 2001, p.182
112. Ang Cheng Guan, op cit, p.4
113. James Goldrick and Jack McCaffrie, op cit, p.193, 194
114. Ibid, pp.195,196
115. Ibid, p.199
116. Ang Cheng Guan, op cit, p.6
117. Ibid
118. James Goldrick and Jack McCaffrie, op cit, p.122
119. Rodolfo C. Severino, 'The Philippines and South China Sea' in Pavin Chachavalpongpun (ed) *Entering Uncharted Waters?: ASEAN and the South China Sea*, Singapore, Institute of Southeast Asian Studies, 2014, pp.169-170
120. Stein Tønnesson, 'The History of the Dispute', in Timo Kivimäki (ed), *War or Peace in South China Sea*, Copenhagen, Nias Press, 2002, pp.14-15
121. James Goldrick and Jack McCaffrie, op cit, p.62
122. Ibid, p.70
123. Ibid, p.75
124. Ibid, pp.92,93
125. For details see Ton That Thien, *India and Southeast Asia 1947-1960: A Study of India's Foreign Policy towards the South East Asian Countries in the Period 1947-1960* Geneve, Librairie Droz, 1963, p.240 and Subhadeep Bhattacharya, *Looking East Since 1947: India's Southeast Asia Policy*, New Delhi, Knowledge World, 2016

126. David C. Hawkins, 'Britain and Malaysia- Another View: Was the Decision to Withdraw Entirely Voluntary was Britain Pushed a Little?, *Asian Survey*, Vol.9, No.7, July 1969, University of California Press, p.548
127. FPDA was a security arrangement among Malaysia, Australia, New Zealand and Britain signed in 1971 which was a British attempt to ally the concern of her dominions and ex-colony Malaysia triggered by the military disentanglement policy of London called East of Suez policy.
128. James Goldrick and Jack McCaffrie, op cit, p.99
129. Cited in ibid, p.100
130. Ibid
131. Ibid, p.101

4

South China Sea Geopolitics: Fall of Soviet and Rise of China in the 1990s

The disintegration of Soviet Union by 1992 formally ended the Cold War leaving USA as the sole super power in the unipolar world order. This was the second major turning point in the international relations since the end of the World War II. The World War when ended the colonial era and founded a new world system of global competition for domination between the two new world powers, the Cold War ended with an overhauling of the international relations erasing the 'camp culture' of the two contesting blocs founding a new global politico-strategic culture centring around the sole super power USA. Many scholars viewed the end of the Cold War as the triumph of the Western liberal democratic principles and capitalist mode of economy which was championed by the Western bloc under USA. Francis Fukuyama called it 'the end point of mankind's ideological evolution and the universalization of Western liberal democracy as the final form of human government.'[1] The world now was more concerned about the economic gains rather than ideological salvation. In other words, the world was moving towards 'common marketization' mission forgoing the 'ideological operations'. The demise of USSR unveiled a new chapter in inter-state relations in Europe with the emergence of 'liberated' states in Eastern Europe and the unification of Germany. Undoubtedly, the Western liberal ideology, both economic and political, was triumphant in Europe. However, what was the scene in Asia, or East Asia precisely?

The post-Cold War Asia interested many international relations theorists regarding her future course in the new world order. Samuel Huntington has described this new order of international politics as departure from the 'Western phase' and the onset of interaction between the West and non-Western civilizations and among the non-Western civilizations.[2] And this was more concentrated in East Asia. The main reason behind this was that when the end of the Cold War brought about changes in the geopolitical structure of Europe, East Asia was unable to shed off the debris of the War. This was most evident in the Korean Peninsula which still remains a partitioned land between North and South, unlike unified Germany. Another reason is the growing power and the supplementary assertiveness of the states of East Asia whose grievances against the neighbours remained second to the Cold War geostrategic objectives of the super powers. In other words, the local tensions were mere tools in the global Cold War tussle. Now, with the end of the War these regional tensions were to shape the post-Cold War geopolitics of East Asia. This was an obvious development since neither the conclusion of the World War II nor that of Cold War actually resolved the local tensions. On the contrary the Cold War used them as fuel to run its war machine. So, the end of the Cold War actually left the local contestants with their unresolved tensions. Moreover, the local powers were now free to pursue their respective national interests which got intertwined with the unresolved inter-state tensions promoting the zeal for 'national security and defence'. Aaron L. Friedberg prophesied that in the new world order when USA, even remaining the single richest and strongest nation, 'will be less inclined to project its power in every corner of the globe' (a prophesy proven wrong in the subsequent years) the other nations will be more competent to act independently to pursue their national interests, *'whether out of ambition or necessity'*. He prophesied that ... 'in the long run it is Asia that seems far more likely to be the cockpit of great power conflict'.[3] Undoubtedly, Asia suffered more of instability than Europe after the end of the Cold War. When both Europe and Asia, during the war, were experiencing similar style of super power tussle impacting the policies of the states of the two regions, big or small, the end of the Cold War diminished the inter-state frictions more in Europe than in Asia. Friedberg puts the credit to the 'spread and consolidation of democracy, increased equality and material well-being promoting social stability, less chauvinism and more inclination to economic interdependence and growing sense of collective identity' for lesser chances of war in post-Cold War Europe. He also identifies the rising cost of war and growth of industry over agriculture as source of wealth generation thereby lessening interests in land acquisition promoting invasions as the reasons for decreasing significance of war.[4] However, these advancements did not happen during the Cold War period. On the contrary, the Industrial Revolution propelled the production of more destructive weapons leading to the advent of the nuclear weapons era which Friedberg also admits.[5] But the significance of the opinions of Friedberg remains in the fact that the Europeans were exhausted by the two consecutive wars and the totalitarian state systems in between. It is undeniable that Europe (and not America) bathed in the blood while splashing it to her Asian colonies. Thus the Europeans dreaded the war and were hunting for a long lasting tranquillity. So they promoted economic interdependence and 'we-feeling' among them to bolster the *Europeanness* rather than nurturing the jingoism which they learnt, from experience, as destructive. In that way the wars matured Europe.

Asia, on the other hand, landed in a different and difficult situation after the end of the Cold War. The end of the war did not end the conflict in Asia. On the contrary, now there was chance for it to get more prominent. This is because the intra-Asian relations are very complicated. The inter-state relations in Asia are marred with tensions, mostly territorial and sometimes sociological or psychological.[6] Moreover, the colonial history and the resultant liberation struggle have generated a strong sense of national identity, sometimes taking shape of jingoism which is a major impediment to the creation of Europe-type collectiveness in Asia. Also, the ethnic and religious issues also tend to communalise the Asian society reflected in the government policies.[7] To quote Friedberg, "...in many parts of Asia, nationalism is rooted firmly in ethnic and racial differences."[8] The history plays a vital part in the formulation of the Asian inter-state relations. The territorial disputes, both land and maritime, are a major feature of the international relations of Asia. Sometimes these disputes have their roots in the history of European colonialism and sometimes even before that. China is feared by her neighbours in East, especially Southeast, Asia not only because of her sheer size and strength but also, in case of Vietnam, because of her occupation of the Vietnamese land in the ancient period, apart from the PRC's invasion of Vietnam in late 1970s. The legacy of Sino-centric East Asian order of the pre-European period is triggering the fear of Chinese domination, especially in Southeast Asia and in Vietnam in particular.[9] Similarly, the Japanese colonial past is a major hurdle in her socialization with East Asia. Sometimes, the governments use the history as a tool to formulate its aggressive foreign policy. The Sino-Japan and Korea-Japan relations are marred with historical references of Imperial Japan's policies. Thus, Friedberg opines that history is the subject of disagreement in Asia with the Asian powers 'constructing a history that serves its own national purposes'.[10]

Even in case of formulating economic policies, the Asian countries are over-cautious. The Chinese, according to Friedberg, are sensitive about 'unequal treaties' catering economic privileges to the foreigners given their history while, the Japanese business class fear 'backlash' triggered by over-dominance of Asian markets.[11] The proposed Trans Pacific Partnership or TPP agreement, forwarded by USA apparently promoting the economic integration among the countries on both sides of the Pacific is suspected as a counter to the Chinese initiative of Asian Infrastructural Investment Bank or AIIB, proposed to boost economic development of Asia. This contention has a reference to the Cold War history where Pacific region, especially East Asia, is emerging as the battleground between dominant USA and rising China, taking Soviet Union's place. Also, the inter-state threat perception is high in Asia than Europe. This is also related to the history, both ancient and recent, of the region. Thus the Southeast Asian countries, especially the South China Sea littorals, are wary and apathetic about either the dominance of any single power in the region (their main concern is China currently) curbing their freedom like what the Japanese did during WWII or the Cold War type tussle disturbing the tranquility in the region affecting their mission of economic prosperity. Also, the strong nationalist feeling, rooted in the colonial history of Asia coupled with economic and technological development, often push states to assertive mode against their neighbours. It is noteworthy here that the Asian states, like any other ex-colonies, fight mainly with their neighbours. Such a trend had been promoted by the big powers throughout the Cold War period. And in the post-Cold War period, the super power involvement in the regional affairs has continued amidst the possible rise of new power, China.

South China Sea geopolitics after the Cold War

The end of the Cold War propelled speedy alteration in the geopolitical landscape of maritime Southeast Asia that is South China Sea region with the withdrawal of the US naval bases from the Subic Bay in the Philippines. On December 27, 1991, the Philippine Government asked the Americans to withdraw from the Subic Bay naval base by end of 1992.[12] Located on the South China Sea the Subic base was a major asset of the American naval fleet to handle the presence of the Soviets in the Cam Ranh Bay on the other side of the Sea. With the withdrawal of the Soviets the Americans were to be dominant naval figure in the South China Sea region. The US and the Philippine governments had concluded an agreement to extend the presence of the US navy in the Subic Bay for another decade in exchange for $203 million in the summer of 1991 but the Filipino Senate rejected the agreement terming the continued American presence as 'vestige of colonialism'[13] and infringement of Philippines' sovereignty. Both the American and the Philippine governments cited the disintegration of the Soviet Union as the reason for the reducing importance of the Subic Bay.[14] However, the Americans were not very keen to withdraw, nor was the Philippine government to force them to leave. This was because the Subic naval presence was a major source of dollars supply in the Filipino economy. In the fiscal year of September 1991, the Subic Bay pumped in $344 million in the economy of the Philippines which received $408 million in connection to all the American bases located in the country.

The importance of the bases to the government can be understood from the initial decision of the then Filipino President Corazon C. Aquino to go for a referendum on the issue after the Senate turned down the agreement but had to succumb to domestic opposition.[15] This development had cast suspicion on the future role of the US in the region. Many scholars expressed doubt regarding the ability of USA to deal with the future developments in the South China Sea region after losing her bases in the Philippines. In a telephonic interview to the New York Times Japanese security policy analyst Masashi Nishihara said that the US would have little chance to 'change the events' in case they develop in South China Sea region, like tension between China and Taiwan or Hong Kong.[16] Thus South China Sea is seemed to be retaining its significance in the post-Cold War East Asian geopolitical scene. In case of the Philippines, it was all the more important since, as Robert Kaplan says, "The sea is the country's economic lifeline for everything from fishing to energy exploration."[17] The Philippines imports all her oil by sea and acquires the natural gas from the offshore oil field near Manila Bay.[18]

However, in the absence of US protection, the Philippines was more vulnerable to Chinese 'aggression'. Within two years of the closure of the Subic Naval Station, along with the Clark Airfield (both in Luzon) in 1992 China occupied Philippines controlled reefs in the Spratlys and started expanding her air and naval forces adopting an aggressive posture in South China Sea.[19] Thus, in the post-Cold War South China Sea region, the Chinese were bothering both USA as well as her allies. In other words, the Chinese were taking the place of the Soviets in the post-Cold War South China Sea region. The fall of Soviet Union might have left USA unchallenged power in most part of the world, and definitely in Europe, but not in East Asia. However, it is undeniable that USA has remained the lynchpin of East Asian or Asia Pacific security since her entry into the World War II in the early 1940s. Such a role got even stronger during the Cold War period with development of alliance network throughout the region, from Japan and Korea in the north to Australia and New Zealand in the south of Asia Pacific. The San Francisco System[20] principle had entangled USA with the vast security and geopolitical network of the Asia Pacific which was the continuation of the war time US defence system. On the other hand the US-Japan treaty was a welcome arrangement for the East Asian countries, who could hardly get over their haunting memories with Imperial Japan, since the treaty was a security guarantee against resurgence of Japanese influence in the region.[21]

Post-Cold War East Asian geopolitics and the question of US protection

The US influence in the entire Asia-Pacific region, since the World War II, has grown manifold. She has well positioned herself in the region to utilize the sea not only to acquire resources but also as a means of transportation and spreading ideas and influence the region.[22] The Americans could set up such a vast network of alliance with the mercy of geography. In the absence of any land border, the Americans are relieved of carrying the baggage of any territorial dispute with any country of the region, USA herself being an 'extra-regional player' which has helped her to act as a broker in dispute settlement.[23] Although in context of East Asia it can be said that the USA has been more a security guarantee rather than a peace broker since no settlement of disputes, most of which are either products of the World War II like the territorial disputes of Korea, China and Russia with Japan or even older like the South China Sea territorial disputes, have taken place yet. It can be said that US' success in East Asia lies in the restraining the small and medium powers of the region from embarking on arms proliferation race against either each other or with any rising power, like China. This is because the US, in the post-Cold War world, is still the strongest power. She maintains the largest fleet as well as strongest air and ground forces (in the East Asian waters), since the WW II. These forces, especially the unmatched naval forces, have acted as the security guarantee to the states of the region. And it is the military bases that the alliances provide to USA which makes her the dominant figure in the East Asian region.[24] However, the immediate aftermath of the end of Cold War in US's Southeast Asia policy was of 'benign neglect and missed opportunities'.[25] The end of the Cold War actually ended the American vision of the Pacific as 'American lake'. This was because from the mid-1980s the East Asian economies were rising while China was growing militarily and both these developments were changing the Asia-Pacific relations.[26] The end of the Cold War apparently ended the strategic reason for American presence in the Southeast Asian waters anymore, especially after the Soviet withdrawal from the Cam Ranh Bay. Many Southeast Asian countries were upset with this fact, particularly after the US withdrawal from the Philippines. Singapore was perturbed regarding the emerging 'new world order' in the post-Cold War period which was 'not a safer place for small states like herself'. Thus, she offered facilities to USA for the latter's warships and military personnel after USA had to wind up from the Philippines.[27]

However, the importance of the presence of US forces in East Asia was realized by many countries including Soviet Union. By the beginning of the 1990s many Soviet officials and academics started viewing US in East Asia as a 'stabilizing force'. They discarded the traditional Soviet opinion that the US military presence in Asia is the primary source of regional tension. In fact all the powers of the region, except North Korea, viewed the continuation of US military presence favourably. While in northeast Asia, South Korea saw the American presence as deterrent towards any North Korean aggression, in Southeast Asia (still coping with the recent tension over Vietnam-Cambodia issue) many saw US presence helpful to counter Vietnam, a modernizing China and a more powerful Japan.[28] At the outset of the post-Cold War era, even China was also opting for US protection against a resurgent Japan who, she feared, could transform her economic power into military strength and try to establish herself as a regional power.[29] On the other hand, that the US was also keen to act as a balancer in the emerging East Asian geopolitical order after the end of the Cold War with waning Soviet strength was clear from the statement of the then US Assistant Secretary of State Richard Solomon who said on 30th October, 1990 that, "the fact is that no power other than the United States is now able or welcome to play the role of regional balancer."[30] Thus, Admiral James Lyons Jr. was contented saying, "...today the balance of power in the Pacific is in our favor economically and militarily."[31] The US Pacific security policy at that time were: 1) protection of US territories and bases, 2) the maintenance of regional deterrent posture vis-à-vis Soviet forces in the Western Pacific, South China Sea and the Indian Ocean, 3) power projection capabilities in the Western Pacific, the South China Sea and the Indian Ocean, 4) security of sea and air lanes of communication and 5) access to and cooperation with regional allies and China.[32] The regional allies were also keen to collaborate with USA. As mentioned earlier, government in Manila reluctantly agreed to ask USA to vacate the Subic Bay. Thailand, a traditional US ally, also wanted the latter to continue her presence in the Southeast Asian waters to protect the nearby important sea lanes (of communication). Malaysia, on the other hand, was not in favour of such presence but signed military access arrangements with USA in 1998, along with Thailand, Singapore and the Philippines while Manila signed Visiting Forces Arrangement with USA separately in 1999.[33]

Obviously, the insurance to the predominance of the US in the Asia Pacific region was established by the concluding phase of the Cold War era. Thus we see that the significance of the US' naval prowess continued in the South China Sea even after the withdrawal of the Soviets from the region. One of the reasons behind this continued US predominance in the South China Sea geopolitics was rising China. The end of the Cold War ended the Sino-US understanding to counter the common threat, Soviet Union. As we have seen in the previous chapter, the Chinese wanted the American presence in the nearby waters to counter the Soviet threat during the Vietnam War. The geopolitics of maritime Southeast Asia was well directed by the Cold War between the two super powers. In the post-Cold War era, such an understanding was irrelevant given the absence of any such challenge to either of the two powers. However, the secret US Defence Department document, *Defence Planning Guidance 1994-1999* which was leaked in 1992, clearly read, *"Our first objective is to prevent the re-emergence of a new military rival..."*.[34] Nonetheless, subsequently it was China who was to challenge the traditional US dominance in the East Asia.

Rising 'dissatisfied' power: China

The concept of 'dissatisfied power' is most associated with the power transition theory. A dissatisfied power is one who is disgruntled with the existing pyramid-type international system (as explained by the power transition theorists), based on hierarchy of states. In this system, a dominant power is at the top, followed by the great powers in the descending tiers with the number of states in each tier increasing.[35] When an ascending power finds the existing structure not beneficial to its interests, such a state becomes *dissatisfied* with the whole international system.[36] The power transition theorists insist on the possibility of war in case of power transition, if peaceful transition is impossible. Emmanuel Wright noted that the major wars have occurred regularly in modern history followed by period of peace and minor wars ultimately establishing peace in the new world order.[37] A.F.K. Organski says that peace is maintained in the international system so long as the dominant power leading the international order maintains the status quo in coalition with other satisfied powers. When the power gap (between the dominant satisfied power and the emerging dissatisfied power) narrows the dissatisfied power challenges to overtake the status quo power promoting the possibility of war.[38] The ascending power is dissatisfied with the system since it impedes its ambition to emerge as a dominant power, or in other words, denies it 'its rightful place' in the world. China can be termed as a dissatisfied power of the twenty first century. When China started rising by the end of the Cold War period, this power transition theory became relevant again. Chinese leadership has long nurtured the 'victim mentality' of 'centuries of humiliation' at the hands of the Westerners. The Chinese Communist Party has fostered the narrative of '100 years of humiliation' (*bainian guochi*) and claims to protect China from both *xihua* or split and *fenhua* or Westernized by the external states. And this victim mentality has made the Chinese extremely sensitive regarding the potential infringement of their sovereignty and territorial integrity.[39] Increasing her power and prestige in the international stage, apart from protecting her territorial integrity, is vital and foremost task of any state especially those who aspire to be a global power, and it is the priority of China.

China's international ambition can be viewed through the *status inconsistency* theory. The theory suggests that the position of a state in the international system is measured firstly by its achieved or objective status that is the power it has accumulated and the ascribed or subjective status that is the amount of respect it is shown by other powers. The state suffering from the inconsistency often tends to get aggressive to achieve the respect it feels it deserves.[40] The cashing on *victim mentality* by the Chinese leaders is an expression of the frustration they have regarding the position of China in the international society, that is China is suffering from 'subjective status'. Undoubtedly, history has played (and is still playing) its part in encouraging this frustration. As Michael Hunt argued 'history is essential and central, not optional or incidental, to an understanding of Chinese foreign policy.'[41] The Western domination of China has been treated as the era of humiliation by all the Chinese leaders, nationalists or communists. Thus, since 1949 'China embarked on the search for its *rightful place* in the universal international society', says Zhang Yongjin.[42] The pre-eminence of the Middle Kingdom memory, the memory of glorious periods before the advent of the Westerners when China was a tall and towering figure in East Asia, has a major impact on the modern Chinese perception of the country's place in the international society. As Wang Gungwu says, "to most Chinese leaders, it is a measure of a world at disequilibrium if China does not have a *place of respect* commensurate with its size and history".[43] This concept of 'place of respect' comes from the Middle Kingdom system where the China-and the rest relations was based on deference and tribute forwarded by the 'junior' states to China while receiving legitimacy and gifts in return. This system placed the Chinese Emperor at the zenith of the Sino centric international system of East Asia. Thus the 'century of humiliation' matters so much to the Chinese leadership where the glory of the Middle Kingdom was crushed under the boot by the Westerners by capturing some Chinese territories and bringing an end to China's glory. It was hard for the modern Chinese leaders to forget this glorified past. Hence from nationalist leader like Sun Yat-sen to the communist leader like Jiang Zemin, all have been determined to erase this mark of humiliation and 'restore China's rightful place as a great power...'.[44] This victim mentality actually fueled the communist struggle and the later international policies of the People's Republic, especially under Mao tse Tung. This mentality has generated the national feeling which Mao utilized to extract domestic support for his external affirmation as well as power consolidation at home.[45] This mission to 'right the wrongs' of humiliating history thwarts China from seeing herself as the status quo power which is not just about remaking China a great power but also about resolving the territorial disputes. China is convinced that altering the territorial status quo is well within her rights even when it is viewed as dangerous by others.[46]

Many scholars invested much on the future role of 'emerging China' in shaping the post-Cold War East Asia. When many of them predicted that small Asian powers would balance rising China, David Kang prophesied that they would 'bandwagon' China. Kang argues that there existed a hierarchical order in intra-Asian relations where China remained at the core.[47] He emphasized that China was no more revisionist or adventurous, as she used to be during the Cold War and that China's military modernization has been very slow and given her potential threat to other Asian countries growing slowly, the conditions for balancing China does not exist.[48] Kang argues that historically, Asia experienced chaos whenever China was weak while order was preserved in Asia with a strong and stable China. Thus he argues that 'rich and strong China could again cement regional stability.[49] Some analysts have pointed to the 'hegemony-prone' character of Asia and opined that China, with her size, population and natural resources, is the natural regional hegemon and, although displaced temporarily, is set to resume her rightful place as Asia's dominant power.[50] Thus, according to this opinion, China is destined to acquire dominance in (East) Asia. Gerald Segal said that only other part of the world where single power is dominating is North America.[51] Samuel Huntington, insisting that East Asian international relations for 2000 years, before the advent of the Western powers, was Sino-centric, has even predicted that the small powers of Asia would have to choose between 'power balanced at the price of conflict' or 'peace secured at the price of hegemony'. He however said that the Asian states would bandwagon China rather than balancing against her.[52] The term 'bandwagoning' refers to joining stronger coalition while 'balancing' means opposing it. Balancing is meant to contain the rising power that is not to defeat the rising power but to prevent it from further expansion.[53] The post-Cold War geopolitics of East Asia has been no doubt nurtured by this bandwagoning-balancing dichotomy in the context of rising China and dominant USA which, as we will see in the following, greatly impacted the South China Sea geopolitics.

China and South China Sea geopolitics in 1990s

The significance of the post-Cold War South China Sea geopolitics lies in the revival of the territorial disputes which now gears up to be the driving force of the local geopolitical activities. And it was China who was the main propeller of this geopolitics. The military modernization programme of China sent ripples of wariness all around her neighbourhood and the small states of Southeast Asia, already in dispute with the giant neighbour over the sovereignty issue in the South China Sea, felt the heat. This was because China was shedding off her traditional continental defence orientation and focusing on upgrading her naval strength. But before delving into the naval strategy of China in the post-

Cold War period, let us analyze how Chinese authority has been seeing the maritime world of South China Sea and whether they had any impact of Mahanian theory of 'sea power' on them.

The importance of the South China Sea lies in the fact that it is crucial for China's economic prosperity. The Chinese communist leadership nurtures the aspiration to gain China her 'central' position in Asia which is key to the communist regime's survival and in this mission South China Sea is vital for them.[54] The economic strength supplements military strength and thus paves the way for gaining aspired geopolitical dominance. China's economic prosperity is vital for her geopolitical ambition and to sustain the prosperity the security of the energy supply is fundamental. And in this case the sea-lanes of South China Sea are crucial for Beijing for the shipment of oil and gas from Africa and West Asia. The end of the Cold War with the withdrawal of both Soviet and US forces from the South China Sea changed the geopolitical landscape of the region. The strategic significance of the region partially diminished in the eyes of USA, the extra regional power, in the absence of the Soviets in the Cam Ranh Bay. On the other hand, the disintegration of Soviet Union by 1992 was undoubtedly a relief for China since the new Russian Federation, emerged from the ashes of the USSR, was no match with the erstwhile Soviet Union. Also, now the new Russia was to remain engaged with internal reconstruction mission getting minimum time to concentrate on reviving the lost Soviet 'Empire'. At the onset of the post-Cold War period, Russia was falling while China was rising. The Deputy Foreign Minister of Russia acknowledged the growing strength of China saying, "...China is a major power...China boosts an impressive military potential' and said that she has 'scored some impressive economic successes'.[55] China had embarked on this path of economic reform, shedding off the Mao era's ideology-oriented policies- both external and internal-with the advent of Deng era. China under Deng Xiaoping initiated the 'Four Modernizations' programme—to transform China's economy, science and technology, education and military base—following Deng's vision announced back in 1978.[56] Deng, in his direction to the Central Committee of the Communist Party in January 1980, had emphasized on the economic growth of China as the means to play greater role in international affairs saying, "If our country becomes more developed and prosperous, we will be in a position to play a greater role in international affairs."[57] Since the end of the Mao era and the beginning of Deng period, China's priority was to promote her economic reforms preparing for the inflow of foreign investments, modernization and growth. This was unprecedented for any country ruled by a communist party and at that point of time (1980s) when Soviet Red Star was twinkling. Since the economic reforms initiated in 1978, the Chinese GDP has grown consistently at average rate of 7 to 8 per cent annually.[58] By the end of the Cold War Deng Xiaoping's policy started showing results. In 1992 China's real GDP growth rate was almost 13 per cent and she attracted $ 11 billion of foreign investment.[59] Thus the 'rise of China' in the post-Cold War period was the most discussed topic at the beginning of the 1990s accompanied by the speculations regarding the future role of the country in the newly emerging world order. However, Deng Xiaoping's advice to his comrades about dealing with new order was: 'to observe calmly, secure our position, cope with affairs calmly, hide our capabilities and bide our time, be good at maintaining a low profile and never claim leadership'.[60] This was the character of initial days of the post-Cold War Chinese foreign policy.

The South China Sea strategy of China, however, did not reflect the advice of Deng. During the Cold War we saw China never hesitated, even with her minimum strength, to get assertive with her claims on the South China Sea islands. China clashed with South Vietnam in January 1974 and with united Vietnam in March 1988, taking advantage of the changing geopolitical situation in her favour, in both the cases (discussed in the previous chapter). So, it is seen that China never restrained from asserting herself, if and when the situation favoured. It is to be remembered that when the 1974 mission was undertaken under Mao's leadership, the 1988 skirmishes happened when Deng was in charge who is hailed as more pragmatic advising to 'hide capabilities and bide time'.[61] Such a strategy vis-à-vis small powers is significant showing the Chinese policy towards asymmetric power relations. In both the cases the super power disentanglement policy (USA vis-à-vis South Vietnam in post-1970s and Soviet Union vis-à-vis united Vietnam in post-1985) left Vietnam defenceless thereby promoting asymmetric power relations with China which provoked Beijing to get assertive. If this was the situation in the Cold War period, the withdrawal of the super powers from South China Sea region after the end of the War leaving China as a formidable power in the region, catered Beijing with greater chance to assert further. There was a fear among many states that the pulling out of extra regional powers, US and USSR, made China a dominant naval force encouraging her to turn South China Sea into a 'Chinese Lake'.[62] It was opined that the Southeast Asian countries were to face 'new realities' resulting from the resurgence of China in the South China Sea.[63]

Undoubtedly, a power vacuum was created with the closure of the naval bases in Cam Ranh Bay and Subic Bay (although, as discussed earlier, US was desired by many local powers, big and small including China to stay back). Nevertheless, the US continued presence in the region was not a guarantee to protection of her allies against Chinese 'aggression'. The US policy towards the territorial disputes of South China Sea was of total neutrality. Although US was in favour of freedom of navigation, the Under Secretary Robert Zoëllick made it clear in 1992 that his country wants 'peaceful resolution of disputes'.[64] The US Embassy (Manila) spokesman was even more emphatic in 1992 refusing any American aid to the Philippines in case of any armed conflict over the Spratly dispute.[65] The US' interest in the South China Sea region had always been in respect to her overall Southeast Asia / Asia-Pacific strategy. During the 1974 Paracel clash (between China and South Vietnam) the State Department opined that the claimants should settle the dispute among themselves. The then US Defence Secretary Harold Brown, in his annual report, mentioned the South China Sea but only in the context of the Soviet interest in the Cam Ranh Bay and Danang.[66] This was the time when the US was gradually disentangling from Southeast Asian commitment following the Nixon Doctrine while remaining concerned about the growing Soviet presence in the South China Sea (discussed in the last chapter) and the South China Sea did not interest USA independent of the Cold War. And thus the China-South Vietnam clash did not interest them even when the latter was their ally in their 'war against communism'. This was also the time when US-China relations got normalized shaping a new form of geopolitics in the South China Sea. Similarly, in the 1990 US Department of Defence's report on US policy towards East Asia emphasized more on Northeast Asia and hardly mentioned South China Sea except mentioning about the US commitment to maintain security of sea lanes of communication throughout the Pacific.[67] Thus a similar kind of a situation got created as we found both prior to 1974 clash and 1985 clash, catering room to China to act as it did in the mentioned previous occasions. US was making phased withdrawal from the Philippines in the early 1990s which left China as a major power in the region. China, on the other hand, was concentrating on her military buildup for quite some time. As mentioned earlier, the Chinese economy was growing since 1978 and a fast growing economy with a 'victim mentality' and a revisionist character will certainly concentrate on modernizing its military to project power to gain its 'rightful place' in the world. Some opinions suggest that China was attempting establish a sea-based air capability apparent from her 'deck landing practices' and flight training from carrier-like platforms in southern China since 1984.[68] Was China following the Mahanian theory?

Alfred Mahan's 'sea power theory' has had influenced all the rising and aspiring powers globally which identifies three pillars-overseas commerce, naval and merchant fleet and naval bases-as the preconditions to emerge as a 'sea power'. The Chinese ambition at the beginning was however limited to the regional ascendancy. The Chinese leadership had seen the advantage of the dominance of the US Seventh Fleet in the Pacific region throughout the Cold War period. The global supremacy of USA in the post-World War II was undoubtedly the product of the US naval strength. The Chinese command of the regional sea also required similar naval build up, commensurate with its naval strategy. Till 1982 the Chinese leadership was concentrating on coastal defence. However, by 1982 Beijing, despite lack of resources and concentration on continental threats, focused on China's larger maritime zone. The PLA (N) Commander Admiral Liu Huaquing directed for offshore defence which was the naval strategy to uphold China regional maritime interests. His mission was to formulate an 'active green-water defence strategy' which was to control the sea between the inshore 'brown water' and the 'blue water' to defend the growing coastal cities from attack.[69] Admiral Liu identified Yellow Sea, East China Sea, South China Sea, the sea around Spratly Islands and Taiwan, the areas inside and outside the Okinawa island chain and northern Pacific as China's offshore area. Since 1980s, the offshore strategy proponents were insisting on defence strategy to secure China's economic interest and defence against foreign threats by expanding China's maritime capabilities beyond the coastal waters. This strategy accommodated China's Central Military Commission's adoption of new military strategy focusing on local wars on China's periphery.[70] Admiral Liu turned to the guidance of Mahan and was called 'China's Mahan' by analysts outside China. He agreed with Mahan's emphasis on strategic value of certain geographic assets and advised for phased naval buildup to control these assets. His prescription for the initial Chinese naval buildup objective (in the 1980s) was to control the maritime zone of the first island chain, stretched from southern Japan to northern Philippines, passing Taiwan. For Admiral Liu the control of the island chains was important to provide his country access to the high seas after which China could concentrate on 'second chain', further out in the Pacific to compete with US Navy.[71]

After the advent of the Gorbachev era in USSR (and the end of the Sino-Soviet hostility) the Military Commission of the Chinese Communist Party instructed PLA to prepare for local, limited war (*jubu zhanzheng*) instead of 'early, major and nuclear war'.[72] The Chinese military journals, during 1986-87 period, identified five types of limited conflict- small scale wars restricted to border territories, conflict over territorial seas and islands, surprise air strikes against strategic targets in China, defence against deliberately limited attacks against Chinese territory and punitive counter attacks launched by China into enemy territory 'to oppose invasion, protect sovereignty, or to uphold justice or dispel threats'.[73] Among these identifications, the conflict over territorial seas and islands was understandably referred to South China Sea islands dispute. It should be remembered here that China clashed with Vietnam over the Spratly Islands in March 1988. This was the early days of Chinese naval modernization and in autumn the same year, Guangzhou Military Region conducted a major naval exercise code-named '*Guangzi*-15' in order to test the navy's ability to defend the coastal territorial waters and also the islands claimed by China.[74] Thus, Chinese military was now focusing on her regional maritime zone and assessing the country's naval capacity to preserve China's local maritime interests. What is noteworthy here is that as the Cold War drew to a close, Chinese leadership focused more and more on the adjacent maritime region. The emphasis on 'offshore coastal defence' and 'local conflicts' since the 1980s, after the Soviet threat was neutralized in the Gorbachev period, signifies the momentous strategic alterations in the overall Chinese neighbourhood policy. At the same time in the early post-Cold War period, China became more assertive with her South China Sea policy. This was evident from not only the emphasis on 'conflict over territorial seas and islands' made in the Chinese military journals in the late1980s but also challenge that China started putting forward to the South China Sea littorals. In September 1991, China accused Malaysia of encroaching upon her sovereignty after Malaysia announced that she was building airstrips in the Terumbu Layang-Layang (in the Spratlys) and was preparing her navy and air force to defend her interests in the Spratlys. China also opposed in January 1992 the Vietnam-Malaysia agreement to jointly develop any economic opportunities in the Spratlys.[75] Thus, China's post-Cold War South China Sea policy was more focused and articulate regarding her claims of sovereignty unlike during the Cold War period when it was twinned with Beijing's over all policy towards Soviet Union. The mutual agreement between Moscow and Beijing to reduce troops at their common border also relieved China of devoting her forces to deal with a next door super power and gave the scope to concentrate more on the maritime areas which were coming up as vital for her national interests. China now could spend more time and potential to deal with the South China Sea issue being the lone 'naval power' in the absence of US or Soviet threat in the region. Also, the changing geopolitical landscape of East Asia with the US decision to reduce forces coupled with the growing urge to socialize with 'reformed China' under Deng worked in China's favour to be assertive. After the initial shock of Tiananmen Square incident of 1989 (where the communist government nipped a major student movement against the authoritarian regime at the bud) the world was keen to engage with China. Even Japan was also insistent on engaging with Beijing at the Paris meeting of 1989.[76] On the other hand US was keen to embrace China to stop her from returning to 'spoiler role' in Asia, said Deputy Secretary of State Lawrence S. Eagleburger in February 1990 who said that 'a modernizing China was vital for east Asian stability'.[77] The American foreign policy elites were ready to overlook the political repression inside China as temporary and transitional and expected the Chinese leadership, both incumbent and future, to adopt moderate policies with passage of time under domestic pressure.[78] Thus, the post-Cold War Chinese leadership expected least international adverse reaction towards any of her 'adventurous mission' in the early 1990s. And the US was not interested in interfering in the South China Sea dispute. So, the situation was in China's favour. But what made South China Sea so vital for China?

With the economic reforms initiated the South China Sea started gaining more importance as the vital sea lanes of communication. This sea lane is the only maritime route that connects China with the Indian Ocean and beyond. The importance of the area as the transit lane between Indian and Pacific Ocean was continually emphasized in the Chinese commentary in the 1980s and 1990s.[79] On the other hand the resources lying underneath the South China Sea, especially oil and natural gas, became important for China in the 1980s after embarking on the economic reforms. Commensurate with the reform and the ambitious coastal development programme, the energy demand shot up leading to discrepancy between the demand and supply. Prior to 1980s, China's onshore oil production was sufficient to satisfy her domestic requirements leaving surplus amount to export. But the growing demand for more energy forced China to look towards offshore areas, including South China Sea.[80] On the other hand, the economic reform and 'open door' policy made the coastal areas of China very important. China's four special economic zones, three open cities and two open areas border South China Sea, important both for coastal development project as well as for using South China Sea as major channel to expand foreign trade.[81] Unlike Mao, who chose on the Chinese heartland (away from the coasts) to build the industries, Deng favoured international trade for economic reforms which were to be conducted from the coasts. China's first economic zone was created in Shenzhen close to Hong Kong in 1980 followed by 14 other coastal cities in 1984. The offshore oil was the first industry opened for foreign investment and China focused on blocks off Hong Kong and Hainan.[82]

Such economic factors added to the strategic significance of South China Sea to Beijing leadership. South China Sea is the bridge between China and maritime Southeast Asia, the region with which China had very uneasy relations throughout the Cold War period. Also, this region houses all the countries who have been most anxious about China since the inception of the People's Republic's rule in Beijing in 1949 and see China's claims on the South China Sea islands as a threat. Throughout the Cold War period, as we have seen in the last chapter, China had to counter the Soviet threat in the South China Sea and hardly got the scope to act freely. During the Cold War the South China Sea geopolitics was guided by the Sino-Soviet tension which directed China-Southeast Asia (maritime) relations. Now, with the absence of Soviet Union and reduced US involvement China got the chance to act freely. The Vietnam War occupied a major portion of China's Southeast Asia policy during the Cold War and it was mainly the Soviet involvement that complicated the matter further for China. With the normalization of Sino-Soviet relations and gradual Soviet withdrawal from the Vietnam affairs leading to resolution of the Cambodian crisis in 1989, China got the scope to frame her Southeast Asia policy afresh. The relation was further boosted with the decline of the ASEAN countries to join regime of sanctions on China after the Tiananmen Square massacre. China appreciated Southeast Asian countries' reticent approach towards the suppression while the government in Beijing passed the Nationality Law in 1989 ending the Chinese claim to authority over ethnic Chinese population in Southeast Asia. Moreover, China's role in resolving the Cambodian problem, apart from her economic development, made her acceptable to ASEAN.[83] Southeast Asia was fast becoming an important factor in Chinese economic booming. The overseas Chinese investment started pouring in China while the region welcomed China as a new economic partner in 1990-91 periods. The later Asian financial crisis also drew the two sides closer with Southeast Asia gaining confidence in China with the latter's currency policy and preferential loans.[84] Also, the China-maritime Southeast Asia trade volume is more than the trade volume with mainland Southeast Asia. And China's 80 per cent of oil imports pass through the Malacca Strait.[85] Thus several factors worked in favour of China-Southeast Asia closeness.

However, another factor that developed the urge especially among the Chinese to get close to Southeast Asia was Japan. With the gradual disentanglement of USA from Southeast Asia after the Vietnam fiasco, Japan saw the chance to take US's place in the region. The Japanese insistence on Asia-Pacific politico-economic regionalism in tripartite system among US, Japan and Southeast Asia triggered alarm in Beijing. This was further intensified after Japan sent peacekeeping forces to Cambodia in 1992 and was suspected of attempting to take Soviet Union's place in Vietnam. China was aware of Japan's critical stand on China's position over Spratly Islands and thus faced challenge in responding to the newly emerging assertive strategy. This development also pushed China closer to Southeast Asia.[86] China's wariness is understandable. Japan's successful entry in Southeast Asia as a replacement of either US or USSR would be not only a diplomatic defeat of China but a pressure as well. In the early 1990s Japan was a major economic power in Asia, being number one, with significant role played in the regional economy. By 1980s, Japan had become an economic super power with significant technological development matching the West and by 1991 Japan was the largest foreign investor in Singapore, Hong Kong, the Philippines and Thailand and second largest in Malaysia, Indonesia and Taiwan.[87] Thus in the beginning of 1990 Japan was a major economic contributor in Southeast Asia what China was not. Also, Japan was instrumental in foundation of ASEAN Regional Forum (ARF) in 1994. All these were enough factors to perturb China. Therefore, both the economic advantages and Japan factor worked behind China's interests in developing cordial relations with Southeast Asia in the post-Cold War period.

With the growing importance of Southeast Asia to China, the strategic significance of the South China Sea also grew, especially in respect to Taiwan. It is to be remembered that Taiwan Island sits at the northern tip of South China Sea and Taiwan has been a major case of irritation for the People's Republic since 1949 as the communists failed to annex the island into the Chinese territory. It is the only territorial dispute that China confronts with the Island itself and no other state puts forward any claim over it. Also, the special relations between US and Taiwan under Taiwan Relations Act (1979)[88] resist mainland government from undertaking any coercive action to occupy Taiwan. Apart from being a 'dream project' to annex Taiwan, it is important to have control over the island to control the Taiwan Straits. Therefore, China's claim over the South China Sea gives fillip to Chinese claim over Taiwan.[89] In this way South China Sea is strategically important to China vis-à-vis her Taiwan project. The 1996 Taiwan Straits Crisis demonstrated the seriousness of the Taiwan issue when China conducted military exercises in the areas close to Taiwan which included missile tests close to the Taiwanese ports of Keelun and Kaohsiung, live ammunition military exercises and large scale amphibious landing exercises. The situation turned critical after US sent two aircraft carrier battle groups to areas near Taiwan. This was the largest US naval movement in the Asia Pacific region since the Vietnam War. This tension continued until the March 1996 Presidential election in Taiwan.[90] Apparently, political in character, the Taiwan Strait Crisis of 1996 was undoubtedly part of larger post-Cold War military strategy of China. As mentioned earlier, since 1985 Chinese military was emphasizing on off-shore defence strategy. The Chinese military had been concentrating in developing its naval capacity since the early 1990s. It conducted amphibious exercises and naval operations in both East and South China Seas in the early 1990s to extend navy's combat capability beyond the coastal defence.[91] Thus the Strait crisis can also be seen as a rehearsal preparing the naval forces for future combats extending beyond the Straits to larger East and South China Sea region. Also, the location of Taiwan in the north of South China Sea is significant. Similarly, it can also be termed as a message to USA, the security provider of Taiwan. Therefore, the Strait Crisis should not be seen independent of China's larger South China Sea strategy. Taiwan is immensely important for China's strategic gains. Taiwan sits on the way of China's maritime route. Beyond it, there is chain of islands extending from the south of Japan to Indonesia. Down south, the South China Sea route begins crossing the island which takes China to the Malacca Straits, Indian Ocean and beyond. The Chinese merchant vessels have to cross this route to reach West Asia and the Persian Gulf to acquire resources. If Taiwan is annexed, the Chinese navy will get an opening further into the South China Sea route. Also, the east-coast ports of Taiwan would be beneficial for the Chinese submarines, the stronghold of the Chinese navy (especially vis-à-vis the US carriers), providing them with deep water disappearing where they could not be detected and could proceed to American coasts.[92] Such an acquisition would also be beneficial for China to manage the combat operations in the South China Sea since it would extend the Chinese territory further inside the South China Sea zone. Currently Hainan Island is the only Chinese base in the South China Sea region. It is noteworthy here that Taiwan played a vital strategic role in Japan's Pacific War during the WWII. It was from Taiwan that Japanese bombers launched the Pearl Harbour attack. The island sustained Japan's occupation of Southeast Asia throughout the war as a staging area and major supply base and even controlled the shipping through the Taiwan Strait. The control over Taiwan would not only give operational facility to China but also would bolster her assertive posture over her territorial and maritime claims in South China Sea against other disputants, the Philippines, Vietnam, Malaysia and Brunei.[93] Thus, the strategic significance of Taiwan to China should not be seen independent of similar significance of South China Sea to China.

The Chinese Territorial Sea Law, 1992

China adopted *The Law on the Territorial Sea and the Contiguous Zone* on 25th February 1992 'to exercise its sovereignty over its territorial sea and its rights to exercise control over its contiguous zone, and to safeguard State security as well as its maritime rights and interests' (Article 1).[94] This was another attempt of China to legalize her claims over the South China Sea region. The territorial sea vis-à-vis Chinese claim is itself debatable given the territories that China claim beyond the mainland and Hainan are disputed by other states. The UN Convention on the Law of the Sea (1982), referring to the territorial sea and contiguous zone, defines the territorial sea saying, 'The sovereignty of a coastal State extends, beyond its land territory and internal waters and, in the case of an archipelagic State, its archipelagic waters, to an adjacent belt of sea, described as the territorial sea' (Part II, Article 2).[95] China's 1992 law identified the offshore islands, Taiwan, and various affiliated islands, Diaoyu Island, Penghu Islands, Dongsha Islands, Xisha Islands Nansha (Spratly) Islands and other islands as part of as territorial lands of China (Article 2).[96] In this way the government in Beijing strengthened itself with a legal weapon to deal with the territorial disputes of the South China Sea. Not only it claimed the islands as parts of China but also prohibited, under Article 6 of the Territorial Sea Law, the entry of foreign military ships into the 'territorial sea' of the PRC without permission while kept the sea open for the 'innocent passage' of the foreign non-military ships, under Chinese law.[97] The law also preserved the right for Chinese government 'to adopt all necessary measures to prevent and stop the passage of a ship which is not innocent to its territorial sea' (Article 8).[98] Such a provision no doubt kept the military option open for the Chinese Navy. Also it is to be remembered that this was the year when US was to withdraw from the Subic Bay (on 24th November, 1992) which left the Philippines defenceless. The departure was accompanied by the discontinuity of the American subsidized funding to the Armed Forces of the Philippines which weakened the Philippine navy and air force. This was a major jolt to the country in dispute with China over the islands sovereignty issue. Also, as mentioned earlier, USA had already declared of being not interested on siding with her allies (i.e. the Philippines) in any South China Sea territorial dispute. On the other hand, Vietnam was also recovering from the just concluded war in Cambodia and after the withdrawal of the USSR from Cam Ranh Bay was also weak. In a way the geopolitical landscape of the South China Sea was fast altering in the early 1990s, and in favour of China. Hence China used this opportunity to assert her claims.

The adoption of the Law can be analyzed in this context also. The post-Cold War Chinese international perception was taking a new shape. When the Cold War era was marked by 'ideology-orientation' of the Mao tse Tung's time till 1978 (Mao died in 1976) and the coexistence of 'pragmatism' and socialism' of the 1980s, the Chinese leadership of the post-Cold War period was concentrating on 'strategy'(*zhanlue*). Their world view now centred on the concept of self-serving combination of deep cynicism about the motives of the rival states and the confidence on their strategic ability to strengthen their national power.[99] The South China Sea geopolitics in the early 1990s was most strategically favourable for China. The overall Asia Pacific post-Cold War geopolitics was closely studied by the Chinese leadership. According to the Chinese analysis in 1992 US was declining in spite of being the sole super power destined to face tough competition from her rivals. Russia on the hand was confused with her security priorities and would soon turn against US while Japan was failing to become a political great power even when triggering alarm in her neighbourhood and being opposed by the US. On the other hand the rise of small but economically dynamic centres between South Korea and Singapore, China had the best chance to spread her influence and thwart the rise of any rival power.[100]

This strategy of China was to reap satisfactory result in Southeast Asia more than in Northeast Asia since in the latter region China had little scope of success in the presence of Japan, a major economic power of the time with US security guarantee. Also, China's pro-North Korea policy was a major irritant. Such a scenario was absent in Southeast Asia where China promoted her economic diplomacy hard, especially in terms of economic investment. First China invited the overseas Chinese to invest in China subsequently inviting the ethnic Southeast Asians. China offered her economic expansion mission to the Southeast Asians which eventually helped the ASEAN countries during the Asian Financial Crisis of 1997.[101] Actually China's 1990s strategy in Southeast Asia was opportunistic in character taking advantage of withdrawal of both US and USSR from the region. Her purpose was twofold- to ally the fear of the small powers of the region about an aggressive China while gradually turning the South China Sea region a 'Chinese lake' to benefit China's economic as well as strategic gains. This she could do firstly by projecting a benign image prioritizing economic bonding over territorial differences taking advantage of the economic difficulties of the countries there. China was ready to sideline territorial differences in engaging with her southern neighbours, including Vietnam with whom she experienced most bitter relations in the region since 1975. As we have seen in the previous chapter Vietnam was the major factor in framing the Cold War geopolitics in the South China Sea region. China felt the urgency to normalize the relation with Hanoi once Vietnam was inducted in the ASEAN grouping and after the former normalized relations with the US.[102] However, the Territorial Law of 1992 and the subsequent developments in the South China Sea proved that China's overtures vis-à-vis Southeast Asia were subject to conditions. China was ready to sideline but not compromise with her territorial/strategic considerations in South China Sea.

The main reason behind this uncompromising stand was the growing economic importance of the sea lanes passing through the South China Sea to sustain the growth of the Chinese economy. Between 1988 and 1989 *Jeifangjun bao* (Chinese newspaper of PLA) carried series of articles which emphasized on the economic importance of the maritime resources for the economic development of China referring to the limited land-based resources of China compared to India, France, Soviet Union and US. One of the articles read, "In order to make sure that the descendants of the Chinese nation can survive, develop, prosper and flourish in the world in the future, we should vigorously develop and use the oceans. To protect and defend the rights and interests of the reefs and islands within Chinese waters is a sacred mission...The defence of the territorial unity and protection of the rights and interests of the oceans are significant to the security and development of a country...."[103] Thus the resources as well as the communication route of South China Sea were important for China. However, the uncompromising stand of Beijing leadership on the sovereignty issue had a domestic as well as foreign root. A compromise on the dispute was to send a wrong signal to the secessionist factions in mainland China, in Tibet and Xinjiang Province, in one hand while was sure to impact China's stand on other boundary disputes she has with her other neighbours, Japan, Russia and India. Thus, a compromise on South China Sea issue would make China lose more than other disputants of the South China Sea issue.[104] Therefore, China's stand on the dispute was (and still is) based on China's overall geopolitical considerations vis-à-vis her neighbourhood policy. Such a mentality of the Chinese leadership does go with the revisionist character of the Chinese state which still feels that her territorial map is unsettled and therefore incomplete.

The very desire of the Chinese leaders, especially in the navy, to raise China as a formidable sea power can also be linked with the dissatisfying territorial structure of China which needs to be rectified and redrawn as well as the aspiration of the leadership in Beijing to get China her 'rightful place' which can be achieved with a sound economic base and a dominant military. In the post-Cold War South China Sea region an apparent power vacuum was created with the withdrawal of both US and USSR, compounded by the declared aloofness of Washington in the South China Sea territorial dispute. When a powerful nation (China was, and is, powerful compared to her neighbours including South China Sea littoral states) finds itself bordering a region with power vacuum it tend to establish its own power to fill up the gap. This keenness is also directed by the fear that if not filled up other powers might intrude.[105] As mentioned before, China was concerned about the rise of Japan in the early days of the post-Cold War period being alarmed of Tokyo sending peacekeeping troops to Cambodia and suspecting some 'designs' in Vietnam after Soviet withdrawal. Thus China was keen to fill up the vacuum. This could only be done with economic diplomacy in which China was successful and by strengthening the naval power. So it is a 'carrot and stick' strategy that China adopted to deal with the South China Sea claims and claimants. This strategy was evident during the 1995 and 1999 island disputes in South China Sea.

The adoption of the Territorial Sea Law in 1992 legalized the China's claims over the South China Sea islands and the region as a whole, in the Chinese eye. Thus China started acting more aggressively in establishing her claims with actions. In May 1992, the Chinese Offshore Oil Corporation and the (American) Crestone Energy Corporation concluded to jointly explore oil in the South China Sea region claimed by Vietnam which triggered a row between Beijing and Hanoi. From mid-1994 China started seizing the Mischief Reef, claimed by the Philippines. The occupying of the Mischief Reef was a significant development since before that China's disputes in the South China Sea was limited with Vietnam only which was a not a member of ASEAN. But the occupation of the Mischief Reef brought in a new disputant, the Philippines, member of ASEAN.[106] The Chinese built four structures on the Reef and called them as fishing shelters. The Mischief Reef, Manila claimed, fell within the Philippines' Exclusive Economic Zone. However, the Philippine Navy, with only a dozen of patrol boats, could not match with the Chinese Navy and thus could not access to that area. It was forced to stay away from the Chinese warships to avoid any major clash in the South China Sea.[107] Although the Philippines was planning to modernize her military but could not implement the programme even after the Military Modernization Act was adopted by the Congress (in 1995). On the other hand the US was no help either, being over engaged with the Bosnian affair and also being upset due to termination of the Subic Bay base. Thus the Philippine government had no military option.[108] So China took the advantage of the weakness of Manila to establish her claim over the disputed territory, just the way she acted against weak Vietnam during the Cold War period. This Mischief Reef incident is all the more significant since now China expanded her tentacles on the eastern side of South China Sea, for the first time, opening a new front against an ASEAN member. Noting the act of Beijing, Singaporean leader Lee Kuan Yew compared China's action with a big dog saying, "a big dog going up to a tree and raising its leg and marking its presence, so that smaller dogs in the region will know that the big dog has been past and will come back."[109] This was undoubtedly a major assertive gesture of China to establish her claims taking advantage of the power vacuum in the South China Sea region in the post-Cold War period. The Chinese interest in the Mischief Reef was the result of two other factors—when it satisfied the 'green water' strategy of Admiral Liu, then key member of the Politburo Standing Committee and Vice Chair of the Central Military Commission, the new Chinese leader and Deng's successor Jiang Zemin, a non-military person, needed support of the PLA leadership and the nationalist factions of the party and thus approved Admiral Lee's Mischief Reef adventure.[110]

China could dare to undertake the military expedition in the Mischief Reef and thereby expand the 'zone of conflict', both in the east and the west of the South China Sea opening two fronts with Vietnam and the Philippines, also because of her growing confidence in her naval capacity. Since 1985, the PLAN naval programmes focused on extending its operational range beyond the coastal defence including amphibious as well as submarine warfare. It conducted several amphibious exercises in the East and South China Seas (in the early 1990s).[111] China developed her naval prowess, although not very dramatically, focusing on some specific mission, primarily to move the navy from coastal defence to off shore operations.[112] Thus by 1995, China prepared herself to undertake any naval expedition in her maritime neighbourhood, in absence of any big power, since by then her naval power was stronger than other navies of the locality. As Paul Godwin said, "Force projection into the South China Sea to enforce China's sovereignty claims is more plausible than it was a decade ago."[113] In 1974, the PLAN lacked logistic reach to move beyond the Paracels, into the Spratlys, a situation that changed by 1990s.[114] The situation not only changed in respect to Chinese naval strength, but also in the geopolitics of South China Sea. The reason China could venture further deep into the South China Sea in the 1990s, as we have discussed previously, was the withdrawal of the big powers, US and USSR, exposing the small and weak local powers to Chinese 'aggression'. Beijing took the advantage of this situation firstly to establish her 'historical' claims on the islands, for both economic and strategic gains, and secondly to emerge as a dominant figure in the post-Cold War geopolitics of South China Sea.

The enlargement of the Chinese focus from Vietnam to the Philippines in the post-Cold War period was also a significant development. The weakness of the Filipino Navy, in the absence of US support, was known to all along with the fact of the US disinterest in the South China Sea territorial disputes despite the US-Philippines Mutual Defence Treaty Arrangement still in vogue. This presumably enthused the Chinese to 'seize the opportunity'. The Commander-in-Chief of the US Pacific Command clarified in 1991 that neither US had any interest to intervene in the Spratly dispute nor she had any contingency plan to go to Spratly if dispute arises.[115] Moreover, in 1996 US and the Philippines suspended all major military exercises until formal agreement is concluded between the two sides regarding the treatment of the visiting US defence and military personnel. This negotiation continued for next two years resulting to the conclusion of the Philippine-US Visiting Forces Agreement (VFA) on 10th February, 1998 which was endorsed by the Philippine Senate in May 1999.[116] Thus we see that the Mischief Reef incident, exposing the helplessness of the Philippines in front of the Chinese assertiveness, did not trigger any urge in Washington to save its ally, despite the Mutual Defence Agreement being operational. This undoubtedly assured Beijing of less or no risk in continuing its strategy in South China Sea. As mentioned earlier, the very lack of interest of USA in the territorial disputes after her withdrawal from the Philippines and due to other engagements did encourage China to get assertive in the South China Sea affair after 1990. So, the Chinese, assured of no major backlash, continued with her Mischief Reef project. In late 1998 the Chinese workers expanded two of the four shelters on the Reef while Manila protested against China building fort-like structure in the Reef.[117] Meanwhile Chinese activities in the South China Sea triggered regular minor clashes with Manila, like in January 1996 three Chinese vessels clashed in gun-battle with the Philippines navy while in 1997 the Philippine navy ordered a Chinese speedboat and two fishing boats to leave Scarborough Shoal in April while the Philippine fishermen removed the Chinese markers and raised their flag in the Shoal. In retaliation, Chinese navy sent three warships to survey the Philippine occupied Panata and Kota Islands.[118] However, these developments did not ring any bell in Washington. When the February 1995 report of the US Department of Defence kept a short paragraph about the Spratlys the November 1998 report made no mention of the South China Sea.[119] That US was not at all concerned about the developments in the South China Sea with the fear of 'China's rise' was clear from the statement of the Commander-in-Chief of the US Pacific Fleet who, in an interview in 1998, even negated the view of Chinese expansionary ambitions saying that 'US did not think so'.[120] Therefore China was free to act in the South China Sea.

Southeast Asian navies amid Chinese expansion in South China Sea

The changing geopolitical scenario in the South China Sea region after the Cold War resulting the withdrawal of the super powers from the region also impacted the overall strategic calculations of the South China Sea littoral states. So far they were under the protection of the contending powers' geostrategic competition in the region. Now they had to face the heat on their own, amidst the rise of China. The southward naval movement of China perturbed them. This was quite a natural reaction given the fact that no state can overlook the presence of a formidable power in its neighbourhood. And the case of South China Sea littorals vis-à-vis China was all the more serious given the traditional uneasy relations, with occasional clashes, that existed between the two sides. Over all China in the post-Cold War period was, as mentioned earlier in the chapter, a rising and dissatisfied power who nurture the aspiration to get herself her 'rightful place' in the world. And it is the neighbouring states, along with the big powers interested in the region, who will be most affected with the rise of a new power.[121] However, as we have seen in the immediate post-Cold War period, the US was not interested in the politics of the region. Thus the littoral states were left to deal with the new geopolitical challenge. And how were they preparing?

The ***Philippines***, as we have seen, was badly affected by the changing geopolitical landscape in the South China Sea region. The non-committed attitude of the US, despite the Mutual Defence Treaty with Manila, made the Philippines helpless in front of Chinese action. The Seventh Feet's protection was not available anymore but she had to defend her claims in the Spratlys. The Military Modernization Act was forwarded to the Senate in 1991 but the government was slow to respond. Meanwhile the US withdrawal from the Subic Bay and other military bases cost the Philippine Navy (PN) repair and maintenance facilities of the US Navy in the country and put the PN in a difficult situation. Also the Senate authorized the spending of only one-sixth of the funds requested. On the other hand the PN deleted the oldest ships, with or without replacement and by 1995 half of the Second World War vintage constructions were scrapped.[122] Thus the PN was in a difficult situation with depleting strength and developing challenges. In a way the naval strength and the war-fighting capability of PN was not matching the growing regional engagements of the Philippines with her forward presence in the South China Sea which the PN was not in a position to support.[123] This was evident in the Mischief Reef incident in 1995. To make-up the loss of US assistance the PN concluded Memorandum-of-Understanding (MOU) with South Korea in 1994 and conducted the naval exercise with the Singaporean Navy in1996, for the first time. Although the Asian Financial Crisis of 1997 was a major hiccup forcing expenditure cuts in defence sector, the continued Chinese activities in the Mischief Reef in 1999 forced the Philippines to concentrate on naval strength. In

July 1999 two Chinese boats sank after colliding with the PN patrol boat while in October the Philippines Air Force (PAF) reconnaissance aircraft spotted seven Chinese ships, including naval auxiliaries, near the Mischief Reef. The Philippines could only deploy light strike aircraft in the Palawan Island and increased naval patrols in the area.[124] The Philippine economy was not fit to sustain and support the required up gradation of the navy. Although the Senate, under pressure, approved 5.5 billion pesos to be available by April 1999, no substantial equipment acquisition was allowed.[125] Thus there was a gap between the requirement and the availability, at the time when Manila had to promote her formidable presence in the South China Sea.

Like the Philippines, ***Vietnam*** was also facing the Chinese challenge in the South China Sea which was becoming a key maritime security challenge to her. And like the Philippines, Vietnam was also losing a key protection with the Soviets withdrawing from the Cam Ranh Bay. China was (and is) a bigger concern for Vietnam given the traditional uneasy relation with the giant neighbour. The important aspect of the Sino-Vietnam relation has been its asymmetric character. And because China is the larger partner, this asymmetry has made Chinese presence much more important to Vietnam than the vice versa and thus Vietnam has had more acute sense of risk and opportunities offered by this relationship.[126] Both sides normalized relations in November 1991 with the visit of the General Secretary of Vietnam Communist Party Do Muoi and Chairman of the Council of Ministers of Vietnam Vo Van Kiet to Beijing following invitation of Chinese leaders Jiang Zemin and Le Peng but it was the beginning of peaceful and not close relations, unlike the 1950-75 period.[127] The Sino-Vietnam relations are marked by tensions and discomfort which is quite natural in an asymmetric relations where the weaker side lives with sense of vulnerability vis-à-vis the larger side. Such feeling of discomfort worsens with the memories of 'historical subjugation' (Vietnam was part of Han Dynasty) and communist China's invasion during the Cold War. But the most consistent and irritant issue between the two sides has been the South China Sea territorial sovereignty dispute.

Despite several financial and technological problems in the 1990s, the defence budget of Vietnam kept increasing in 1992 and 1993 given the country's interests in the South China Sea. On the other hand, even when the Soviet presence in the Cam Ranh Bay ended in May 1992, the Vietnamese leadership, in 1994, agreed to allow the new Russian State to continue in Cam Ranh Bay temporarily on revised terms. The Russian Commander-in-Chief of the Pacific Fleet, who visited Vietnam in 1996, opined that his country should both retain and develop the Cam Ranh Bay.[128] So we see that Vietnam was lucky not to counter a grim security scenario, like what we saw in case of the Philippines, in the face of Chinese 'threat'. As we have seen in the previous chapter, the Soviet presence in the Cam Ranh Bay was a security guarantee to Vietnam against the Chinese and the continuation of the presence by less powerful Russia was significant since Russia, even then, had much to offer to Vietnam. Vietnam concluded an agreement in 1998 with Russia ensuring future arms supply.[129]

In the meantime both Vietnam and China engaged in physical as well as verbal clashes over their sovereignty claims in the South China Sea. It should be remembered that within three months after visit of Vietnamese leaders to Beijing in November 1991on the latter's invitation, Beijing adopted the Territorial Law of the Sea in February 1992 legalizing China's claim over the South China Sea region and its islands. Thus it was evident that China's normalizing gesture was not at the cost of her 'sovereignty claims'. The PLA Navy blockaded a Vietnamese drilling ship in July 1994 while in 1996 a Chinese ship allegedly captured two Vietnamese patrol boasts in the northern islands of Co To. Thus the Vietnamese Navy had to prepare its vessels according to the Chinese activities in the South China Sea. The Brigades formerly located in the north were positioned in Da Nang, Cam Ranh Bay and Vung Tao to focus on the Spratly Islands, especially to protect Bach Ho and Dai Hung oilfields.[130] So the Vietnamese navy was to keep itself ready for any adverse situation. Although the Navy had ex-USN and Soviet amphibious ships, it needed modernization because the break up of the Soviet Union disrupted the supply chains and necessitated new source of supply but ultimately they had to rely on Russian supply. Meanwhile the Vietnamese Defence Minister, citing the concerns of China and South China Sea, insisted in 1996 on modernizing the navy to defend Vietnam's territorial waters, deploy military forces and Vietnam's maritime economy. A Vietnamese Coast Guard was founded in 1998 under the navy which ultimately was entrusted with much of the maritime enforcement mission. The Navy also emphasized on submarine force to deal with China and got the delivery of two midget submarines from North Korea in 1997. Russia also offered Vietnam second-hand Kilo-class submarines in 1998.[131] Thus, Vietnam was formulating her naval defence policy in line with the Chinese activities in the South China Sea in 1990s.

The other two South China littoral states, Malaysia and Indonesia, were not very prominent in the geopolitical scene in the region unlike Vietnam and the Philippines. They were not the claimants like the other two but started featuring in the regional dispute as the Cold War came to a close. It was in 1980 when ***Malaysia*** declared formally a 200 mile EEZ (Exclusive Economic Zone) encompassing much of the Spratlys. As we have seen in the last chapter how the Malaysian Navy announced to increase patrolling in the South China Sea following the Sino-Vietnam clash in 1988 and later engaged in disputes with Manila over fishing rights. These were the preface of the growing Malaysian presence in the changing South China Sea geopolitics at the concluding phase Cold War. The RMN was most interested acquiring submarine since 'any underwater capability would be better than none'.[132] However, Malaysia found the creation of submarine force very expensive in the early 1990s limiting within the Sixth Five Year Plan (1991-95). However, the RMN enacted a 20-year Expansion and Modernization Programme (1990-2010) to double the size of the Navy. There were plans to construct naval bases in Kota Kinabalu and Sabah.[133] Both these locations are the littorals of the South China Sea. However, apparently, these developments in the RMN did not have any link with the South China Sea dispute since Kuala Lumpur was never involved in the territorial dispute with China, unlike Vietnam or the Philippines. Also, given the maritime distance between Malaysia and China and the then PLAN's naval capability or even its declared objective, Malaysia had nothing to worry. Nevertheless, the declaration of the EEZ by Malaysian government encompassing Spratlys Islands and the adoption of the Territorial Law of the Sea by China in 1992 extending Chinese 'territorial claim to the Spratlys and its adjoining waters did overlap the claims of both the countries. It is to be remembered here that Malaysia occupied Ambon Cay in 1979 and Swallow Reef in 1983 and also kept on building structures on its claimed features in late 1990s triggering reactions from both China and the Philippines.[134] Yet Malaysia welcomed the economic engagement of China with Southeast Asia in the 1990s. Malaysian leader Mahathir Mohammad claimed that China was not a 'threat' and strongly advocated for engaging, instead of containing, her. He emphasized the non-existence of history imperial expansion of China, similar to that of the West.[135] However, Malaysia kept on making constructions on the geographical features in the disputed islands under her possession. In the late 1990s, the government was constructing a two-storey concrete building on the Investigator Shoal which Manila objected to. Also, the country built a helipad, radar and a pier which China described as encroachment on her territory.[136] So Malaysia was also making her contribution in the post-Cold War developments in the South China Sea.

The country, apart from Vietnam and the Philippines, who was affected by China's 1992 Law was ***Indonesia***. The Law extended the Chinese territorial jurisdiction to include the part of Indonesia's EEZ around the Natuna Islands which triggered anxiety in Jakarta. Like Vietnam and the Philippines Indonesia also had uneasy relations with Beijing, especially during the Suharto era. The Natuna Islands was important for Indonesia because she was beginning to exploit the rich and extensive gas deposits in the islands.[137] Indonesia however could not do much during that time since she was more engaged with the East Timor issue and also the Asian Financial Crisis impeded her military acquisition programme. Also the concern for the resources of oil and gas in the Timor Gap forced Indonesia to do patrolling, jointly with Australia, in the region.[138]

ASEAN and the South China Sea geopolitics

The geopolitical tension rising between China and the small littorals of South China Sea expedited the necessity to mitigate the tension arising in the Southeast Asian scene since the end of the Cold War. It was the all the more important in the absence of the big players in the regional tussle. Now the onus was on the regional parties to resolve their differences on their own. And this gave ASEAN a chance to play a major role, something it seriously lacked during the Cold War era. Now it was the litmus test for the Association which was apparently constituted to resolve the regional issues of Southeast Asia in the 'ASEAN Way'.

ASEAN or Association of South East Asian Nations was founded on 8th August, 1967 with the objective of providing security to the region amidst the severe Cold War centring the Vietnam War and the communist threat. It was the product of the anxiety of the regional leaders with a common perception of handling the communist adventurism, both internally and externally. Also they were puzzled about the future role of China in the aftermath of the British withdrawal from the region. However, the main purpose of the Association was to ensure regional security and stability of Southeast Asia. The handful of Southeast Asian leaders had been trying to develop a regional platform to address regional issues, sometimes independent of the big power influence since the 1960s. The foundation of the Association of Southeast Asia (ASI, with Thailand,

Malaya and the Philippines) in 1961 and MAPHILINDO (Malaysia, Philippines and Indonesia) in 1963 were the predecessors of ASEAN which however floundered due to internal differences. The ASEAN was last and the successful initiative for regional stability. Nevertheless, the Association did not get much scope to be a deciding factor in the Southeast Asian geopolitical scene during the Cold War since it was high jacked time to time by the super powers. The end of the Cold War and the absence (and reluctance) of the US, the victorious and the lone super power, to meddle in the regional affairs gave ASEAN the chance to act. Another reason for the sudden activeness of ASEAN was the economic success of its members, (especially Malaysia, Indonesia, Thailand and Singapore) which poured confidence in the Southeast Asian leaders, like Malaysian Prime Minister Mahatir Mohammad and Singaporean Prime Minister Lee Kuan Yew who preached about the virtues of the 'Asian values'.[139]

Yet it would be a mistake to conclude that the ASEAN in the post-Cold War era attempted to insulate Southeast Asia from the big extra-regional power, USA. On the contrary, as we have discussed before, in the aftermath of the US withdrawal from the Philippines, many ASEAN members developed closeness with USA insisting on the latter's continuous presence in the region. One of the reasons behind this gesture was the rise of China. There was a growing concern among many ASEAN states that China might pose a threat to their sovereignty. This feeling was endorsed further after China adopted the law on territorial waters and contiguous areas extending jurisdiction over South China Sea.[140] It can be said that the developments in the South China Sea over the frictions between China and other claimants in the dispute in the 1990s did put the credibility of ASEAN to ensure stability in the region at test.

The disputes in the South China Sea in the 1990s along with the US and Soviet withdrawal creating a power vacuum in the region and paving the way for China's chance to fill the empty space forced ASEAN to formulate a coherent policy. The ASEAN members were concerned that a hegemonic China might attempt to settle the disputes in the South China Sea by force (in the absence of any big power to balance her).[141] So it is seen that the ASEAN countries, none of whom except the Philippines had a direct clash with China in the troubled South China Sea (Vietnam joined the group in 1995), were anyway perturbed by the rise of China amidst power vacuum in the post-Cold War South China Sea geopolitics. This uneasiness is anything but unnatural given the fact that small states are seldom satisfied and comfortable with the presence of a giant neighbour with high power potential. And this is all the more possible when there exist historical tensions with the neighbour. Almost all the member countries of the ASEAN, except Thailand and Singapore, have had territorial issues with Beijing.[142] Moreover, the 1992 territorial waters law of China inducted areas in the South China Sea, claimed by four of the then six ASEAN members—the Philippines, Malaysia, Indonesia and Brunei—within the Chinese territorial jurisdiction.[143] But the countries were not in a position to counter China physically. Also China was becoming important economic partner of ASEAN states during this time. Thus the ASEAN members adopted an 'engage to contain' China approach being incapable to deal with China militarily.[144] The ASEAN countries were in favour of 'constructive engagement' with Beijing promoting mutually beneficial economic and political cooperation. The ASEAN preferred step-by-step engagement with China first making her a guest at the ASEAN Ministerial Meeting (AMM) in 1991, the consultative partner of ASEAN Regional Forum (ARF) in 1994 and finally a dialogue partner in 1996. However, ASEAN used these occasions to express its concerns regarding the Chinese activities in the South China Sea.[145] Thus even when promoting the engagement with China the ASEAN was doing its duty to cater its displeasure to China about her assertiveness in the disputed areas without making the issue a flashpoint in the developing Sino-ASEAN relations.

On the other hand individual ASEAN states were also in action to pacify the tension through engagement with China. Indonesia organized an informal workshop at Bali in January 1990 involving ASEAN government officials and academics to discuss the matter and following this meeting, the Indonesian Foreign Minister Ali Alatas summoned another similar meeting inviting the claimants like China, Vietnam and Taiwan (Vietnam being outside the ASEAN bloc at that point of time). There were two other meetings, one in Bandung in 1991 and the other in Jogjakarta in 1992. These meetings were held to convert the maritime zone (of South China Sea) from zone of conflict to zone of cooperation on the basis of common interest and mutual benefits.[146] Thus it is seen that the ASEAN was now attempting to mitigate the tension arising in its vicinity via dialogue with China in order to thwart any unpleasant scenario developing which would certainly impact the tranquil ambiance of the region needed for the economic development of the regional states. Even China was also cooperating (without of course compromising with her claims) since at that point of time Chinese economy also required a tranquil neighbourhood with strong economic bonding.

Nonetheless, the ASEAN was also not in a mood to give China space to act freely. Thus after China passed the territorial law of the sea in 1992 ASEAN responded with 'Declaration on the South China Sea, 1992' (also called Manila Declaration) which referred to the core principles of the Association of amity and cooperation and urged all the disputants to resolve the disputes through peaceful means 'without using force'.[147] The Declaration suggested that the Association was 'conscious that any adverse developments in the South China Sea directly affect peace and stability in the region.'[148] It also urged to exercise restraints and positive climate to resolve the disputes.[149] It is noteworthy here that the Philippines was chairing the Association. This attempt of Manila to use the ASEAN platform to contain Chinese activities threatening its sovereignty claims in the South China Sea islands can be seen as an important strategic initiative. Since the Philippines could not handle China single-handed it was beneficial for her to combat Beijing collectively via ASEAN. The striking part of this whole event was that Chinese Foreign Minister Qian Qichen was present in Manila as the guest of the ASEAN Chair who, in spite of the insistence of the ASEAN members, refused to sign the Declaration, for China not being involved in the draft-preparation, but assured that China subscribed to the declaration's principles.[150] This was strategic gesture on both sides. When Manila, by inviting China at the ASEAN meeting as the chair of the Association engaged the powerful disputant in the multilateral dialogue process thereby limiting China's scope to bully her less-powerful opponent in a one-to-one show, China also expressed her readiness to consider the suggestions of the Declaration principles displaying her apparent cooperative mood which was essential to pacify the fears of her small and less powerful neighbours regarding their giant neighbour's hegemonic temper while also refusing to sign the Declaration kept China's options open. However, it seemed that both sides were coming on terms with each other, until further development.

ASEAN's engaging gesture with China did not yield desired result which got evident with the Mischief Reef incident of 1995 when the Philippines and China faced each other. Following the discovery of the Chinese made steel structure with Chinese flag and a parabolic antenna atop of it in the Mischief Reef by Manila in March 1995, ASEAN foreign ministers issued a statement on 18th March expressing serious concerns over the developments which they claimed affected peace and stability of the South China Sea. They also urged the concerned parties to adhere to the Manila Declaration which emphasized on resolution of disputes through peaceful means and also advised the contenders to address the disputes through various fora like Indonesia sponsored Workshop Series on Managing Potential Conflicts in the South China Sea. ASEAN also questioned China over the Nine-Dash Line[151] issue on the Chinese maps skirting the Natuna Islands of Indonesia and her presence in the Mischief Reef at the China-ASEAN meeting held in April 1995.[152] However ASEAN was not ready to confront China on the issue despite four of its members-the Philippines, Malaysia, Indonesia and Vietnam (which became a member in 1995)-were parts of the disputes. It was still opting for dialogue as means to restrain China. That is why, even after the second Mischief Reef incident in 1999, it remained contented at the China-ASEAN meeting in Kunming, China from 4-8 April, 1999, with Beijing agreeing to give 'serious' and 'earnest' consideration to the Philippines proposal for a new code of conduct with regards to South China Sea.[153] This code of conduct was also the weapon of the ASEAN to bind the Chinese into a legal framework in executing actions in the disputed waters of South China Sea. ASEAN endorsed the idea for a regional code of conduct in the South China Sea at a meeting in July 1996. This code was meant to promote understanding among the regional states and emphasized on 'freedom of navigation', keeping the regional trading nations in mind, and self-restraints.[154] In a way these approaches seem to be 'appeasing' in character in the face of aggressive and defiant attitude of China although it is natural for a regional organization to act like this putting peace and stability as the only viable option for dispute resolution. However, the physical weakness of the individual members of the Association in respect of the strength of China should also be considered. And that is the reason, they were pushed towards the US as a counter weight. Since 1995 the US started reappearing in the South China Sea with the US Navy making visits, exercises and often being invited. This was further bolstered by the ratification of the Visiting Forces Agreement (VFA) between USA and the Philippines in 1999 which was a major military accord between the two countries since the closure of the Subic Bay.[155]

Thus we see that the disputant members of the ASEAN could hardly rely on the capacity of the ASEAN in defusing the tension with China by bringing the latter on board. The uncompromising attitude of China is undoubtedly the reason for this situation since her intransigence gave no reason to the weaker disputants to be satisfied with the ASEAN initiatives. On the other hand China was never in favour of bringing in the extra regional powers as a backup measure by the weak contestants since that would hinder the Chinese aspirations in the region. China was never comfortable with USA and suspected the Japanese intensions in the post-Cold War Asia Pacific geopolitical scene. While this discomfort of China was well capitalized by the small ASEAN countries, their requirements gave the chance to the US to re-enter the South China Sea geopolitical scene in the late 1990s.

The death of Soviet Union apparently ended the tug of war between the super powers affecting the global geopolitical scene. Nevertheless, the situation in East Asia was different. The geopolitics of East Asia was never dependent on the Cold War developments only. The inter-state tensions in this part of the world have a historical root. Most of the countries here were the colonies of the Western powers which have triggered strong sense of nationalism, sometimes compounded by the territorial disputes with neighbours. That is why the end of the Cold War did not end the inter-state tensions in East Asia. Moreover the rise of China, a revisionist state with 'victim mentality', has complicated the situation further. The withdrawal of the big powers in South China Sea altered the regional geopolitics which acted in the interests of Beijing, initially. It was easier for China to handle the Southeast Asian disputes better than in Northeast Asia given the presence of economically strong Japan enjoying US security guarantee in the region. The Chinese wanted to fill up the power vacuum in the South China Sea. This sent ripples of anxiety around the region and the small and weak states got cautious. However, they chose to handle China through engaging her in order to contain her and that too via ASEAN since they could not do so single handed. In this way the ASEAN, for the first time since its foundation in 1967, featured prominently as a mediator. China also acted as a collaborator apparently to defuse tension. But given her uncompromising stand on the dispute displayed in her activities throughout the 1990s triggering tensions with other claimants, the capacity of ASEAN as a reliable entity to soothe tension was limited. This paved the way for the US to re-enter the scene in the concluding phase of 1990s. However, two major features of the post-Cold War geopolitics of South China Sea were- firstly, the emergence of China as the sole major power locally. Secondly, the emergence of ASEAN as a medium of communication, however unsuccessful as dispute resolution mechanism, was a significant development of the post-Cold War South China Sea geopolitics where the small and weak states found a platform to handle China jointly thereby making their voices heard separately, something which remained suppressed under the roaring of the super powers during the Cold War. The most important development of the post-Cold War geopolitics of South China Sea was that now the politics was directed by the local developments with the rise of a local power China initiating a local Cold War between her and the other disputants. In a way the South China Sea geopolitics, in the post-Cold War period, became more localized with the rise of China and the resultant uneasiness among her neighbours.

END NOTES

1. Francis Fukuyama, 'The End of History?', in Richard K. Betts (ed), *Conflict After the Cold War: Arguments on Causes of War and Peace*, New York, Pearson Longman, 2008, p.6
2. Sameul P. Huntington, 'The Clash of Civilizations', ibid, p.35
3. Aaron Friedberg, 'Ripe for Rivalry: Prospects for Peace in Multipolar Asia', *International Security*, Vol.18, No.3, 1994, p.6, 7 emphasis added
4. Ibid, pp.11-15
5. Ibid, p.14
6. The dispute over 'comfort women' issue (where Japanese colonizers supplied their military with Korean women as sex workers during the colonial rule) between Japan and South Korea or the Chinese and Korean objections to Japanese version of World War II history and the visit of Japanese leaders to Yoshukuni Shrine, a Japanese war memorial, are more psychological and sociological than political, even the Japanese WWII history is equally contentious to many Southeast Asian countries who were colonized by Japan during the war.
7. The ethnic tensions have been a major issue in Myanmar, Thailand, Malaysia, the Philippines in Southeast Asia apart from Sri Lanka and Pakistan (between its eastern and western wings) in South Asia
8. Aaron Friedberg, op cit, p.17
9. Barry Buzan and Gerald Segal, 'Rethinking East Asian Security', *Survival*, Vol. 36, Summer 1994, p.6
10. Aaron Friedberg, op cit, p.18
11. Ibid, 21
12. 'Philippines Orders U.S. to Leave Strategic Naval Base at Subic Bay', *The New York Times*, December 28, 1991, http://www.nytimes.com/1991/12/28/world/philippines-orders-us-to-leave-strategic-navy-base-at-subic-bay.html?pagewanted=all (accessed on 11.01.2016)
13. The Philippines was an American colony from 1898 to 1946, the Americans took her over from the Spaniards after defeating Spain in the war of 1898
14. *The New York Times*, December 28, 1991, op cit
15. Ibid
16. Cited in ibid
17. Robert D. Kaplan, *Asia's Cauldron: The South China Sea and the End of a Stable Pacific*, New York, Random House, 2014, p.127
18. Ibid
19. Ibid, p.126
20. This system, the term coined by John W. Dower, originated from the peace treaty with Japan signed in San Francisco in 1951, was a bilateral security

arrangement of USA with Japan. The treaty was signed when the Cold War era was starting at a high pitch with communist victory in China, Soviet nuclear test and unfolding of Korean War. The significance of the event lies in the fact that by this treaty USA delinked Japan from all her neighbours by not inviting either China (communist or nationalist) or Korea, who were the victims of wartime Japan's aggression, to the peace conference. In a way it was an American sponsored anti-communist alliance system. For details read John D. Dower, The San Francisco System: Past, Present, Future in U.S.-Japan-China Relations, *The Asia-Pacific Journal*, Vol 12, Issue 8, February 28, 2014

21. Javed Maswood, 'The Rise of the Asia-Pacific', in Anthony McGrew and Christopher Brook (eds), *Asia-Pacific in the New World Order*, London and New York, Routledge, 1998, p.64
22. Patrick C. Bratton, 'The United States as a Pacific power', in Geoffrey Till and Patrick C. Bratton (eds), *Sea Power and the Asia Pacific: The Triumph of Neptune?*, London and New York, Routledge, 2012, pp.19, 20
23. Ibid, p.20
24. Ibid
25. Diane K. Mauzy and Brian L. Job, 'U.S Policy in Southeast Asia: Limited Reengagement after years of benign neglect', *Asian Survey*, Vol.XLVII, No.4, July/August, 2007, p.623
26. Anthony McGrew, 'Restructuring foreign and defence policy: the USA', in Anthony McGrew and Christopher Brook (eds), op cit, p.160
27. Diane K. Mauzy and Brian L. Job, op cit, p.627
28. Donald S. Zagoria, 'The End of the Cold War in Asia: Its Impact on China', *Proceedings of Academy of Political Science*, Vol.38, No.2, The China Challenge: American Policies in East Asia, 1991, p.4
29. Ibid, p.6
30. Cited in ibid, p.4
31. Cited in Rakesh Gupta, 'Games on the High Seas', Rakesh Gupta (ed), *India's Security Problems in the Nineties*, New Delhi, Patriot Publishers, 1989, p.71
32. Ibid, p.72
33. Diane K. Mauzy and Brian L. Job, op cit, pp.626, 627
34. Cited in Anthony McGrew, op cit, p.172, emphasis added
35. David Rapkin and William R. Thompson, 'Power Transition, Challenge and the (Re) Emergence of China', in Leszek Buszynski (ed), *Asia Pacific Security*,Vol.1, London and New York, Routledge, 2014, p.23
36. Eminent theorists like A.F.K Orgnaski, Arnold Tyonbee, Quincy Wright, Paul Kennedy and Robert Gilpin, among many others, have introduced the power transition theory. Orgnaski's *World Politics*, first published in 1958, was first to lay the foundation of the theory including the notion of a hierarchical international order and stages of transition that affect the relative power among nations.
37. Cited in Zhiqun Zhu, *US-China Relations in the 21st Century: Power transition and peace*, London and New York, 2006, p.11
38. Cited inibid, p.13
39. Evan S. Medeiros, *China's International Behavior: Activism, Opportunism and Diversification*, Santa Monica, Rand Corporation, 2009, p.10, http://

www.rand.org/content/dam/rand/pubs/monographs/2009/RAND_MG850.pdf (accessed on 25.03.2016)

40. Zhiqun Zhu, op cit, pp.20-21
41. Cited in David Scott, *China Stands Up: The PRC and the international system*, London and New York, Routledge, 2007, p.7
42. Cited in ibid, p.6, emphasis added
43. Cited in ibid, p.8, emphasis added
44. Ibid, p.12
45. Ibid, p.13
46. Barry Buzan and Gerald Segal, op cit, p.6
47. Read David C. Kang, 'Getting Asia Wrong: The Need for New Analytical Framework', *International Security*, Vol.27, No.4, 2003The MIT Press
48. Ibid, p.64
49. Ibid, pp.66, 67
50. Aaron Friedberg, 'Will Europe's Past Be Asia's Future?', *Survival*, vol.42, no.3, 2000, p.150
51. Gerald Segal, 'East Asia and the "Constrainment" of China, *International Security*, Volume 20, No.4, 1996, MIT Press, p.109
52. Cited in Aaron Friedberg, op cit, p.151
53. Randall L. Schweller, 'Managing the Rise of Great Powers: History and Theory', in Alastair Iain Jonston and Robert Ross (eds), *Engaging China: The Management of Emerging Power*, London and New York, Routledge, 1999, pp.9,10
54. James R. Holmes and Toshi Yoshihara, 'China's Caribbean in South China Sea', *SAIS Review of International Affairs*, Volume 26, No.1, John Hopkins University Press,2006, p.80
55. Cited in David Scott, op cit, p.100
56. Ibid, p.76
57. Cited in ibid, p.77
58. Andy Yee, 'Maritime Territorial Disputes in East Asia: A Comparative Analysis of the South China Sea and East China Sea', *Journal of Current Chinese Affairs*, 2011, 40, 2, p.171
59. Peter Harrold and Rajiv Lall, 'China: Reform and Development in 1992-93' *World Bank Discussion Papers*, China and Mongolia Department, 215, 1993, p. xi
60. Cited in David Scott, p.85
61. Even Mao himself, while introducing Deng to Soviet leader Nikita Khrushchev in 1957, hailed him as 'very intelligent' and prophesied that 'he has a great future ahead of him', cited in 'Deng Xiaoping is Dead at 92: the Modern Architect of China', *The New York Times*, February 20, 1997, http://www.nytimes.com/1997/02/20/world/deng-xiaoping-is-dead-at-92-architect-of-modern-china.html?pagewanted=all (accessed on 21.01,2016)
62. Tridib Chakrabarti, 'The Territorial Claims in South China Sea: Probing Persistent Uncertainties', in Arun Kumar Banerji and Purushottam Bhattacharya (eds), *People's Republic of China at Fifty: Politics, Economy and Foreign Relations*, New Delhi, Lancer Books, 2001, p.173
63. Ton That Thien, 'South East Asia Post Cold War Geopolitics', *Global Affairs:*

The American Journal of Geopolitics, Vol.VIII, No.1, Winter, 1993, http://www.tonthatthien.com/wp-content/uploads/2015/07/1993-Southeast-Asias-Post-Cold-War-Geopolitics-The-New-Realities.pdf (accessed on 21.01.2016) p.1

64. Cited in ibid, pp.6,7
65. Cited in ibid, p.7
66. Ang Cheng Guan, 'The South China Sea Dispute Re-visited', *Institute of Defence and Strategic Studies (IDSS)*, Singapore, Rajaratnam School of International Studies, August, 1999, p.13
67. Ibid
68. Ton That Thien, op cit, p.2
69. Bill Hayton, *The South China Sea: The Struggle for Power in Asia*, New Haven and London, Yale University Press, 2014, p.80
70. A Modern Navy with Chinese Characteristics, *The People's Liberation Army Navy*, August 2009, pp.5,6, http://fas.org/irp/agency/oni/pla-navy.pdf (accessed on 21.01.2016)
71. James R. Holmes and Toshi Yoshihara, op cit, p.83
72. Paul H.B. Godwin, 'From Continent to Periphery: PLA Doctrine, Strategy and Capabilities towards 2000', *The China Quarterly*, No.146, Special Issue: China's Military Transition, Jun, 1996, pp.464
73. Ibid, p.467
74. Ang Cheng Guan, op cit, pp.6-7
75. Tridib Chakrabarti, op cit, p.186
76. Donald S. Zagoria, op cit, p.7
77. Ibid
78. Ibid, p.8
79. Andy Yee, op cit, p.172
80. Tridib Chakrabarti, op cit, p.178
81. Ibid, p.180
82. Bill Hayton, op cit, p.80
83. Bronson Percival, *The Dragon looks South: China and Southeast Asia in the New Century*, Connecticut and London, Praeger Security International, 2007, p.7
84. Gilbert Rozman, *Chinese Strategic Thought towards Asia*, New York, Palgrave Macmillan, 2010, pp.202, 203
85. Bronson Percival, op cit, p.52
86. Gilbert Rozman, op cit, p.203
87. Kenneth Pyle, 'Restructuring foreign and defence policy: Japan', in Anthony McGrew and Christopher Brook (eds), op cit, pp.127-128
88. The Taiwan Relations Act, enacted April 10, 1979, is an act of the United States Congress. Since the recognition of the People's Republic of China, the Act has defined the non-diplomatic relations between the United States and the governing authorities on Taiwan.The Taiwan Relations Act potentially requires the U.S. to intervene militarily if the PRC attacks or invades Taiwan. The act provides Taiwan with arms of defensive character and empowers USA to resist any resort to force or any other forms of coercion that would jeopardize the security, or social or economic system, of the people on Taiwan. (Taiwan relations Act, American Institute of Taiwan, http://www.ait.org.tw/en/taiwan-relations-act.html, accessed on 22.01.2016).

89. Tridib Chakrabarti, op cit, p.179
90. Chen Qimao, 'The Taiwan Strait Crisis: Its Crux and Solutions', *Asian Survey*, Vol.36, No.11, Nov.1996, p.1055
91. Paul H.B. Godwin, op cit, p.474
92. John F. Copper, 'Why We Need Taiwan', *The National Interests*, August 29, 2011, http://nationalinterest.org/commentary/why-we-need-taiwan-5815 (accessed on 25.01.2016)
93. Joseph A. Bosco, 'Taiwan and Strategic Security', *The Diplomat*, May, 15, 2015, http://thediplomat.com/2015/05/taiwan-and-strategic-security/ (accessed on 25.01.2016)
94. *The Law on the Territorial Sea and the Contiguous Zone* on 25th February 1992, http://www.un.org/depts/los/LEGISLATIONANDTREATIES/PDFFILES/CHN_1992_Law.pdf (accessed on 15.01.2016)
95. Part II, 'Territorial Sea and Contiguous Zone', Section 1: General provisions, *United Nations Convention on the Law of the Sea*,http://www.un.org/depts/los/convention_agreements/texts/unclos/unclos_e.pdf (accessed on 25.0102016), p.27
96. February 1992, op cit
97. Ibid, pp.1,2
98. Ibid, p.2
99. Gilbert Rozman, op cit, p.68
100. Ibid, p.71
101. Bronson Percival, op cit, p.9
102. Gilbert Rozman, op cit, p.205
103. Cited in John W. Garver, 'China's Push Through The South China Sea' in Leszek Buszynski (ed), *Asia Pacific Security*,Vol.3, London and New York, Routledge, 2014,pp.325-326
104. J.N. Mak, 'The Asia-Pacific Security Order', in Anthony McGrew and Christopher Brook (eds), op cit, p.110
105. Randall L. Schweller, op cit, p.3
106. Ang Cheng Guan, op cit, p.9
107. Tridib Chakrabarti, op cit, p.194
108. Bill Hayton, op cit, pp.86-87
109. Cited in ibid, p.87
110. Ibid, p.88
111. Paul H.B. Godwin, op cit, p.474
112. Ibid, p.478
113. Ibid, p.484
114. Ang Cheng Guan, op cit, p.8
115. Cited in Ibid, p.14
116. Ibid, p.12
117. Tridib Chakrabarti, op cit, pp.194, 195
118. Ibid, p.196
119. Ang Cheng Guan, op cit, p.15
120. Cited in ibid
121. Randall L. Schweller, op cit, p.7

122. James Goldrick and Jack McCaffrie, *Navies of South-East Asia: A Comparative Study*, London and New York, Routledge, 2013, p.125
123. Ibid
124. Ibid, pp.129,130
125. Ibid, pp.128-129
126. Brantly Womack, *China and Vietnam: The Politics of Asymmetry*, New York, Cambridge University Press, 2006, p.1
127. Ibid, p.8
128. James Goldrick and Jack McCaffrie, op cit, pp.200,201
129. Ibid, p.201
130. Ibid, p.204
131. Ibid, pp.206,207
132. Ibid, p.102
133. Ibid
134. Ishani Naskar, 'The South China Sea Issue: India's Interests and Approach', *Policy Brief* No.1, Institute of Foreign Policy Studies, University of Calcutta, December 2012, p.4
135. Bronson Percival, op cit, p.55
136. Tridib Chakrabarti, op cit, p.197
137. James Goldrick and Jack McCaffrie, op cit, p.83
138. Ibid, p.82
139. Allan Collins, *Security and Southeast Asia: Domestic, Regional and Global Issue*, Singapore, Viva Books Pvt. Ltd., 2005, p.140
140. Ibid, p.170
141. Tridib Chakrabarti, op cit, p.197
142. Vietnam was not the member of ASEAN until 1995
143. Christopher B. Roberts, 'ASEAN: The challenge of unity in diversity' in Leszek Buszynski and Christopher B. Roberts (eds), *The South China Sea Maritime Disputes: Political, legal and regional perspectives*, London and New York, Routledge, 2015, p.131
144. Allan Collins, op cit, p.170
145. Lee Lao To, 'East Asian Assessments of China's Security Policy', *International Affairs*, Vol.73, No.2, Asia and the Pacific, Apr.1997, p.259
146. Tridib Chakrabarti, op cit, pp.197-198
147. Christopher B. Roberts, op cit, p.131
148. '1992 ASEAN Declaration on the South China Sea', Adopted by the Foreign Ministers at the 25th ASEAN Ministerial meeting in Manila, Philippines, 22nd July 1992, http://cil.nus.edu.sg/rp/pdf/1992%20ASEAN%20Declaration%20 on%20 the%20South%20China%20Sea-pdf.pdf (accessed 01.02.2016)
149. Ibid
150. Rodolfo C. Saverino, 'ASEAN and the South China Sea' in Leszek Buszynski (ed), *Asia Pacific Security*,Vol.III, London and New York, Routledge, 2014, p.343
151. The nine-dash line was originally an eleven-dash line first shown on a map published by the government of the then Republic of China in December 1947 to justify its claims in the South China Sea. In 1949, the line was adopted and

revised to nine by the new communist regime. Discussed in the proceeding chapter

152. Rodolfo C. Saverino, op cit, p.344, 345
153. Ang Cheng Guan, op cit, p.16
154. Rodolfo C. Saverino, op cit, p.346
155. Tridib Chakrabarti, op cit, p.199

5

South China Sea Geopolitics in the New Millennium

The economic development of East Asia since the mid 1980s, with the rise of South Korea, Japan, Taiwan and Singapore, subsequently spread to other areas of the region, especially in Southeast Asia while the performance of China in this field was most noteworthy. This economic booming was seen by many as the rise of new Asia, brimming with economic potentiality. Such a development is significant in the context of the geopolitical history of East Asia which came a long way from the zone of coercion since the dawn of the last century, surviving the colonial and imperial conflicts of the World War II and that of the Cold War, to a region of cooperation by the end of the century tying itself in the web of regional organizations promoting regional cohesion and cooperation. Asia was now getting directed by the Asians with her economy gaining a distinct place in the world. Yet the growing economic interactions and burgeoning trade when in one hand ensured prosperity of the local participants, both large and small, they hardly acted as a mode of unity among them. In a way the international relations of East Asia remained transactional in character lacking the urge for genuine regional unity. And the main reason behind this failure is the continuation of the inter-state sovereignty disputes. Such political disputes now mingled with the economic requirements of the emerging regional economies who are now hungry of resources to sustain their economic growth. And the most significant trend observed among the disputants is their rising military expenditure, with their burgeoning economy, in order to 'prepare themselves for any adverse situation'. As Robert Kaplan says, "It is the very steepness of Asia's economic rise from the 1970s through the first decade of the twenty-first century that causes its leaders *to pound their chests militarily*."[1] Such a tendency is more noticed, apart from China, among the maritime Southeast Asian states, the disputants of the South China Sea. On the other hand the rising economic clout of the region further pulls in extra regional powers shaping a new form of geopolitics in the South China Sea region in the new millennium.

With the economic prosperity gaining priority in the fiscal policies of the South China Sea littoral states and China, the importance of the sea lane and the disputed territories of the Sea also gained importance. The safety of the passage is important for all the disputants, and even to the outsiders, which we will discuss in details subsequently, since it is the only maritime route they have to contact with the world outside. China surpassed Japan to become number one user of the Malacca Straits.[2] Also the resources lying underneath the Sea and around the claimed islands are also important for the resource hungry economies like China and other disputants. There are also rich fisheries resources and it is believed that there are huge oil and gas reserves beneath the sea bed. According to a much publicized Chinese study, the South China Sea could hold as much as 213 billion barrels of oil, or equivalent to 80 per cent of Saudi Arabia's known reserves. The British Petroleum (BP) estimated that the entire region (of South China Sea) may contain 2 quadrillion cubic feet of natural gas which is five times more than the known reserves of Latin America.[3] Thus the importance of the entire sea, and not just the islands, to resource hungry China, and others, is understandable. China has been hunting for energy since the 1990 because her inland oil reserves at Daqing was becoming insufficient as a supply source given the rising demand (for resources) after the new economic policies unveiled by Deng Xiaoping.[4] Therefore, since the beginning of the post-Cold War period, China has been concentrating on the usage of the South China Sea as the potential source of energy. Thus we have seen the growing assertiveness of China in the disputed islands and their vicinity throughout the 1990s. On the other hand the South China Sea became important for China as the sole maritime lane of communication with the western Asia, especially the Gulf region which is the main oil supplier to China. China imports 80 per cent of her crude oil through South China Sea. As a result South China Sea grew in strategic importance to China by the turn of the new century while the 'chest pounding' of Beijing with her military prowess growing also got reflected in her South China Sea strategy. And in this way China plays a major role in the twenty-first century geopolitics of South China Sea.

China being a dissatisfied and revisionist country has traditionally opted for military solution to any dispute, irrespective of her own military capacity. This was well articulated during the Korean War when a new born weak regime in Beijing, still struggling hard to pull China out of the decades of devastating civil war, compounded by the World War II, took an adventurous step to fight the mighty US forces at her doorstep.[5] And today standing on a strong economic base with disputes to solve, it is natural for her to strengthen herself militarily. Moreover, a state hunting for her 'rightful place' in the world and herself experiencing the enthroning of a revolutionary regime at home via bloodshed will naturally build up herself militarily being convinced of the global rivalry for power. Also, the affection of the Chinese leaders, both military and civil, with the *Art of War* (ancient Chinese literature on universal war technique) written by Sun Zi is noteworthy which is considered as superior Chinese contribution to the history of strategic thought.[6] The dissatisfaction of the Chinese leadership with the international system at the dawn of the twenty-first century was evident from the Chinese Defence White Paper of 2000 which stated,

> "...in today's world, factors that may cause instability and uncertainty have markedly increased. The world is far from peaceful. There is a serious disequilibrium in the relative strength of countries. No fundamental change has been made in the old, unfair and irrational international political and economic order. Hegemonism and power politics still exist and are developing further in the international political, economic and security spheres. Certain big powers are pursuing "neo-interventionism," "neo-gunboat policy" and neo-economic colonialism, which are seriously damaging the sovereignty, inde-pendence and developmental interests of many countries, and threat-ening world peace and security."[7]

Clearly China was frustrated with the international order directed by USA. The end of the Cold War, although reduced the US interests in the East Asian, especially Southeast Asian, scene, however, did not vanish the lone super power from China's neighbourhood. China was upset with the emerging geopolitical scenario of the larger Asia Pacific at the turn of the new millennium. Her 2000 defence paper expressed Beijing's disgust with the scenario in the following words:

> "There are new negative developments in the security of the Asia-Pacific region. The United States is further strengthening its military presence and bilateral military alliances in this region.... Encroachments on China's sovereignty and interests in the South China Sea are not infrequent, and some extra-regional countries are attempting to interfere in this issue."[8]

Given this regional situation, the Chinese leadership, in the 2000 Defence White Paper, emphasized on defending state sovereignty, unity, territorial integrity and security as the main aspects of China's defence policy in the new millennium and even vowed to enhance China's capability 'to defend its sovereignty and security by military means'.[9] Some might view the emphasis on defence of territorial integrity in relation to China's Taiwan policy, but given the revisionist character of the Chinese state and the intransigent attitude of the leadership in Beijing towards the South China Sea territorial sovereignty dispute, it won't be a mistake to consider the reference of territorial sovereignty in respect of South China Sea as well. Moreover, the developing Chinese interests in the Mahanian theory of sea power with the growing importance of the maritime neighbourhood in China's 'rise', economic as well as strategic, is equally remarkable. The Chinese defence White Paper *China's National Defense* 2004 directed the PLA-Navy to build new warships, especially amphibious vessels, to acquire special purpose aircraft and insisted on the maximum use of precision weaponry and information technology.[10] The command of the sea became vital for China since the end of the Cold War with the commerce taking place of conflict. The post-Cold War world catered to China the opportunity to enhance her economic strength by integrating with the emerging East Asian economy, especially Southeast Asia, as we have discussed in the previous chapter. Also, with economy booming, China became more and more energy hungry, desperate to ensure unhindered energy supply, especially oil from the Gulf. Thus the security of the sea lanes of South China Sea was vital for her. However, the presence of USA in the vicinity with the growing interests among the small and medium local powers of the South China Sea region to re-engage USA, amidst the growing military prowess of China with her resultant assertive posture, kept the Chinese suspicious about the unhindered supply of the resources. Also, the rich natural resources like oil and gas lying underneath South China Sea was an added attraction, facilitated by the absence of formidable challengers like USA, which influenced the strategy makers in Beijing. Control of oil and gas provides power which ensures security, from both external and internal threats, required for stability and prosperity.[11] Therefore, China's aspiration to have control over the resources of South China Sea, plus the supply from the Gulf, both are important for her prosperity which will enhance her power catering to her regional as well as global aspirations in the long term. However, the reappearance of US in the South China Sea challenges the regional aspiration of the 'Middle Kingdom'. All these made the command of the sea, following Mahan's hundred years old advice, essential for China.

China's naval strategy has evolved over the time. Initially, the naval priority was the coastal defence or the 'near coast defense' (*jiñan fangyu*) till the mid 1980s followed by 'near seas active defense' (*jinhai jiji fangyu*) after mid-1980s and then 'far seas operations' (*yuanhai zuozhan)* by mid-2000s.[12] The naval strategy has evolved from the limitation of coastal defence to the expansion in the large ocean beyond over the decades. Such evolution was part of the changing character of the geostrategic and security concerns of Chinese leadership since the inception of the communist rule in 1949. Initially, in the 1950s and 1960s, one of the concerns of the mainland China's authority was the reunification with the Taiwan Island. It should be remembered that the communist leadership of China considers Taiwan as an incomplete chapter of China's post-revolution territorial set up. The case has worsened further for China with the conclusion of special relations between Taiwan and USA under the Taiwan Relations Act (mentioned in the previous chapter). The Chinese leadership wants to convince the world that Taiwan is an integral part of China and the reunification of Taiwan with mainland China is the 'sacred mission' for the Chinese people.[13] Thus the initial naval strategy of coastal defence included the concern for Taiwan and its reunification case. However, given the lack of naval potential, it was difficult for mainland China to launch an attack on Taiwan. On the contrary the leadership was concerned about possible coastal invasion by the Kuomintang forces based in Taiwan.[14] So initially the Chinese naval strategy was defensive in character. With the introduction of the near-seas defence strategy in the late 1980s which entrusted the PLA-Navy (PLAN) with the larger duty to defend larger sea areas or the 'near seas' of China. The main purpose of the 'near seas' defence strategy was to reunite Taiwan, restore the disputed maritime territories, protect China's maritime resources and sea-lanes of communications (SLOCs) during war time and to defend against foreign aggression. On the other hand, the Taiwan Straits Crisis of 1996 convinced the Chinese planners the need to establish local sea-control for sea-crossing and amphibious operations.[15] Thus, with time the priority of the PLAN also altered and its periphery of actions expanded.

Map 5.1: China's Near Seas Zone

It was in the beginning of the new century that Chinese leadership looked beyond the Taiwan Island as a zone of activities of PLAN. President Hu Jintao's emphasis in 2004 on expanded role of the PLA safeguarding China's expanding national interests and ensuring world peace catered new roles for the PLAN. The mission broadened the security parameter of China to include new geographic and functional areas beyond the traditional territorial security missions of PLA which would prepare PLAN for new roles beyond Taiwan like safeguarding China's SLOCs.[16] China's Defence White Paper 2004 emphasized on the development of the operational strength 'with priority given to the Navy, Air Force and Second Artillery Force....'.[17] The defence white papers of 2006 and 2008 also highlighted missions outside the traditional sphere. The 2008 paper even uttered China's intention to gradually develop capabilities to operate in the 'open ocean'.[18] Thus we see that the PLAN has been expanding its focus further away from the coastal China into the ocean. As the Chinese economy expanded, the demand for resources also shot up while the growing commercial connections with the outside world were also enhanced, all making the 'near seas' important for China whose security became more and more important for Beijing. As the map above shows the near seas are the opening maritime route of China to the world beyond her coasts. Thus the importance of the PLAN increased with the increasing significance of the SLOCs via South China Sea.

There was another side of the naval strategy vis-à-vis South China Sea. It should be remembered that compared to the naval strength of China, the navies of the South China Sea littorals are weak and ill-prepared to combat any major adversary. Also, the economies of the littoral states are incapable to promote any major naval build up. So, it is prudent and logical for China to exploit the situation to gain upper hands in the naval competition in order to turn the South China Sea geostrategic ambience in her favour. This is a situation (or an opportunity) in contrast to what China encounters in Northeast Asia, where she has similar territorial dispute with Japan in the East China Sea. Since Japanese economy has been powerful and the fact that she enjoys US protection under a defence treaty with US and the latter's bases stationed on Japanese soil, China has lesser chance to direct the East China Sea geopolitics. Also, given the history of Japanese 'imperialism' in the early twentieth century subjugating China and rest of East Asia, too much aggressiveness of Beijing might provoke Tokyo to embark on similar militarization policy again which is undesirable for China. South China Sea is thus a better option, although China's 'Near Seas' zone covers, as we see in Map 5.1, both East and South China Seas.

The Nine-Dash Line

The one of the most important developments of the twenty-first century South China Sea geopolitics is the submission of the *note verbale* in the United Nations (UN) in 2009 by China claiming the 'indisputable sovereignty right and jurisdiction' over the South China Sea waters and islands in response to a Submission by Vietnam and Malaysia urging for expansion of their maritime territories in the southern South China Sea. This was for the first time when the rivals, China and Vietnam, were making their case at an international forum. Along with the letter, Chinese Government attached a map with 'U-shaped line' denoting the areas which fall within the Chinese territorial jurisdiction, as claimed by China. It is seen that in the map China claims the entire South China Sea.

The submission of the *note verbale* was in response to the joint submission of Malaysia and Vietnam to the Commission on the Limits of the Continental Shelf (under UN) on 6th May 2009. The Joint Submission by the two littoral states of South China Sea, which were referred to as 'coastal States', informed the Commission regarding the unresolved

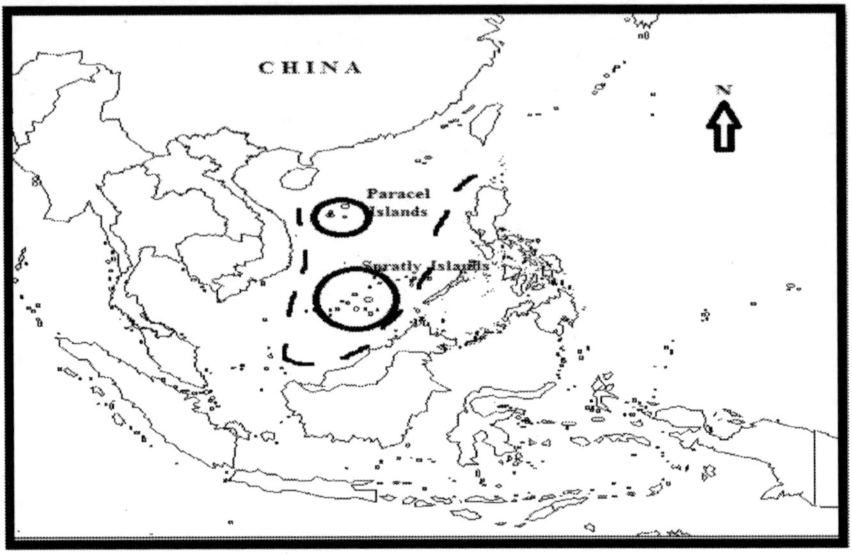

Map 5.2: China's Nine-Dash Line map of South China Sea

disputes in the 'Defined Area' that is the continental shelf 'which is entirely landward of the outer edge of the two coastal States continental margin'.[19] In this Submission both sides sought to extend their continental shelves into the South China Sea beyond 200 nautical miles.[20] The Submission requested the Commission to 'establish the limits of the continental shelf appurtenant to Malaysia and Socialist Republic of Vietnam *beyond 200 nautical miles* from their baselines from which the breadth of their respective territorial seas is measured in respect of the southern part of the South China Sea...'.[21] Following this submission, China filed a *note verbale* on the following day (7th May, 2009) to the same Commission which declared, "China has the indisputable sovereignty over the islands in the South China Sea and the adjacent waters, and enjoys sovereign rights and jurisdiction over the relevant waters as well as the seabed and subsoil thereof (see attached map)."[22] She also insisted that the above mentioned Submission by Vietnam "has seriously infringed China's sovereignty, sovereign rights and jurisdiction in the South China Sea" and requested the Commission "*not* to consider the Submission by the Socialist Republic of Viet Nam."[23] What is notable here is that in spite of the fact that the Submission was a joint endeavour of Vietnam and Malaysia, China only mentioned Vietnam in her note. This can be interpreted in terms of the Sino-Vietnam traditional bilateral tensions and the occasional frictions that both sides experienced since 1974 in the South China Sea. On the other hand Malaysia has always kept a low profile in placing her claims in the disputed waters and never chose to confront China openly. China, already occupied in dealing with Vietnam and the Philippines, also must have been reluctant to open a new front with Malaysia over the issue. This must have helped Malaysia to dodge the Chinese radar. China perhaps considered Vietnam a bigger challenge than Malaysia and China had reason to think so given the growing closeness between Hanoi and Washington. It should be remembered here that Vietnam holds the record of entertaining big powers like Soviet Union in the past to counter China. However, the attached map with the diplomatic note triggered confusion concerning whether the term 'relevant waters' refers to the EEZs and continental shelf of the islands claimed by China or the entire water areas marked within the 'U-shaped line'. It was suspected that China would claim the entire area with islands and waters as her historical territory.[24] Chinese foreign ministry however, clarified to the embassies, but only behind the closed doors, that China claims only the land features and the adjacent EEZs.[25] Thus China avoided making her stand official and public.

It is mention worthy here that China's Kuomintang regime, during its last phase of rule, internally circulated an atlas in 1947 showing eleven-dash line to mark the area of authority of China over South China Sea. Later in 1953 two dashes were removed by the new communist regime in Beijing reducing the line to nine-dashes. By this, China excluded the Tonkin Gulf between China and northern Vietnam. This was an attempt, according to Bill Hayton, to favour the 'brother Communists' of Vietnam who were fighting for independence (during that time against the French colonizers).[26] The Chinese map of the South China Sea submitted to the UN Commission with nine dash lines comprise islands, waters and other features of the Sea. The line encircles some 2,000,000 square miles of maritime area of the South China Sea which equal to 22 per cent of China's land area. The dashes denoted in the map are not uniform but are separated from one another by 106 and 274 nautical miles. Also the lines are drawn close to the mainland coasts and coastal islands of the South China Sea littorals.[27] Definitely the drawing of the dashes in close proximity to the coasts and islands of the South China Sea claimants establish the uncompromising attitude of the Chinese Government regarding its claim over the area. Also the maritime area mentioned within the 9 dash lines actually symbolizes the Chinese aspiration of over lordship over her maritime neighbourhood. This also serves the strategic purpose of China to strengthen her military capability as a pretext of safeguarding her 'territorial sovereignty' in the entire South China Sea maritime zone amidst the claims of other littoral states. Maritime lawyers underline that Beijing routinely outlines the scope of its claims in the South China Sea with reference to the so-called nine-dashed line that takes in about 90 percent of the 3.5 million square kilometer South China Sea on Chinese maps. However it is difficult for Beijing to substantiate its nine-dash line conclusion even when it possesses historical evidences about its territorial links with the islands and reefs of the Sea.[28] Therefore the nine-dash line can be treated as an ascribed phenomenon of the Chinese claims. Even the Chinese themselves are not sure about the historical aspect of such claim as was evident from a report of US Embassy in Beijing that revealed that a senior Chinese government maritime law expert had "admitted" that he was unaware of the historical basis for the nine dashes. This information was delivered in response to US diplomatic cable of September 2008, as exposed by the WikiLeaks.[29]

In response to the Chinese letter on 7th May, 2009, Vietnam submitted a similar diplomatic note to UN clearly stating that, "The Hoang Sa (Paracels) and Troung Sa (Spratlys) archipelagos are parts of Viet Nam territory."[30] It also said that Vietnam has indisputable sovereignty over these archipelagos and nullified the Chinese map submitted as having 'no legal, historical and factual bases.[31] Thus both sides were now registering their respective claims officially to the UN. The actions and the reactions of both sides over the territorial disputes in the South China Sea signify the mood of the disputants determined not to compromise over the territorial gains.

The uncompromising mood of Beijing was more evident when the Chinese military emphasized on "indisputable sovereignty" over the South China Sea in 2010. The Ministry of Defence spokesman Senior Col. Geng Yansheng, said that "China has indisputable sovereignty of the South Sea, and China has sufficient historical and legal backing" to support its claims.[32] The interesting part is this that such a comment came as a response to US Secretary of State Hillary Clinton's comment that a peaceful resolution of territorial disputes over the South China Sea is in the "national interest" of the United States. She also lobbied for a multilateral solution to the question.[33] This comment she made while visiting Hanoi. *The Washington Post* commented that such a statement 'was music to Vietnam's ears'.[34] Certainly the smaller disputants were looking of extra-regional protection in the face of growing Chinese might.

As we have seen before, countries like Vietnam and the Philippines have been re-engaging USA in the latter half of the 1990s as was evident from the conclusion of the Visiting Forces Agreement (VFA) between Washington and Manila in 1999. And this did not please China who now was getting more assertive with her claims. The growing assertiveness on the part of Beijing over the sovereignty issue in the South China Sea at the beginning of the new century can also be seen as a response to the growing possibility of US reengagement in the South China Sea affairs.

Meanwhile, there were reports that China called South China Sea disputes as one of her 'core interests' during a private meeting with the US officials in March 2010 and a US official said that the term 'core priority' and not 'core interest' was used by the Chinese. However, the refusal of the Chinese officials to negate the rumour, apart from the rising of the speculation itself, added to the concern of the growing assertiveness of the Chinese.[35] The Chinese have never been clear with their policies and they love to keep them under the veil. The term 'core interest' is important in the context of China since the Chinese use this term in reference to the more uncomfortable issues of the Chinese authority—Tibet, Xinjiang and Taiwan. But the Chinese researchers opine that China has not taken the South China Sea dispute to the level of Taiwan to call the former 'core interest'.[36] Certainly the Taiwan issue is much closer to China since it is the sole trace of defeat of mighty communist force who failed to annex the island after establishing its rule over the vast mainland and has got determinant day-by-day to complete the task. Comparatively, South China Sea dispute has been less serious an issue for them. Moreover, China knows she needs to prepare herself militarily with the geopolitical ambience of the region turning to her favour in order to act decisively. Also, there are many other claimants to counter, unlike in case of Taiwan. And in the turn of the century they all are becoming formidable challenge.

The challenge is not in the external field only since the leadership in Beijing has to cope with the internal pressure also to act on the South China Sea issue, sometimes aggressively.

Internal actors and obligations of China affecting her South China Sea policy

China's assertiveness in the South China Sea is mainly seen in the light of the revisionist character of the Chinese state. However, the Chinese decision is sometimes directed by the domestic compulsions also. There are many back-screen actors in China who act as pressure groups directing China's policy.

A close study of the South China Sea politics vis-à-vis China will show that China's activities in the disputed waters are also directed by pressure groups and sometimes are result of provincial governments' policies. There are several actors whose interest are more directly linked with the South China Sea and therefore are more interested in securing China's jurisdiction over the Sea. These actors include Fisheries Administration, China Marine Surveillance, the local governments, PLA-Navy (PLAN) and the foreign ministry.[37] Sometimes, these actors' activities are independent of the direction from the central government seated in Beijing whose actions may not reflect Beijing's strategy but the central leadership sometime has to bear the responsibility. This is so since some of these actors, as we shall see, possess forces who implement the strategies of the local governments, sometimes not approved by the central leadership. Apart from them, the national oil companies of China like China National Petroleum Corporation (CNPC), China Petroleum Corporation (Sinopec) and China National Corporation (CNOOC) also contribute in directing China's South China Sea policy.[38]

Bureau of Fisheries Administration

The Bureau of Fisheries Administration of the agriculture ministry is entrusted with the duty of law enforcement in the maritime zone of China including the disputed territory. The Chinese Fisheries Law Enforcement Command, apart from regulating the domestic fishing industry, also ensures protection to the fishing vessels and restricts, and if necessary repulses, the approaching of the foreign vessels near the claimed territories in the maritime zone. In the past, the Command was used in occupying the Mischief Reef by China.[39] Thus it is seen that the Bureau is empowered to maintain forces to smoothen its maritime activities of fishery and the South China Sea is rich in fishery resources. The Bureau has the South Sea Region Fisheries Administration Bureau in charge of South China Sea which it oversees with the South Sea Fisheries Law Enforcement Command. This Command has been involved in clashes with The Philippines and Vietnam. Previously working under the provincial level administration under the State Council and the Central Military Commission, the Command was taken over by the agriculture ministry in 1984.[40] It is to be noted here that it was in the 1980s that the South China Sea started featuring as an important aspect of Chinese economic policy when the PLA was also concentrating on its naval empowerment and strategy. The Fisheries Command have been equipping itself with patrol vessels and even decommissioned military vessels from the PLAN upgraded for fishery control mission while the passage of EEZ law by China in 1998 has enhanced the importance of the command which has increased its patrols and even escort the fishing boats to the disputed Spratly Islands.[41]

China Marine Surveillance

The China Marine Surveillance, another maritime law enforcement agency of China, is conducted by the State Oceanic Administration. One of the duties of the Administration is to defend sovereignty of China's claimed maritime area. The State Oceanic Administration had been involved in the South China Sea affairs in the 1970s and 1980s to explore the feasibility of establishing observation posts and set up the Marine Surveillance in 1998. Since 2001 the defence of China's claims in the South China Sea has become a priority and it has started conducting regular patrols in the disputed waters around China, including South China Sea, since 2008. The agency has been involved in several incidents at the Sea in 2009 like clashing with Vietnamese forces and also with USNS *Impeccable* while it was also involved in the Sino-Philippines standoff in the Scarborough Reef in 2012.[42] In April 2012 a Filipino vessel was engaged in a standoff with Chinese surveillance ships in the South China Sea. The Philippines said its warship tried to arrest Chinese fishermen anchored at the Scarborough Shoal, but was blocked by the two surveillance boats. The Philippines' Ministry of Foreign Affairs stated that the naval vessel, the Gregorio Del Pilar, found eight Chinese fishing vessels at the shoal when it was patrolling the area. The Chinese ships arrived immediately. And this was the time when Manila was preparing for a joint naval exercise with USA near the disputed area.[43]

Provincial governments

China is a regime with one party system. The Chinese Communist Party is the sole governing entity of the country with no recognized opposition party. There is a general perception that in such system the decision taken at the top of the structure is followed and implemented by the rest, including the local governments, without any expression of disagreement, let alone contradiction. In case of the South China Sea dispute, the activities of China in the disputed waters are generally seen as the act of the leadership sitting in Beijing implemented by its forces at the borders. However, in respect to the coastal areas of China, like in Hainan, Guangdong and Guangxi, the governments of the respective provinces play a distinct role in fomenting the South China Sea dispute. The coastlines are very important for China's economic wellbeing. And it is all the more important for the economic growth of the provinces which is promoted by the local governments. For example, the Chinese government announced in 2009 that it would convert Hainan into 'an international resort destination, on par with Hawaii' by 2020. Besides, Hainan is the largest of all the economic zones of China.[44] As we have mentioned earlier, the open-door policy of China in the 1980s emphasized on the economic development of the coastal areas. Four special economic zones of China, three open cities and two open areas border South China Sea which are important for the coastal development project of China and also to promote the maritime trade.[45] On the other hand, the local governments are eager to expand their economic activities, like fisheries and tourism, into the disputed areas of South China Sea even with possibility of confrontation in order to promote their provinces' GDP growth to facilitate the political system.[46] The provincial governors in China are equal in authority to the ministers and their governments enjoy considerable freedom of action in handling local issues with the help of the local law enforcement forces. Sometimes, their actions create unfavourable outcomes for the central authority, especially in respect to dealing with the neighbouring countries.[47] This is so because the coastal provinces and the islands governments have direct access to the adjacent waters and clashes are inevitable if the water's jurisdiction is disputed like in case of South China Sea where the Hainan provincial government is most active, theoretically governing Paracel and Spratly Islands and their surrounding waters since the province's establishment in 1988. The Hainan government has repeatedly attempted to establish a governing body in these islands or develop them as high-end tourism industry.[48] The authority of Hainan over the disputed islands of South China Sea is declared in the official website of the Hainan provincial government which reads: "The Hainan Province administers three cities, 16 counties, as well as the islands and reefs of the Xisha Islands, Nansha Islands and Zhongsha Islands and seawaters around them."[49]

Chinese Navy

The navy is supposed to perform the duty of protecting the country from any maritime aggression and play primary role in forwarding any maritime claims of the country. However, the People's Liberation Army-Navy or PLAN seems to perform secondary role in forwarding the South China Sea claims of China. It is said that since 2005, the PLAN has not been directly involved in any clash with other claimants in the troubled waters even though it has been engaged in the patrolling of the waters. On the contrary, when clashes take place, the PLAN chooses to refrain from interfering and allows the civilian law enforcing and paramilitary forces to do its job.[50] Therefore, it is seen that only the civilian law enforcing agencies have 'defended the sovereignty claims' of China in the South China Sea. To an extent the usage of paramilitary forces can be seen as a welcome alternative to military force since while they perform the functions of the conventional navy, these forces are seen as less threatening. There can also be another explanation to this strategy of the Chinese leadership. The South China Sea is claimed by China in almost its entirety. Therefore, using of the civilian and paramilitary forces, instead of the navy, in dealing with the challenges in this 'internal' water body of China bolsters China's sovereignty claims since navy is used normally in external confrontation. Also, the non-involvement of the navy relieves the central leadership in Beijing of bearing the blame of 'stirring up troubles' in the region directly on its shoulders. However, the comparative freedom of exercises by the local governments and concerned authorities to act according to their respective interests, with forces available at hand, also adds to the trouble.

Nevertheless, the Chinese leadership, as we have discussed already, has invested in strengthening the PLAN. The South Sea Fleet of the PLAN is the strongest with advanced fleet destroyers. To facilitate the Fleet, the Yulin Naval Base in Sanya, Hainan has been expanded to include underground facilities for growing number of nuclear and conventional submarines.[51] Sanya is on the southern coast of Hainan island and faces the South China Sea. The Chinese nuclear submarine base in Hainan has always been a matter of concern for all China-wary countries in the region and outside. In 2008 *The Telegraph* reported that China has secretly built underground nuclear submarine base opining that it could 'threaten Asian countries and challenge American power in the region'.[52] It is said that the development so close to the sea lanes vital to Asian economies "can only cause concern far beyond these straits".[53] The Telegraph also said that the location of the base off Hainan will also give the submarines access to very deep water exceeding 5,000 metres within a few miles, making them even harder to detect.[54] Thus, the Chinese central authority was not solely depending on the forces of its local provinces to defend its South China Sea claims but was simultaneously preparing its national forces for future use.

The Maritime Safety Administration, under the transport ministry, is another law enforcement agency of China which plays a major management role in the South China Sea. It is responsible to ensure smooth operation in the sea lanes of communication by conducting anti-piracy operations. Between 2006 and 2010 the force, which aspires to play bigger role in the South China Sea affairs, has acquired three large vessels of 1000 tonnes with helicopters.[55] Hainan Maritime Safety Administration launched a patrol (in the South China Sea) on Sept. 25 (2015) in which seaplanes and cruising vessels both participated.[56]

Apart from these forces, there are others like the pressure groups who play their part in keeping the South China Sea issue alive in the Chinese leadership's policy. The national oil companies like China National Petroleum Corporation (CNPC), China Petroleum Corporation (Sinopec) and China National Corporation (CNOOC) also contribute in directing China's South China Sea policy. CNOOC wants the Chinese central government to fund and approve energy exploitation in the disputed waters since, according to them, such actions would buttress China's sovereignty claims there. However, Beijing has been unwilling to support them.[57] In 2008, the CNOOC declared to invest $32 billion over ten to twenty years in developing South China Sea which it declared as a 'priority'. At the National People's Congress the CNOOC delegate urged the government for financial support and insisted to enhance the policy as an urgent task since the other claimants are engaged in 'predatory exploitation' in the Chinese waters.[58] On the other hand the National Tourism Administration, which is responsible for promoting tourism sector of China, promotes tourism to South China Sea islands as demand for such visits rises in the domestic circle of China. The central government of China also promotes such role of the Tourism Administration since it bolsters the sovereignty claims.[59]

Thus we see that there are many actors in the South China Sea activities and policies of China which are not the exclusive jurisdiction of the communist leadership sitting in Beijing. It can be termed as a mixture of strategy and compulsion where the central leadership sometimes is under pressure from the oil companies to act assertively while in most of the cases, related to the skirmishes in the sea, it is the local forces of the provincial governments or agencies responsible to perform functions of safeguarding respective interests which trigger tensions for which the central government is not directly responsible. On the other hand it can also be a strategy of the government in Beijing to let the local authorities to carry on with their mission to safeguard their interest, sometime resulting to clashes which they handle with their law enforcing forces while keeping the PLAN, directly under the central military command, aloof. On the other hand there seems to be consistent pressure from the oil companies who want the government to act fast given the growing activities of the other claimants in the disputed waters. They themselves have been involved in the exploitation activities already. Among the leading oil companies of China, CNPC, CNOOC and Sinopec are termed as 'three buckets of oil'. These National Oil Companies (NOCs) have their top executives, who are also the party cadres, appointed by the central Organization Department of the Chinese Communist Party.[60] Thus the exploration in the South China Sea cannot be done without the approval of the central party authority providing policy support. Such approval from the central leadership comes as China goes richer, powerful and hungry for energy resources. That the Chinese leadership is emphasizing on similar exploration mission is evident from the Twelfth Five Year Plan for the Development of National Strategic Emerging Industries of 2012 issued by the State Council declaring the goal of obtaining indigenous capability for the design and manufacture of deep-water resource exploitation equipment by 2015.[61] Thus as Chinese economy gets stronger, the central leadership also gets assertive about the requirements to address the growing needs of resources even from the disputed regions.

Ministry of Foreign Affairs irrelevant?

We have seen so far the role the other actors, apart from the foreign ministry of China, have been playing in the South China Sea policy of Beijing when China has to counter other countries in dealing with the affair which directly falls within the jurisdiction of the country's foreign ministry. The question then arises what role the foreign ministry plays in the affair. However, the Ministry of Foreign Affairs (MFA) is not the supreme player in the South China Sea affairs since other players perform significantly in the scene. Sometimes their authority is equal to that of the MFA enjoying relevance and autonomy and they, considering themselves equal to that of the foreign ministry, resent being advised and coordinated by the MFA. The local actors do not inform the MFA about their activities claiming that the bureaucrats in the ministry do not understand the situation on the ground. Also, the domestic issues like economic growth and political stability, being prioritized over the foreign affairs, also promote the role of the actors directly concerned with the issues thereby reducing the significance of the MFA in the leadership role. As the Chinese economy has grown over the years the domestically oriented agencies (dealing with economic affairs), like commerce ministry, finance ministry, state security ministry and National Development and Reform Commission, have gained additional foreign powers declining the relevance of the MFA.[62] This is natural because as China prioritized her internal development mission related to economic prosperity and that too within a time frame, the agencies dealing with it will certainly get priority. The external affair always comes second to internal affairs. Moreover, it is unnatural that China will consider the South China Sea issue an external affair exclusively since she considers the disputed islands and the adjacent waters as her own territory and therefore referring it to MFA is illogical to her.

On the other hand sometimes the handling of the affair by the PLA makes the issue all the more complicated for the MFA. The Central Military Commission is equal in status to the State Council (a political body) while the MFA falls below it. Neither the military directly report to the Politburo about nor the MFA has any access to such information. This is all the more important since the military plays significant role in the formulation of China's international role in general and the South China Sea in particular. Sometimes, the MFA has to rely on the Western reports about the PLAN's activities in the South China Sea.[63] The PLA has traditionally held sway in China's foreign policy matters related to defence, particularly with respect to policies related to strategic arms, territorial disputes and national security.[64] The military is now relieved of the political duty of spreading the political teachings of Marxism and communism and it is no more entitled to export revolution to other countries. It is now 'depoliticised'. Chinese leadership now makes the conventional use of the military, practised in all other countries, that is to promote the national interests. Day-by-day as the Chinese economy flourishes the need for resources as well as unhindered navigation through her maritime neighbourhood also becomes important and given the fact that the ambience of cooperation does not exist in the neighbourhood, China will certainly look for military option to ward off any challenge to her national interests. This makes the PLA, especially PLAN, all the more important for the Chinese leadership. Thus with economic power soaring, money will be funnelled into the military and will be allocated on the basis of priority. The military modernization is the result of such mission. Such growing importance to of the PLA will no doubt reduce the importance of the MFA.

Therefore we see that the Chinese policy towards South China Sea is not mere expression of hunger for power and the urge for dominance of neighbourhood but a result of many factors directly related to the internal economic policy of the country. The Chinese leadership in the capital acquiesce to the demands of the different pressure groups and even grant them free hand to act independently firstly because their policies are in tandem with the overall economic prosperity of the country and secondly, the involvement of the provincial law enforcement actors in the confrontations save the national military, and thereby the central leadership, from bearing the blame directly on their shoulders. The engagement of the PLAN might invite the big powers involvement in the region which China currently wants to avoid. However, the PLAN is not aloof from the affair. Over the past several years the PLAN has stretched out its presence in South China Sea. China has increased the rate of her presence missions in the area by both surface and sub-surface vessels. Apart from developing bases at Sanya in Hainan Island (located in the north of South China Sea) in 2007, China has also expanded her facilities in the Paracels (especially in Woody Islands) and in the Spratlys. According to Chinese media, PLA regularly conducts integrated exercises over South China Sea whose size and sophistication has increased since 2010.[65] Several high-ranking officers of the Chinese Navy have urged the government to promote scope for building military infrastructure in the disputed islands.[66]

The case of the other claimants

Like China, other claimants of the South China Sea territorial sovereignty are also getting assertive since the dawn of the new century. In the last few years countries like Vietnam and the Philippines, the traditional contenders, have risen their voice against the 'Chinese expansionism' in South China Sea while others like Indonesia and Malaysia, who have maintained low profile so long, have also started appearing in the scene.

Vietnam is the forerunner in challenging China in the South China Sea. As we have seen so far the Sino-Vietnam tension has directed the mode of the South China Sea geopolitics since 1975, after the unification of Vietnam. Even after the Cold War was over the Sino-Vietnam rivalry continued and it complicated further with the Vietnamese economy flourishing and her hunger for resources increasing, just like China. However, it should be mentioned here that China had a significant contribution in thriving the Vietnamese economy in the initial days. Since 1990 both sides have been engaged in confidence building measures which included border agreement with China. When Russia relinquished Cam Ranh Bay in 2002, Hanoi assured Beijing that the Bay would be used only for commercial, and not military, purposes. Appeasing and assuring Beijing became the top priority of the then Vietnamese leadership.[67] China granted loans to promote Vietnam's agricultural and industrial sectors.[68] However, Hanoi remained anxious about Beijing's consistent objection to any joint exploration endeavour between Vietnam and any other country in the South China Sea warning 'unspecified consequences'.[69] Nevertheless, South China Sea, which Vietnamese call 'East Sea', is equally important for Vietnam's economic development. It has important maritime trade routes connecting Northeast Asia and Southeast Asia. It is also the shortest shipping route from the Pacific to the Indian Ocean (for the Vietnamese and for the rest).The *East Sea* is the 'adjusting valve' for trade flow, especially oil from the Middle East (West Asia).[70]

Since the introduction of the economic reforms called *Doi Moi* initiative in the mid-1980s, the Vietnamese leadership has been interested in maintaining status quo in the neighbourhood to promote the country's economic development. For this, Hanoi overhauled its foreign policy towards diversification and multilateralisation to create conducive ambience in the neighbourhood helpful for its economic development. As a part of this mission, Vietnam initiated process of concluding boundary agreements with her neighbours in the South China Sea. In June 1992 Vietnam signed agreement with Malaysia for joint development of the area of overlapping continental shelf claims in the south-west of Vietnam and in 2000 signed an agreement with China on maritime boundaries and an agreement on fishery cooperation in the Gulf of Tonkin (north-east of South China Sea). In 2003 she inked an agreement with Indonesia on delimiting the continental shelf boundary north of the Natuna Islands (claimed by Indonesia).[71] These initiatives of Hanoi were meant to clear the ambience of the tensions in the neighbourhood which could impede the economic mission of post-Cold War Vietnam. During the *Doi Moi* period, Vietnam started putting emphasis on her maritime areas under her jurisdiction. Vietnam assumed to be possessing 1 million square kilometres of the sea area under the UNCLOS (United Nations Law of the Sea).[72]

As the economic development mission got priority the maritime zone became important for Vietnam. South China Sea is the only maritime opening for the country to the rest of the world. It is the only maritime trade route Vietnam has to head towards the Pacific and the Indian Ocean. Besides, Vietnam's 3,000 kilometres coastline and thousands of islands offer natural advantages for aquaculture, shipbuilding and sea tourism.[73] Strategically also South China Sea is important for Vietnam. The Cam Ranh Bay, Danang and other important locations are situated on the South China Sea shore which played an important role in containing China against Vietnam during the Cold War with the presence of the Soviet Navy, as we have already discussed before. The 8th National Party Congress of the Vietnamese Communist Party stated in 1996 that, "The maritime and the coastal areas, which are strategically important in terms of economy, security and defense. These areas have advantages for economic development and serve as the gate for the country to connect with the world and main attraction for foreign investments."[74] Thus the South China Sea got intertwined with the economic prosperity and security of Vietnam in the post-Cold War period.

Not only in terms of connectivity, South China Sea is an important source of natural resources and livelihood for the Vietnamese as well. It was estimated that seas around Vietnam (which is South China Sea) hold a reserve of 1.2 billion barrels of oil equivalent, fish stock of 2,744,900 tons (allowable catch of 1,372,400 tons) and a great deal of other resources.[75] Also, the fishery reserves of the Sea are important source of livelihood of the Vietnamese fishermen community. It is said that with the depleting sources of fish stock in the nearby shore the Vietnamese fishermen are compelled to sail deep into the sea beyond the EEZ of Vietnam into the disputed waters of the Paracel Islands which has triggered clashes in the recent years.[76] The burgeoning Vietnamese economy is hungry of resources. The soaring food prices, weakening confidence in currency and stagnating job markets are forcing the government to develop energy resources in the South China Sea to improve Vietnam's economy.[77] In September 1997 the Politburo of the Vietnamese Communist Party issued direction to industrialize and modernize Vietnam's maritime economy. This was in response to the analysis that Vietnam has not been successful in controlling her maritime domain resulting to increased violation against her national security, sovereignty and national interests while the navigational safety has become more complex. There was proposal for development of offshore fisheries and between 1997 and 2001 the government allotted US$ 94 billion for the offshore fishery programme. In 2007 the government adopted resolution on Vietnam's maritime strategy to 2020 where the main emphasis was on maritime economy which would contribute up to 53-55 per cent of Vietnam's GDP and 55-60 per cent of the country's exports by 2020.[78] Therefore we see how South China Sea emerged as an important sector in Vietnam's economic development mission by the beginning of the new century. This obviously affected the country's security strategy vis-à-vis China's policy towards the region.

As Vietnam moved ahead with her economic development mission, she became more and more assertive about her claims in the South China Sea since the safeguard of her maritime interests is important for the success of her economic mission. And this has put the country in direct clash with China. That Vietnam is uncomfortable and anxious about the challenges in the South China Sea was evident from the country's 2009 Defence White Paper which stated,

> "Concerning the disputes over sovereignty, sovereign rights and jurisdiction over the territories in the East Sea, the complicated developments so far have seriously affected many activities and the maritime economic development of Vietnam."[79]

In order to boost the economic prosperity of the country the Vietnamese leadership decided to strengthen the country's defence structure as well. The 2009 White Paper thus stated that to support the cause of industrialization and modernization and rapid sustainable economic development Vietnam has adopted the policy to concurrently develop her socio-economic and defence capabilities and coordinate defence-security and diplomatic activities.[80] Thus it is implied that the strengthening of the defence is required for the socio-economic development of the country and the country is to promote both simultaneously. Given the challenges that Vietnam faces especially in the maritime zone which is emerging as a vital aspect of the economic prosperity such dual emphasis is understandable. The White Paper further states, "Proactively preventing and repulsing the dangers of wars are among the essential tasks of Vietnam's national defence in peacetime in order to realize the optimal national defence strategy of protecting its sovereignty, unity, territorial integrity and other national interests without resorting to war fighting."[81]

It implies the emphasis of the defence policy of Vietnam to thwart any possibility of emergence of war like situation in the region which endangers the country's sovereignty and territorial integrity. This can be seen in the context of the 'expansive and assertive' activities of China in the South China Sea posing challenge to Vietnam's case of territorial sovereignty in the disputed waters. Thus the Paper emphasized on the 'whole nation's tradition of patriotism and fighting against the foreign aggression' in reference to strengthening the armed forces and developing the Vietnamese military arts to meet the demands of the modern wars by upholding the values of Vietnamese military sciences.[82] Vietnam's history is marred with the events of foreign invasion with special reference to China both in the pre-colonial as well as the modern period (1979 invasion). The Vietnamese have never been comfortable with their giant neighbour. Similar determination to counter aggression was reflected in the 2004 Defence White Paper of the country where it was said, "...Vietnam is prepared for self-defense against any action encroaching upon the territory, air-space and territorial waters, and its national interests."[83] It also emphasized on the necessity to build national defence to strengthen self defence.[84] Thus, by the beginning of the new century, Vietnam embarked on the up gradation of her military in view of challenges posed against her 'national interests'.

Citing factors like China and South China Sea the Vietnamese Defence Minister General Doan Khue said in 1996 that his country needs a modern navy to defend its territorial waters, to deploy military forces and develop marine economy.[85] The Vietnamese Coast Guard was constituted in 1998 under the Navy for maritime enforcement mission. The Coast Guard procured aircraft from Poland under an agreement signed with the country in 2003. By the beginning of 2000 the Defence Minister of the country emphasized on restructuring the armed forces spending more on technology weapon system and hinted the expansion and modernization of the navy depending on the economic strength.[86] Vietnam's defence budget grew from $910 million in 2003 to $1.327 billion in 2008. Vietnamese navy has gained the maximum of the increased budget expenses in the context of Hanoi's 'East Sea' policy.[87] For the ten years (since 2000) Vietnam's economy grew at an average annual growth rate of 7.3 per cent and 2010 the growth rate was 6.5 per cent which, according to the International Monetary Fund (IMF), was mainly due to the rise in foreign direct investment (FDI) and in 2010 the defence spending was estimated $2.3 billion.[88] In 2012, the defence spending grew to $3.3 billion which was 16.1 per cent real increase on the budget of 2011. Also in August 2012 Vietnam took the delivery of the first of three Airbus Military C-212 light transport aircraft modified for the maritime patrolling.[89]

The emphasis on the maritime zone by the Vietnam leadership was both economic and strategic in character. Safeguarding the 'national interests' can be seen in the context of the alleged 'Chinese expansion' in the South China Sea. The growing assertive stance of Beijing about its sovereignty claims in the disputed waters of South China Sea is directing the Vietnamese leadership to safeguard its sovereignty claims in the Sea. This cannot be seen as a mere economic concern even when the emphasis on the maritime zone of Vietnam is the product of the economic rejuvenation mission. No country will be comfortable with its neighbour acquiring formidable power, especially when the relation with that neighbour has traditionally been tensed. As a Vietnamese foreign ministry official said, in reference to Vietnam-China relations, "the two countries are old friends and old enemies".[90] In Vietnam there exists uneasiness about the activities of China in the South China Sea which is viewed as act of domination. This author's impression after talking to some scholars at a research centre in Hanoi in 2015 corroborates such view. In the context of the Chinese activities in the South China Sea one of the scholars opined such activities as 'Chinese aggression' against Vietnam and that this policy existed from the time of the Kuomintang regime. He suggested that China wants to dominate the entire sea, from South China Sea to East China Sea. However, due to the US' strategic alliance with Japan and South Korea and special security relations with Taiwan, China cannot intrude in the Pacific. In this situation the *East Sea* is most advantageous for Chinese expansion to realize her 'oceans outreach' given the fact that the littorals of the Sea are small countries with minimum naval capacity, according to one Vietnamese scholar.[91]

Another South China Sea littoral state most anxious about the Chinese 'expansion' in the South China Sea is **the Philippines**. Like Vietnam, the Philippines is also upgrading her defence to uphold the strength in the context of the tension with China over South China Sea dispute. As we have discussed in the previous chapter the country experienced Chinese 'aggression' in the Mischief Reef in 1999 which established the weakness and vulnerability of the Philippines naval strength against Chinese action. The Philippines was anyway weakened with the withdrawal of the US from the Subic Bay, as mentioned earlier. However, even with the umbilical cord with the US protection cut off, Manila continued its claims over the Spratlys with its forward presence in the South China Sea, which the Philippines Navy (PN) was not in a position to support. This was the reason why the Philippines could not stop the Chinese from making constructions on the Mischief Reef in the Spratly Islands in 1995, within 200 nautical miles of the her EEZ. On the other hand, China targeted the Philippines, the country being the weakest of all the claimants.[92] The 1999 tension with China necessitated the credible presence of the PN in the South China Sea. The Senate was asked to allot 7.8 billion pesos to the Navy which was earlier reserved for the Armed Forces but it could only release 5.5 billion pesos in 1999.[93] Thus the PN was very ill-prepared in the context of the challenges it faced in the South China Sea.

At the turn of the new century, the Chinese pressure in the South China Sea continued with China deploying fishing boats in January 2001 which was a test for the new government in Manila under President Gloria Macapagal-Arroyo. The new government sought a defence budget allotment of US$ 1.17 billion in 2002, a 16.5 per cent high over the 2001 allocation.[94] However, the financial challenges kept on haunting the Philippine armed forces while the country dithered between the internal and external security with the rising maritime terrorism conducted by the Abu Sayyaf Group (a domestic Islamic insurgent group) which abducted 20 people from the resort of Palawan Island on 27th May, 2001when the PN did not have any asset to counter the threat in the area.[95] Thus the Philippines was getting engaged with the domestic security challenges in the southern part of the country amidst the growing Chinese challenge in the South China Sea. Meanwhile the tension between the two countries steadily revived in 2011 after the new President Benigno Aquino III took charge of office in 2010. The previous government of Arroyo was less inclined in antagonizing China and was ready to compromise with its claims in the disputed islands. The Arroyo government even attempted an understanding of secret joint survey of large swathes of South China Sea in 2005 with China and Vietnam under the Joint Marine Seismic Undertaking (JMSU) which was seen by the new President to have 'encouraged greater Chinese forcefulness'. The publication of the understanding triggered strong protests in Manila accusing President Arroyo of 'trading Philippines' territory to China'.

The Philippine officials opine the agreement had weakened Philippines' territorial claims by giving China and Vietnam areas previously not disputed. After the JMSU expired, the Philippines started to look for hydrocarbons in her claimed areas which resulted in clashes with China in early March 2011 after China increased her patrolling vessels around Paracel and Spratly Islands. There were five skirmishes reported in the first five months of 2011.[96] Meanwhile Manila seemed to very assertive with its claims when the Filipino President declared in July 2011, "what is ours is ours".[97]

In the beginning of the second decade of the new century, the situation of the South China Sea became more complicated with the Chinese moves and counter moves of the other South China Sea littorals. In 2012, China enraged her South China Sea neighbours by reiterating her claims over the disputed islands by publishing their maps in her reprinted passports. The Xinhua news agency reported that 'it is the first map that reflects the geological information of China's Sansha City and South China Sea islands in a comprehensive, accurate and specific manner, according to a statement issued by its publisher'.[98] This shows that China is very clear in asserting her sovereignty claims over the Sea. Sansha city was developed as prefectural city in the Hainan Province to administer Xisha, Zhongsha and Nansha islands and their surrounding waters in South China Sea. This project was approved by China's State Council in June (2012).[99] No doubt this was an attempt of China to bolster her claims on the disputed islands and the adjacent waters. Such a move of China automatically triggered strong protests from other claimants. The Philippines sent a note to Chinese embassy in Manila protesting against the image while her Foreign Minister Albert del Rosario said that China's claims included an area that is "clearly part of the Philippines' territory and maritime domain". The Vietnamese government said it had also sent a diplomatic note to the Chinese embassy in Hanoi that called on Beijing to remove the "erroneous content" printed in the passport. China only reacted to the row by assuring that the map in the passport did not target any particular country.[100] Such a reaction from Beijing was expected since it is unimaginable that China would admit her 'mistake' and do the necessary rectification. However, the response from the Chinese foreign ministry was very calm and instead of asserting the 'right' of China to show any part of 'her territory' in her passport, the ministry opted for an assuring gesture to pacify the anger of the other claimants without changing the stand on the claims. Both Vietnam and the Philippines refused to stamp the new Chinese passports. This was also a counter assertive move by the disputants articulating their determination not to surrender to the 'mighty neighbour' implying that the Chinese have no scope to direct the South China Sea strategic landscape on its own.

Meanwhile, China commissioned her first aircraft carrier *Liaoning* in September 2012, a reconstructed version of *Varyag*, a Ukrainian carrier. This was a big achievement for China, longing for developing blue water navy which is a significant exhibition and achievement of maritime prowess. The aircraft carrier is not only a sign of national prestige, something the Chinese, like others especially with colonial past would be eager to earn, but also an important weapon in bolstering the naval capacity of an aspiring power in the wider maritime geostrategic arena. Given the maritime territorial disputes China has been involved in her neighbourhood, from north to south, the aircraft carrier undoubtedly added to her required naval competence. It is to be remembered that although initially the main concern behind China's naval modernization mission was Taiwan crisis with the island enjoying US protection, opting for blue water navy is part of Chinese strategy to counter US in the distant waters in the Pacific and in South China Sea region. It is reported that China is building her second carrier and wants to exert her presence in the South China Sea amidst 'provocations' from US.[101] China is not comfortable with the growing involvement of USA in the South China Sea affairs. The China Daily wrote in 2012 that Washington was using the Philippines and Vietnam 'as pawns' and prophesied that the South China Sea disputes 'are likely to evolve into a Sino-US strategic competition'.[102]

In this background China was also preparing herself. The People's Liberation Army held a series of preparedness drills in Shenyang, Jinan and established Sansha in Hainan, the city created by Beijing to oversee disputed islands in the South China Sea in January 2013. It included soldiers from the South Sea Fleet stationed on Chenhang, in the Duncan Islands group in the Paracels. Ni Lexiong, director of the sea power and defence policy research institute at Shanghai University of Political Science and Law, said that 'all the drills took place in cities along the South China and East China seas, where our maritime territorial disputes with neighbouring countries are still unresolved'.[103] This was a significant development since now China was preparing her military for any adverse situation and the inclusion of the soldiers from the Paracel islands indicates that such preparedness includes the dealing with the 'challenges' posed in the South China Sea. Another Chinese assertive move was authorization of the Chinese patrol ships in the disputed waters from January 1, 2013 and to 'board ships' alleged of 'trespassing' and force the foreign ships to change courses.[104] These patrol ships were of the border police (and not the PLA-Navy) who were authorized following a territorial law passed by the Hainan Province in November 2012 to allow actions against foreign ships illegally entering the island's sea areas. Before this in June the same year the State Council of China incorporated the resource-rich but nearly uninhabitable islands as an administrative unit known as Sansha under Hainan's administration. It includes islands known in English as the Paracel Islands, the Spratley Islands and the Macclesfield Bank, reported *Los Angeles Times*.[105]

Therefore we see that the provincial governments are also contributing in the framing of China's South China Sea policy. Such actions are anyway endorsed by the central government of China which is clear firstly from the annexation of the islands by the central State Council of China and also by the backing of enactment of such law by the central government. The Chinese Foreign Ministry, in support of the law, said that China has the right to implement the new regulations insisting that "Carrying out maritime management according to law is the justified right of a sovereign country."[106] However, China assured that there is no problem with the navigation in the South China Sea. The Foreign Ministry said that, "China attaches importance to the South China Sea and there is no problem in this regard at the moment".[107] Nevertheless, the term *'at the moment'* is significant which implied the non-permanent character of such assurance.

The other alternatives

The other claimants are also getting prepared to counter Chinese moves. As we have discussed earlier, Vietnam embarked on her military modernization amidst growing Chinese assertive posture in the disputed waters while there was a growing tendency in Hanoi to get closer to Washington. Since the dawn of the new century, the US and Vietnam started coming closer by exchanging high-level visits and holding series of defence and security dialogues on a regular basis. It started with the visit of US President Clinton to Hanoi in 2000 followed by his Secretary of State Colin Powell in 2001 to attend the ASEAN Regional Forum meeting while in 2003 the Vietnamese defence minister Pham Van Tra paid a visit to US. In 2006 after US Defence Secretary Donald Rumsfeld visited Vietnam the Bush administration permitted the US companies to supply Vietnam with limited defence articles and in October 2008 both sides held the first-ever bilateral Political, Security and Defence Dialogue at the vice-ministerial level in Hanoi.[108]

On the regional diplomatic front Vietnam kept on pushing the issue as the chairman of the ASEAN in 2010 which forced China to attend two meetings of the ASEAN-China Joint Working Group on the South China Sea while discussions on the issue were held at the ASEAN Regional Forum for the first time.[109] So, knowing well that it is hardly possible for a comparatively weak country like Vietnam to handle China on her own, especially militarily if necessary, Hanoi opted for a balance game. Firstly, by engaging with USA Vietnam was shielding herself behind a super power protection which, even though is not a physical protection anyway like the Cold War defence treaty with the Philippines, was a way of thwarting any adverse Chinese move given the latent rivalry that exists between the emerging and the status quo powers. On the other hand by using ASEAN Vietnam attempted to handle China multilaterally also by engaging the regional states many of whom share similar concern about China's 'rise to power'. China agreeing to concede to Vietnam's arrangement for such multilateral engagement also showed that China was ready to compromise for the time being given the fact that China always favours bilateral over multilateral dialogue over the disputes insisting that South China Sea dispute does not concern all the ASEAN members. Vietnam also opted for bilateral settlement with China by signing an agreement on six basic principles guiding the settlement on maritime disputes. This was an attempt of Vietnam not to anger China since she had been 'too vocal in her opposition to China', according to a Vietnamese diplomat.[110]

However, Vietnam was not giving up her exhibition of sovereignty rights in the disputed waters. In 2012, Vietnam passed a maritime law articulating her jurisdiction over disputed Paracel and Spratly Islands asked the foreign ships to seek her permission to enter the South China Sea.[111] In May 2011, Hanoi decided to deploy civilian-led patrols, supplemented by marine police and a border force, from Jan. 25, to stop foreign vessels that violate fishing laws within Vietnam's waters. This followed similar Chinese move in the region in the form of the Hainan law. China, apart from protesting against this move, also protested the unilateral oil exploration of Vietnam. Vietnamese Foreign Ministry criticized China for violating its sovereignty and accused Chinese boats of sabotaging an exploration operation that was being carried by

Vietnam's state oil firm Petrovietnam,[112] Thus we see that Vietnam was balancing against and engaging with China without compromising with her claims, following Beijing's footsteps. In response to this move, China announced to establish the prefectural city Sansha to be controlled by central government in Beijing rather than the Hainan government.[113]

Meanwhile the Philippines seemed to be less inclined to engage with China to contain her but rather opted for international arbitration. In January 2013 Manila decided to refer the dispute with China to UN International Tribunal for the Law of Sea in accordance with the dispute settlement provisions of UNCLOS of which she is a signatory. She issued a Notification and Statement Claim in accordance with the settlement provision which was rejected by China.[114] The arbitration filing accused China of violating Philippines' exclusive economic zone which is 370 kilometres away from the country's coastline calling China's claim of entire South China Sea 'illegal'. On the other hand China rejected the arbitration saying that Philippines' actions make numerous 'historical and legal errors' which China cannot accept.[115] That Manila is trying hard to establish its position on the South China Sea dispute became clear when its ambassador to Argentina presented Philippines' case at the Argentine Council of International Affairs explaining how of 'indisputable sovereignty' over waters and features of South China Sea falls within the country's EEZ.[116] The Chinese Foreign Minister Wang Yi said during his visit to Manila to attend the Asia-Pacific Economic Cooperation (APEC) meeting in November 2015 that Philippines' case against China at the arbitration tribunal has strained relations between the two sides and it was up to the Philippines 'to heal the rift'.[117] So, like Vietnam, the Philippines also prepared for a diplomatic assault against 'Chinese assertion'. What is noteworthy in both the cases of Vietnam and the Philippines is that both, being small and weak power, opted to handle China diplomatically and in a multilateral way, Vietnam via ASEAN and the Philippines through United Nations. This was obvious since both the countries are militarily weak compared to China. The Defence Chief of the Philippines Voltaire Gazmin had admitted in 2013 the Philippine government had no power to thwart Chinese ships entering Scarborough Shoal.[118] So, engaging and containing China multilaterally is the only option for them. However there appear some changes in Philippines' South China Sea strategy with the advent of new government in Manila.

The South China Sea strategy of the newly elected Rodrigo Duterte Government in Manila (elected in June 2016) is certainly going through some overhaul. Unlike the previous Benigno Acquino regime, the new regime is clearly not in favour of being too much hostile to China on the sovereignty issue. As the current president Duterte said during his election campaign that if elected his administration will hold talks with Beijing and even welcomed joint exploration of South China Sea resources with China. He even proposed for direct talks with Beijing on the South China Sea in case the ongoing multilateral efforts fail within two years.[119] Apparently the current regime is not putting much hope in the multilateral approach Moreover Duterte had already informed, after being elected as the President, that his government would reduce Philippines' long term security alliance with Washington, hinting reduction of US-dependence in dealing with China.[120] Apparently the new government in Manila is less interested to add too much hype to the sovereignty dispute of South China Sea and complicating its relation with the giant neighbour. This was clear from the outcome of the maiden visit of President Duterte to China in October 2016 where both the leaderships decided to 'temporarily put aside' their differences over South China Sea, as suggested by Chinese President Xi Jinping.[121] Duterte regime clearly wishes to avoid any hostility with Beijing. First of all China is undoubtedly, being a major economic power, useful to the emerging economies of the Southeast Asian region as a source of investment. China is contributing in development of ASEAN countries like Laos and Cambodia. The Philippines is also looking for investment and economic reform is one of the priorities of the Duterte Government. In this case China can be useful for Manila as Duterte himself had said during his election campaign that he would seek Chinese assistance in building rail line between Manila and Mindanao, the southern island.[122] Moreover the Manila administration has bigger concerns regarding internal security of the country. The Philippines is countering insurgency for decades in the south of the country. Therefore the new regime gives more priority to the internal troubles than external disputes and it was clear from the statement of the new defence minister of the country, Delfin Lorenzana, in June 2016 who said crushing Islamic militants 'will take precedence over territorial disputes in South China Sea.'[123]

Nonetheless the fact that resolution of South China Sea dispute is a distant dream and no country, let alone the Philippines, is in a position to 'wrest its share' from China, either peacefully or militarily even with some external assistance, can be a reason for the new regime to relinquish aggressive posture on the issue. This is undoubtedly a practical solution to opt for alternative route to solution of the dispute. This is more so because even when Manila won its case at the UN tribunal it will hardly have any effect given that China has consistently refused to accept the tribunal's verdict. Thus there is no way to compel China to give up her adamant and uncompromising stance towards South China Sea dispute.

While **Malaysia's** claim in the South China Sea is not too much heard in the South China Sea, unlike Vietnam and the Philippines, the country mentioned key strategic priorities as territorial defence, in her 2010 defence policy. Here the policy mentioned South China Sea Exclusive Economic Zone, sea and air lanes between eastern Malaysia and the Malaysian Peninsula and Malacca and Singapore Straits. The naval and the air assets of Malaysia are largely meant for the defence of its territorial waters and its airspace and also for limited regional power projection.[124] Malaysia claims eleven maritime features in the Spratly Islands and occupies eight of them. These are important for the country's prosperity. Malaysia derives a significant part of her oil and gas resources from the South China Sea, the country being the second largest producer of oil and natural gas in Southeast Asia.[125] However, Malaysia cannot be overtly assertive with her South China Sea claims. Her navy does not possess any aircraft carrier or destroyers limiting its blue water capability. Also, given the Sino-Malaysian economic ties growing since the end of the Cold War it will naturally be against her interests to engage in open spat with China. Malaysia was the first ASEAN member to normalize relation with China. Malaysia had welcomed China's engagement in ASEAN+3, ASEAN Regional Forum and East Asia Summit. By the end of 1990s the official view of Kuala Lumpur was that China posed no threat to the country.[126] Malaysia was the largest trading partner of China in 2010 and any disruption in Chinese trade and investment or tourism boycott would badly affect Malaysian economy.[127] Thus Malaysia needed to be cautious about her strategy with her South China Sea claims vis-à-vis China.

Nevertheless, given her maritime interests in the region, Malaysia cannot ignore the need to strengthen herself in order to counter any adverse situation in future. It is to be remembered that although China is not a 'threat' to Malaysia, Chinese assertive stand in the South China Sea cannot let Kuala Lumpur relax for long since China claims the entire Sea which overlaps with Malaysia's EEZ. Besides open commercial activities and overall freedom of navigation in the Sea is required for Malaysian economy to prosper, apart from the fact that the presence of a mighty power, especially a neighbour, is not a fact to cope with very easily. Thus, keeping the options open, the Malaysian Defence Minister

Hishamuddin Husain, declared on Oct, 10, 2013 that Malaysia will build a new naval base in Bintulu Division of Sarawak, only 100 kilometres away from James Shoal, in the southernmost point of the Spratly Islands.[128] Malaysia is situated at the mouth of the Malacca Straits and thus any single power domination of the South China Sea will be detrimental to her economic wellbeing. Meanwhile Malaysia was shocked with the two Chinese naval exercises in 2013 and in 2014 around James Shoal, off Sarawak island state. The reef lies outside Malaysia's territorial waters but inside its 200 nautical mile exclusive economic zone. Although the Malaysian navy chief said that the ships were 'far off from the Malaysian waters', there were reports the three Chinese warships almost certainly took place at or close to James Shoal.[129] This shows that officially the Malaysian government was still reluctant to openly charge China which confirms it's 'maintain low profile in claims' stand. This is certainly because Malaysia's naval capacity is not in a position to counter any Chinese challenge. Nor it is prudent for the country to spoil diplomatic relations with China, the major partner of the former's economic growth. However, instead of sitting idle, Kuala Lumpur quietly stepped up cooperation with the Philippines and Vietnam.[130] Thus Malaysia chose to collate regional support from the other claimants in order to counter China. This is interesting since these countries' maritime territorial claims also overlap but they chose to get united to counter a bigger 'threat'. Thus it can be said that China is the prime security priority for the small and weak littorals of the South China Sea.

Indonesia, on the other hand, is also coming up as an actor in the South China Sea geopolitics. As mentioned earlier the Natuna Islands of the country is located in the disputed waters. Traditionally Jakarta maintained a neutral stand on the dispute and never took part in the South China Sea geopolitics in a mention worthy manner. However, it acted as mediator in resolving the disputes since 1990s and summoned a conference on the issue in 1991. In the 1993 workshop, the Chinese delegation presented a map illustrating its country's "historic waters" that showed that China's claimed areas overlapped with Indonesia's EEZ adjacent to the Natuna Islands. Indonesia asked for clarification from China regarding the claim, but China offered no explanation. Instead, China offered a negotiated solution that Indonesia rejected, since Indonesia does not see the need for maritime negotiation with China. Indonesia also rejected China's 'nine-dashed line' alleging that 'it lacks international basis and upsets the UNCLOS 1982'.[131] Thus Indonesia also started 'raising her head' among the group of disputants to counter the Chinese. In late 2015 Jakarta even went ahead threatening China to drag her to the international tribunal if the disputes are not resolved through dialogue. The country's chief security minister Luhut Pandjaitan, said Indonesia's small Natuna islands on the southern edge of the South China Sea could be affected by China's maritime claims.[132] He said that, "We don't want to see any power projection in this area."[133] This is a significant act of Indonesia in which the country openly expresses concerns about China's assertiveness, something she never did previously. This was also significant since the minister shared Indonesia's concern about the China's 'nine-dash line' with other disputants saying, "The nine-dash line is a problem we are facing, but not only us. It also directly (impacts) the interests of Malaysia, Brunei, Vietnam and the Philippines".[134] Presumably the minister was attempting to bind other disputants together with Indonesia by sharing his concerns about the Chinese assertiveness with others. Indonesia is acting on her own to assert her 'territorial rights' in her claimed areas of South China Sea. Indonesia's state-owned energy company *Pertamina* has planned to explore for oil and gas in areas close to Indonesia's maritime border in the South China Sea to assert the country's territorial rights.[135]

ASEAN: A Divided House

As we discussed in the previous chapter the growing friction over the territorial sovereignty issue in the South China Sea caters the appropriate opportunity to ASEAN to emerge as the true arbiter, the objective with which the Association was founded almost fifty years back (ASEAN will celebrate 50 years of its foundation in 2017). The ASEAN Charter vows to 'respect the fundamental importance of amity and cooperation, and principles of sovereignty, equality, territorial integrity, non-interference and consensus and unity and diversity.'[136] Article 1 of the Charter declares to 'maintain and enhance peace, security and stability and further strengthen peace-oriented values in the region'.[137] The South China Sea dispute challenges both the principles of sovereignty and territorial integrity while threatens the peace, security and stability of the region. Thus it is a litmus test for ASEAN. The Association has been playing its role as a regional dispute management mechanism for a long time and its importance undoubtedly grew in the post-Cold War period in the absence of big power geopolitics of the Cold War. The ASEAN is certainly a body which was founded to manage the Southeast Asian affairs in 'ASEAN Way'. It was created following the critical intra-Southeast Asian duel of *Konfrontasi* policy of Indonesia against newly founded Malaysia and after the failure of previous similar attempts of regional cohesion building measure with Association of Southeast Asia (ASA, 1961) and MAPHILINDO (Malaysia, Philippines, Indonesia, in 1963). Thus it is a fact that the Southeast Asian countries were serious about regional stability. The Cold War period did not allow the ASEAN to leave its marks in the complex regional affairs. This can be explained in the light of the lack of confidence among the member states to manage the regional affairs as well as the involvement of the super powers considering the regional affair as part of larger global Cold War duel. Also, the ASEAN was incomplete with the absence of mainland Southeast Asia in its Association. Thus, ASEAN was weak and given the availability of the super power protection from any inter-state conflict during the Cold War period reduced the dialogue, based non-violent option for debate resolution, as unattractive to the concerned parties.

In the post-Cold War period, the importance of ASEAN for dispute management, and not resolution, grew in the absence of the security guarantee of the big powers following their decision to withdraw. Also, regional stability became important for all the countries aspiring for economic prosperity. This was crucial for both China and the disputant members of ASEAN. Thus China, which viewed ASEAN as object of US strategy to encircle her during the Cold War, decided to mingle with it in the post-Cold War period. China proposed for comprehensive economic cooperation with ASEAN in 2000 Summit including China-ASEAN Free Trade Agreement and in 2002 ASEAN and China signed Comprehensive Economic Cooperation Agreement establishing China-ASEAN Free Trade Agreement (CAFTA).[138] On the other hand, ASEAN also attempted to pacify the simmering tension in the South China Sea region amidst the assertive postures of the disputants. In July 2000 meeting of the ASEAN Regional Forum (ARF) Thai Foreign Minister, Surin Pitsuwan, said, "The (foreign) ministers encouraged the exercise of self-restraint by all countries concerned and promotion of confidence-building measures in this area...".[139] He also praised the efforts of both China and ASEAN to 'develop and adopt the Regional Code of Conduct for the South China Sea'. This was also affirmed by Chinese Foreign Minister who urged ARF to take helpful position.[140] Thus both sides agreed to cooperate on the issue.

However, it is difficult for ASEAN to pacify the tension, let alone resolve the dispute. The most important issue with ASEAN is that the South China Sea dispute does not concern all the members of the grouping. Four out of ten members, Vietnam, the Philippines, Malaysia and Indonesia, are directly affected by the developments in the South China Sea while the rest six members have nothing to be concerned about (although Brunei can face the heat in future being the littoral of the South China Sea). This is why Beijing always insisted on bilateral management of the dispute rather than via multilateral forum. This is beneficial for China with a scope to direct the dispute handling mechanism in her own way, respective of the strength of the other side. Thus ASEAN is a divided house on the issue. Moreover, the 'divide-and-rule' policy of China vis-à-vis the ASEAN members is also noteworthy. This China is doing with her economic leverage. China is a major trading partner of many ASEAN states. China's investment in Greater Mekong Sub-region (GMS) to upgrade the poor countries like Myanmar, Laos and Cambodia through the Strategic Framework for Next Ten Years of the GMS Programme (2012-2022) and Plan of Action for Trade and Transportation Facilitation are parts of China's economic diplomacy to advance her interests in Southeast Asia.[141] China's economic diplomacy works better in the mainland Southeast Asia where some of most underdeveloped member states of ASEAN are located. So they are reluctant to act against China on the South China Sea issue, especially when the issue does not concern them. This was evident in 2012 when Cambodia opposed ASEAN's united stand on the Scarborough Shoal incident where China and the Philippines clashed. Thus the Phnom Penh Summit of ASEAN in July 2012 ended without a joint communiqué for the first time in ASEAN's history (the Association decides on consensus). This was because Cambodia refused to include the territorial disputes in the communiqué which Vietnam and the Philippines insisted. While Manila accused Phnom Penh for 'blocking any mention of the dispute', Cambodia insisted that the 'failure' to issue the statement was on all the members of ASEAN. The Cambodian Foreign Minister insisted that ASEAN Foreign Ministers' Meeting 'is not a court, a place to give a verdict about the dispute'.[142] The frustration of the Philippines over the issue was clear with Manila 'deploring ASEAN's failure to address the worsening row' while her Foreign Minister, Albert del Rosario, without mentioning China, said, "The increasing assertion by this member state over the disputed and non-disputed areas poses a threat to the peace and stability in the Asia-Pacific region".[143] On the other hand Indonesia also expressed her disappointment over the failure with her President Susilo Bambang Yudhoyono expressing concern on the issue. He expressed fear that the failure might 'lead to a misperceptions or false depiction about ASEAN' although he insisted that "ASEAN is not shattered and there is no disunity despite existing issues that must be resolved".[144]

In the recent years the summit statements of the grouping, although expressed concern regarding the escalation of tension in the South China Sea region and emphasized on the freedom of navigation, however have seldom gone to the specifics. It is seen that China has been successful in dividing the house over the issue. Given this weakness of the Association, the member states also lack much confidence in it as an arbiter of the dispute. In conversation with this author in Hanoi, one scholar opined that the ASEAN and its other wings like ARF and Defence Ministers Meeting Plus (DMM+) are mere 'information desks which have no ability to resolve the dispute'. He said that the members of the forums do not comply with the forums' decisions and the treaties concluded there are 'chaos treaties' with differing views. Thus it is seen that the ASEAN has miserably failed to garner much confidence. This became more evident when Manila referred the South China Sea dispute to the UN tribunal for arbitration in 2013 which was no doubt an expression of its 'no confidence on the ASEAN' and its 'trouble-shooting mechanism'. In 2013 Manila approached the international tribunal accusing China of violating UNCLOS-designation of a country's exclusive economic zone, which is 370 kilometres from its coastline. The Filipino Foreign Minister Albert del Rosario called this arbitration under Annex VII and part XV of UNCLOS as 'a peaceful and durable way of resolving maritime disputes'.[145]

However, Manila has been cautious about not underestimating the ASEAN. Thus a top diplomat of the country assured that the arbitral proceedings initiated by Manila to challenge China's excessive maritime claims 'do not undermine the consultations between the Association of Southeast Asian Nations (ASEAN) and Beijing for the crafting of a Code of Conduct (COC) on the South China Sea'.[146] Such an assurance is necessary otherwise ASEAN would lose its significance. Nevertheless, Manila's action has exposed the weakness of the Association as a reliable dispute-resolution mechanism. Also, it is noteworthy that even when the ASEAN as a regional association promotes stability and tranquillity, the members individually prepare themselves militarily for any future adverse situation. This is evident from the burgeoning defence budget of the disputants like Vietnam and the Philippines. However, even when they expect little help from ASEAN, they find the Association a platform which can thwart the Chinese 'expansionism' or at least slacken its speed. That China today is the part of larger ASEAN institutions like ARF, East Asia Summit and ADMM+ is a remarkable development which puts Beijing leadership in a difficult position to embark on any unilateral policy vis-à-vis South China Sea dispute. China on the other hand also needs the cooperative ambience in her East Asian neighbourhood for both her economic as well as strategic benefit. When the market of ASEAN is required for China (just the way ASEAN needs enhanced trade relations with China) similarly Beijing has the obligation to clear its name as an aggressor and an unfriendly and troublesome neighbour. This China can do only by acquiescing to the ASEAN regional cooperative initiatives. On the other hand by bringing in extra regional powers, like Japan, India and most importantly USA, within its institutional ambit, ASEAN wants to balance the 'Chinese threat'. However, the disputants, both China and others, are not relying completely on the ASEAN initiatives since ASEAN, as we have seen, is not strong enough to thwart China nor is successful yet to at least discourage Beijing from embarking on military modernization programme. So, they are also encouraging extra regional powers, especially USA, to re-engage with emerging South China Sea geopolitics.

USA and the recent developments in the South China Sea

The US' policy towards South China Sea dispute has been of clear aloofness. Despite the involvement of her ally the Philippines, USA was not interested to entangle in the dispute at the conclusion of the Cold War in early 1990s. Yet, since the dawn of the new century, USA started taking interest in the South China Sea affairs, amidst the 'rise of China'. US has been interested in the South China Sea as a strategic target since the 19th century when she turned the 'East Sea' (South China Sea) into her 'strategic lake' after colonising the Philippines.[147] As we have discussed before in the book, during the Cold War period, the US Seventh Fleet was a big support for her allies fighting against communist China, and later USSR. The renewed interests of USA in South China Sea arose with China posing challenge to the US interest in the region. The death of Soviet Union left USA as the world's sole super power. This power status USA enjoyed throughout the 1990s, in East Asia, until the new century began which is seeing the 'rise of China'. However, Robert Ross opines that East Asia is bipolar because China is not a rising power but established regional power while USA is not a regional hegemon but 'shares with China great power status in the balance of power'.[148]

The presence of US naval bases in Japan and South Korea has kept Northeast Asia under the US protection while Southeast Asia remained exposed to 'threats' in the post-Cold War period. Thus, China, as we said earlier, got a better chance to 'intrude' in the Southeast Asian region. In the new century with China strengthening her military prowess, keeping an eye on US, Washington is getting cautious. The Chinese interest in the South China Sea is matter of concern for USA since three of US' ten sea lanes of communication pass through West Pacific Ocean and Malacca Strait. Also, US's close allies, Japan and South Korea, depend on the sea lanes of the South China Sea (East Sea) for importing oil and other resources. Moreover, the littorals of the Sea are important trading partners of USA while the Sea itself is rich in oil.[149] Thus, the US interest in the South China Sea is not only to safeguard her own interests but also her allies in East Asia. Moreover, the rise of China is a concern for USA since this poses a challenge to the existing geopolitical framework of East Asia.

The 'Asia pivot policy' of the Obama administration in Washington re-engaged USA with Asia Pacific region once more, after being engaged for too long with West Asia, especially in Iraq and Afghanistan. Referring to the 'Asia-Pacific Rebalance', the State Department said,

> "Recognizing that America's future prosperity and security are intertwined with the East Asia-Pacific region, President Barack Obama made a strategic commitment to rebalance our efforts and investments toward Asia. The United States will remain a strong, reliable, and active partner in the region and is investing diplomatic, public diplomacy, military, and assistance resources in a way that is commensurate with our comprehensive engagement. We continue to emphasize economic development, energy cooperation, people-to-people exchanges, youth, and education in our programs."[150]

The US wants a peaceful East Asia with no dominance of any adverse power challenging the US dominance in the region, especially in the maritime zone where the US is the supreme power till the date. The South China Sea is an important chain of US' coastal military network stretching from the Persian Gulf to Korean peninsula, passing through the East Sea which serves as an 'iron belt' to contain China, maintain Taiwan status quo and bolster the US alliance system in the region. As China's military build up strengthens, the US feels to increase her presence in the Sea.[151]

The latest addition to the South China Sea row is the reclamation of land by China in the disputed waters. In mid August 2015, Pentagon reported that China has reclaimed more land in the disputed Spratly Islands of the South China Sea than previously known. The report said Beijing was in the process of completing a runway on one of its seven man-made outposts. Once the airstrip on Fiery Cross Reef is operational, China could potentially use it as an alternative runway for carrier-based planes, allowing the Chinese military to conduct "sustained operations" with aircraft carriers in the area, the report said.[152] Actually China began her land reclamation in December 2013 and since then she claimed more than 2,900 acres of land as of June 2013, according to the report.[153] Previously the Chinese declaration of air defense identification zone (ADIZ) in the East China Sea in 2013 was criticized by USA and the declaration sent ripples of anxiety all over the region. This was also significant since Chinese ambassador to Manila Ma Keqing, while defending China's decision to establish ADIZ in the area between China, Japan, Taiwan and South Korea, said that it is Chinese government's prerogative to decide 'where and when to set up such zone', in response to questions about the concern that China might set up such zone over South China Sea also.[154] So China now gets assertive with her sovereignty claims over the disputed waters of East Asia, from north to south. The US Ambassador to Manila, Philip Goldberg, said, "We do not believe that this is a move intended to build confidence or in any other way improve the situation but instead, will create tension and the possibility of miscalculation."[155] Thus the geopolitics of East Asia, including South China Sea, is fast getting mingled with the geopolitical rivalry of emerging power China and existing power USA. Such a rivalry is fast spreading its shadow over the South China Sea, a reminiscent of the Cold War period.

The situation worsened further with US sending her naval guided-missile destroyer *USS Lassen* within 12 nautical miles of an artificial island constructed by China in the South China Sea in October 2015. US, although has maintained her neutrality over the sovereignty disputes among the South China Sea littoral states, has been in favour of freedom of navigation. This is natural for a country who is an integral part of the larger East Asian geopolitics. USA has been dominating the East Asian scene since the World War II. Throughout the Cold War period, as we have seen, the US Seventh Fleet was positioned in the Pacific under the charge of the US Pacific Command (USPACOM). The Area of Responsibility of USPACOM 'encompasses about half the earth's surface, stretching from the waters off the west coast of the U.S. to the western border of India, and from Antarctica to the North Pole'. With allies and partners, USPACOM is committed to enhancing stability in the Asia-Pacific region by promoting security cooperation, encouraging peaceful development, responding to contingencies, deterring aggression, and, when necessary, fighting to win. This approach is based on partnership, presence, and military readiness.[156] Its headquarter is in Honolulu island. Thus we see that with USPACOM the US controls the geostrategic as well as geopolitics of the entire Indo Pacific belt. Therefore, freedom of navigation is vital for the movement of the US fleets in the 'USPACOM waters' which undoubtedly includes South China Sea. So, the Chinese attempts to expand in these waters certainly challenge the long 'domination' of US in the region.

Moreover, the US interests in the South China Sea is also to safeguard the economic as well as a strategic interests of her allies, Japan, South Korea and the Philippines, not to mention Taiwan, who depend on the East Asian waters, East as well as South China Sea for their commercial requirements, especially importing oil and gas from the western Asia. Moreover, given the reserve of oil, natural gas and other natural resources in the South China Sea, the ownership of China over the region is detrimental not only to the other claimants' economic interests but also USA who can garner profit from the economic burgeoning of her allies who are and will be depended on US for physical security especially against China in the near future. So, US will always insist on 'freedom of navigation' in the South China Sea. During her visit to Hanoi in 2010, US Secretary of State Hillary Clinton had categorically said, "The United States, like every nation, has a *national interest in freedom of navigation*, open access to Asia's maritime commons, and respect for international law in the South China Sea."[157] Explaining the need for the freedom of navigation the US Defence Department, in its 2015 report, said, "Maritime Asia is a vital thruway for global commerce, and it will be a critical part of the region's expected economic growth. The United States wants to ensure the Asia-Pacific region's continued economic progress."[158] Referring to the South China Sea it says, '30 percent of world's maritime trade transits through South China Sea annually, including approximately $1.2 trillion in ship-borne trade bound for the United States.[159] Thus any dominance of an adverse party in the South China Sea is detrimental to US interests. Chinese growing naval might, supplementing her aspirations for 'domination' in regional waters, both for strategic and economic gains, is unacceptable to USA. Therefore sending *USS Lassen* in the South China Sea is a significant move. In response to this the Chinese embassy in Washington said that 'the concept of freedom of navigation should not be used as an excuse for muscle-flexing and that the United States should "refrain from saying or doing anything provocative and act responsibly in maintaining peace and regional stability'.[160]

Later in December 2015, an American B-52 bomber on a routine mission over the South China Sea flew within two nautical miles of an artificial island built by China. When Pentagon maintained that such a flight was 'unintentional', Beijing filed a formal diplomatic complaint with the U.S. Embassy in Beijing. China's Defense Ministry said that both of the American B-52 bombers on Dec. 10 (2015) "entered without authorization the airspace around the relevant islands and reefs" of the Spratlys, but didn't specify the precise area. The ministry said this and other U.S. operations in the area were "serious military provocations" that endangered Chinese personnel and could cause the militarization of the South China Sea. It added that the Chinese military would take "all necessary measures" to protect China's sovereignty.[161] The Global Times, the Chinese daily in English, termed the US action as 'mild' but 'aggressive'. It wrote that the B-52 flew within 2 nautical miles of the islands built by China 'which severely threatened the security of the islands.' It opined, echoing the response of the defence ministry, that such US moves will undoubtedly propel China to accelerate militarizing it's newly built islands and make them capable to cope any direct military threat from US.[162] Such a statement clarifies the Chinese intension to prepare for military actions against USA in future. This is certainly an addition to the tension and is detrimental to the pledge of the other small South China Sea disputants to opt for peaceful resolution of the dispute. Moreover such determination of China, expressed in a paper which is assumed to reflect the views of the Chinese leadership, will certainly encourage the small powers to opt for physical protection from the big powers like USA and embark on military modernization programme to counter any adverse situation in future.

The South China Sea geopolitics is taking a new shape in the new century in the form of the Sino-US tug-of-war for domination in East Asia. The emergence of China is the major development of the twenty-first century. The growing economy of China raises the demand for more resources from different corners of the world. For that hassle-free maritime commerce is needed. Moreover, the hunger of resources are raising the importance of the South China Sea, containing abundant quantity of natural resources underneath, where the possession of the islands becomes important since under UN maritime law the certain areas of the adjacent waters of the possessed islands fall within the territorial jurisdiction of the country occupying the islands in the form of exclusive economic zone. Thus China needs the islands more because of their economic zones. However, the mostly uninhabited islands offer scope to be converted to military bases as well which will help China vigil over the South China Sea. With the economic strength growing, China is spending more on her defence modernization programme, construction of the airfields in some disputed islands within China's possession in the Sea is part of the programme. In a way China is getting assertive in the new century about her position in East Asia, especially in the disputed regions. However, China is expressing her inclination to collaborate with her neighbours on the dispute as 'a good neighbourly gesture' thus attending the ASEAN meetings on South China Sea while entangling further with the developing larger East Asian institutional mechanism like East Asia Summit and ASEAN Defence Minister Meeting Plus which engage the extra-regional powers, like India and USA, in the regional geopolitics of East Asia, and much to the displeasure of Beijing. Nonetheless, knowing her challenges/unacceptability in the US dominated East Asia, China keeps her military option open. Guided by the Middle Kingdom mentality, China aspires to 'rule her neighbourhood', especially East Asia where her main challenge is USA. China is yet to supersede the military, especially naval, might of America which has made the latter invincible in the waters of East Asia. Moreover, establishing her possession in the disputed South China Sea, which houses some traditional as well as emerging US allies, is also important to regain the 'prestige of the Middle Kingdom'.

On the other hand, the small disputants of South China Sea, aware of the Chinese 'dream', are also getting prepared to sabotage the mission. They are also preparing themselves to defend their sovereignty. And they could do this, apart from opting for diplomatic solutions, by investing in their military as their economic strength improves. We can see that the South China Sea dispute is impacting the defence policies of the claimant states although the nature of the impact varies. When Vietnam and the Philippines seem to be investing more in their respective military potentials (although Manila's policy under new Duterte regime is currently de-emphasizing alliance with USA and apparently insists dialogue with China), Malaysia and Indonesia are still opting for diplomatic solutions. However they all confront with the same requirements, like China, in the South China Sea. Like China, they are also on the path of economic revivalism which makes the maritime zone equally important for them. On the other hand like China they also need natural resources to sustain their economic growth and thus eye on South China Sea and her islands.

Apart from these purely materialistic reasons, the case of nationalism also plays its part, in case of Vietnam and the Philippines. Governments both in China and in other claimant countries sometimes give in to the nationalistic sentiments or even utilize them for political gains. The Chinese make a good use of this with the 'victim mentality' of 'Century of Humiliation'. This nationalism is useful for China to counter the arguments of other countries regarding their legislatures' refusal to compromise. Also, the US support to the other claimants over the dispute strengthens China's argument of being a weaker party and victim in disputes.[163] Same is the case with Vietnam and the Philippines. This author's impression following interaction with some scholars in Hanoi suggests that there exists tremendous amount of anti-China feelings among a section of the academia of the country. Chinese actions in South China Sea sometimes trigger anti-China demonstrations in Vietnam as happened in 2014 when protesters staged an anti-China demonstration against Beijing's deployment of a deep-water drilling rig in contested waters. This demonstration included war veterans and students with one veteran calling it the largest anti-China demonstration in Hanoi.[164] Similarly in June 2015, on the Philippines Independence Day, the leftist protesters decried the Chinese claims in South China Sea.[165] Sometimes, the governments have to heed to such public sentiments. The most noteworthy aspect of the twenty-first century South China Sea geopolitics is the emerging role of the smaller South China Sea littoral states who are rising as a separate entity in the South China Sea geopolitics of the new century. When during the Cold War they were mere tools of super power geopolitical game in the region, now they are the vital driving forces directing the game itself. This they are doing, firstly, by strengthening themselves militarily with their economic power growing, and secondly, being aware of their strength, by engaging extra-regional powers to balance against China. In that way USA is re-appearing in the scene giving a new look to the developing geopolitics of South China

Sea. The US is finding her traditional East Asian domination under threat with China emerging. Thus by siding with the China-wary states of the region, she is creating a Cold War type ambience in the region. The current South China Sea geopolitics is revolving around four countries—China, Vietnam, the Philippines and USA. However, gradually the US is bringing in other extra regional powers in the emerging twenty-first century South China Sea geopolitics, the countries who share wariness of USA regarding China's rise and also feels the need of a freely navigable South China Sea without any domination of China. USA wants to share the burden of 'handling China' with others actively involved in the region like Japan, Australia and India.

END NOTES

1. Robert Kaplan, *Asia's Cauldron: The South China Sea and the End of a Stable Pacific*, New York, Random House, 2014, p.33, emphasis added
2. Anders C. Sjaastad, 'Southeast Asian SLOCs and security options', Chong Guan Kwa and John K. Skogan (eds), *Maritime Security in Southeast Asia*, London and New York, Routledge, 2007, p.3
3. Subhadeep Bhattacharya, 'The Maritime Border Dispute of South China Sea: Factors Impeding Solution', Arpita Basu Roy and Subhadeep Bhattacharya (eds), *India and South East Asia: States, Borders and Culture*, Delhi, Shipra Publications, 2015, pp.50,51
4. Bill Hayton, *The South China Sea: The Struggle for Power in Asia*, New Haven and London, Yale University Press, 2014, pp.121,122
5. Andrew B. Kennedy focuses on the 'martial efficacy beliefs' of Mao Tse Tung based on his revolutionary experiences, in this context. The *martial efficacy beliefs* are those national efficacy beliefs which refer to the ability of a nation to overcome material disadvantages on the battlefield. For details see Andrew Bingham Kennedy, *The International Ambitions of Mao and Nehru: National Efficacy Beliefs and the Making of Foreign Policy*, New York, Cambridge University Press, 2012
6. Richard D. Fisher Jr., *China's Military Modernization: Building for Regional and Global Reach*, Stanford, California, Stanford University Press, 2010, p.7
7. 'China's National Defense in 2000', Embassy of People's Republic of China in the Republic of Estonia, 2004/05/20, http://www.chinaembassy.ee/eng/ztlm/zfbps/t112926.htm (accessed on 03.02.2016)
8. Ibid
9. Ibid
10. James R. Holmes and Toshi Yoshihara, 'China's Caribbean in South China Sea', *SAIS Review of International Affairs*, Vol. 26, No.1, John Hopkins University Press,2006, p.84
11. Sigfrido Burgos Caceres, *China's Strategic Interests in the South China Sea: Power and Resources*, London and New York, Routledge, 2014, p.35
12. Nan Li, 'The Evolution of China's Naval Strategy and Capabilities: From

"Near Coast" and "Far Seas" to "Far Seas", Phillip C. Saunders, Christopher Yung, Michael Swaine, Andre Nien-Dzu Yang (eds), *The Chinese Navy: Expanding Capabilities, Evolving Roles,* Washington D.C., National Defense University Press, 2011, p.109

13. Richard D. Fisher Jr, op cit, p.42
14. Nan Li, op cit, p.111
15. Ibid, p.118
16. The People's Liberation Army navy, 'A Modern navy with Chinese Characteristics', August 2009, http://fas.org/irp/agency/oni/pla-navy.pdf p.9 (accessed on 04.02.2016)
17. 'National Defense policy', China's National Defense in 2004, http://www.china.org.cn/e-white/20041227/ (accessed on 0402.2016)
18. The People's Liberation Army Navy, op cit, p.9
19. Part 1, Executive Summary, 'Joint Submission to the Commission on the Limits of the Continental Shelf pursuant to the Article 76, Paragraph 8 of the United Nations Convention on the Law of the Sea 1982 in respect of the southern part of the South China Sea', Malaysia, Socialist Republic of Vietnam, May, 2009, p.1, http://www.un.org/depts/los/clcs_new/submissions_files/mysvnm33_09/mys_vnm2009excutivesummary.pdf (accessed on 05.02.2016)
20. 'Stirring up the South China Sea'(I), Crisis Group Asia Report, N° 223, 23rd April, 2012, p.3
21. HA24/09, http://www.un.org/depts/los/clcs_new/submissions_files/mysvnm33_09/mys_re_chn_2009re_mys_vnm_e.pdf (accessed on 05.02.2016), emphasis added
22. CML/18.2009, http://www.un.org/depts/los/clcs_new/submissions_files/vnm37_09/chn_2009re_vnm.pdf (accessed on 05.02.2016)
23. Ibid, emphasis added
24. Jian Zhang, 'China's South China Sea policy: Evolution, claims and challenges', Leszek Buszyniski and Christopher B. Roberts (eds), *The South China Sea Maritime Dispute: Political, legal and regional perspectives*, London and New York, Routledge, 2015, p.71
25. Stirring up the South China Sea'(I), op cit
26. Bill Hayton, op cit, p.59
27. 'Limits in the Seas, China: Maritime Claims in South China Sea, No.143, Office of Ocean and Polar Affair, Bureau of Oceans and International Environmental and Scientific Affair, United States Department of State December 5, 2014, pp.4,5 http://www.state.gov/documents/organization/234936.pdf (accessed on 05.07.2016)
28. David Lague, 'Analysis: China's nine-dashed line in South China Sea', *Reuters,* May 25, 2012, http://in.reuters.com/article/us-china-sea-boundary-idUSBRE84O07520120525 (accessed on 05.07.2016)
29. Ibid
30. Permanent Missions of the Socialist Republic of Viet Nam to the United Nations, No.86/HC-2009, 8th May, 2009, http://www.un.org/depts/los/clcs_new/submissions_files/mysvnm33_09/vnm_chn_2009re_mys_vnm_e.pdf (accessed on 05.02.2016)
31. Ibid

32. 'Beijing claims indisputable sovereignty over South China Sea', *The Washington Post*, July 31, 2010, http://www.washingtonpost.com/wp-dyn/content/article/2010/07/30/AR2010073005664.html (accessed on 05.02.2016)
33. 'Clinton wades into the South China Sea dispute',*The Washington Post*, July 23, 2010, http://voices.washingtonpost.com/checkpoint-washington/2010/07/clinton_wades_into_south_china.html (accessed on 05.02.2016)
34. Ibid
35. Stirring up the South China Sea (I), op cit, p.4
36. Ibid
37. Ibid, p.14
38. Subhadeep Bhattacharya, op cit, p.61
39. Stirring up the South China Sea (I), op cit, p.8
40. Ibid, pp.8,9
41. Ibid, p.9
42. Ibid
43. 'Philippine warship in stand-off with Chinese vessels', *BBC News*, 11 April, 2012, http://www.bbc.com/news/world-asia-17673426 (accessed on 08.02.2016)
44. 'Foreigners Wanted', *The Economist*, Aug 28th, 2014, http://www.economist.com/blogs/gulliver/2014/08/hainan-province (accessed on 08.02.2016)
45. Tridib Chakrabarti, 'The Territorial Claims in South China Sea: Probing Persistent Uncertainties', in Arun Kumar Banerji and Purushottam Bhattacharya (eds), *People's Republic of China at Fifty: Politics, Economy and Foreign Relations*, New Delhi, Lancer Books, 2001, p.180
46. Stirring up the South China Sea'(I), op cit,p.10
47. Ibid
48. Ibid
49. Brief Introduction to Hainan Province Government, http://en.hainan.gov.cn/englishgov/Government/201001/t20100107_40311.html (accessed on 08.02.2016)
50. Stirring up the South China Sea (I), op cit, p.10
51. Ibid, p.11
52. 'Chinese nuclear submarine base', *The Telegraph*, 01 May,2008, http://www.telegraph.co.uk/news/worldnews/asia/china/1917167/Chinese-nuclear-submarine-base.html (accessed on 08.02.2016)
53. Ibid
54. Ibid
55. Stirring up the South China Sea (I), op cit, p.13
56. *Xinhua*, 'Maritime Safety Administration launches patrol in South China Sea, September 26, 2015, http://en.people.cn/n/2015/0926/c90882-8955832.html (accessed on 08.02.2016)
57. Stirring up the South China Sea (I), op cit, p.12
58. Stirring up the South China Sea (IV): Oil in Troubled Waters, *Crisis Group Report*.N°275, January 2016, p.6
59. Stirring up the South China Sea (I), op cit, p.12
60. Stirring up the South China Sea (IV), op c it, p.5

61. Ibid, p.6
62. Stirring up the South China Sea'(I), op cit, p.14, 15
63. Ibid, p.15
64. Linda Jakobson and Dean Knox, 'New Foreign Policy Actors in China', *SIPRI Policy Paper* 26, Stockholm International peace research Institute, September 2010, p.13
65. Subhadeep Bhattacharya, op cit, pp.55,56
66. Tridib Chakraborti and Subhadeep Bhattacharya, 'South China Sea Imbroglio: Problems, Outcome and India's Stand', Institute of Foreign Policy Studies, *Policy Brief*, No.5, December 2012, p.6
67. Bronson Percival, *The Dragon looks South: China and Southeast Asia in the New Century*, Connecticut and London, Praeger Security International, 2007, p.43
68. Stirring up the South China Sea'(II); regional Responses, *Crisis Group Asia Report N°229*, 24 July, 2012, p.3
69. Ibid
70. Tran Khanh, 'Current East Sea Disputes: Possible Solution', *Southeast Asian Studies*, Institute of Southeast Asian Studies, Vietnamese Academy of Social Sciences, 2013, p.3
71. Do Thanh Hai, 'Vietnam's evolving claims', Leszek Buszynski and Christopher B. Roberts (eds), *The South China Sea Maritime Dispute: Political, legal and regional perspectives,* London and New York, Routledge, 2015, pp.87,88
72. Ibid, p.88
73. Ibid
74. Cited in ibid
75. Ibid
76. Tridib Chakraborti and Subhadeep Bhattacharya, op cit, p.4
77. Ibid
78. Do Thanh Hai, op cit, p.89, 90
79. 'Vietnam National Defence', Socialist Republic of Vietnam, Ministry of Defence, Hanoi 12, 2009, p.18
80. Ibid, p.20
81. Ibid, pp.20,21
82. Ibid, p.20
83. 'Vietnam's National Defense in the Early Years of the 21st Century, Socialist republic of Vietnam, Ministry of Defense, Hanoi, 2004, p.14
84. Ibid
85. Cited in James Goldrick and Jack McCaffrie, *Navies of South-East Asia: A Comparative Study*, London and New York, Routledge, 2013,p.206
86. Ibid, pp.207,208
87. Subhadeep Bhattacharya, op cit, p.56
88. 'Defence Economic Trends in the Asia pacific 2010', *Defence Intelligence Organisation*, http://www.defence.gov.au/dio/documents/det_10.pdf, p.27 (accessed on 10.02.2016)
89. Defence Economic Trends in the Asia pacific 2013', *Defence Intelligence Organisation, DIO Reference Aid 13-04,* http://www.defence.gov.au/dio/documents/DET_13.pdf, p.27 (accessed on 10.02.2016)
90. Cited in Crisis Group Asia Report N°229, op cit, p.4

91. Tran Khanh, op cit, p.5
92. James Goldrick and Jack McCaffrie, op cit, pp.125, 126
93. Ibid, p.128
94. Ibid, p.130
95. Ibid, p.131
96. Crisis Group Asia Report N°229, op cit, p.6, 7
97. Cited in ibid, p.7
98. 'China publishes map of Sansha, South China Sea islands', English.news.cn, 2012-11-23, http://news.xinhuanet.com/english/china/2012-11/23/c_131995195.htm (accessed on 11.02.2016)
99. Ibid
100. 'China passports claim ownership of South China Sea and Taiwan', *The Guardian*, 23rd November, 2012, http://www.theguardian.com/world/2012/nov/23/china-passports-ownership-sea-taiwan (accessed on 11.02.2016)
101. 'China builds new aircraft carrier in show of strength to Washington', RT, 31 Dec, 2015, https://www.rt.com/news/327562-china-build-aircraft-carrier/ (accessed on 11.02.2016)
102. 'Building a peaceful environment', China Daily,2012-12-25, http://www.chinadaily.com.cn/world/2012-12/25/content_16054506.htm (accessed on 11.02.2016)
103. 'PLA carries out defence drills in Shenyang, Jinan and Sansha', *South China Moring Post*,4 January, 2013, http://www.scmp.com/news/china/article/1119355/pla-carries-out-defence-drills-shenyang-jinan-and-sansha (accessed on 11.02.2016)
104. 'Naval Patrols to Expel Ships in South China Sea', *The New York Times*, Nov 30, 2012, http://www.nytimes.com/2012/11/30/world/asia/naval-patrols-to-expel-ships-in-south-china-sea.html (accessed on 12.02.2016)
105. 'Law enhances Chinese police's power in disputed South China Sea', *Los Angeles Times*, November 30, 2012, http://articles.latimes.com/2012/nov/30/world/la-fg-wn-law—police-powers-south-china-sea-20121130 (accessed on 12.02.2016)
106. 'New Chinese law Allows for Search, Expulsion of Foreign Ships', *Voice of America (VOA) News*, November 29, 2012, http://www.voanews.com/content/china-border-partols-to-search-expel-illegal-foreign-ships/1555049.html (accessed on 12.02.2016)
107. 'No problems with South China Sea navigation: China', *Zee News*, November 30, 2012, http://zeenews.india.com/news/world/no-problems-with-south-china-sea-navigation-china_813853.html (accessed on 12.02.2016)
108. Murry Herbert, Phuong Nguyen and Gregory B. Poling, 'A New Era in US-Vietnam Relations: Deepening Ties Two Decades after Normalization',*Center for Strategic and International Studies*, 2014, pp. 4,5
109. Crisis Group Asia Report N°229, op cit, p.4
110. Ibid, p.5
111. Ibid
112. 'South China Sea: Vietnam Clash Over Oil Exploration, Fishing', *International Business Times*, 12.06.2012,http://www.ibtimes.com/south-china-sea-china-vietnam-clash-over-oil-exploration-fishing-923341 (accessed on 12.02.2016)

113. Crisis Group Asia Report N°229, op cit, p.5
114. Jay J. Batongbakal, 'Arbitration 101: Philippines V China', *Asia Maritime Transparency Initiative*, January 21, 2015, http://amti.csis.org/arbitration-101-philippines-v-china/ (accessed on 12.02.2016)
115. 'Philippine to Forge Ahead with Sea Dispute Arbitration', *Voice of America*, February 21, 2013, http://www.voanews.com/content/philippines-to-forge-ahead-with-sea-dispute-arbitration/1607849.html (accessed on 12.02.2016)
116. Subhadeep Bhattacharya, op cit, p.58
117. 'Indonesia brandishes legal stick at China over SCS', *The Statesman*, 12 November 2015, p.10
118. 'Govt can't stop Sino ships entering Shoal', *The Standard*, April 13, 2013, http://manilastandardtoday.com/news/-main-stories/93218/govt-cant-stop-sino-ships-entry-in-shoal.html (accessed on 12.02.2016)
119. Jeremy Page and Treffor Moss, 'Philippine Front-runner Duterte Floats New Tactic in South China Sea Dispute', *The Wall Street Journal*, May 4, 2016, www.wsj.com/articles/philippines-front-runner-floats-new-tactic-in-island-dispute-1462402735 (accessed on 08.07.2016)
120. 'Philippines president-elect says won't rely on United States on South China Sea dispute with China'1 Jun, *Straits Times*, Jun, 2016, www.straitstimes.com/asia/se-asia/ Philippines-president-elect-says-wont-rely-on united-states-on-south-china-sea-dispute (accessed on 08.07.2016)
121. 'Philippines, China close ranks. 13 pacts pave way for calm on seas', *The Statesman*, 21st October, 2016, p.10
122. Richard C. Paddock, 'Rodrigo Duterte Poised to Lead Philippines, Is Expected to Take New Approach to China', *The New York Times*, May 11, 2016, www.nytimes.com/2016/05/12/world/asia/philippines-election-rodrigo-duterte-html?_r=0 (accessed on 08.07.2016)
123. Manuel Mogato, 'New Philippines defense chief says militant threat more pressing than South China Sea', Reuters, June 29, 2016, www.reuters.com/articles/us-philippines-security-idUSKCN0ZF0WX (accessed on 08.07.2016)
124. Subhadeep Bhattacharya, op cit, pp.58,59
125. Prashanth Parameswaran, 'Playing it Safe: Malaysia's Approach to the South China Sea and Implications for the United States', *Maritime Strategy Series*, Center for a New American Society, February 2015, p.4
126. Bronson Percival, op cit, p.55
127. Crisis Group Asia Report N°229, op cit, pp.10-11
128. Cited inSubhadeep Bhattacharya, op cit, p.59
129. 'Insight-China's assertiveness hardens Malaysian stance in sea dispute', *Reuters*, Feb 26, 2014, http://uk.reuters.com/article/uk-malaysia-china-maritime-insight-idUKBREA1P1Z020140226 (accessed on 12.02.2016)
130. Ibid
131. Made Andi Arsana, Denpasar, RI's position in South China Sea dispute, *Jakarta Post*, September 29, 2012,http://www.thejakartapost.com/news/2012/09/29/ri-s-position-south-china-sea-dispute.html (accessed on 12.02.2016)
132. 'Indonesia Invokes International Tribunal in South China Sea Dispute; Suggests move if dispute can't be resolved through dialogue', *Wall Street Journal*, Nov 12, 2015, http://www.wsj.com/articles/indonesia-invokes-

international-tribunal-in-south-china-sea-dispute-1447260065 (accessed on 12.02.2016)

133. *The Statesman*, 12 November 2015, op cit, p.10
134. Ibid
135. 'Indonesia's Pertamina plans to develop South China Sea border areas', *Reuters*, April 12, 2016, http://www.reuters.com/article/indonesia-pertamina-ma-idUSL3N17F1EL (accessed on 12.04.2016)
136. 'The ASEAN Charter', Association of Southeast Asian Nations (ASEAN), Jakarta,Public Affairs Office, ASEAN Secretariat, 2008, p.2
137. Ibid, p.3
138. Bronson Percival, op cit, p.96
139. Cited inTridib Chakrabarti, op cit, pp.200-201
140. Ibid, p.201
141. Subhadeep Bhattacharya, op cit, p.60
142. 'Asean nations fail to reach agreement on South China Sea', *BBC News*, 13 July, 2012, http://www.bbc.com/news/world-asia-18825148 (accessed on 15.02.2016)
143. 'SE Asia meeting in disarray over sea dispute with China', *Reuters*, July 13, 2012, http://www.reuters.com/article/us-asean-summit-idUSBRE86C0BD20120713 (accessed on 15.02.2016)
144. 'ASEAN's communiqué failure disappoints SBY', *Jakarta Post*, July 16, 2012, http://www.thejakartapost.com/news/2012/07/16/asean-s-communiqu-failure-disappoints-sby.html (accessed on 15.02.2016)
145. 'Arbitration process a peaceful way to solve maritime disputes', *The Philippine Star*, July 12, 2013, http://www.philstar.com/headlines/2013/07/12/964500/arbitration-process-peaceful-way-solve-maritime-dispute (accessed on 16.02.2016)
146. Ibid
147. Tran Khanh, op cit, pp. 5,6
148. Robert Ross, 'Geography of the Peace: East Asia in the Twenty-first Century', *International Survey*, Vol.23, No.4, (Spring 1999), p.83
149. Tran Khanh, op cit, p.6
150. 'The East Asia-Pacific Rebalance: Expanding U.S. Engagement', Bureau of Public Affairs, U.S. Department of State, December 16, 2013, http://www.state.gov/r/pa/pl/2013/218776.htm (accessed on 16.02.2016)
151. Tran Khanh, op cit, p.6
152. 'China's land reclamation in South China Sea grows; pentagon report', *Reuters*, August 21, 2015, http://www.reuters.com/article/us-southchinasea-china-pentagon-idUSKCN0QQ0S920150821 (accessed on 16.02.2016)
153. Ibid
154. 'Envoy says China has right to establish air defense zone in another disputed region', *Fox News*, December 2, 2013, http://www.foxnews.com/world/2013/12/02/envoy-says-china-has-right-to-establish-air-defense-zone-in-another-disputed.html (accessed on 16.02.2016)
155. 'Obama tells Philippines, Asian allies; West stand with you', *The Philippine Star*, December 3, 2013, http://www.philstar.com/headlines/2013/12/03/

1263727/obama-tells-philippines-asian-allies-we-stand-you (accessed on 16.02.2016)

156. 'US Pacific Command', USPACOM, http://www.pacom.mil/AboutUSPACOM.aspx (accessed on 17.02.2016)
157. Press Availability, Hillary Rodham Clinton, National Convention Center, Hanoi, Vietnam, U.S. Department of State, July 23, 2010, http://www.state.gov/secretary/20092013clinton/rm/2010/07/145095.htm (accessed on 17.02.2016), emphasis added
158. 'Asia-Pacific Maritime Security Strategy; Achieving US National Security Objectives in a Changing Environment', Department of Defense, United States of America, p.1, http://www.defense.gov/Portals/1/Documents/pubs/NDAA%20A-P_Maritime_SecuritY_Strategy-08142015-1300-FINALFORMAT.PDF (accessed on 17.02.2016)
159. Ibid
160. 'U.S. warship sails within 12 miles of Chinese-built island in South China Sea', *The Washington Post*, October 26, 2015, https://www.washingtonpost.com/world/us-warship-sails-within-12-miles-of-chinese-built-island-in-south-china-sea/2015/10/26/a178497b-7033-4e4c-a328-0f3c980cf193_story.html (accessed on 17.02.2016)
161. 'U.S Bomber Flies Over Waters Claimed by China', *The Wall Street Journal*, Dec, 18, 2015, http://www.wsj.com/articles/u-s-jet-flies-over-waters-claimed-by-china-1450466358 (accessed on 17.02.2016)
162. 'US actions prompt island militarization', *The Global Times*, 2015-12-21, http://www.globaltimes.cn/content/959609.shtml (accessed on 17.02.2016)
163. Crisis Group Asia Report, N°223, op cit, p.27
164. 'Vietnamese protests against China gather pace, fuelling regional tension', *theguardian*, 11 May, 2014, http://www.theguardian.com/world/2014/may/11/vietnamese-protests-against-china-gather-pace (accessed on 17.02.2016)
165. 'Philippines Protesters Decry China Sea Claims', *Voice of America*, June 12, 2015, http://www.voanews.com/content/philippines-independence-day-protest-decries-chinas-sea-claims/2819052.html (accessed on 17.02.2016)

6

India in the Emerging South China Sea Geopolitics

As the eastern gateway of Indian Ocean, South China Sea is India's strategic left frank. India is not a South China Sea littoral and has no territorial claims in the region. However, being an extra-regional power, like others, the stability and freedom of navigation are the two important factors which India emphasizes in South China Sea region. The sea lane is vital for India's commercial link with East Asia. Fifty-five per cent of India's trade with Asia passes through this strategic sea-route, including crucial energy supplies.[1] The South China Sea is an economic security life-line of India. It serves as the strategic link between the Pacific and the Indian Ocean and the smooth flow of trade through the region is vital for India's sea-borne trade with East Asia. Being the signatory of UNCLOS India supports both the right to freedom of navigation and right to innocent passage through the territorial sea. Therefore, any obstruction to safe navigation is undesirable to India, both in legal terms as well as in terms of her economic interests.[2] One of the main objectives behind India's engagement with South China Sea littorals is the exploitation of the energy resources underneath the Sea. Like the littoral states of South China Sea, including China, Indian economy is also soaring. Thus, she has to look for resources like oil and gas from sources including in Southeast Asian countries, like seeking extraction rights from Vietnam. On the other hand, India's Look East-turned Act East Policy is emphasizing on the expansion of India's strategic sphere of influence to Southeast and then larger East Asian and Asia Pacific world. It is to be remembered that India's contact with Southeast and larger East Asia is maintained via the maritime route. As we will discuss later in the chapter, the twenty-first century sees India's growing emphasis on the maritime zone in her neighbourhood. In 2000, India's the then Defence Minister George Fernandes said that India's area of interest extended from 'the north of the Arabian Sea to the South China Sea".[3] The South China Sea is fast getting integrated with the emerging East Asia strategy of India whose growing emphasis in her maritime policy leads her to focus on naval prowess.

India and her maritime policy

George Tanham opined that India's strategic thinking has traditionally been land oriented since Indian subcontinent had been repeatedly invaded through the lands which gave a 'strong strategic land orientation with little orientation to the ocean.'[4] It is noteworthy that India experienced invasions, one after another, from the north-western route of today's Pakistan, Iran and Central Asia. There is no record of any such devastating invasion via the sea route although like the land, the sea opened India's gate to the world outside. India played a vital role in the vibrant Indian Ocean trade as a major economic power of Asia before the advent of the Europeans in the fifteenth century. Nevertheless, Indian history does not bear any record of massive invasions on the subcontinent, comparable with the atrocities conducted by the invaders in the northern plains, originating from the maritime zone of India. This has given birth to a land-oriented defence perception in India, inherited from the British who were the masters of the sea in the eighteenth and the nineteenth century but were concerned with Russian threat to the Indian subcontinent via Afghanistan. When the British were concerned with the Russians beyond Afghan border, partition created a new (and perhaps permanent) threat to independent India next door in the form of Pakistan. The invasion of Kashmir in 1947 by Pakistan initiated a new chapter of India's defence policy with an addition of Chinese invasion of Tibet in 1950 and the subsequent war of 1962 with India. Thus hostile Pakistan in the west and expanding China in the north directed India's defence and strategic deliberations towards the northern and western land borders since 1947.

The sea in the south was no threat to Indian security. However, two incidents during the Cold War period can be considered as sea-borne threat to India. During the India-Pakistan war of 1965, Indonesia dispatched a naval flotilla to deter India, as a mark of support for Pakistan, which was perceived as a threat of opening a second front in the Andaman and Nicobar Islands. Secondly, during the war of 1971 against Pakistan, the visit of USS *Enterprise* in the Indian Ocean upset New Delhi.[5] These are the two cases which might contradict the 'no sea-borne threat' perception. However, these cannot be termed as a security threat equal to one emanating from Pakistan and China. Apart from the fact that India never experienced any sea-borne invasion (although the occupation of Andaman and Nicobar Islands by the Japanese during the World War II was undoubtedly tantamount to invasion and it definitely posed a threat to the British Raj in India), the very presence of the British Royal Navy in the Indian Ocean with bases from Aden in the west to Singapore in the east ensured physical protection to India. Moreover, for ten long years after independence, British naval officers headed the Indian Navy, till 1958 when Admiral Ram Dass Katari became the first Indian to head the Indian Navy. In a way India's maritime defence was ensured by the Royal Navy with its presence in the Indian Ocean, or the 'British Lake' as it was called. It is said that India is a beneficiary of a largely benign maritime strategic environment.[6] India does not have any major maritime dispute which would force the country's leadership to consider the formidable naval strategy. Also, naval build up requires large investment. Given the economic health of India with social obligations, compounded by the pressure of defence of the land borders, it was a luxury for the Indian leadership to invest in the navy in the initial years after independence, and that too unnecessarily, in the absence of any maritime threat and presence of the friendly Royal Navy. So, for long since her independence India never considered to develop a maritime strategy. The waterways in India's maritime areas like Straits of Hormuz, Straits of Malacca, Ten Degree Channel and two hypothetical choke points between Lakshadweep Islands and mainland India and the Indira Point in the Nicobar Islands western edge of Sumatran Island bear economic as well as military importance for India.[7] The vast Indian Ocean lying at the foot of India is an important maritime highway connecting the wide Indo-Pacific area. This region serves as the 'umbilical cord of the economies of several Asia Pacific and European countries'.[8] As India's economy strengthens this sea lane becomes important for her. The sea lane from the east coast of Africa and the Gulf region to East Asia passing through the Malacca Straits and the South China Sea is the economic lifeline of India.

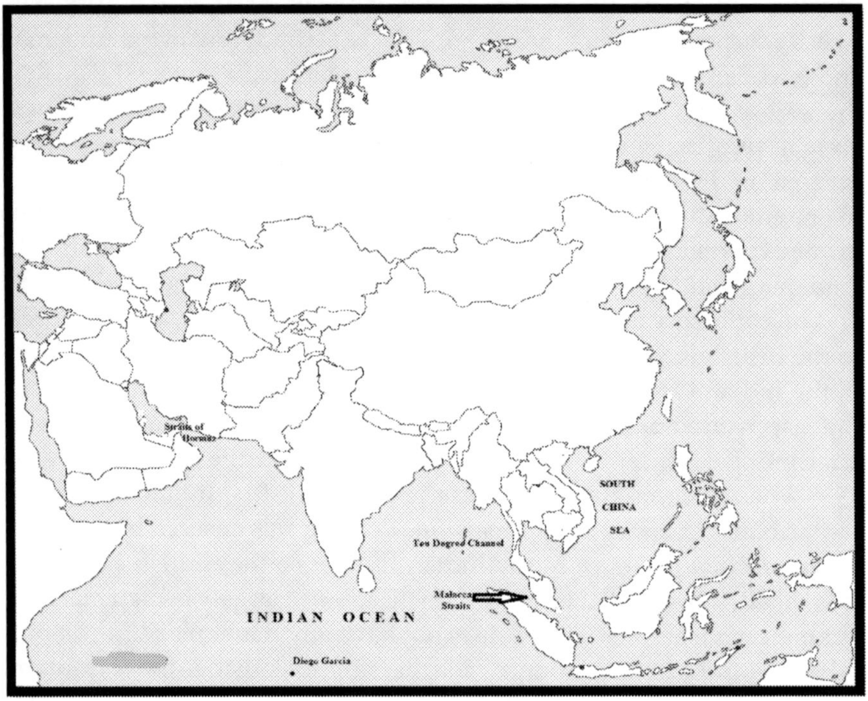

Map 6.1

India developed her maritime policy not before the dawn of the new century. Nonetheless, India's maritime concern began at the later stage of the Cold War with the rise of Chinese naval strength. The main concern of India's maritime policy is the growing presence of the PLA-Navy or PLAN in the Indian Ocean. There were opinions in the concluding phase of the Cold War about China concentrating on the development of blue water navy in the twenty-first century after the Chief of Chinese Naval Staff Zhang Liazhong stressed on it at the concluding phase of the Cold War. There was suggestion that the Chinese naval combat in the Spratlys and the Paracels Islands clashes (in South China Sea) should be an eye opener for the Indian Navy in the context of threat of similar actions that China might take in the Andaman and Nicobar Islands given the fact that the Indian navy was weaker than its Chinese counterpart although the Soviet bases from the Cam Ranh Bay and Da Nang (in South China Sea) restrained the passage of the Chinese naval vessels.[9] This was undoubtedly a welcome arrangement for India. On the other hand, the US was inclined to welcome the growth of Chinese blue water navy (during the Cold War) 'as being a deterrent to Soviet navy'. The US was also keeping the Pakistani navy ahead of its Indian counterpart as a capable deterrence force expressing doubt about the success of any Indian carrier escorted naval strikes against Pakistan coastline.[10] Thus India was not having a 'benign maritime environment' in her maritime neighbourhood during the Cold War as is generally perceived. Moreover, the presence of the US base in the Diego Garcia, in the middle of the Indian Ocean (see Map 6.1), was also not a welcome situation for New Delhi. The US involvement in the Indian Ocean increased in the 1960s and 1970s and it was early 1960s the US Navy realized the importance for logistics base in the Indian Ocean to carry out contingency operations in the region. They chose Diego Garcia of the Chagos archipelago of the Indian Ocean. Located 970 nautical miles away from the Indian mainland, this island was seen as a potential military base of the British. In the light of possible British withdrawal from the region, USA initiated discussions with London in early 1960s for shared Anglo-American defence facility. Following this, Diego Garcia was combined with three more islands taken from the Seychelles as a British crown colony of the British Indian Ocean Territory (BIOT) in 1965 and entire BIOT was made available for defence purposes of both US and UK governments. Diego Garcia was being developed by US from 1971 following the British withdrawal and the entrance of the Soviet navy in the Indian Ocean region.[11] It is to be remembered that this was the time when India-Soviet relationship was getting warmer with conclusion of friendship treaty signed between the two sides and the Soviet Union supported India's war against Pakistan in the latter's eastern wing. India was very uncomfortable with this American military presence in her neighbourhood. The Lusaka Summit of NAM (Non-Aligned Movement) of 1970 warned against possible increase in super power tussle in the Indian Ocean region and adopted the Indian Ocean 'zone of peace' resolution. The non-aligned countries insisted on the removal of foreign military bases from Indian Ocean region. Even Indian Prime Minister Indira Gandhi mentioned the presence of US bases in Diego Garcia at the New Delhi Summit of NAM in 1981which was although objected by Sri Lanka.[12] These developments undoubtedly forced the strategists in India to focus on the country's naval power. However, the unveiling of the Look East policy by India in the aftermath of the Cold War actually emphasized more on the need for India's naval empowerment.

Look East Policy and the maritime strategy

The Look East Policy, introduced in the beginning of 1990s, is widely seen as an economic initiative of the Indian policymakers to address the chronic economic crisis at home. Economic considerations occupied the lion's share of the post-Cold War global diplomacy of India redirecting the mode of her new foreign policy. India emphasized on economic relations since the economic security became the priority at the time. India encountered gigantic level of balance of payment crisis leaving her foreign exchange reserves with only two weeks' requirement. This chronic economic crisis forced the Narsimha Rao government to liberalize the economy through reforms. On the other hand, with the death of Soviet Union, India not only lost a prime international support but also was exposed to a new international geopolitical situation which she had to deal with on her own. So India now had to look for new friends and in this mission, her neighbourhood, far and near, became important. The Look East Policy was such a gesture in the east. Southeast Asia was also important from the strategic view point. India shares both land and maritime border with the region. The Nicobar Islands of the Andaman and Nicobar archipelago are few nautical miles away from Indonesian island of Sumatra. Moreover, these islands are most strategically situated at the gate of the Malacca Straits, gateway to South China Sea and beyond.

As India's trade relations with the east grew, this maritime region gained strategic significance for India. On the other hand, with the commerce intensifying with the east, maritime policy claimed a major share of India's Look East strategy. In a way Indian Ocean and the adjacent maritime zone of Asia has become strategically as well as economically very important for India. In 2004, India's Prime Minister Dr. Manmohan Singh proclaimed, "Our strategic footprint covers the region bounded by Horn of Africa, West Asia, Central Asia, South-East Asia and beyond..."[13] The twenty-first century Act East Policy of India (former Look East policy was renamed as Act East policy by the second NDA government which came to power in 2014 under Prime Minister Narendra Modi) attempts to act in the entire Asia Pacific region, extending from Japan in the north to Fiji and Australia in the south. In this mission both maritime and 'sea' powers are the most important factors.[14] Given the challenges that India faces in the geopolitical landscape in her neighbourhood, a strong naval prowess is necessary to promote India's maritime power. And in that case, India needs to have a definite maritime strategy in the form of Maritime Doctrine. The importance of the maritime zone and the complimentary naval power was realized fast by the Indian government at the dawn of the new century. Prime Minister Atal Behari Vajpayee, while addressing Annual Combined Commanders' Conference in 2003, said,

> "...As we grow in international stature, our defence strategies should naturally reflect our political, economic and security concerns, extending well beyond the geographical confines of South Asia... Our security environment ranges from the Persian Gulf to the Straits of Malacca across the Indian Ocean, includes Central Asia and Afghanistan in the North West, China in the North East and Southeast Asia. Our strategic thinking has also to extend to these horizons."[15]

Similarly, his successor Dr. Manmohan Singh said that 'India's growing international stature gives it strategic relevance in the areas from Persian Gulf to the Straits of Malacca'.[16] Thus it is seen that the Indian governments started putting emphasis on India's maritime neighbourhood as it concentrates more on the global performances which requires the need to strengthen the country's naval power since the beginning of the new century.

However, the change in the mindset of the government vis-à-vis the need to focus on the waters around started occurring in the concluding phase of the last century. The Indian Navy conducted Strategic Defence Review in 1998 openly articulating the service's desired ends, ways and means for the use of sea power with four major roles identified for the navy: sea-based deterrence, economic and energy security, forward presence and naval diplomacy.[17] India embarked on naval modernization mission in the late 1990s to turn the navy into a consequential force in the Indian Ocean region. This was the result of the realisation of the political leadership of the country about the importance of the maritime power and thus the Indian Navy, which was treated as 'Cinderella service' for long, could not be ignored anymore. However, the ambitious naval modernization programme, announced in 1990, could not be materialized due to resource crisis at home and the loss of Soviet Union.[18] Thus it is seen that the Indian government pondered on the naval build up in the immediate conclusion of the Cold War although it yielded no result due to lack of resources and support. It is to be remembered that, as we have seen in the previous chapters, China had already started concentrating on her naval up gradation since the mid-1980s and India's concentration on similar mission is noteworthy in this context. However, nothing significant happened until the concluding phase of the last century with the conduct of Defence Review of 1998. Subsequently, the maritime strategy doctrines were published by the Indian Navy of which the Indian Maritime Military Strategy titled *Freedom to Use Seas* of 2007. The then Indian Navy Chief, Admiral Suresh Mehta, wrote in the forward of the Strategy that,

> "Current projections indicate that India will be foremost centres of power-economic, technological and cultural, in the coming decades. ...Our primary national interest therefore is to ensure a secure and stable environment, which will enable continued economic development and social upliftment of our masses...Therefore, within this overall national and defence framework, our primary maritime military interest is to ensure national security, provide insulation from external interference, so that the vital task of fostering economic growth and undertaking developmental activities, can take place in a secure environment..."[19]

The document pronounced the duty of the Navy to support India's foreign policy saying, "The Maritime Military Strategy recognized that the major task of the Indian Navy during the 21st Century will be to use warships to support national foreign policy".[20] C Raja Mohan gives the credit of the government's emphasis on the maritime policy to the BJP-led NDA government which was elected to power in 1998. Referring to its stress on strong national security programme, he argues that the Foreign Minister Jaswant Singh, National Security Adviser Brajesh Mishra and Defence Minister George Fernandes were 'strong supporters of expanding India's maritime profile and fully backed modernization of the navy'.[21] Following this initiative, the budget allocation for the navy climbed up from 14 per cent during 1999-2000 to 18.9 per cent in 2008-2009.[22] Prime Minister Dr. Manmohan Singh of the successive UPA government remarked in 2004 that India's 'strategic footprint covers....Southeast Asia and beyond' following which the then Indian Navy Chief Admiral Arun Prakash said in 2005, "it is imperative for India....to retain a strong maritime capability in order to maintain a balance of maritime power in the Indian Ocean, as well as the larger Asia Pacific region."[23] Even his successor Admiral Suresh Mehta echoed his viewpoint saying that, "(the Navy's area of) interest is not restricted to the Indian Ocean."[24] Thus the Indian Navy was expressing its solidarity with the government's foreign policy while assuring its readiness to promote it. As mentioned earlier, the initial thrust of India's Look East Policy was economic and the maritime route plays vital role in sustaining this policy. Thus the significance of the sea lanes of communication (SLOC) is understandable.

Since 1990, India's economic engagement with ASEAN increased with annual trade growing from \$2.4 billion to \$30 billion in 2007.[25] Between 2009-10 periods it rose to \$44 billion and to \$74 billion in 2013-14 periods.[26] In 2014-15 periods the trade amounted to \$76.52 billion.[27] Thus we see that India-ASEAN trade grew significantly in the years following the unveiling of Look East Policy. Nevertheless, apart from the economic consideration, the strategic concerns also played important role in India's interests in developing closeness with ASEAN countries. Both sides have convergence of security and strategic interests. It is noteworthy here that during the Cold War years India-ASEAN relations experienced many hurdles due their respective association with the two contending super powers even when both sides shared strategic concerns. Nonetheless, in 1966 Singapore urged India to contribute in the 'Asian Monroe Doctrine', with possibility arising of British military disentanglement under East of Suez policy, and hoped that India would play viable long-term role in the security of Southeast Asia, especially in Malaysia and Singapore. But India was unable to respond to Singapore's request at that point of time following her engagement with South Asian affairs vis-à-vis Pakistan and China. Even Singapore understood India's precarious situation and thus talked about assistance from a long term perspective.[28] This shows that India was counted as a strategic tool by Singapore, one of the founders of ASEAN, even during the Cold War period, in absence of British protection. However, the overall India-ASEAN relations were marred by the larger contesting geopolitics of the Cold War where both sides became hostage of their respective super power patronisers, most evident in the Cambodian affair.[29]

India was not in a position to reach out to Southeast Asian waters with her weak naval strength nor she had any economic reason (or even strategic reason) to do so during the Cold War time. The end of the Cold War altered the situation faster with India losing Soviet Union and USA reducing her interest in the Southeast Asian affairs. India and Southeast Asia came closer with India joining ASEAN Regional Forum in the early 1990s. One common strategic and security concern of both sides was the rise of China. GVC Naidu argues that China factor started concerning the ASEAN countries amidst the US withdrawal from the Philippines and the emergence of the South China Sea dispute as a major security concern for the ASEAN countries. Balveer Singh also attributes the India-Southeast Asia closeness in the security arena in the post Cold War period to the China factor.[30] As we have seen in the previous chapters China started emerging as a 'threat' to many South China Sea littorals in the post Cold War period with Beijing acting assertively on her sovereignty claims over the disputed islands and waters around since the concluding phase of the Cold War with her National People's Congress passing the territorial law in 1992. We have discussed in chapters before that China has always been opportunistic in asserting her sovereignty claims in South China Sea appearing in the scene when the super power domination waned. Also there was urge among the claimants to engage the extra regional powers more and more to balance the 'Chinese threat' where India started featuring day-by-day. We should also remember that compared to China, India took a late entry in the ASEAN affair. By the time India appeared in ASEAN business, China was already an influential power. India had the urge to compete with China for influence. As GVC Naidu opines, "It is in India's interest to ensure that Southeast Asia would not be dominated by any regional power once it became obvious that the super powers were going to build down their presence...".[31]

The India-China relations have remained a matter of competition and containment (on India's part) vis-à-vis Southeast Asia since the 1962 war. After the war India initiated the mission to contain China in her backyard just the way China wants to corner India in South Asia by engaging India's small and medium neighbours like Nepal, Sri Lanka and Bangladesh who are uneasy with India's 'dominance' on the sub continent and 'empowering' Pakistan, India's arch rival and a major security threat. Thus the strategic aspect of India's Look East Policy is partially a tit-for-tat approach vis-à-vis China's South Asia/Indian Ocean policy. This can also be viewed from the Kautalyan model where the state looks for weaker allies or partners as help to neutralize the designs of distant opponent, China in this case. The strategy of mounting forward defence in South China Sea also adheres to British Viceroy Lord Curzon's prescription to create geographic buffers against external threats, applying it in the nautical milieu.[32]

South China Sea and India

In April 2000, India announced her plan to conduct unilateral naval exercises in the South China Sea. Following this announcement, Indian Navy sent warships, tankers and submarines to Japan, South Korea, Indonesia and Vietnam for bilateral exercises.[33] India's interest in South China Sea are directed both by economic as well as strategic concerns. Freedom of navigation in a tranquil Southeast Asian ambience is essential for India's commerce with East Asia, a major concern of India's Look East Policy. As we have said in the beginning of this chapter South China Sea is the economic lifeline for India. Apart from being the trade highway between India and the Pacific world, South China Sea is also a major source of energy for the hungry Indian economy. The exploration of energy resources from the South China Sea is thus a priority of India. In October 2011, India signed an agreement with Vietnam to explore oil from the South China Sea. Vietnam invited India to explore oil and gas in Blocks 127 and 128. In reaction to this, China issued a demarche to India in November 2011 underlining the requirement of China's permission to conduct the explorations in the said blocks. New Delhi ignored the demarche and her state-owned company ONGC-*Videsh* expressed its desire to strengthen contacts with Vietnam.[34] Again in 2015 *China Daily* termed New Delhi's plan to restart oil exploration off the Vietnam coast as 'illegal' and said, "India's intention to once again explore for oil in the disputed waters of the South China Sea is an unwise move, as it will further complicate the maritime disputes and do a disservice to maintaining the positive momentum that has been achieved in China-India ties".[35] It said, "...since India began to covet oil reserves in the disputed waters in recent years and has sought to cooperate with Vietnam to extract them, the issue has been looming over the generally stable and improving relations between China and India".[36] Thus, the paper links India's oil exploration in the disputed waters in collaboration with China's leading challenger Vietnam, with the geopolitical dispute of South China Sea. Although India made it clear that she is 'not a party to the dispute'. India's Minister of State for External Affairs, E. Ahmed, said in 2012 that 'Sovereignty over areas of South China Sea is disputed between many countries in the region. India is not party to the dispute," but maintained "Government has said that it supports freedom of navigation, right of passage and access to resources in accordance with accepted principles of international law and these should be respected by all".[37] Thus India has made it clear that her concern is not the dispute but the right to unhindered access to the sea route. The sea route is important for India since she imports oil from the faraway Sakhalin (in Asian Russia) which is transported to Mangalore through the sea routes.[38] Therefore her interest is in tranquil conflict free South China Sea.

On the other hand, given the latent Sino-India rivalry for influence in the Southeast Asia and larger Asia Pacific region, it is important for India to contain China from acquiring dominance in the South China Sea region. India's naval diplomacy with the South China Sea littoral states, who are also the parties to the sovereignty disputes, is noteworthy in this context. The ships of Eastern Fleet of the Indian Navy comprising Navy Ships *Rana, Khukri, Ranvir, Kora* and *Udaygiri* were deployed for 'Presence-cum-Surveillance Missions' in Malacca Straits, Sunda Strait and South China Sea in May 2003 while INS *Ranvijay, Ranjit, Godavari, Kirch, Sukanya* and *Jyoti* sailed into South China Sea and the West Pacific Ocean from 1st October to 20th November 2003. During this trip, the ships visited Pusan (South Korea), Tokyo (Japan), Jakarta (Indonesia) Manila (the Philippines) and Ho Chi Minh City (Vietnam).[39] All these countries have uneasy relations with China and are concerned with her military modernization mission. Selecting these countries did have a geopolitical and geostrategic message. This modernization issue was repeatedly mentioned in India's annual defence reports since 2000.[40]

The naval diplomacy with these kinds of port visits to the countries with traditional uneasiness with China is significant. In 2006 Indian Navy's Eastern Fleet sent ships *Rana, Rajput, Jyoti, Kirpan* and *Kulish* to South China Sea where they conducted naval exercises with several navies.[41] Thus India maintained her presence in the disputed water body and associated herself with China-wary countries.[42] Not only visiting the disputed zone, Indian government also prepared the Indian island territory to promote such movements. In 2005 the Indian Navy established Far Eastern Naval Command (FENC) in the Andaman and Nicobar Islands, located between Bay of Bengal and the Straits of Malacca which opens the gate of South China Sea and beyond to India. The airfields in the Andaman bring the Straits and larger portions of the South China Sea within the operation range of the Indian fighter aircrafts like SU-30K Sukhoi and SEPECAT Jaguar.[43] India inaugurated an air marine station *Baaz* in the Andaman islands in 2012 which enables India to conduct surveillance operations in the South China Sea. According to Indian defence officials India is building longer airstrips at the top and bottom of the Andaman and Nicobar chain, partly for long-range surveillance planes. One is at Campbell Bay on Great Nicobar Island in the south, 240 km (150 miles) from the mouth of the Malacca Straits. They said that India also expects the number of naval vessels based in the island chain to double to 32 before a targeted timeframe of 2022.[44] However, having said this, India, at least in 2012, was not putting South China Sea into her priority list. The then Chief of Indian Navy, Admiral Nirmal Verma, said, "...the primary areas of interest to us is from the Malacca Strait to the (Persian/Arabian) Gulf in the west, and to the Cape of Good Hope in the south... the Pacific and the South China Sea are of concern to us, but activation in those areas is not on the cards."[45] The up gradation programme in the Andaman Nicobar Islands definitely directs to India's priority on Indian Ocean Region which is her undisputed and so far tranquil maritime home.

However, the port visits to the area prior to 2012 tells a different story. It is true that Indian Navy is yet to acquire the strength to actively participate in the South China Sea. Besides, such a move might not be welcomed by the local powers. When India embarked on naval expansion mission in the 1980s with Soviet help, following the unhindered entry of USS *Enterprise* in her maritime vicinity during the Indo-Pak war of 1971, many ASEAN countries were upset especially with the rumours about New Delhi's intentions of building bases in the Great Nicobar Island, 80 nautical miles away from Indonesian island of Sumatra. The expansion of naval facilities in the Andaman was seen as Indian attempt of projecting capability to control Malacca Strait and other crucial straits of the region. Indonesia reported against such naval build-up in the Andaman and Greater Nicobar Islands in 1986.[46] Thus India needs to be cautious about her strategy in the South China Sea region. Moreover, Indian Ocean houses India where she is the local power with most powerful navy. So it is natural for India to put Indian Ocean above South China Sea. However, South China Sea is her maritime neighbour, equally important, both economically as well as strategically. That is why the Indian governments since 2000, have included South China Sea into India's 'maritime zone of interests'. And China is the major factor in India's South China Sea relations.

India, China and South China Sea

C. Raja Mohan writes, "*...a rising China and an emerging India are turning to the sea in ways that they did not before.*"[47] The two neighbouring ancient civilizations-turned-modern day rivals of Asia are now facing each other in the new front, the Asian maritime area. Having been the contesters on land for fifty years, India and China are now contesting each other in the waters of their respective neighbourhood, Indian Ocean and South China Sea. Such a development is natural since both strategic rivals are emerging economies and aspiring powers (China is already considered a major Asian player being number one economy of the continent and number two in the world) and both the economies depend heavily on maritime trade route and thus need secured sea lanes of communication. Therefore, both are witnessing the 'intrusion' of one another in 'their waters' with China creating the 'string of pearls' around India developing port facilities in Pakistan, Sri Lanka and Djibouti (the latest in the Horn of Africa) in Indian Ocean while India making port visits in the South China Sea littoral states and deciding to build satellite tracking stations in Vietnam. When China is preoccupied with securing the sea lanes from any hostile power, India is concerned with growing Chinese presence in Indian Ocean.

There are opinions that both the countries are influenced by the Mahanian theory arguing however that the relevance of the theory to both lies on the relation between the emerging power with global interests and its maritime strategy rather than doctrine of naval battles on high seas.[48] China plays a very important part in India's Look East/Act East policy. Since independence, China factor played a major role in India's Southeast Asia policy and since 1962 India's Southeast Asia strategy is directed by the challenge from China.[49] Besides, there is a general view among the Indian policy makers that in the long run China will be India's competitor, economic and possibly military.[50] Nevertheless, it will be wrong to view India's maritime expansionist agenda in the East Asian waters in the context of her relations and rivalry with China only. Apart from the strategic calculation vis-à-vis Chinese naval ambitions, India needs to expand her zone of maritime activity to boost her economy as well. However strategic the Act East Policy seems to have the economic consideration which played a vital part during its unveiling in the early 1990s is also relevant. Both China and India are transforming into major economic powers and this economic orientation of both coupled with their rapid globalization since the end of last century have been the principle source of navalism in Beijing and New Delhi. The unhindered acquisition of resources has become a national security priority of both the countries. Both Beijing and New Delhi focus on the reliable transportation of resources and are concerned about disruptions of the supply. Such a situation compels them to focus on their naval strength to protect sea lanes of communication.[51]

However, it is also to be remembered that both the countries aspire to be global player and for that they have to expand their zone of influence and activities. This is needed for both economic as well as strategic reasons. To be a global power one has to, first, strengthen its economy which requires unhindered supply of resources as well as vast global market thus to invest in maritime power. And second, to sustain the maritime power, strengthening one's naval power is important. Thus two powers, maritime and naval, are complementary to each other. Both India and China are pursuing this strategy and it is taking the shape of competition for influence since the two are traditional rivals. Hence, when both the countries are working to promote their economic strength, the strategic rivalry cannot be ruled out given the fact that both aspire to be major global powers. On the other hand both the countries were subject to hostile power presence in their respective maritime vicinity, with US sending its ship to the Indian Ocean during 1971 war and to Taiwan Strait in 1996 which exposed the vulnerability of their coasts to any enemy attack. When the Taiwan Strait incident influenced the Chinese leadership to develop the navy in order to thwart any such intervention in future, the 1971 incident underlined India's need for powerful navy.[52] Such a defensive policy subsequently poses threat to the neighbours, especially when there exists traditional suspicion. Today, China's economic interest lies in India's vicinity while India's lies in China's and in this way South China Sea opens a new front between India and China. Both India and China are aspiring naval powers and possess the potential to rule the Asia-Pacific waters. There is undoubtedly a rise in maritime competition between the two to influence the East Asian waters resulted by the conflict of interest.

This strategic competition became the cornerstone of India's East Asia / Asia Pacific maritime policy with the unveiling of the new century where South China Sea started featuring prominently in India's East Asia policy. And in that way the Indian Navy became the main benefactor. The government in New Delhi under Prime Minister Vajpayee in late 1990s embarked on ambitious project of naval acquisition as part of the 'forward leaning' policy emphasizing on India's access and political leverage from East Africa to Asia Pacific region. However, India's maritime strategy doctrine of 2004 focused on the arc from Persian Gulf to Malacca Strait as the area of interest.[53] Malacca Strait is the gateway to South China Sea and the Pacific world from the west. Till 2000 it was assumed that India would limit her maritime interests between the Gulf of Aden and Malacca with no intension to play larger role in the western Pacific Ocean. Such a perception was shaken after the Indian Navy appeared in the South China Sea in late 2000 which initiated the process of frequent and wide ranging naval exercises between India and the South China Sea littorals. Not only this, the significant contribution that Indian Navy made in the 2004 tsunami relief efforts in the Indian Ocean region also gave the message of the Navy's preparedness in handling any future humanitarian crisis in Southeast Asia.[54] Such efforts are parts of the naval diplomacy that India initiated since the late 1990s. This is the way India attempted to gain the confidence of the South China Sea littoral states.

In the 1990s India developed close defence and strategic relations with the Southeast Asian states, especially the South China Sea littoral states. The naval diplomacy was part of this new gesture. Shedding decades old military isolationism, India paid special attention to military engagement with many Southeast Asian countries. India began to expand her joint naval exercises with the Southeast Asian countries concentrating on improving relations with the eastern navies. From 1995 India, in a mission to promote sub regional maritime togetherness, started organizing naval interactions with *Milan* naval exercise at Port Blair in the Andaman Islands. This exercise was started with the navies of Indonesia, Singapore, Thailand and Sri Lanka as a Confidence Building Measure (CBM) firstly to mitigate the fear that arose among some Southeast Asian countries about India's naval expansion policy and secondly to counter the emerging presence of China in India's adjacent waters.[55] This was the curtain-raiser of India's twenty-first century naval diplomacy in the Southeast Asian waters as part of the second phase of India's Look East Policy which transcended the economic orientation of the initial days and embraced the larger geostrategic and security considerations. This was made clear by Foreign Minister Yashwant Sinha who said in 2003 at the India-ASEAN Business Summit, "India's Look East Policy has now entered Phase II. Phase I was primarily on the ASEAN countries and on trade and investment linkages...Phase II marks a shift in focus from exclusively economic issues to economic and security issues including joint efforts to protect sea lanes, coordination and counter terrorism etc..."[56] This statement was made after the 9/11 incident in USA which unveiled the period of series of terrorist attacks all over the globe, including Southeast Asia. Thus the inclusion of the security aspect is understandable. In the post 9/11 world national security became the corner stone of the foreign policy, replacing the sole consideration of economic benefits which was the trend in the early days of the post Cold War period.

Considering that 80 per cent of the global trade is conducted via sea, the issue of maritime security at the choke points of Malacca Strait and the harbours around the world became a priority. The hijacking of the ship at Malacca Strait in 1999 and attack on the *USS Cole* and *MV Limburg* by Al Qaida at Yemeni port of Aden in 2002 put the maritime security issue at the forefront.[57] Thus security of the sea lanes became vital for both India and Southeast Asia. However, this should not be seen as the sole reason behind India embarking on naval diplomacy. China's Indian Ocean policy of the twenty-first century also played its part. It is to be remembered that when India's interest in South China Sea lies in freedom of navigation to ensure unhindered commercial connections with East Asia and the Pacific, China also requires similar arrangement in Indian Ocean to cater to the need for unhindered connections with West Asia, specially the oil rich Gulf region. On the other hand both India and China consider the two water bodies as their respective zones. And by the beginning of the twenty-first century India well established her presence in the East Asian geopolitical framework through her association with several ASEAN-sponsored institutions like ARF, East Asia Summit and ADMM+ (ASEAN Defence Ministers Meeting Plus). This was India's diplomatic endeavour to 'intrude in the Chinese zone'. David Scott suggests that, 'Whereas India perhaps seeks pre-eminence in the Indian Ocean, it also seeks to deny similar pre-eminence to China in South China Sea'.[58]

There is no doubt that India is in competition with China for influence in the latter's neighbourhood. Like other neighbours, India is also anxious about the growing power of China although Prime Minister Manmohan Singh claimed that that India and China are not in competition and that 'there is enough economic space for us to grow'.[59] However it does not mean that India is going to give 'enough space' to China to act freely. India's interest in the South China Sea is apparently economic in character, nonetheless it does have strategic connotation as well. India has been active in the Sea for almost a decade. Indian carrier INS *Viraat* made a maiden visit to the South China Sea ports—Klang in Malaysia, Singapore and Jakarta in Indonesia—in 2005.[60] This visit was termed by the then Navy Chief Admiral Arun Prakash as 'friendly mission' insisting that it was a reflection of India's 'commitment' to these countries 'in the very limited sense of engaging them...in maritime sense...and not committing military sense'.[61] Thus India at this point of time was eager to project a benign image in the region where she was unveiling a 'military adventure' for the first time. The Navy Chief also put forward the proposal for navy-to-navy talks with Malaysia and Indonesia to 'explore "areas of cooperation without military collaboration'.[62] This shows that the Indian navy was reluctant to display its power and emphasized on regional cooperation with the local navies to ensure its interest in the region. Although the main focus of this visit was Malacca Strait whose security is important for India as it is the gateway to both the Pacific and the Indian Ocean, given the fact that the states the Navy chose to visit are all the littorals of South China Sea and are uneasy with China's rise, such a visit was significant. Keeping the Malacca Strait region within control, in collaboration with the local powers, will definitely serve India's interests in thwarting China's move into the Indian Ocean region.

However, as mentioned earlier India does not limit her maritime interest within the Indian Ocean since she is 'looking East' and for that she has to get into the South China Sea. In 2012 the then Navy Chief, Admiral D.K. Joshi, firmly asserted that India will protect her interests in the disputed South China Sea waters. Declaring 'concern' about China's naval modernization mission, Admiral Joshi said, "Not that we expect to be in those waters very frequently, but when the requirement is there for situations where country's interests are involved...".[63] He insisted on freedom of navigation as the priority of India's interest in the South China Sea.[64] This is significant in the sense that with passage of time India started becoming assertive with her interests in the South China Sea region. Such assertiveness was attached to India's growing energy interests in the South China Sea which she started exploring causing much displeasure to Beijing. *Global Times* reported that Chinese foreign ministry issued objection to India's unilateral oil exploration in the South China Sea asking the relevant countries 'to respect China's sovereignty and national interests'. Such a statement came following the remarks made by Admiral Joshi.[65] Analysts however see India's growing 'assertiveness' vis-à-vis her interests in the South China Sea reflected in Admiral Joshi's statement, firstly, in terms of her economic interest and secondly as the reflection of India's changing regional and global status. It is argued that conflict between Vietnam, the Philippines and China over the South China Sea dispute will 'internationalize' the dispute bringing in US as arbiter and India's deployment of her navy to safeguard her energy interest in the region will contribute to such internationalization.[66] Thus India's policy in the South China Sea, apparently to safeguard her economic interest, is viewed as a part of larger geopolitical game plan formulated with USA. Although it is difficult to justify such an argument given India's fixation with independent foreign policy exercise, nonetheless the US guarantee is undoubtedly helpful, as we will see later, in sustaining India's interest in the South China Sea region.

India's growing importance in the Southeast Asian geopolitics was established when the ASEAN urged India to intervene to resolve the South China Sea disputes in 2012 which was however turned down by India saying that the issue did not require India's intervention.[67] This was interesting in the sense that it showed in one hand the growing willingness among the small Southeast Asian countries to involve India in the local affairs, undoubtedly as an act of balance against China, and India's unwillingness to involve in the affairs annoying China, on the other. This can be analyzed in the context of China's South Asia policy where China might increase her involvement as counter to India's 'overactive' posture in Southeast Asia. But this does not mean that India was ready to leave South China Sea to the Chinese whims.

David Scott argues that from strategic viewpoint India's strengthening of position in the South China Sea is an attempt 'to *compensate* for not being able to stop China's appearance in the Indian Ocean.[68] This argument is interesting since both China and India are destined to 'intrude' into each others' maritime zone of influence after they embarked on economic development and reform. However, India need not have to focus on South China Sea, the only maritime route to East Asia from India, if she had not embarked on the Look East Policy where the economic policy is complimented by the strategic considerations. China, on the other hand, has to look at the Indian Ocean it being the sole maritime supply route for her. Also, India's position in the Indian Ocean region is much better compared to China's in her maritime vicinity. This is, firstly, because of India's predominant naval power in the Indian Ocean region and her vast Peninsula that juts into the larger part of the Ocean and secondly, and most importantly, India's maritime neighbourhood is free of territorial dispute and her small neighbours do not overtly challenge the predominance of the Indian naval strength in the region although they do attempt to balance against India by engaging with China. China lacks such ambience. When in one hand she has major maritime territorial disputes with her neighbours, such a situation is compounded by the presence USA as a security guarantee to them, herself being the major challenge to China's regional as well as global aspirations. Such precarious situation of China is undoubtedly helping India's strategy in the East Asian region of which South China Sea is a vital part.

It is to be remembered that the major strategic priority of India's East Asia policy is to contain China in her own area. Even the Chinese sources argue that the strategic objective behind India's involvement in the South China Sea is to 'pin down China in the area'.[69] Such an objective is natural for India to undertake since, apart from her East Asia strategy, China is the major hurdle in India's regional aspirations in South Asia where China attempts to wean the small South Asian states like Nepal, Sri Lanka and Bangladesh away from India with Pakistan already within China's grip. It is mention worthy here that Pakistan and Bangladesh are the leading customers of Chinese defence products. Moreover the construction of port facilities in South Asia—Gwadar in Pakistan (already operational), Humbantota in Sri Lanka and Chittagong in Bangladesh—by China ensure China's strengthening presence in the South Asian region, home of India. The Commander of PLAN's guided missile destroyer No.132 commented that China did not recognize that Indian Ocean belongs to India.[70] So India's move into the South China Sea region can be seen as a strategic countermove. Since China is investing heavily in diplomatic and military capital in the Indian Ocean even not being an Indian Ocean power, India, even not being a South China Sea power, is 'working overtime to project itself as one.'[71] Like China developing closeness with India-wary countries of South Asia, India has also developed similar closeness with the China-wary countries of South China Sea region, and Vietnam tops the list.

India-Vietnam geostrategic alliance and South China Sea

The India-Vietnam relations have to be specially analysed in the context of South China Sea geopolitics vis-à-vis India. India's relation with Vietnam has been traditionally guided by the latter's equation with China. During the Cold War period India's relations with ASEAN, that time constituted only by the pro-US countries of the region, were directed by New Delhi's relation with Hanoi. India had to earn severe criticism from ASEAN following her support to Vietnam's Cambodia policy. Although such a policy should be seen through the larger Cold War geopolitical prism with India being tied to Soviet knot who was also the main supporter of Vietnam against both US and China, countering Chinese influence in the Indochina region was another objective of India which she did relying upon the Moscow-Hanoi alliance.[72] Thus India always valued her relation with Vietnam in countering China since their strategic and geopolitical interests converge over the issue. Vietnam has come up as a major strategic partner in India's Look East Policy. Harsh Pant identifies Vietnam as the lynchpin in India's move towards East Asia as a counter to China's expansion in South Asia and Indian Ocean and citing the Sino-Vietnam tension opines that, "...in some quarters of New Delhi, Vietnam is already seen as a counterweight in the same way Pakistan has been for China".[73] David Scott also suggests India-Vietnam strategic partnership acts as counterweight to the Sino-Pakistan nexus.[74] Developing strategic relations with Vietnam is also helpful for India, firstly because Vietnam is the South China Sea littoral state and is in possession of some of the islets of the disputed water which will serve India's economic objectives and secondly because of Hanoi's uneasiness about China's rise which converges with India's concerns. If India can thwart Chinese expansionist activities in the South China Sea with Vietnam's help that can ensure India's interests in the Indian Ocean region. Since 2000 India has deepened defence cooperation with Vietnam. Defence Minister George Fernandes signed a defence protocol with Vietnam in 2000 which included naval exercises between the two navies and coastguard and training of Vietnamese air force pilots by India.[75]

It is undeniable that India-Vietnam strategic closeness has developed in the shadow of China's rise. Apart from this China-concern, the strategic closeness is important for India given the necessity to keep the sea lanes of South China Sea free of hindrance which may arise for India if it slips into the hands of China. Vietnam also suffers from similar concern since apart from the sovereignty issue the sea lane itself is important for her as it is the only maritime opening for her to the world outside. Thus Harsh Pant argues, "The two nations (India and Vietnam) also have stakes in ensuring security of sea lane as well as shared concerns about Chinese access to the Indian Ocean and South China Sea."[76] It is in India's interests that the sea lanes of the eastern waters remain in friendly hands. China is a major factor in India-Vietnam relations and it is natural for both to develop bold strategic relations due to this factor. That is why the Vietnamese President Tran Duch Luang said in 2000, while receiving the Indian Defence Minister, "Vietnam treats India with strategic importance."[77] India considers Vietnam as the major barrier against the southward expansion of China. Besides, given Vietnam's geostrategic setting in China's neighbourhood, it is suggested that she can contribute in future strategy to contain China's rise in the Asia Pacific region.[78]

Apart from the strategic considerations, India's urge for closeness with Vietnam also has economic connotations. As it is known that India, being a rising economy, is hunting for energy resources especially oil and Vietnam is proving to be very helpful in this regard. India faced difficulties in importing oil from the Gulf region and Middle East (West Asia) during the Gulf War of 1991. Given the requirement of meeting the growing energy demands following the economic reforms of 1990s India looked for alternative source of energy supply which drew India's attention to the South China Sea's oil and natural gas reserves. However, India's ONGC (Oil and Natural Gas Corporation) *Videsh* Ltd (OVL) was already engaged in the oil exploration arrangements with Vietnam. India's oil exploration in Vietnam dates back to the 1980s when she started oil exploration in the country in 1988 with Soviet Union. It was only in the post Cold War period when India started exploration of oil in South China Sea after Vietnam opened its oil and gas sector to foreign companies in 1990 and 1992.[79] Vietnam was her first partner country since late 1980s. In 1988 OVL inked an agreement with PetroVietnam on petroleum sharing contract. It conducted explorations jointly with British Petroleum (BP) and PetroVietnam in the South China Sea in 1992 and 1993. In 2006 OVL got offshore exploration blocks, 127 and 128, which fall within Vietnam's EEZ as an operator with 100 per cent stake.[80] In 2001 India's oil fields in Vietnam were the largest overseas possession in the energy sector with ONGC holding 45 per cent share in its joint venture with BP group.[81] This oil exploration rights serves India's economic objectives of her relations with Vietnam. However, this takes a strategic turn when China opposes such ventures of India and warns strong repercussion. In 2011 China objected to India's oil exploration which India vowed to continue in the two blocks near the Paracel Islands. The Chinese foreign ministry, while reiterating China's "indisputable sovereignty" over the South China Sea islands, said without naming India directly, that "Any country engaging in oil and gas exploration activities in this jurisdiction without the approval of the Chinese government constitutes an infringement upon China's sovereignty and national interest."[82] China's allegation of India's 'infringement' with her sovereignty can be compared to similar allegation levelled by New Delhi against Beijing following the latter's construction of Economic Corridor in Pakistan which passes through portion of India's Kashmir territory under occupation of Pakistan. China paid no heed to such objections of India. Thus it gives the logic to India to return the 'favour' to China in South China Sea. India and Vietnam signed a fresh exploration deal in 2014 during Indian President Pranab Mukherjee's visit to Vietnam.[83]

The India-Vietnam relations have improved further in the context of the South China Sea issue, after India re-launched her Look East Policy as 'Act East Policy' in 2014. During Vietnamese Prime Minister Nguyen Tan Dung's visit to India in October 2014 ONGC signed a Heads of Agreement with Petro Vietnam Exploration Production Company Ltd. (PVEP) for exploration in Blocks 102/10, 106/10 and 128. The agreement called for ONGC to take 40 percent equity in Block 102/10 and 50 percent in 106/10, both of which lie outside the waters claimed by China and Vietnam assured India of security in the South China Sea.[84] The joint statement issued by the two sides emphasized on freedom of navigation and read that over flight in the South China Sea should not be 'impeded' and called for parties 'to exercise restraints and avoid threat or use of force and resolve disputes through peaceful means in accordance with universally recognized principles of international law, including the UNCLOS-1982'.[85] The emphasis on exercising restraints and avoidance of using force to resolve the disputes undoubtedly refers to China which, for the past two decades, have not only risen as the most powerful among the claimants South China Sea disputes but does not hesitate to project her power at times. The frequent clashes that occur between the patrolling vessels in the disputed waters where the fishermen are sometimes subject to suffering are taken as the Chinese way of showing strength and can be seen as ominous signs. Given the current strength of Vietnam it is not possible for her to handle China single handed. Thus Prime Minister Dung, in an interview with Press Trust of India (PTI), called on India to play a more active diplomatic role in addressing territorial disputes in the South China Sea saying "Vietnam hopes that India, as a major power in the region and the world, will actively support the parties concerned to peacefully resolve all disputes."[86] The latest development in the India-Vietnam strategic relations has been the installation of a satellite station in Vietnam's Ho Chi Minh City. The Indian Space Research Organisation (ISRO) has set up a Data Reception and Tracking and Telemetry Station in Ho Chi Minh City, which will be activated soon and linked with another station in Biakin, Indonesia. It is termed as the most important strategic asset for India in the South China Sea region.[87] The Chinese experts, however, have termed this development as India's attempt 'to stir up trouble in the region to serve its (India's) own ends, which is to counterbalance China's influence'.[88]

India takes an uncompromising stand on ensuring her interest in the South China Sea region without taking any stand on the dispute. Her main concern is to ensure unhindered access to the sea lanes with freedom of navigation ensured. India is expanding her zone of activities beyond the confines of South Asian waters in tandem with her economic progress which necessitates the unconstrained supply of resources to sustain the development. On the other hand India's growing active engagement in the Southeast Asian region is part of her larger geostrategic consideration in the context of her covert competition with China for power and influence. This strategy of India is generating hope among the China wary countries of the region like Vietnam about India's balancing act against the giant neighbour. This is clear from the open urge of the Vietnamese Prime Minister that India should play significant role in the resolution of the dispute despite the fact that India is reluctant to take sides in the matter and is unwilling to be an arbiter in the dispute. This author's interactions with the Vietnamese experts in Hanoi also echoed the government's position in this context, in a more direct manner. They insisted on India's increasing appearance in the disputed waters suggesting that India's and other big powers' presence in the 'East Sea' (the Vietnamese name for South China Sea) can be helpful in containing China. They said that India's Act East Policy can break the Chinese circle. However, during the interaction with this author, the Vietnamese experts expressed reservation regarding India's 'peaceful policy' vis-à-vis South China Sea tension which, according them, is not sufficient to counter China who is 'very aggressive'. They emphasized on the requirement of a security treaty between India and Vietnam insisting that both these countries know China 'more than any other country'. Such an enthusiasm about India is natural given the fact that Vietnam has been the victim of Chinese aggression, like India. On the other hand such high expectation about India's contribution in the resolution of the dispute lacked among some experts in Singapore who, during interaction with this author, expressed doubt about any significant role that India can play in the South China Sea geopolitics.

The emerging South China Sea strategy in India's Act East Policy

As India's economy grows, her maritime neighbourhood gains more and more significance in her strategy formulation. This growing economic interaction with the world has increased the importance of India's maritime neighbourhood since seaborne trade is the backbone of India's economic growth. 90 per cent by volume and 70 per cent by value of India's external trade today is conducted via sea.[89] On the other hand the growing importance of the sea lanes of communication has increased the importance of its security, especially in the context of the growing maritime challenges from both state and non-state actors. And with the growing economic strength the urge to expand her sphere of influence grew as well. India has always considered herself a major player in the global politics and central to Asian international relations. India's first Prime Minister Pandit Jawaharlal Nehru suggested, "...India is curiously situated from geographical view as well as many other points of view. It belongs to Southeast Asia, it belongs to South Asia, it belongs to West Asia. It just depends in which way you look at it because it happens to be the centre of these..."[90] Sandy Gordon points to this opinion of the Indians regarding how they place their country in the global politics saying, '*Indians have always known that their nation has the potential to be a significant power in a way in which citizens of nations with smaller populations do not*.'[91] The Indian leaders, from Nehru onward, have always placed India at the centre of the Asian politics. Nehru did involve India significantly in the international politics of Southeast Asia in the troublesome days of 1950s (contrary to the general perception that India only 'looked East' after the Cold War) when the region was in severe turmoil combating the 'menace of communist revolution' in the aftermath of the birth of 'Red' China in 1949. India's engagement undoubtedly got a new thrust with the unveiling of the Look East Policy formally in the early 1990s with trade taking the front seat. This was the result of the economic emergency of the post Cold War period. In the long twenty years since the introduction of the Policy, India's trade with the region has made India the sixth largest trade partner for ASEAN with trade standing at US$ 76.52 billion in 2014-15.[92] Gradually, as we have discussed before, India's Look East Policy expanded its scope to induct the security considerations at the turn of the new century. However it is to be remembered that India's Southeast Asia policy never detached itself from the strategic considerations evident in the promotion of the naval diplomacy which got a boost in the new century.

On the other hand, India has established herself as a player in the larger East Asian geopolitical scene with her association with several ASEAN sponsored institutions. In this way India has entangled herself firmly with the larger East Asian geopolitical landscape. This was further boosted by the introduction of the Act East Policy in 2014. Defining the Policy, the External Affairs Ministry writes, "Under the new leadership in Delhi, India's Look East policy has morphed into a *proactive* Act East policy, which envisages accelerated across-the-board engagement between the two growth poles of a vibrant Asia."[93] The Indian government under Prime Minister Narendra Modi has been emphasising on India's connection with East Asia and the Act East policy was first mentioned by Prime Minister Modi at the opening address of the 12 India-ASEAN Summit held in Myanmar capital Nay Pyi Taw in November 2014. He said, "...Externally India Look East Policy has become Act East Policy."[94] This policy is meant to expand and boost India's larger East Asia policy, where she has to compete with China for influence. China is the prime challenge to India's journey beyond the confines of South Asia, especially in the East, where they meet in a new front of Asia, the maritime front and the South China Sea is such a front.

India has traditionally kept a safe distance from the South China Sea dispute and the related geopolitics only emphasizing on the freedom of navigation. However significant development is noticeable in India's South China Sea policy since 2014 after the unveiling of the Act East Policy by the Narendra Modi government. It considers the South China Sea as an important element of New Delhi's relationship with the East, for both trade and strategic reasons.[95] It is to be remembered that India's connection with Southeast Asia has historically been maritime in character. The creation of the so called 'Greater India' in Southeast Asia had a significant contribution of the maritime connection between India and Southeast Asia in the ancient period. Also, the trade between India and Southeast Asia, from ancient to the modern time, has been conducted via sea. And the South China Sea featured prominently in this exercise. Today, when India is attempting to 'Act East', she has to concentrate on her maritime network with the region and which passes through the South China Sea. Therefore it is the priority of India to keep the Sea out of the reach of any 'hostile hand' and China's growing assertiveness is undesirable to her. On the other hand, India wants to project herself as a reliable security actor in Southeast Asia.[96] As already mentioned, this author also got the impression about similar expectation about India's role in the South China Sea dispute in the context of China's activities in the region during his conversation with the scholars in Hanoi. The experts are of the opinion that the South China Sea dispute will have pervading impact on China's relations with ASEAN, US and India since the dispute is geopolitical in character which involves interest of extra regional powers like US and India. They expect India to be more active in South China Sea. However, given the naval power of India at the time of the writing of this book, it is not possible for her to deny the dominance of South China Sea to the Chinese single handed. In this context India's problem with other China wary South China Sea littoral states is identical. Thus India is opting for diplomatic alternative by trying to engage with the extra-regional powers with common interest in thwarting Chinese expansion in the South China Sea.

India's interest on freedom of navigation in the South China Sea converges with the similar interest of the extra regional powers like US, Japan and Australia. Japan is experiencing similar maritime sovereignty dispute with China in East China Sea and, like India, is uncomfortable with China's growing might. On the other hand Australia, even being the major trading partner of China, is not very delighted with Beijing's growing prowess either and these two countries are the traditional allies of USA. This is clear from the recently published Defence White Paper of Australia 2016 where, referring to South China Sea and without directly referring to China, the Paper has notified Australia's concern about land reclamation and construction activity by the claimants which 'raise tension in the region'. Mentioning that two-thirds of Australia's exports pass through South China Sea, the Paper mentions Australia's opposition to 'any assertion of associated territorial claims and maritime rights which are not in accordance of international law.' It has called upon claimants to halt land reclamation and construction activity.[97] And India is investing on US' 'Asia Pivot' policy to forward her Act East strategy vis-à-vis South China Sea. This became clear when the South China Sea featured for the first time in the Indo-US joint statement in 2014 after Prime Minister Modi met US President Barak Obama. In the statement it was said,

> 'The leaders expressed concern about rising tensions over maritime territorial disputes, and affirmed the importance of safeguarding maritime security and ensuring freedom of navigation and over flight throughout the region, especially in the South China Sea. The Prime Minister and President called on all parties to avoid the use, or threat of use, of force in advancing their claims. The two leaders urged the concerned parties to pursue resolution of their territorial and maritime disputes through all peaceful means,in accordance with universally recognized principles of international law, including the United Nations Convention on the Law of the Sea'.[98]

Indo-US relations have never been easy. On the contrary the relations, throughout the Cold War period and even in the first decades of the post Cold War era, have been marred with mutual suspicion, irritation and discomfort. India's non-alignment policy never matched with the US's alliance-oriented anti-Soviet global policy. Also India's gradual tilting to the Soviet camp in the 1970s following the US-China-Pakistan rapport widened the chasm even further. Situation did not improve much after the Cold War. President Clinton referred to Kashmir in his UN address in 1993 saying, "...we must also recognize that serious threats remain. Bloody ethnic, religious, and civil wars rage from Angola to the Caucasus to Kashmir".[99] This created uneasiness in Indo-US relations. Situation further deteriorated with India's testing of nuclear weapons in 1998 and the resultant US sanctions. However, the relations appeared to be altering for better since the turn of the new century with the Bush administration coming to power in Washington. By that time China started causing headache for US. Thus the latter was looking for alliance to contain Beijing. This was evident in the statement of US Secretary of State Dr. Condoleezza Rice who said, "I really do believe that the US-Japan relationship, US-South Korean relationship, the US-Indian relationship, all are important in creating an environment in which China is more likely to play a positive role rather than a negative role...".[100] The current Obama administration's 'Asia Pivot Policy' also gave due importance to partnership with India which was clear from the strategic guidance document of the US State Department on January 3, 2012 which emphasized on India's partnership in the US' Asia Pacific policy saying, "the United States is also investing in a long term strategic partnership with India to support its ability to serve as a regional economic anchor and provider of security in broader India Ocean region."[101] The changing geopolitical landscape in the Asia-Pacific region with the emerging possibility of China replacing US' decades' old dominance has forced both India and USA to find points of convergence.

Since 2014 India has developed a strategy of engaging with the regional as well as extra regional powers involved in the Asian waters who share similar concern about China's growing 'expansionist strategy'. In this case US seem to be the most favourable. US is very concerned about the recent military build-ups by China in the South China Sea. China started converting the reefs in the Spratly archipelago into artificial islands and building airfields and other facilities on some of them lately. This has triggered concerns in US and in the Southeast Asian region suspecting China trying to militarize the South China Sea region. However China has consistently claimed that such constructions are necessary to ensure the country's national defence and protection of those islands and reefs.[102] In this situation US has adopted a 'collaborative containment' strategy vis-à-vis China involving all the China wary countries of the entire Indo-pacific region. There was report about possible Indo-US joint patrolling exercise in the South China Sea which got floated with a US defence official claiming in February 2016 that the two sides (India and US) discussed joint patrols, both in India Ocean as well as South China Sea. However, spokesperson of the Indian Navy asserted that India only joins UN led international military effort and there is no change in government's policy.[103]

It is a fact that India will be reluctant to be part of any US-led strategy overtly. India will never opt to be a junior partner of USA and tag around with her in any global mission, even if that includes cornering China. It won't be prudent for her to do it either. After all China is India's next door neighbour while USA is a distant help. Also, with the lack of any such alliance relation in the traditional India-US relations, marred with mutual distrust and suspicion (especially regarding Washington's military aids to Pakistan), it is not possible for New Delhi to rely on Washington. Apart from these considerations, India nurtures a definite East Asia policy which is to make India more relevant in the larger geopolitics of the region. This India cannot do as a partner of US strategy. Even the 'small and medium powers' of the Southeast Asian region prefer an *'omni-enmeshment'* strategy to contain China's rise involving all the extra regional powers, including India, in the East Asian geopolitics, rather than the balancing strategy against China by hiding behind the US.[104] This multi polar approach goes with India's policy where she prefers to contain China through larger collaborative efforts involving all the relevant powers. Instead of singling out USA for her 'contain China' mission, India prefers to exercise the strategy taking it to a multilateral dais of like-minded powers. This was evident when India joined US and Japan in a first-ever trilateral dialogue forum, held in September 2015, where it was emphasized that the maritime disputes should be settled in a peaceful manner while freedom of navigation and unimpeded lawful commerce have to be ensured. India's foreign minister Sushma Swaraj insisted on freedom of navigation in the sea lanes of Asia Pacific region (which includes South China Sea) calling them 'lifeline of India's trade and commercial externalities'.[105] China on the other hand has always insisted that the extra-regional powers should not 'militarize' the South China Sea region. Reacting to the reports of US and India mulling on joint naval patrols in the South China Sea, Beijing said that such interference threatens peace and stability in the region. It said that, "Countries from outside the area must stop pushing forward the militarisation of the South China Sea..."[106] China, however, expressed hope that India can play a 'positive role' in the South China Sea affairs. Without directly naming India, China's Foreign Ministry opined in November 2015 that, "We hope that countries who really care about freedom of navigation in the South China Sea can play constructive and positive role in peace and stability of the region." This was in response to India's Defence Minister Manohar Parikkar's opinion about tension in South China Sea between US and China who said at the ASEAN Plus Defence Ministers' Meeting held in Kuala Lumpur, Malaysia (in November, 2015) that, "The situation in South China Sea and the recent developments there have attracted concern...This is natural since freedom of navigation are of concern to us all."[107] In a way such a comment of China is significant. This can be interpreted as the Chinese attempt to separately treat India's role in the South China Sea geopolitics as a possible contributing factor, independent of US strategy, given the traditional Indian policy to act independently in foreign affairs.

Calling South China Sea 'an important shipping route' and reiterating India's support for emphasis on freedom of navigation, India's former Foreign Secretary Nirupama Rao said in 2011 that 50 per cent of India's sea borne trade is East bound.[108] Thus India's concern about Chinese activities in the South China Sea is understandable. Apart from the concern of Chinese dominance, the possibility of severe tussle among the participants of the South China Sea sovereignty row can disturb the tranquillity of the region which is also undesirable for India. The growing assertive stance of China and the resultant military preparedness of the small states of the region, along with the encouragement of USA are no doubt complicating the situation further. Such a situation jeopardises India's commercial activities in not only the ASEAN countries but also rest of East Asia. Therefore India prefers a balance against China's assertiveness, although in collaboration with the China wary powers of the region, including USA. On the other hand, South China Sea is fast becoming an integral part of India's Act East Policy which is a 'proactive' stance of India's East Asia/Asia Pacific policy. On February 2013, Ms. Nirupama Rao, who was the then Indian Ambassador to USA, said, "... We want the Indian Ocean and the Asia-Pacific regions to develop into a zone of cooperation rather than one of competition and domination...".[109] Clubbing the Indian Ocean and the Pacific Ocean region into the emerging concept of *Indo-Pacific* region, India wants to remain active in a vast maritime zone of Asia. Thus the South China Sea maritime zone is featuring very prominently in India's emerging maritime strategy.

India is lately developing her maritime strategy, a reflection of her growing interest in her maritime neighbourhood. The Maritime Security

Strategy 2015 suggests that "As India moves forward in the 21st Century, its development and prosperity will remain closely linked to the maritime domain."[110] The 2007 Maritime Strategy doctrine of India also emphasized on the resurgence of India's maritime power and freedom to use seas for India's national purposes 'under all circumstances'.[111] In this way South China Sea becomes important to India since India's economic prosperity is linked with the East also. This is also important to push India's aspiration to be a major player in the wider Asia Pacific scene. And China's growing might and assertiveness in the South China Sea region is becoming an impediment to such aspirations. India's Act East Policy vis-à-vis South China Sea has both economic as well as strategic connotation. When sustaining her trade with ASEAN and beyond is primary to India's policy, containing China is also vital. No power can disregard China's relevance in the East Asian geopolitical scene since China's position in East Asia is identical to India's position in South Asia. And given the decades old suspicion and rivalry existing between the two giant neighbours of Asia, compounded by their competition for resources and influence globally, India and China are becoming rivals for position in each others' 'zone of influence'. However, for India the geopolitical landscape of East Asia is favourable given the fact that she is not the only challenger to emerging Chinese dominance and has super, big, medium and small powers, all ready to thwart Chinese 'expansion'. The South China Sea is the starting point of the mission. Thus the Sea is vital for India, a non-claimant extra regional power, to promote her geostrategic mission in East Asian region through her Act East Policy.

END NOTES

1. Tridib Chakrabarti and Subhadeep Bhattacharya, 'South China Sea Imbroglio: Problems, Outcome and India's Stand, Institute of Foreign Policy Studies, *Policy Brief*, No.5, December 2012, p.6
2. Ishani Naskar, 'The South China Sea Issue: India's Interests and Approach, Institute of Foreign Policy Studies, *Policy Brief*, No.1, December 2012, p.7
3. Cited in Subhadeep Bhattacharya, *Looking East Since 1947: India's Southeast Asia Policy*, New Delhi, KW Publishers, 2016, p.149
4. George K. Tanham, *Indian Strategic Thought: Am Interpretive Essay*, Santa Monica, C.A., Rand Corporation, National Defense Research Institute, 1992, p.3
5. Vijay Sakhuja, *Asian Maritime Power in the 21st Century: Strategic Transactions, China, India and Southeast Asia*, Singapore, Institute of South East Asian Studies, 2011, p.66
6. James R. Holmes, Andrew C. Winner and Toshi Yoshihara, *Indian Naval*

Strategy in the Twenty-first Century, London and New York, Routledge, 2009, p.9

7. Vijay Sakhuja, op cit, p.57
8. Ibid
9. See V.D. Chopra, 'India's Security Perspectives in the Nineties', Rakesh Gupta (ed), *India's Security Problems in the Nineties*, New Delhi, Patriot Publishers, 1989, p.59
10. Rakesh Gupta, 'Games on the High Seas', ibid, p.73
11. Andrew S. Erikson, Walter C. Ladwig III, Justin D. Mikolay, "Diego Garcia and the United States' Emerging Indian Ocean Strategy', *Asian Security*, vol.6, no.3, 2010, p.221, 223
12. Renu Srivastava, *India and the Nonaligned Summits: Belgrade to Jakarta*, New Delhi, Northern Book Centre, 1995, p.95
13. Cited in Subhadeep Bhattacharya, op cit, p.149
14. *Maritime power* is the state that makes greater access to the seas and sea resources for economic purposes that in turn provide the state with significant position in its power relations, while *sea power* is a state that has formidable naval capabilities (ships, submarines, shipping in support of the military for specific missions). Sea power may not be a maritime power although one follows from the other. See Vijay Sakhuja, op cit, p.4
15. Cited in ibid, p.91
16. Cited in ibid
17. James R. Holmes, Andrew C. Winner and Toshi Yoshihara, op cit, p.62
18. C. Raja Mohan, *Samudra Manthan: Sino-Indian Rivalry in the Indo-Pacific*, Washington D.C., Carnegie Endowment for International Peace, 2012, pp.57-58
19. Indian navy, *Freedom to Use Seas; Indian Maritime Military Strategy*, p.iii, https://ifr16.indiannavy.gov.in/writereaddata/images/pdf/maritime_strat.pdf (accessed on 24.02.2016)
20. Ibid, p.11
21. C. Raja Mohan, op cit, p.58
22. Ibid
23. Cited in Walter C. Ladwig III, 'Delhi's Pacific Ambition: Naval Power, "Look East" and India's Emerging Influence in the Asia-Pacific", *Asian Security*, vol.5, no.2, 2009, p.91
24. Cited in ibid
25. Ibid, p.94
26. RCEP pact to boost India-ASEAN trade to $200 by 2022, *The Economic Times*, March 11, 2015, http://articles.economictimes.indiatimes.com/2015-03-11/news/60008745_1_asean-india-free-trade-agreement-rcep-india-asean-trade (accessed on 26.02.2016)
27. 'ASEAN-India Summit: Terrorism, trade, sea dispute to be top agenda', The Indian Express, Nov 21, 2015, http://indianexpress.com/article/india/india-news-india/asean-india-summit-terrorism-trade-sea-dispute-to-be-top-agenda/ (accessed on 26.02.2016)
28. Subhadeep Bhattacharya, op cit, p.58
29. During the Cambodian crisis, India backed the Hanoi-installed Heng Semrin

regime in Phnom Penh, supported by USSR, which was opposed by ASEAN and US, and also China. Things became complicated when China invaded Vietnam in 1979 while Indian Foreign Minister Atal Behari Vajpayee was in Beijing and Deng Xiaoping compared the invasion with the one that China conducted in 1962 on India. For details see ibid, pp.75-79

30. Cited in ibid, p.86
31. Cited in ibid, p.89
32. James R. Holmes, Andrew C. Winner and Toshi Yoshihara, op cit, p.154
33. Subhadeep Bhattacharya, op cit, p.135
34. Tridib Chakrabarti and Subhadeep Bhattacharya, op cit, p.9
35. 'India should rethink its oil exploration plan', *ChinaDaily*, 2015-09-01, http://www.chinadaily.com.cn/opinion/2015-09/01/content_21764279.htm (accessed on 26.02.2016)
36. Ibid
37. 'India not party to the dispute over areas of South China Sea: Govt', *The Indian Express*, Aug 30, 2012, http://indianexpress.com/article/india/latest-news/india-not-party-to-dispute-over-areas-of-south-china-sea-govt/ (accessed on 26.02.2016)
38. Ishani Naskar, op cit, p.8
39. Subhadeep Bhattacharya, op cit, pp.136-137
40. Ibid, p.137
41. Annual Report 2006-2007, Ministry of Defence, Government of India, p.30
42. Subhadeep Bhattacharya, op cit, p.137
43. Walter C. Ladwig III, op cit, p.95
44. 'From remote post, India looks to check China's Indian Ocean thrust', *Reuters*, July 14, 2015, http://www.reuters.com/article/us-india-andamans-military-idUSKCN0PO2N120150714 (accessed on 26.02.2016)
45. 'Navy Chief says Indian Ocean is priority and not South China Sea', *Business Standard*, August 8, 2012, http://www.business-standard.com/article/economy-policy/navy-chief-says-indian-ocean-is-priority-not-south-china-sea-112080802019_1.html (accessed on 26.02.2016)
46. Subhadeep Bhattacharya, op cit, p.91, 92
47. C. Raja Mohan, op cit, p.1
48. Ibid, p.40
49. Read Subhadeep Bhattacharya, op cit
50. Walter C. Ladwig III, op cit, p.89
51. C. Raja Mohan, op cit, pp.40, 43
52. Ibid, p.42
53. Walter C. Ladwig III, op cit, p.90
54. C. Raja Mohan, op cit, pp.97,98
55. Subhadeep Bhattacharya, op cit, pp.94,95
56. Cited in ibid, p.117
57. Ibid, p.126
58. David Scott, 'India's Role in South China Sea: Geopolitics and Geoeconomics in Play', *India Review*, vol.12, no.2, 2013, p.53
59. Cited in ibid, p.52

60. C. Raja Mohan, op cit, p.98
61. 'Aircraft carrier on a friendly mission', *The Hindu*, Aug 03, 2005, http://www.thehindu.com/2005/08/03/stories/2005080302231300.htm (accessed on 02.03.2016)
62. Ibid
63. 'India will protect its interests in disputed South China Sea: Navy Chief', *The Economic Times*, Dec 3, 2012, http://articles.economictimes.indiatimes.com/2012-12-03/news/35568724_1_south-china-sea-interests-chinese-navy (accessed on 02.03.2016)
64. Ibid
65. 'China warns India against oil exploration', *Global Times*, 2012-12-05, http://www.globaltimes.cn/content/748314.shtml (accessed on 02.03.2016)
66. Hooman Peimani, 'India's claims in South China Sea further polarizes rows', *South China Morning Post*, 11 December, 2012, http://www.scmp.com/comment/insight-opinion/article/1102286/indias-claim-south-china-sea-further-polarises-rows (accessed on 02.03.2016)
67. 'Asean wants India's help in China disputes',*South China Morning Post*, 21 December, 2012, http://www.scmp.com/news/asia/article/1109717/asean-wants-indias-help-china-disputes (accessed on 03.03.2016)
68. David Scott, op cit, p.54, emphasis added
69. Ibid, p.53
70. Cited in Vo Xuan Vinh, 'India's Stand on the East Sea Disputes and its Impacts on Vietnam-India Relations', *Southeast Asian Studies*, Institute of Southeast Asian Studies, Vietnam Academy of Social Sciences, 2013, p.46
71. Rajeev Sharma, 'China and India jostle in Indian Ocean', *Global Times*, 2012-10-18, http://www.globaltimes.cn/content/739276.shtml (accessed on 02.03.2016)
72. Subhadeep Bhattacharya, op cit, p.79
73. Harsh V. Pant, 'India-Vietnam Axis', *The Wall Street Journal*, September 22, 2011, http://www.wsj.com/articles/SB10001424053111903791504576584653465899250 (accessed on 03.03.2016)
74. David Scott, op cit, p. 60
75. Subhadeep Bhattacharya, op cit, p.138
76. Harsh V. Pant, op cit
77. Cited in Subhadeep Bhattacharya, op cit, p.138
78. Tridib Chakraborti, 'India and Vietnam: The Historical Strategic Friendship in Asian Domain', in Arpita Basu Roy and Subhadeep Bhattacharya (eds), *India and South East Asia: States, Borders and Culture*, New Delhi, Shipra Publication, 2015, pp.130, 132
79. S.D. Muni, 'The Turbulent South China Sea Waters: India, Vietnam and China', Singapore, ISAS Insight, No.40, 11 October, 2011, *Institute of South Asian Studies*, National University of Singapore, p.8
80. Vo Xuan Vinh, op cit, pp.47,48
81. S.D. Muni, op cit, p.8
82. 'South China Sea projects an infringement on sovereignty, says China', *The Hindu*, September 19, 2011, http://www.thehindu.com/news/international/

south-china-sea-projects-an-infringement-on-sovereignty-says-china/article2468317.ece (accessed on 03.03.2016)

83. 'Vietnam, India to Expand Oil Exploration in Contested South China Sea', *The Wall Street Journal*, Sep15, 2014, http://www.wsj.com/articles/vietnam-india-to-expand-oil-exploration-in-contested-south-china-sea-1410777168 (accessed on 03.03.2016)
84. Carl Thayer, 'India and Vietnam Advance their Strategic Partnership', *The Diplomat*, December 11, 2014, http://thediplomat.com/2014/12/india-and-vietnam-advance-their-strategic-partnership/ (accessed on 03.03.2016)
85. 'Joint Statement on the Visit of the Prime Minster of Socialist Republic of Vietnam to India (October 27-28, 2014), Ministry of External Affairs, Government of India, October 28, 2014, http://www.mea.gov.in/bilateral-documents.htm?dtl/24142/Joint+Statement+on+the+State+Visit+of+Prime+Minister+ of+the+ Socialist+ Republic+ of+Vietnam+to+India+ October+2728+2014 (accessed on 03.03.2016)
86. Cited in Carl Thayer, op cit
87. 'New base: Satellite monitoring station in Vietnam to give India room in South China Sea region', *The Economic Times*, Jan 04, 2016, http://economictimes.indiatimes.com/news/defence/new-base-satellite-monitoring-station-in-vietnam-to-give-india-room-in-south-china-sea-region/articleshow/50431099.cms (accessed on 03.03.2016)
88. 'India installs satellite station in Vietnam to monitor Beijing', *Pakistan Defence*, January 12, 2016, http://defence.pk/threads/india-installs-satellite-station-in-vietnam-to-monitor-beijing.418116/ (accessed on 03.03.2016)
89. Statement by Navy chief Admiral R.K Dhowan, Ensuring Secure Seas: Indian Maritime Security Strategy, October 2015(Forward), Naval Strategic Publication (NSP)1.2, http://indiannavy.nic.in/sites/default/files/Indian_Maritime_Security_Strategy_Document_25Jan16.pdf, p.i (accessed on 04.03.2016)
90. Cited in Subhadeep Bhattacharya, op cit, p.4
91. Sandy Gordon, *India's Rise to power in the Twentieth Century and Beyond*, London, Macmillan Press Ltd, 1995 and New York, St. Martin's Press, Inc, 1995, p.1
92. 13th ASEAN-India Summit and 10th East Asia Summit in Kuala Lumpur, Malaysia, *Ministry of External Affairs*, Govt. of India, November 18, 2015, http://www.mea.gov.in/press-releases.htm?dtl/26038/13th+ASEANIndia+Summit+and+10th+East+Asia+Summit+in+Kuala+Lumpur+Malaysia (accessed on 04.03.2016)
93. Manish Chand, Act East: India's ASEAN Journey, *Ministry of External Affairs*, Govt. of India, November 10, 2014, http://www.mea.gov.in/in-focus-article.htm?24216/Act+East+Indias+ASEAN+Journey/ (accessed on 04.03.2016), emphasis added
94. Cited in Subhadeep Bhattacharya, op cit, p.145
95. Darshana M. Baruah, 'Asia's Nightmare: Could India and China Clash over South China Sea?', *The National Interest*, July 14, 2015, http://nationalinterest.org/blog/the-buzz/asias-nightmare-could-india-china-clash-over-the-south-china-13333?page=show (accessed on 04.03.2016)

96. Ibid
97. 2016 Defence White Paper, *Department of Defence*, Australian Government, pp.57.58 http://www.defence.gov.au/WhitePaper/Docs/2016-Defence-White-Paper.pdf (accessed on 07.03.2016)
98. Joint Statement during the visit of Prime Minister to USA, *Ministry of External Affairs*, Govt. of India, September 30, 2014, http://www.mea.gov.in/bilateral-documents.htm?dtl/24051/Joint+Statement+during+the+visit+ of+ Prime+Minister+to+USA (accessed on 04.03.2016)
99. Address by President Bill Clinton to the UN General Assembly, U.S Department of State, September 27, 1993, http://www.state.gov/p/io/potusunga/207375.htm (accessed on 04.03.2016)
100. Cited in Subhadeep Bhattacharya, op cit, p.173
101. Cited in ibid, pp.173-174
102. 'China won't cease building on SCS isles', *The Statesman*, 23 November 2015, p.10
103. 'US, India to post joint vigil in choppy Seas',*The Statesman*, 11 February 2016, p.9
104. See Evelyn Goh, 'Great power and Hierarchical Order in Southeast Asia: Analyzing Regional Security Strategies', *International Security*, Vol.32, No.3, Winter 2007/2008
105. 'US, India, Japan to Chart Safe Sea lane',*The Statesman*, 1 October, 2015,p.9
106. 'China warns Against US-India Vigil in Turbulent Asian Waters', *The Statesman*, 12 February, 2016, p.10
107. 'India can play constructive role, positive role in SCS, says China',*The Statesman*, 6 November, 2015, p.10
108. 'Address by FS on 'Maritime Dimensions of India's Foreign Policy', *Ministry of External Affairs*, Government of India, July 28, 2011, http://www.mea.gov.in/Speeches-Statements.htm?dtl/53/ (accessed on 04.03.2016)
109. Cited in Subhadeep Bhattacharya, op cit, p.176
110. Ensuring Secure Seas: Indian Maritime Security Strategy, October 2015, op cit, p.2
111. Ibid

7

Understanding South China Sea Geopolitics

South China Sea tension is the part and parcel of the emerging twenty-first century East Asian geopolitics. Asia (East) is a distinctively maritime region where shipping plays very important role. The region has key points connecting the Indian and the Pacific Oceans which are used as shipping lanes economically and strategically important for the economies of Northeast Asia, United States and the emerging Asian maritime powers.[1] Thus the maritime world of Asia is fast emerging as the zone of conflict in the new century. The emerging concept of the Indo-Pacific (gradually replacing the old Asia Pacific notion) is significant in this regard since it implies the maritime world of the Indian and the Pacific Oceans. The concept clubs the two neighbouring regions, East and South Asian maritime zones, into a single geopolitical and geo-economic entity as the Indo Pacific world. And this world is gaining significance with the rise of the resource hungry power centres along its shores who have undertaken the mission of economic growth. And the maritime activities are integral to this growth. With ninety per cent of the world trade conducted via sea route, the maritime region of Asia is regaining its significance in the policies of its littoral states. The South China Sea region is such a region. The countries of the South China Sea are undergoing the economic transformation where maritime commerce and supply are becoming important day-by-day. Thus the South China Sea is becoming integral to their economic growth. On the other hand the shadow of historical animosity and associated mutual fear and suspicion are creating a tensed ambience in the region. Thus the growing economic might of the regional powers is gradually being reflected in their defence policies while the asymmetrical power relations is paving the way for meddling of the extra regional entities who also have vested interest in the sea lane. However, given the history of the South China Sea region, this 'interfering' policy of the extra regional powers is not unnatural. There remains a consistency in the geopolitical character of the South China Sea region which has always been the joint ventures of the big and small powers, both from inside and outside the region. Today, the geopolitics of the region is more concentrated on the local developments attracting the outsiders and it seems to be centred around the activities of the emerging powers of East Asia, including China.

The world academia has been debating about the future of Asian international politics in the twenty-first century since the end of the Cold War when it was certain that the economic power of the world is shifting from the Atlantic to the Pacific, with special reference to rise of China. The process however started long back with the rise of Japan, from the ashes of the World War II, as the leading economic powerhouse of Asia in 1960s, raising herself to the level of developed Western powers of the time. This was followed by the rise of 'Four Asian Tigers'—South Korea, Taiwan, Hong Kong and Singapore—followed by China. China's economic empowerment is the most widely discussed topic today since the once underdeveloped and authoritarian state is now world's number two economy holding the highest foreign currency reserve in her pocket today. China's economic development has been the most outstanding achievement of the communist regime of the country. China's per capita income doubled in just one decade after the economic take off in late twentieth century which Britain took six decades to achieve it following the industrial revolution of the eighteenth century while the Americans took five decades following the civil war of the nineteenth century.[2] Thus the rise of China was faster in the Asian international politics than any other power. However China's rise currently is discussed more in the context of her military empowerment and alleged muscle flexing. Japan could have risen to this position long back if she was not shackled by the treaty obligations following her surrender in the WW II and in the absence of any US security guarantee. China's rise in the concluding phase of the Cold War triggered curiosity among the Asia-observers about the future trend of Asian international politics. This is because according to Kenneth Waltz, "A general theory of international politics is necessarily based on great powers."[3] China has risen herself to the stature of a great Asian power and aspires to be so globally. Thus any discussion on twenty-first century Asian power politics should start with reference to China. But how far China can be successful in dominating the Asian power politics? This issue became all the more important in the context of the simultaneous economic prosperity of many other Asian states. By the time China took off, Japan was already an economic power of Asia while there were other power houses like South Korea, Taiwan, Hong Kong and Singapore. Therefore the rise of China was an addition to the emerging Asian power dynamics. Then, why Chinese case is treated specially? This is because firstly China's sheer size and her resources make her a potential power centre, in every sense. Chinese military power is the biggest in Asia which is not constrained from empowering itself by any treaty obligation, unlike Japan, nor she enjoys any security guarantee. Further the vast Chinese territory extends to all over Asia. However, these factors would not have mattered much if China was not a revisionist state. China suffers from 'victim mentality' considering herself deprived of her 'rightful place' in the world in the existent global system and it starts from her neighbourhood. China nurtures the territorial problems she has with all her neighbours as fodder for her military empowerment. On the other hand, this rise of China is triggering uneasiness among her neighbours forcing them to be protective about their existence. All these are creating a complex international order in Asia in the twenty-first century.

Scholars differ on what shape Asian geopolitics will take in the new century with this rise of China and its repercussions and the most interesting debate on the issue exists between the two leading Asian scholars, David Kang and Amitav Acharya. David Kang opines that the Asian states will bandwagon China, negating the Western opinion of balancing against her propelling arms race in the region. He claims that barring a few states like North Korea and Taiwan, other Asian states 'do not fear for their survival'. Citing history Kang suggests that hierarchy of power has always remained in Asia where China remained at the top with small 'secondary' states surrounding her. Thus, so long as China remains dominant in Asia, there is little need for interstate wars.[4] This theory of Kang has been rejected by Amitav Acharya who negates any possibility of hierarchy in Asia suggesting that 'there can be no bandwagoning in Asia without China usurping or balancing US power.' On the contrary, he claims that China's neighbours never approved an hierarchical regional orders citing the statement of the Burmese delegate at the Asian Relations Conference held in 1947 (in India) who said, 'It was terrible to ruled by Western power, but it was even more so to be ruled by an Asian power.'[5] Acharya opines that China's relations with US, Japan and Southeast Asia actually 'constrains Chinese strategic options'.[6] Certainly bandwagoning China seems to be out of question in the present context of Asian geopolitics where China's rise has unveiled the era of diplomatic manoeuvring as well as military preparedness going hand in hand. However, Northeast Asia seems to be inclining towards balancing tactics against North Korean as well as Chinese 'threat', while Southeast Asia is more vulnerable to conflict between emerging China and dominant US centring the South China Sea conflict. This is because the South China Sea littoral states are weaker and divided, compared to that of Korean Peninsula, which makes the case of possible Chinese hegemony easier. On the other hand such a possibility illustrates the importance of the US presence depicting the cost of the US decline or withdrawal from the region.[7]

Historically, South China Sea has remained at the centre of Southeast Asian international relations and geopolitics. Robert Kaplan depicts the significance of the Sea in the following words:

> "South China Sea functions as the *throat* of the Western Pacific and Indian oceans-the mass connective economic tissue where global sea routes coalesce. Here is the heart of Eurasia's navigable rimland, punctuated by Malacca, Sunda, Lombok, and Makassar straits. More than half of world's annual merchant fleet tonnage passes through these choke points, and a third of all maritime traffic worldwide."[8]

Being the 'throat' of Indian and Pacific Ocean network, South China Sea provided a major maritime route of the traders moving in both directions. Traders from the west and the east traversed this route making the Sea the lifeline of East Asian economy. From the pre-colonial period of Southeast Asian history, South China Sea has been the centre of major commercial activities. Commerce has always been vital to Southeast Asia. Southeast Asia's location along the trade route between China in the east and India, West Asia and Europe in the west made the region an important trading hub. Passage through Southeast Asia by international traders became important in the second century AD as the central Asian caravan routes, the previously preferred connecting link between East and West commercial networks were disrupted by internal strife. And this passage was the South China Sea maritime route. The maritime ancient kingdoms of Southeast Asia were the gifts of the South China Sea. The trade in the South China Sea maritime zone boosted the economy of its littoral states and brought Southeast Asia at the centre of the East Asian commercial history. No East Asian commercial activities could take place bypassing South China Sea. And that flourished the maritime kingdoms of Southeast Asia. The Kingdoms of *Funan, Champa* and *Sri Vijaya* were the creations of South China Sea trade. And this trade was mainly conducted between China in one side and the Arab world and India on the other in the pre-colonial period. In that way China has historically been an integral and important part of South China Sea history. The *Nanhai* trade characterized China's maritime commerce with the world outside. Initially a coastal trade, it expanded from localised commercial network to become an important part of maritime Asian trade which extended to the Indian Ocean region. This trade was done via South China Sea. Apart from the economic importance, South China Sea carried political significance for the Chinese since this was the route gained political legitimacy for China. The vassal states of Southeast Asia acknowledged their subordinate status by sending annual tribute to the Chinese court which was sent with the purpose of acquiring trading prerogative from China along with Chinese goods. The kingdoms which sent tributes to China were the South China Sea littoral states and thus South China Sea was the source of political legitimacy for the Chinese emperors. Not only the local or regional powers, South China Sea attracted the 'extra-regional' powers like the Arabs, the Japanese and ultimately the Europeans in the later period.

The advent of the Europeans introduced the theme of geopolitics in the South China Sea. The European rivalry for dominance and economic benefits in the emerging commercial network globally brought the competing European powers one after another to the shore of South China Sea. Being introduced by Marco Polo in the late thirteenth century, Southeast Asia and China soon became the commercial destination of the European powers, starting with the Portuguese, who were then gradually exploring by sea the world beyond the frontier of Europe. The Portuguese settled themselves in certain pockets in Asia, starting with Goa in India, moving further east in Malacca and at Macao in China which is located at the extreme south of China in the north of South China Sea. The Spaniards, who followed the Portuguese, came from the opposite direction crossing the Pacific Ocean after occupying Latin America and found stiff opposition from the latter. Subsequently other European powers like the Dutch, French and the British crept in the scene. This triggered the severe competition among them over the control of the Southeast Asian trade conducted via South China Sea. And this trade was conducted between India and China. The main thrust of the South China Sea trade was with China. With the coming of the Europeans the maritime Southeast Asia got intertwined with the global commercial channels extending from Asia to Europe with Indian Ocean and South China Sea as the main highways of transaction. The Indo-Pacific commerce which existed between the Indian Ocean and the Pacific Ocean world prior to the advent of the Europeans got extended further connecting Europe directly where the Europeans gradually emerged as the master of the Indo-Pacific-European trade. And the South China Sea became the bridge between the two worlds of the Indian Ocean and the Pacific Ocean. This maritime trade boosted the importance of the trade routes and the choke points in between this maritime highway and thus Malacca Strait, the gateway to both the oceans gained the strategic significance. The importance of this Strait, midway between the Chinese and the Indian trading network, became the seat of the Portuguese trading empire in the region for 130 years since its seizure by the latter in 1511. Later the Dutch and the Portuguese fought over the Malacca Strait while the British appeared in the scene in 1786 settling themselves at Penang in the Malayan Peninsula. In this way the Malacca Strait experienced great power struggles in the early modern era. Realizing that the fierce competition over the trade monopoly was unsustainable, the Dutch and the British concluded to divide the Strait region among them and following the Treaty of London in 1824 the British took possession of the Malay Peninsula while the Dutch got the Indonesian archipelago.[9] This was a classic example of extra-regional power struggle over the control of the South China Sea trade of the modern era which was settled with a treaty of territorial jurisdictional division. The subsequent establishment of the trading centres in the South China Sea region gave further shape to the emerging geopolitical struggle among the European colonisers over the regional maritime trade. Singapore became the British tool to counter the challenges emanating from the Dutch trading activities in the South China Sea clashing with that of the British. The foundation of Singapore was meant to control the trade in the Malacca Strait by the British.

The main objective of the European missions in the South China Sea region was to control the maritime commercial highway and this framed the geopolitical struggle in these waters. Such a situation was compounded by the territorial claims of the colonisers in the colonial era. The Westphalian concept of territorial sovereignty which settled

European power struggle in their homeland was imported in Asia by the European colonisers. By the end of the nineteenth century, the South China Sea region was colonised by the European powers and the foundation of the colonies with definite borders initiated the measurement of maritime frontiers. This initiative was the result of the exploration of the maritime resources. It is to be remembered that the European colonisers were basically traders whose main objective behind establishing colonies in the world was to harness the economic benefits from the colonies by exploiting their natural resources like the British attempt to extract guano from the Spratly Islands in the 1870s. On the other hand, the French attempts to construct light house in the Paracel Islands, off the then French Indochina coast, and the patrolling of the French vessels in the nearby waters (like what the Chinese and the Vietnamese do in present days) were attempts to establish control over the islands as bases to overlook the South China Sea trade. However, it was not until the appearance of the Chinese in the scene in the late nineteenth century that the 'dispute' over the territorial sovereignty issue actually got inaugurated. Such disputes, in the form of claims and counter claims by the claimants of the islands, were local in character. Although the European colonisers were outsiders, they were fighting as the masters of the South China Sea littoral states.

World War II and South China Sea geopolitics

So far South China Sea remained as a local affair of territorial sovereignty dispute. Nevertheless, the onset of the World War II raised the maritime zone above its local character and linked it with the global geopolitical framework. This new *avatar* of South China Sea happened with the Japanese seizure of entire East Asia during the war throwing out the European colonisers from the region and delinking them from their source of supplies in Southeast Asia. The occupation of the maritime routes of South China Sea by Japan showed the importance of the sea lanes of communication in the geopolitics of East Asia. The Japanese not only established their pre-eminence in the South China Sea region but also their access to the resources there which the Europeans were exploiting since the eighteenth century and prospering themselves. Japan could flourish during the war since she had in her possession the Chinese coast as well as the South China Sea littorals, both of which were keys to prosperity in the region. When the pre-colonial maritime kingdoms of Funan, Champa and Sri Vijaya flourished as the economic hubs on the way to China, the Europeans' prime target in the initial days of their Asian trade was also China. The significance of the Japanese occupation of the South China Sea region also lied in its associated strategic aspect. When Indochina provided the Japanese a base from where they could launch attack both on mainland and maritime Southeast Asia, the Japanese could also control the air and sea routes of the South China Sea. In this way the old maritime trade route took its place in the map of geostrategic considerations of not only the incumbent but also the future players of the region. The Japanese established the fact that who controls South China Sea controls the maritime world of East Asia and in that way it was also established how important the issue of freedom of navigation is in the context of other powers' interests in this sea lane. The Japanese successful adventure in the South China Sea made it the key to the future geopolitical successes for the powers interested in the East Asian region, regional as well as extra regional. It proved that the Sea slipping into the hands of any major power can be detrimental for others' prosperity. Such a notion framed the core of South China Sea geopolitics and directed it in the Cold War period, and beyond.

Cold War and South China Sea geopolitics

During the Cold War period, South China Sea became an integral part of the larger global geopolitical considerations. With the shifting of position the Cold War sun its reflection also shifted in the South China Sea waters. Initially the US-Soviet tussle framed the geopolitics of the South China Sea region. The Soviet Union was mainly concerned about the strategic nuclear forces of the United States and thus in the post war period, the Soviet leadership concentrated in constructing vessels to counter the formidable sea-based nuclear weapon systems of the Western navies, especially USA. The post-war naval strategy of the Soviet Union was to secure the sea routes of the world. Her priority was firstly to secure the maritime zones in her neighbourhood, the Northern, Baltic and the Black Sea and then the Pacific. The emphasis on strengthening the Pacific Fleet followed the Soviet entrance in the Indian Ocean region in the late 1960s, apart from the Soviet interest in regional and security objectives in the Pacific region where the US Seventh Fleet was already in position. The Americans had involved themselves in the East Asian maritime geopolitics since their occupation of the Philippines as a colony in 1898 and it got intense further during the WW II. The Cold War geopolitical impact on South China Sea was not to become prominent until the

Vietnam War which involved Moscow on North Vietnam's side. This geopolitical tussle was the result of two major alterations in the overall Cold War framework: the apparent Sino-Soviet ideological rift and subsequent rapport between Washington and Beijing and it was best displayed in the Vietnam crisis. The interesting part in the context of Vietnam was that the Soviet entry in the crisis was the result of the traditional Sino phobia of Vietnam and the Soviet visit to South China Sea did not happen before the Sino-Vietnam war of 1979. There happened surge in port visits of the Soviet ships to Vietnam and by the end of 1980 Vietnam became the second most visited country by the Soviet Navy in the Pacific, after Singapore. The Soviet policy in the South China Sea was to contain the Chinese rather than handling the USA. Another noteworthy point was the timing of the Soviet appearance in the region, which was only after the dissociation of USA from the region after the defeat in the Vietnam War in 1975 and the emergence of China. The Chinese were also uncomfortable with the presence of the Soviet Navy in the South China Sea. They accused USSR of an expansionist and aggressive policy in South Asia and Indian Ocean route which, they asserted, got exposed with Moscow's support of Vietnam during the war. The South China Sea geopolitics of the Cold War era was directed by the ups and downs of the Sino-Soviet relationship establishing the importance of China as a major factor (and not power) in the local geopolitics. The disentanglement policy of Gorbachev regime since the mid 1980s was also the result of the urge of the Soviet leadership to normalize relations with China.

However, it will be wrong to conclude that US was not vigilant about Soviet policy in the South China Sea politics. The growing Soviet interests in Southeast Asia since the WW II did perturb policy makers in Washington who were concerned with the growing nationalist-communist tussle fearing to lose the resources and communication lines to Kremlin. During the second phase of the Vietnam War in the 1960s the US extensively utilized the South China Sea as a naval frontline for action. Nevertheless, the Soviet appearance in the South China Sea did not happen until the US withdrawal from the region handing over the 'responsibility of Southeast Asia' to China following the Sino-US normalization of relations in 1971. This paved the way for 'rise of China' in the post Vietnam War geopolitics of South China Sea. The striking feature of the US strategy in the region after the conclusion of the Vietnam War was her reluctance of any military engagement in the Southeast Asian region after the war which was reflected during the Sino-Vietnam War which promoted Soviet naval deployment in the South China Sea region. On the other hand the US wanted to contain Soviets in the South China Sea even when not directly present in the scene. In this case she opted for the Chinese help given the growing Sino-Vietnam tension where the Soviets started featuring as Vietnam's ally against China.

Throughout the Cold War period, until the Gorbachev era, the South China Sea geopolitics reflected the Sino-Soviet tension. China saw the Soviet involvement in the Southeast Asian affairs as an 'intrusion' in her zone of influence. The Chinese attempted to counter the 'Soviet encirclement of China' with the help of the American and the Japanese, economically, politically as well as militarily. The striking part of China's South China Sea policy during the Cold War was the emphasis on freedom of navigation under threat from the Soviet domination which was reflected in Beijing's support for Malaysia-Indonesia joint proposal for South China Sea remaining open for international shipping. Today, Chinese strategy in the same waters is just the reverse. China is currently concerned of US domination in 'her waters'. Today the concern for the freedom of navigation is expressed more by the others, especially the outsiders, than China. Thus it can be said that the fear of domination of the South China Sea by any single power has been a traditional aspect of the regional maritime geopolitics and this fear can be traced in the WWII experience when Imperial Japan ousted the great powers of Europe from the East Asian scene occupying the entire East Asian region and its sea lanes. Secondly, China mattered in the South China Sea affairs as an important factor of the Cold War geopolitics of South China Sea. It is also noteworthy here that China's policy towards South China Sea territorial disputes was also shaped in tandem with the changes in the super powers' strategy in the disputed Sea. The Chinese clashed with the South Vietnamese in the Paracel Islands first in 1974, the time when the latter was losing the US protection guarantee following the Nixon Doctrine. Again in 1988 the Chinese clashed with the Vietnamese at the time when the Soviets were preparing to withdraw from Vietnam. So it is seen that the Chinese strategy towards South China Sea has been guided by the non-interference guarantee of the big powers of the Cold War time. Today however, the situation is different where the Chinese are getting assertive in spite of the growing US involvement in the region. This can be analyzed in the context of the growing naval strength of the PLA Navy (PLAN). The strength of Navy of the 1980s and that of today is different. With the growth of Chinese economy, its dependence on import of resources has also grown. And to sustain the growth China has invested in her Navy since the mid 1980s. As the PLAN developed, the confidence in handling the nearby waters also developed among the Chinese policy makers. The current assertiveness in the South China Sea by China can be seen as the reflection of that confidence.

South China Sea geopolitics in the post Cold War period

The post Cold War was an interesting period for both the regional and the extra-regional powers interested in the South China Sea.The end of the Cold War propelled speedy alteration in the geopolitical landscape of maritime Southeast Asia that is South China Sea region with the withdrawal of the US naval bases from the Subic Bay in the Philippines. Amidst this arising power vacuum in the region, the 'rise of China' was prominently visible. China was anyway a major power among the small and medium 'powers' of East Asia. It is noteworthy here that in the absence of US Seventh Fleet and its bases in the Asia Pacific region China is the lone formidable force in the region. The only country that holds the potentiality to challenge her is Japan (given her show of might since the dawn of the 20th century till the end of the World War II) but she is shackled by Article 9 of her post-war 'pacifist constitution'.[10] Moreover the 'victim mentality' of China has been a fodder to the Chinese quest for power and status ensuring her 'rightful place' in the international order. This was stimulated by the growing need for unhindered supply of resources to sustain the Chinese mission of economic progress. The initial years of post Cold War era witnessed the ripples generated in the South China Sea by the Chinese assertive posture in the absence of the Soviet threat and the receding US power projection in the region and the counter moves by the regional powers to contain Chinese 'expansionism'. China now had the best opportunity to establish her dominance in her neighbourhood, a status symbol in the international community of powers. As we have seen during the Cold War period, China exhibited her opportunistic attitude again when in 1994 she seized the Mischief Reef in the South China Sea defeating the Philippines. This incident was important since here China took the advantage of defenseless Philippines after the US withdrawal, reminiscent of the 1974 and 1988 clashes with defenseless Vietnam. Also by this China opened another front in the South China Sea battleground against the Philippines, an old contender ignored so far by Beijing. Apart from undertaking hard power diplomacy to establish her sovereignty claims,

China also opted for legal fillip for such moves by enacting the *The Law on the Territorial Sea and the Contiguous Zone* in 1992 to exercise its sovereignty over its territorial sea and its rights to exercise control over its contiguous zone, and to safeguard State security as well as its maritime rights and interests. In this way China rooted her claims on firm legal grounds which gave her the reason to undertake 'legal' measures in order to safeguard her 'sovereignty and territorial integrity'. Such assertive moves were the proofs of China's growing obligation to ensure her strategic as well as economic interests in the South China Sea. With the economic reforms unveiled the South China Sea started gaining more importance as the vital sea lanes of communication. This sea lane is the only maritime route that connects China with the Indian Ocean and beyond. On the other hand the resources lying underneath the South China Sea, especially oil and natural gas, became important for China to boost her energy requirements. However, living in a friendless neighbourhood with territorial disputes, both land and maritime, China felt the need to ensure protection of her interests unilaterally. Such unilateral actions worsened the ambience further. On the other hand the leadership in Beijing sometimes becomes the victim of internal pressures like the military and local governments. Sometimes the Chinese local governments' law enforcement forces act on their own to safeguard the economic interest of their respective coastal provinces clashing with the foreign vessels. Therefore, in a way the communist regime seated in Beijing is not the sole decision maker in the South China Sea issue. However it can also be seen as the strategy of the central government of China to forward the provincial forces to ensure the territorial interest without involving the PLAN directly which might trigger wider repercussions at the international level. The Chinese oil companies also undertake pressure tactics to force the government shape and re-shape its South China Sea policy according to their interest. Such activities have become more prominent in the post Cold War era with economic progress becoming the priority. The difference between the Cold War and the post Cold War geopolitics in the South China Sea vis-à-vis Chinese policy is that previously the strategic considerations of defeating Soviet forces in the region was the priority while in the post Cold War era, it is safeguarding the sea lanes for unhindered supplies and the exploitation of resources underneath the Sea is the precedence. Thus previously it was politico-strategic in character while now it is economic-strategic.

However, the desire of the Chinese leadership to exhibit its prominence of growing power to the neighbours and the world, especially

USA, cannot be ruled out. China is a revisionist character with tremendous urge to prove her power potentiality to the world. Moreover, China is dissatisfied with the 'US-dominated' international order and wants to alter it, at least in her nieghbourhood. Thus the altered geopolitical situation in the South China Sea region catered the opportunity to China to establish her prominence in the region. China eyes on South China Sea region that is maritime Southeast Asia mainly because it is easier to handle the comparatively weaker and divided claimants in the disputes in the absence of any US security guarantee unlike prevailing in East China Sea that is Northeast Asian maritime region where her main contenders in the similar territorial disputes are South Korea and Japan, both formal US allies with her military bases. This can be construed as a strategic move by Beijing. Moreover China used her economic diplomacy in the early 1990s to entangle the Southeast Asian countries, including the disputants, into a thick web of economic interdependence boosting her indispensability in the regional economic order. This is also a post Cold War diplomatic development in which China, instead of playing one state against another, attempted to embrace all in order to fasten the nuts firmly in the region. This however did not alter the Chinese stand on the South China Sea issue and instead she emphasized on bilateral negotiations with the disputants.

Another important development of post Cold War was the changing tactics of the other claimants of the South China Sea disputes, notably Vietnam and the Philippines. These are the two countries that have been most vocal against the growing Chinese assertiveness in the South China Sea. Also, these are two countries who lost the security guarantee of the two super powers with the end of the Cold War and were exposed to the Chinese 'expansionism'. When the Philippine Navy (PN) was in serious war-fighting potentiality challenges with depleting naval capacities and without US security umbrella, Vietnam was comparatively in a better position enjoying the presence of the new Russian State to continue in Cam Ranh Bay, after the Soviet withdrawal. This can be seen as the reason the Chinese chose the Philippines over Vietnam as the target in 1994. And that is the reason the Vietnamese were seen in the frontline to challenge the Chinese activities in the disputed waters throughout the 1990s. Russia was also a consistent supplier of arms to the Vietnamese during this time. Thus it can be construed as the continuation of the Cold War tussle between Russia and China in the South China Sea where Vietnam started playing more prominent role as a direct player and not a mere base of operations of a super power which she was during the

Cold War. This was the indication of the rising role of the local powers in the post Cold War South China Sea geopolitics.

In a way the South China Sea geopolitics was now getting more localized in the immediate aftermath of the Cold War, in the 1990s. This development got all the more prominent with the appearance of new challengers, Indonesia and Malaysia, who, although not related to the dispute like the other two littoral states and concerned about emergence of any hostile ambience in the region, did not feature at all in the geopolitical game of South China Sea during the Cold War. This was mainly because of their weak naval capacity. Also, the Chinese were no direct threat to these two countries, unlike to Vietnam and the Philippines. However, the territorial law of China enacted in 1992 included the Natuna Islands of Indonesia, a major source of rich and extensive gas deposits, within its ambit while the declaration of the EEZ by Malaysian government encompassing Spratlys Islands and the adoption of the Territorial Law of the Sea by China in 1992 extending Chinese 'territorial claim to the Spratlys and its adjoining waters did overlap the claims of both the countries. Thus these two countries were almost dragged into the South China Sea feud by China in the post Cold War period. Thus we see that the local factors were shaping the South China Sea geopolitics in the post Cold War era. On the other hand, when China's role in the Cold War geopolitics in the region was intertwined with the larger Sino-Soviet ideological duel during the Cold War where the local powers only played side roles, in the post Cold War age it was China versus the local powers.

As the geopolitics of South China Sea got localized at the end of the Cold War, the significance of ASEAN rose as the regional torchbearer of peace and tranquillity. Undoubtedly ASEAN encountered the challenge of upholding its significance and fulfilling the objectives with which it was founded in 1967. The primary focus of the ASEAN was 'to accelerate economic growth, social progress and cultural development in the region'.[11] In the post Cold War period, with the gradual disentanglement of the big powers and the emerging geopolitics in South China Sea region with the rise of China and the associated regional anxious developments, ASEAN had to face the new situation on its own. The ASEAN countries were in favour of 'constructive engagement' with Beijing promoting mutually beneficial economic and political cooperation. The ASEAN opted for gradual engagement with China first making her a guest at the ASEAN Ministerial Meeting (AMM) in 1991, the consultative partner of ASEAN Regional Forum (ARF) in 1994 and finally a dialogue partner in

1996. However, ASEAN used these occasions to express its concerns regarding the Chinese activities in the South China Sea. ASEAN members were concerned about the possible Chinese threat to their sovereignty in the post Cold War period, especially in the context of the growing assertive posture of China in the South China Sea evident in her enactment of the territorial waters law in 1992 which appeared to extend Beijing's sovereignty jurisdiction over the entire South China Sea. In this situation, ASEAN opted for 'to engage to contain' strategy vis-à-vis China, given firstly its incapability to counter Chinese move militarily and secondly the growing importance of China as an economic partner.[12] This *omni-enmeshment policy* which is a process of engaging with a state so as to draw it into deep involvement into the international or regional society is embraced by Southeast Asian countries to engage China by political and economic means through bilateral efforts as well as multilateral institutions.[13] This is a major post Cold War development initiated by ASEAN in order to thwart any outbreak of major conflict in the Southeast Asian region in the context of China's growing power and assertive stances in the South China Sea and also to buy security guarantee for its member countries. This endeavour goes with the ASEAN objective to maintain regional tranquillity especially with the existing asymmetric power relations between China and the small and weak ASEAN states and the associated uneasiness among them regarding the 'Chinese threat'. Even the adoption of 'Declaration on the South China Sea' or Manila Declaration in 1992 in response to Chinese enactment of the territorial law of the sea emphasizing on peaceful resolution of the South China Sea dispute can also be termed as the ASEAN way ensuring security guarantee to its members while conveying message to China regarding its unified stand on the issue. However, given the fact a united ASEAN can hardly dissuade China from getting assertive, the Association brought in the extra regional powers relevant as balancing factor against China through *omnidirectional* strategy by pushing for regional security structure since 1990s involving as many big powers as possible (including US and China) in the regional institutions.[14] In the context of South China Sea tension such an initiative is helpful in a way that not only it engages China thereby reducing the possibility of any Chinese 'aggression', the involvement of US acts as a balance against China as well. And in order to give the initiative a multidirectional look, it has also engaged medium Asian powers like India and Japan, from the extended neighbourhood, who also have equal interest in thwarting China's rise. In this way when ASEAN attempts to check China's assertiveness and the associated fear of military solution of big powers (USA) it also attempts to keep itself relevant as the main arbiter organization in the regional affairs of Southeast Asia. However, the geopolitics of South China Sea started taking a new turn at the outset of the new millennium.

The South China Sea geopolitics in the new millennium

The major development in the South China Sea geopolitics in the new century is the impact of the economic growth of the disputants on their respective defence policies. China's military preparedness and the reciprocal actions of other claimants are making the situation very critical. It should be remembered that like China, other claimant countries' economies are also growing fast as a result of their emphasis on economic development in the post Cold War period. Thus like China they also require resources and hazard free maritime trade routes. So their respective claims of the islands and the adjacent territorial waters of the South China Sea are becoming all the more important for them. Moreover, the Chinese investment in the PLAN is making the small claimants jittery who are opting for military preparedness to counter any adverse situation in the future, near or far. Over the past several years PLAN has extended its presence in the South China Sea by increasing the rate of its 'presence missions' in the area by both surface and sub-surface vessels. In 2007 China built a naval base in the Hainan Island which boosted these naval activities in the South China Sea. In the island underground facilities are made for submarines and piers capable of accommodating a mix of sub surface and large surface vessels, including amphibious landing ships and aircraft carriers. Similarly, facilities are constructed in the Chinese controlled Woody Islands of the Paracels archipelago and also in the Spratlys. The PLAN regularly conduct exercises in the South China Sea and the sophistication of these exercises have increased since 2010 which is part of China's 21st century naval policy.[15] China has realized that her destiny in this century lies in the sea. Long confined with the continental obligations, China is now looking to the sea, both for economic as well as strategic objectives.

As we have seen while discussing the South China Sea in the pre-colonial period that China was the prime destination for trade in Asia which raised the importance of South China Sea as the most important sea lane in East Asia, today China's urge for connectivity with the rest of the world, for trade and resource supply, is giving new the importance to the South China Sea lane. China's 'Maritime Silk Road' project, which the Chinese President floated as a proposal during his address to the Indonesian Parliament in October 2013, intends to revive the ancient maritime trade connectivity with Southeast Asia which adds to the importance of South China Sea. The 21st Century Maritime Silk Road project intends to tighten the economic knot between ASEAN and China and the priority of ASEAN in China's neighbourhood policy is clear with the announcement of the proposal by the Chinese President in one of the major actor of the ASEAN grouping, Indonesia. *Jakarta Post* wrote that 'In building the 21st Century Maritime Silk Road, China, together with ASEAN, will provide a new platform and opportunity for forging a closer community and shared future between China and ASEAN'.[16] This project emphasizes trade, investment and connectivity. The project is designed to go from China's coast to Europe through the South China Sea and the Indian Ocean in one route, and from China's coast through the South China Sea to the South Pacific in the other.[17] Thus this project brings South China Sea at the core. On the other hand this initiative undoubtedly promotes China's economic diplomacy of entangling with her maritime Southeast Asian neighbours which the other side has been pursuing since 1990s.

On the other hand this project can also be seen as the Chinese attempt to place herself as the sole dominant economic power in the South China Sea region. The project is part of China's grand 'One Belt One Road' (OBOR) project which encompasses 4.4 billion people, 64 countries, and a combined economic output of $21 trillion.[18] However, the success of the OBOR depends on the success of the Maritime Silk Road project and the tension existing between China and some ASEAN states over the South China Sea issue with associated intransigent attitude of Beijing to continue with its unilateral activities in the disputed waters is putting the future of the project under doubt. It should be remembered that China's main hurdle is her failure to garner support and confidence of her neighbours and China's revisionist character is to be blamed for this. China never took any compromising posture vis-à-vis her neighbours, especially in the South China Sea region. On the contrary her unquenchable desire for power projection has put her at odds with her neighbours. On the other hand it is also true that China herself feels insecure in the presence of the formidable US prowess in her neighbourhood, compounded by the latter's special defence relations with Taiwan, whose annexation to the mainland still remains unfinished in the eyes of the leadership in Beijing. Thus much of China's naval strategy is formulated keeping Taiwan case in mind but today China looks beyond Taiwan. South China Sea is important for China since, according to Robert Kaplan, not only the Sea provides spatial configuration for Chinese expansion but also is the route through which China's overwhelming share of energy imports come from the 'Middle East by way of various Indonesian Straits'.[19] Kaplan has also cited the importance of South China Sea vis-à-vis Taiwan whose seizure, according to him, will provide Chinese naval planners to concentrate their energies on the wider South China Sea, which he terms the 'antechamber to the Indian Ocean' where China wants to have her naval presence to ensure supplies from the Middle East.[20] Thus, China's South China Sea policy should be seen in the wider perspective of the Indo-Pacific region which is emerging as the vital economic and strategic zone for China in the 21st Century.

China's investment in the naval build up can also be viewed from this angle where the distant maritime zone is fast integrating with China's economic mission whose security is thus becoming important to her. However, given the revisionist character of China and her dissatisfaction with the US dominated global order, especially in Asia Pacific region, China's interest in developing her naval strength to ward off 'American threat' is understandable. Moreover, China has a hostile neighbourhood in the entire Indo-Pacific region, from Japan to India, which is a challenge for her 'rise to power'. That is why China is strengthening her navy and formulating a proper maritime policy to ensure protection to her emerging maritime interest. *The Japan Times* writes, 'China is shifting resources to the navy and air force. Those services will be responsible for dealing with the main perceived threats to China's interests—a conflict over control of the South China Sea and a move by self-governing Taiwan toward formal independence that China has threatened to respond to with force'.[21] So both the economic necessity as well as desire of acquiring 'the rightful place in the world community' is directing China's South China Sea policy. China's desire to be a power was clear when in November (2015) her President Xi Jingping said that China is shifting from a "large country to a large and powerful one."[22]

China's military preparedness is encouraging other claimants to embark on similar path of modernization. Currently Vietnam and the Philippines are the two vocal opponents of China 'expansionist strategy' in South China Sea. One high ranking official from one South China Sea littoral state commented that China is equally tough towards both the countries since when Vietnam is in fierce competition with China, both historically and geographically, the Philippines is a weak state that can be intimidated.[23] Undoubtedly, these two countries are most uncomfortable with China's rise. Vietnam's case is not only related to contemporary development, it is deep rooted in the country's history of animosity with her giant northern neighbour. And it is all the more interesting since both are governed by communist party and Ho Chi Minh's Vietnam received support from Mao Tse Tung's China against the common enemy, USA. Today, Vietnam is looking for US assistance to counter Chinese menace. Vietnam is the classic example of hostile neighbourly relations that prevails when asymmetry exists in the power relations, compounded by history of aggression on small by the big. During conversation with this author some scholars in Hanoi expressed suspicion about China's Maritime Silk Road project as a new 'power' game of China with hidden geopolitical objectives. They opined that the project is meant to turn the South China Sea into 'China's Sea'. To counter China's growing naval might, Vietnam unveiled her own military modernization programme. Vietnam is modernizing her navy with foreign, mainly Russian made, military hardware which has gained maximum from increased budget expenses.[24] Vietnam was counted as one of the top 20 arms importers in the world between 2010 and 2014 in Stockholm International Peace Research Institute (SIPRI).[25] Vietnam's special emphasis on naval empowerment is certainly in reference to the South China Sea and China's threat in the waters. Vietnam is operating four Russian-made, Kilo-class submarines from a purpose-built base in Cam Ranh Bay in south-central Vietnam and is also acquiring Russian-designed ships equipped with anti-ship missiles and other weapons. Vietnam has also strengthened its coastal defenses with anti-ship artillery batteries and the mobile Bastion K-300P system, equipped with Orynx cruise missiles.[26]

On the other hand, the Philippines also opted for legal as well as military solutions to counter China. Manila's decision to refer the dispute with China to UN International Tribunal for the Law of Sea in 2013 can be analyzed from two angles. Firstly, this action clearly depicts the lack of confidence of the Philippines on ASEAN as a reliable arbiter which is certainly a blow to the Association's image and credibility and secondly, it was an attempt of a weak party to look for legal source to put the stronger one in a difficult position. The verdict which delivered went against China, however not binding on her, was an embarrassment for Beijing. On the other hand, Manila's re-engagement with the US as a security guarantee, following US President Obama's 'Asia Pivot' policy which re-directs US' focused on the Asia Pacific region amidst rise of China. Situation, however, changed with the election of Rodrigo Duterte as the country's new President in June 2016. The new administration seems to be reluctant to follow the overt anti-China policy of the previous government. On the contrary the new President seems more in the mood to resolve the differences with the Chinese diplomatically and bilaterally and less to depend of USA for any assistance.

Meanwhile the emergence of Malaysia and Indonesia in the scene as latest and newest development has made the South China Sea geopolitics more complex given the fact that neither these two states have been known China wary states (although their policy towards China during the Cold War were not very friendly and even fluctuated in case of Indonesia) although they have not been very comfortable with the Chinese empowerment. Their interests in the South China Sea are more economic in character given the sea lane which is vital for their economic activities. Malaysia's defence policy 2010 mentioned the strategic priorities of the South China Sea Exclusive Economic Zone and the sea lanes between Eastern Malaysia and Malaysian Peninsula as well as the Malacca and Singapore Straits.[27] Also, these two countries, especially Indonesia, never approved any single state domination in their neighbourhood. Thus China's assertive posture in the South China Sea will not be approved by them. Meanwhile the new administration in Jakarta under President Joko Widodo is emphasizing on Indonesia's long neglected maritime policy. It aims to revive Indonesia's maritime culture, uphold the country's 'food sovereignty' by managing the country's oceans and fisheries and boost maritime economy and bolster its security while opt for maritime diplomacy to eliminate breaches of sovereignty, territorial disputes, illegal fishing and others.[28] President Widodo, popularly known as Jokowi, in his inaugural address after taking charge of Presidency in 2014, said, "We have to work really hard to return Indonesia's status as a maritime nation. Oceans, seas, straits and gulfs are the future of our civilization. We have been showing our backs too long to these seas, to these oceans, to these straits, and gulfs. This is the time for us to return them all, therefore *Jalesveva Jayamahe*, it is at the sea we are glorious, as the motto of our ancestors, may ring once more."[29] Thus such a policy will certainly clash with China's maritime assertive policy in the South China Sea. There was an indication of this when the Indonesian President claimed that China's main claims to the majority of the South China Sea had no legal basis in international law.[30] However, the President has clarified his country's neutral stand on the South China Sea dispute and offered mediation to deescalate the tension.[31] Indonesia might pose a challenge to China's South China Sea ambition in future given her growing interest in the maritime zone.

Thus China's maritime neighbours in the South China Sea zone, including the Philippines, are not ready to offer China an open playground to exercise her will freely. Yet they are incapable to contain China on their own. Here the role of extra regional powers is becoming important.

Extra regional powers shaping the contour of the South China Sea geopolitics

The growing assertive behaviour of China and the resultant anxiety generated among her weak neighbours are paving the way for the greater involvement of the extra regional powers in the South China Sea geopolitics of the twenty-first century. Feeling vulnerable to the possible Chinese aggression and the strong urge to keep the region free of the giant neighbour's domination, especially of the sea lanes of communications, for both economic and strategic dividends, is pushing the small neighbours towards the security of the global China-wary network of states.

The role of the extra regional powers in the East Asian affairs has been a historical fact. The region attracted the 'outsiders', for economic purpose both during the pre-colonial as well as colonial period. However the advent of the European traders-cum-colonisers in the East Asian theatre since the fifteenth century changed the character of the region. The European colonisers divided the South China Sea region among themselves demarcating the territories' boundary following the Westphalian norm implied in Europe. Their prime objective was to thwart any one of them to emerge too powerful to be handled. This is identical with the European system where no single power ever dominated the landmass.[32] This shaped the geopolitics of South China Sea region where not only the outside powers integrated with the region without any single party domination, the regional powers also encouraged such mingling in order to prevent any regional power to be too dominant in the region. This was well articulated during the World War II when the local anti-Japan forces secretly collaborated with the Allied forces to challenge Japanese occupation while during the Cold War the local powers were eager to thwart the contending Russians and the Chinese.

What is noticeable is that no single power ever dominated the entire East Asian world until the emergence of the Imperial Japan during the Second World War. Robert Ross writes that since 1970s, until the end of the Cold War, a 'strategic triangle' existed in East Asia between Russia, US and China.[33] In a way these powers shaped the Cold War geopolitics of East Asia as did the Japanese and the Allied Powers during the World War II. The local powers hardly played any decisive role in this geopolitical game of the Cold War in East Asia because they were weak and fearful of neighbours and therefore dependent on 'outsiders' for physical protection. In this way the role of the extra regional powers got too deep rooted to be negated or challenged. Moreover, given the weakness of the small powers and their fear about possible Chinese domination in the South China Sea region, the expectation from the interested extra regional powers is also rising. The disputants of the South China Sea case are weak and vulnerable to Chinese aggression and therefore want to involve the powers from outside, especially USA, as a counterweight. This is also generating interest among the powers outside since apart from their discomfort with the Chinese rise, the 'security of the South China Sea lane' is vital for their economic sustainability. The emphasis of the outsiders has been on the 'freedom of navigation' in the sea lanes rather than the dispute itself. Their insistence on the peaceful resolution of disputes without using force is mainly meant to ensure that the tranquillity is maintained in the waters which are their main commercial highway in the region. However, it is undeniable that the growing assertive stand of China in the South China Sea, which is best articulated from her recent constructions in the disputed islands, is stimulating the powers, both local as well as of outside the locality, to align against China and the growing role of the US in this regard is noteworthy.

US, according to Robert Ross, is a great power along with China in the East Asian geopolitical scene. Ross, while calling East Asia a bipolar system between China and USA after the demise of Soviet Union, opines that US is *not a hegemon* in the region while China is an established regional power. He has characterised the East Asian geopolitics as divided between China-dominated mainland East Asia and US-dominated maritime East Asia.[34] In this situation China's naval empowerment is challenging the decades old US dominance in the East Asian waters. Although US has refrained from taking any side overtly in the sovereignty disputes, her main interest in the South China Sea has been to stop it slipping into the hands of any hostile power as happened during the World War II. Since the defeat of Imperial Japan in the World War II, USA has kept a vigilant eye on the waters of East Asia from her bases in Guam and Hawaii and from the bases in the foreign lands in the region also. US currently has access to bases in Singapore, Brunei, Indonesia and Malaysia.[35] Undoubtedly US has been the dominant naval power in the East Asian waters since the last world war and it should be remembered that the Soviet interest in the South China Sea grew only after the US dissociated herself from the Southeast Asian affairs after the Vietnam fiasco. Also, the Chinese dared to get assertive in the disputed waters only after the Americans withdrew. The Pacific world, which extends from the western coast of the American continent to the Asian coast in the east, has been a play ground of USA since the end of the last world war. Bordered by weak powers, the region catered to the US the opportunity to develop military power in strategic isolation and focus strategic resources on naval power projection into distant regions.[36] For decades US has remained an invincible power in the Pacific waters.

Thus, the growing investment of China in her navy, evident in the commissioning of China's first aircraft carrier as well as the constructions in the disputed reefs in the South China Sea, apart from the declaration of Air Defence Identification Zone in East China Sea in 2013, all are seemed as ominous signs to Washington. However, China still needs to go long way before she could be in position to challenge US dominance in her maritime neighbourhood. US' dominance as a great power in the East Asian bipolar system will remain intact for next quarter century. US' naval power, along with her strategic depth and isolation, enable her to dominate the coastal waters and penetrate the air space of any country, including China. All these capabilities empower USA to neutralize the naval capability of any great power competitor and ensure security to her international resources.[37] The Chinese view the US as a hegemonic power in the East Asian waters. There is a widespread belief in Beijing that it is US who 'attempts to keep Asia under its thumb and arrogantly throws its massive power projection capacity around.' According to Chinese reasoning it is US, and not China, who is the 'agitator' in the South China Sea disputes, and therefore needs to be 'deterred'. The counter argument suggests that because China is fundamental to Asia geographically, her military and economic power must be hedged against in order to protect the small Asian allies of USA. Such a strategy is termed as containment by Robert Kaplan.[38] Containment is a very common strategy in international power politics. It is defined as the strategy 'not to defeat the rising power but to prevent its further expansion in order to maintain the balance'.[39] This is a new trend that emerged in the post Cold War global geopolitics where the potential challenger is balanced against via alignment with its neighbours, not to isolate it or corner it but making its expansion-cum-domination more difficult.[40]

US is worried about the Chinese 'emergence to power' not only because she might pose a challenge to her decades old domination in the Asian waters, but also this might make her East Asian allies, especially in Southeast Asia, vulnerable to Chinese aggression . And the US lack of interest in helping them to contain China will surely put the US credibility at stake pushing many to the 'Chinese camp'. Such a situation is most undesirable for Washington given her strategic as well as economic interest in the Asian waters. Also, the dissociation of USA from the East Asian region might encourage the local China-wary countries to venture for self empowerment which will destabilize the local geopolitics. In this case Japan's rise to power will be most destabilizing, reminiscent of Imperial Japan. Such a situation is certainly not desirable to USA. Moreover, no existent power (in this case USA) will ever be ready to relinquish its dominance unless otherwise finds it too much a pressure on exchequer, as we found in case of British withdrawal from the East of Suez, or the region's situation is too difficult for it to handle, as we saw in US venture in Iraq and Afghanistan. Even in that case also, the dominant power will leave the region in the hands of some 'responsible local power(s)' which will manage the scene in its absence. This is not only to safeguard its interests but also as a mark of assurance to the states dependent so far on its security. The Five Powers' Defence Agreement of 1971 among UK, Singapore, Malaysia, Australia and New Zealand, was such an arrangement made by the British in the aftermath of its withdrawal. Even if it is true that the US is not interested to contain China, which is hard to conclude given her recent activities in the South China Sea like the *Freedom of Navigation* operations she conducted in the South China Sea in October 2015, US has little scope to dissociate from the region since there is hardly any 'responsible power' to take up her job. From the economic perspective also it is difficult for USA to disentangle with the region. The US sponsored TPP or Trans-Pacific Partnership pact of which four South China Sea littoral states, Vietnam, Malaysia, Singapore and Brunei are signatories, will enhance the importance of the East Asian maritime zone, including South China Sea, if the pact comes to effect.

However, instead of dealing with matters singlehanded, US now wants collaboration with the local powers with efficient naval capacity to jointly handle the China affairs in the South China Sea and in its neighbourhood. USA announced to give more than $250 million of maritime aid to her Southeast Asian allies and an offer of a warship to the Philippines when President Obama visited Manila last November (2015).[41] US decision to sell arms worth $1.83 billion to Taiwan in December 2015 is also important in this respect which was seen significant in the light of the recent South China Sea tension.[42] The Taiwan case is very significant in the context of China's naval empowerment programme. China longs for occupation of the island but has failed so far due to lack of necessary naval strength. Apart from the nationalist zeal to capture Taiwan to complete the 'map of China under communist rule', the strategic importance of Taiwan also matters. According to Robert Kaplan, "Taiwan is the cork in the bottle of the South China Sea, controlling access between Southeast Asia and Northeast Asia, the two security and conflict systems of the Pacific Rim."[43] Moreover, given the fact that Taiwan occupies major portion of Chinese naval strategy formulation, US will definitely try to use Taiwan to contain mainland China empowering the former with weapons, even if she was not compelled to do so under any treaty obligation. This is also contributing to the geopolitical landscape of South China Sea region. To handle Taiwan affairs China's military would invest more for better submarines, surface warships and fighter jets and better trained crews to operate them. And in foreseeable future the US Navy and Air Force might be unable to defend Taiwan from China.[44] In that case China's power will extend beyond the Taiwanese Island to the larger South China Sea region affecting the geopolitical system of the region tremendously. Thus it will be difficult for US to handle China singlehanded in future. Also handling the challenges of East Asia single handed is too much a pressure for USA. Hence USA wants to involve the extra regional powers with identical interests in the South China Sea region and equal anxiety about China. The reference of the South China Sea dispute and the 'growing convergence of their respective countries interests in the Indo-Pacific region' during the meeting between the foreign ministers of Japan and India with their US counterpart in September 2015 are indications in this direction.

There is a fear among the neighbours of the South China Sea region, like Japan, Australia and India, that China's growing naval strength can be threatening to their vested interest in the South China Sea. Therefore they take growing interest to involve more in the South China Sea region to assist the countries there to tackle the 'emerging maritime security concerns'. Japanese Foreign Ministry's white paper emphasizes on securing the sea lanes of the region including that around those of the ASEAN member countries calling the regional bloc 'extremely important from both political and economic perspectives'. The white paper declares that Japan will support the (ASEAN) countries' efforts to improve maritime security and build infrastructure.[45] Australia sent one of her flight on a 'routine maritime patrol' over South China Sea from November 24 to December 5 (2015) following the Chinese construction of man-made islands on the reefs of the Spratly Islands including 3000 metre long airstrip in one of them. Australia even played down the Chinese objections to such patrolling with her Defence Minister Marise Pyne insisting that Australia 'always navigate in a very constructive way in the region'.[46]

India's strategy in South China Sea is manifold. Apart from containing China within her backyard in order to thwart her further expansion in her own zone of influence in the Indian Ocean region, the security of the sea lanes of East Asia, especially South China Sea, is vital for India's economic interest. With more than fifty per cent of her East Asian trade passing through this sea lane and the supply of oil from Sakhalin of Russian Far East, the South China Sea is vital to India's economic sustenance. On the other hand India is involved in the oil exploration in the region which is also important for her energy hungry economy. Also, from the strategic angle, the South China Sea caters to India an important scope to remain relevant in the larger East Asian geopolitical scene. There is no doubt that India is considered as a major player in the region. India's strategic interest there converges with that of other major players interested in the region. Like others India also insists on freedom of navigation in the South China Sea. Like other extra regional powers, India is equally upset with the growing might of China in the South China Sea region. The outright defiant mood of China in the context of the rising international as well as regional worry regarding her recent construction of artificial islands in the disputed reefs in the South China Sea under China's occupation, does add to the uneasiness of India. This has been all the more worrisome after China placed surface-to-air missile launchers in one of the islands (Woody Island) in the disputed maritime zone.[47] Such a move is threatening to the sea lane and the freedom of navigation through it. Keeping South China Sea free of Chinese dominance is important for India in respect to the latter's growing presence in the Indian Ocean region. India, however, is not in a position to forward her interests in the South China Sea region, which is fast integrating with the emerging larger geostrategic sphere of Indo-Pacific, single handed. Therefore, it is vital for India to join with other regional and extra regional powers with identical interest vis-à-vis Chinese assertiveness as well as importance of the sea lanes in order to balance China. Indian observer Brahma Chellaney insists on unified action among India, ASEAN States and Japan, without leaving the matter to China and US 'to address through a great power modus-vivendi'.[48] India's current interest in empowering her naval strength does highlight the growing importance of India's maritime zone in New Delhi's foreign policy priorities. India's Act East policy also integrates her economic and strategic interests in the East Asian theatre where she always wanted to remain relevant. With passage of time as the concept of the Indo-Pacific encompassing the Indian and the Pacific Ocean world will take shape, the sea lanes of the region will occupy relevant place in India's external policy where South China Sea will be vital. According to Brahma Chellaney '...the South China Sea has become critical to the contest for influence in the Indian Ocean and the larger Indo-Pacific region'.[49]

South China Sea occupies a major part of India's maritime future. Therefore India's Act East Policy, which will turn more strategic in character with time, will concentrate more on the South China Sea where India will look for like-minded partners to deal with the emerging complex geopolitics of the twenty-first century. And here Vietnam can play a major role. Vietnam is fast becoming an important partner of India's resource exploration mission in the disputed waters since the late 1980s. Vietnam is the only country in the region which encourages India's involvement in her economic activities in the disputed waters. The state-owned Oil and Natural Gas Commission Videsh Ltd (OVL) of India has been associated with the oil exploration activities in the South China Sea since 2003 after acquiring the license from Vietnam in 1988. Despite strong objection of Beijing New Delhi continued with the exploration in the waters which shows its determinant mood to defy any Chinese threat. That India is not ready to confuse the sovereignty issue over South China Sea with her economic interests was clear from the statement of India's Minister of State for External Affairs, E. Ahmed, who stated in Indian Parliament in 2012 that 'Government has clearly conveyed that such activity by Indian companies is purely commercial in nature and that ONGC's decisions are taken entirely on techno-economic criteria. Sovereignty issues must be resolved peacefully by the countries which are parties to the dispute in accordance with international law and practice'.[50] India signed another deal with Vietnam to explore oil in two blocks in the disputed water body in 2014. India also decided to sell naval vessels to Vietnam, agreed during the visit of the Vietnamese Prime Minister to India in 2014.[51] It is evident that India sees Vietnam as an important partner in her Southeast Asia strategy vis-à-vis China given the convergence of interests of the two sides on the issue. Also the oil exploration benefit catered to her by Hanoi serves India's economic interest as well. Therefore it can be said that Vietnam will feature more and more in India's Act East strategy in the coming decades, especially in case of South China Sea.

When the extra regional powers are interested in involving in the South China Sea affairs, the regional powers are also keen to involve them in the affairs. Given the asymmetrical power relations between China and her South China Sea rivals, the latter parties look for a healthy balancing arrangement in the involvement of the big powers. Most striking part of this is the growing concerns of the states, like Malaysia and Indonesia, who have traditionally kept low voice over the disputes, openly advocating for more involvement of the outsiders. Malaysia's navy chief advocated for patrolling of the international community in the disputed waters under the Code for Unplanned Encounters at Sea (CUES) amid the ongoing disputes and militarization in the South China Sea.[52] CUES was concluded by the Asia Pacific naval chiefs at the Western Pacific Naval Symposium in 2014, which included China, in the context of the rising clashes over territorial disputes in the South and East China Seas. The code defines ways for naval ships and aircraft to manoeuvre and communicate when they meet "casually or unexpectedly", according to Wall Street Journal.[53] Malaysia's defence minister Hishammuddin Hussein wished to consult his Australian counterpart about China's military build up in the disputed South China Sea. He openly said that the military build up and placement of military assets in the islands by China will 'force us to pushback against China'.[54] However Malaysia knows her incapacity to thwart China in the disputed region alone and therefore wants to work in collaboration with other China-wary countries like Vietnam and the Philippines. At the same time the statement of the defence minister emphasizing on joint actions by ASEAN 'to curb the actions of the superpowers, whether it is China or the United States'[55] is significant in the sense that Malaysia wants to adhere to her principle of non-alignment even when attempting to balance against China. It is to be remembered here that many ASEAN countries like Malaysia and Indonesia do not like any single power dominance in their neighbourhood, but at the same time prefer to balance against any emerging power, especially China in the region, by engaging with any formidable challenge to her, mainly USA. This is mainly because given their weak naval strength they are aware of their vulnerability and thus look for protection from any big power. However for countries like Malaysia and Indonesia apathy to 'tag around' any big power to counter any foreseeable threat can be termed as a dilemma. When they know they are too weak to counter any threat single-handed, they are the captives of their principles of non-alignment. Most ASEAN countries are uninterested in leaving the decision of their regional security to 'external powers', as was opined by the Singapore Prime Minister Go Chok Tong in 1995 while Malaysian leader Mahatir Mohamad warned against ASEAN becoming 'pawn' in global politics.[56]

Since the dawn of the post Cold War period, changes have taken place in the geopolitics of the South China Sea region, especially with the growing power of China. Today, China, with her unrelenting assertive stand over the South China Sea territorial dispute, coupled with installing missiles in the islands under her control, is giving a new face to the geopolitics of South China Sea making the involvement of extra-regional powers evident which is welcomed by the weak local powers. In this way the South China Sea geopolitics is fast transcending its localized character of the post Cold War period and associating itself with the larger emerging Indo-Pacific geopolitics involving the powers like USA, Japan, Australia and India as major players to balance China. Moreover, the growing defence expenditure of the South China Sea claimants, apart from China, is also significant. From this it becomes evident that the countries are keeping the military option open in the light of the military modernization of China. This they can do given their economic growth allowing them to spend more on military which is natural for any country living in hostile neighbourhood with uneasy relation with neighbours. And in this mission they are becoming dependent on the extra regional suppliers making their presence in the affairs more prominent. On the other hand knowing the challenge China has to face from US naval strength in case of her expansion the maritime zone of East Asia, China is also preparing herself accordingly. It can be said that when China's concern in East Asia is US, more than her allies, the local US allies of the South China Sea region are worried about China. So China's worrisome response is pushing her local rivals more to the US camp.

In this connection it is relevant to refer to the apparently changing character of the Philippines under President Rodrigo Duterte, at the time of writing of this book, which seems to be inclining towards China.

However, this change can be seen more in terms of balancing rather than bandwagoning, which Manila had traditionally been performing with USA. This is clear from the visit of the Filipino leader to Japan after visiting China in October, 2016. Duterte regime does not want the Philippines to tag along with USA any more as an anti-China pawn but to handle the China affair on its own. That the Philippines under Duterte wishes to divorce the US was clear from the announcement of the President himself during his maiden visit to China in October 2016 where he said, "I announce my separation from the United States."[57] Not only that the Filipino President announced that he wants the US troops stationed in his country to leave within next two years and even went to the extent of expressing his desire to scrap defence deals with Washington.[58] However, this anti-US policy of the new government in Manila is more due to the clash between the US-led Western governments and the new regime over Duterte's war against his drug mafia resulting to the extra-judicial killings allegedly conducted by the Duterte government in the country. The US, European Union and the United Nations have condemned these extra-judicial killings in the Philippines where police have killed 1,578 people while 2,151 have died under unexplained circumstances. President Duterte rebuffed these critics a 'fools' vowing not to stop until "the last pusher, the last drug lord is taken away."[59] China, being an authoritarian regime itself, refrains from making such allegations like USA.

During Duterte's visit to China the leadership of the two countries decided to 'temporarily put aside' their differences over South China Sea, as suggested by Chinese President Xi Jinping. Chinese leader insisted on dispute resolution bilaterally. He said, "As long as we stick to friendly dialogue and consultation, we can frankly exchange views on any problem, manage differences, discuss cooperation and temporarily put aside what is hard to reach by consensus."[60] Clearly he was referring to the ASEAN, which work on consensus, whose interference in the South China Sea affairs China does not approve. Previously Manila used the Association to target China. The regime's emphasis on internal economic development and security challenges (emanating from the southern Philippines) will naturally encourage it to be less hostile to an external power like China. On the contrary the economic benefits of associating with China can be helpful for the new regime. It should be remembered that China has successfully utilized her economic largess to lure the small and weak economies like Cambodia. The regime in Manila realizes the economic pressure that investment in its anti-China preparation will create which will paralyze its internal economic development. However, what final shape Philippines' South China Sea policy vis-à-vis China and USA will take finally is yet to be seen.

However, it will be improper to conclude that other China-wary countries are preparing for a war-like situation in East Asia. On the contrary, to ensure that the East Asian stage does not plunge into a Cold War type zero-sum duel, there is an urge to divert the situation away from US-China one-to-one confrontation by involving the other regional 'medium powers' like Japan, Australia and India. Here the role of ASEAN matters the most. Since the demise of the Soviet Union ASEAN has been the main instrument of preserving regional tranquillity. This it did by embracing its Cold War rival Vietnam and expanding its periphery as wide as possible encroaching upon the whole of Southeast Asia. It has been able to perform its duty successfully till recently since it did not face any formidable challenge to the security of the region, until the rise of China and the resultant clash with the existing power USA. It should not be forgotten that since the last world war, USA has been the security provider of the East Asian world and the ASEAN could flourish because of US presence. No ASEAN state is in a position to ensure its own physical security, let alone the security of the region and unlike European Union, ASEAN has not been able to emerge as a supra-national body transcending the barrier of nationalism.[61] Also, the bilateral strategic relations of each of the individual ASEAN state with USA vary where the Philippines (until recently) and Vietnam have less interest in projecting a neutral stand vis-à-vis big extra regional powers (given their history of alignment with superpowers during the Cold War) than Malaysia and Indonesia. However, ASEAN as a whole takes a united 'omni-directional' strategy involving all the big powers, including US and China, to keep itself relevant in the East Asian geopolitics. But it still is unable to garner confidence of its own members as a reliable dispute resolution mechanism evident in Manila's approach to international tribunal for dispute resolution rather than raising it with ASEAN. On the other hand the 'all-embracing' strategy of ASEAN is helpful for US also who will prefer in sharing the burden of balancing tactic with other likeminded powers, worried of China's rise. So, ASEAN's policy commensurates with the larger Indo-Pacific policy of USA.

South China Sea geopolitics has consistently been integral to the global politics of big powers. Given its strategic and economic importance, the Sea can never remain outside the calculations of the players outside

Southeast Asia. From the pre-colonial time the region attracted outsiders whose activities shaped the regional politics and economics of South China Sea. When the trade with China shaped the destiny of the local maritime powers in the pre-colonial Southeast Asia, the advent of the Europeans and their introduction of territorial sovereignty concept gave a new shape to the South China Sea international relations in the colonial period which continues even today. The World War II on the other hand pointed to the immense strategic importance of the region directing to the vulnerability of the extra regional powers to the consequences emanating from a single power's seizure of the sea lane of communication bridging the Indian and the Pacific Ocean world. Throughout the Cold War period, the South China Sea geopolitics was shaped by the super power global rivalry while today the region is subject to local rivalry fast taking global shape. Contrary to the Cold War period when the outsiders' policies shaped the South China Sea geopolitics involving the local players for the formers' benefit, today the policy of the local players are attracting the outsiders. The growing economic strength of the local powers and their fear of China's rise are now shaping the destiny of the South China Sea region and it will be interesting to see how the emerging geopolitics of the region will shape the larger geopolitical game of East Asia in the coming days. However, one thing remains constant in the South China Sea geopolitics and that is the relevance and the inevitability of the extra regional powers' involvement. Also, the geopolitics has been China centric ever since the end of the last world war given that geopolitics is played among the big powers.

END NOTES

1. Joshua H. Ho, 'Introduction', Joshua H. Ho and Sam Bateman (eds) *Maritime Challenges and Priorities in Asia: Implications for regional security,*London and New York, Routledge, 2012, p.1
2. Robert D. Kaplan, *Asia's Cauldron: The South China Sea and the End of a Stable Pacific*, New York, Random House, 2014, p.33
3. Cited in David C. Kang, 'Getting Asia Wrong: Need for New Analytical Frameworks', *International Security*, Vol. 27, No.4, Spring 2003, p.57
4. Ibid, pp.58, 63, 67
5. Amitav Acharya, 'Will Asia's Past be Its Future', *International Security*, Vol. 28, No.3, Winter 2003/04, p.155, 156
6. Ibid, p.157
7. Robert D. Kaplan, op cit, p.24
8. Ibid, p.9
9. Robert D. Kaplan, *Monsoon: The Indian Ocean and the Future of American Power*, New York, Random House Trade Paperback Edition, 2011, pp.262, 263

10. Pacifism is the soul of Japan's post-war foreign policy. Article 9 of the post-war constitution, which was drafted under U.S. occupation in 1947, declares that the Japanese people "forever renounce war as a sovereign right of the nation" and pledges that "land, sea, and air forces, as well as other war potential, will never be maintained" by Japan, and that "the right of belligerency will not be recognized." However, the current Shinzo Abe government in Tokyo is attempting to reorient the decades old pacifist military-cum-foreign policy through legislations for wider military activities of the Japanese Self Defence Forces under changed regional situation with rise of China and growing North Korean threat.
11. Allan Collins, *Security and Southeast Asia: Domestic, Regional and Global Issues*, Singapore, Viva Books Pvt. Ltd., 2005, p.129
12. Ibid, p.170
13. Evelyn Goh, 'Great Powers and Hierarchical Order in Southeast Asia: Analyzing Regional Security Strategies', *International Security*, Vol.32, No.3, (Winter 2007/2008), p.121
14. Ibid, p.122
15. Subhadeep Bhattacharya, 'The maritime Border Dispute in South China Sea: Factors impeding Solution' in Arpita Basu Roy and Subhadeep Bhattacharya (eds), *India and South East Asia: States, Borders and Culture*, New Delhi, Shipra Publications, 2015, pp.55, 56
16. Xu Bu, 'Maritime Silk Road can bridge China-ASEAN cooperation', *Jakarta Post*, August 5, 2015, http://www.thejakartapost.com/news/2015/08/05/maritime-silk-road-can-bridge-china-asean-cooperation.html (accessed on 16.03.2016)
17. 'China's trade with Maritime Silk Road countries rises 18 pct annually', *Xinhua*, 2016-02-11, http://news.xinhuanet.com/english/2016-02/11/c_135089988.htm (accessed on 16.03.2016)
18. Feng Zhang, 'Beijing's Mater Plan for South China Sea', *Foreign policy*, June 23, 2015, http://foreignpolicy.com/2015/06/23/south_china_sea_ beijing_retreat_ new_strategy/ (accessed on 16.03.2016)
19. Robert D. Kaplan, op cit, p.20
20. Ibid, p.13
21. 'How China is transforming its military, especially in the air and at sea',*The Japan Times*, March 5, 2016, http://www.japantimes.co.jp/news/2016/03/05/asia-pacific/china-transforming-military-especially-air-sea/#.VtvL0EJ97IU (accessed on 16.03.2016)
22. Ibid
23. Cited in Robert Kaplan, op cit, p.12
24. Subhadeep Bhattacharya, op cit, p.56
25. The Top 20 Arms Importers 2010-2014, http://www.sipri.org/googlemaps/2015_of_at_top_20_imp_map.html (accessed on 16.03.2016)
26. 'Factbox: Inside Vietnam's military modernization', *Reuters*, Dec 18, 2015, http://www.reuters.com/article/us-vietnam-china-conflict-factbox-idUSKBN0U10SE20151218 (accessed on 16.03.2016)
27. Subhadeep Bhattacharya, op cit, p.59
28. Adelle Neary, 'Jokowi Spells Out Vision for Indonesia's Global Maritime

Nexus', *Centre for Strategic and International Studies,* Mar 16, 2016, http://csis.org/publication/jokowi-spells-out-vision-indonesias-global-maritime-nexus (accessed on 16.03.2016)

29. 'Jokowi Focuses on Maritime in Inaugural Address', *The Maritime Executive,* 2014-10-21, http://www.maritime-executive.com/article/Jokowi-Focuses-on-Maritime-in-Inaugural-Address-2014-10-21 (accessed on 16.03.2016)
30. 'Joko Says China Has No Legal Claim to South China Sea', *JakartaGlobe,*http://jakartaglobe.beritasatu.com/news/joko-says-china-no-legal-claim-south-china-sea/ (accessed on 16.03.2016)
31. 'Jokowi Clarifies: Indonesia Still Neutral in S. China Sea Dispute', *JakartaGlobe,*http://jakartaglobe.beritasatu.com/news/jokowi-clarifies-indonesia-still-neutral-s-china-sea-dispute/ (accessed on 16.03.2016)
32. Aaron Friedberg argues that since no single power could assemble sufficient material power and the acquire legitimacy for hegemony in the post Westphalian state system, Europe never experienced any single power domination, see Aaron L. Friedberg, 'Will Europe's Past be Asia's Future', *Survival, Vol. 42, No.3,* Autumn 2000, p.150
33. Robert Ross, 'The Geography of Peace: East Asia in the twenty-first century', in Leszek Buszynski (ed), *Asia Pacific Security,* Volume 1, London and New York, Routledge, 2014, p.55
34. Ibid, emphasis added. Ross, referring to William Fox, defines the regional powers as 'those who enjoy... great power status' but 'their interests and influence are great only in a single theatre of power conflict'. See p.54. Following this definition China can certainly be termed as a regional power whose power projection is currently confined in the East Asian region.
35. Ibid, p.56
36. Ibid, p.62
37. Ibid, p.63
38. Robert D. Kaplan, op cit, pp.166-167
39. Randell L. Schweller, 'Managing the Rise of Great Powers', in *Engaging China: The Management of an Emerging power,* Alastair Iain Johnston and Robert Ross (eds), London and New York, Routledge, 1999, p.10
40. However,India's Southeast Asia policy under Prime Minister Nehru, which was directed strategically, by the China factor, also followed this 'to engage-to-contain' policy vis-à-vis Mao's China. See Subhadeep Bhattacharya*Looking East Since 1947: India's Southeast Asia Policy,* New Delhi, KW Publishers, 2016
41. 'US, China fight for influence at APEC Summit', *The Statesman,* 19 November, 2015, p.5
42. 'US Arms Taiwan in Mega Firepower Sale' *The Statesman,* 18 December, 2015, p.10
43. Robert D. Kaplan, op cit, p.143
44. Ibid, p.151
45. 'Japan to increase aid to Asia amid China's growing maritime assertiveness', *The Japan Times,* March 9, 2016, http://www.japantimes.co.jp/news/2016/03/09/national/politics-diplomacy/japan-increase-aid-asia-amid-chinas-growing-maritime-assertiveness/#.VuqonNJ97cs (accessed on 17.03.2016)
46. 'Australia says no plan to stop surveillance flights over South China Sea',

Reuters, Dec, 17, 2015, http://www.reuters.com/article/us-southchinasea-australia-surveillance-idUSKBN0U00I720151217 (accessed on 17.03.2016)

47. 'Beijing places missile launchers on disputed South China Sea island', *The Guardian*, 17 February, 2016, http://www.theguardian.com/world/2016/feb/17/china-places-missiles-woody-south-china-sea-islands (accessed on 17.03.2016)
48. Brahma Chellaney, 'Japan and India need to deal with South China Sea dispute', *Hindustan Times*, Jan 20, 2016, http://www.hindustantimes.com/analysis/japan-and-india-need-to-deal-with-the-south-china-sea-dispute/story-t62xmr3Is5MCUtNtXqkeCP.html (accessed on 17.03.2016)
49. Ibid
50. Q. 4532 Oil exploration in South China Sea, Rajya Sabha, May 17, 2012, *Ministry of External Affairs, Government of India*,http://www.mea.gov.in/rajya-sabha.htm?dtl/19717/Q4532+Oil+Exploration+in+South+China+Sea (accessed on 18.03.2016)
51. 'Vietnam and India Sign Oil, Naval Agreement Amid South China Sea Disputes, Angering Beijing, *International Business Times*, 10/29/14, http://www.ibtimes.com/vietnam-india-sign-oil-naval-agreement-amid-south-china-sea-disputes-angering-beijing-1715677 (accessed on 18.03.2016)
52. Prashanth Parameswaran, 'Malaysia Wants Expanded Naval Protocol Amid South China Sea Dispute', *The Diplomat*, December 4, 2015, http://thediplomat.com/2015/12/malaysia-wants-expanded-naval-protocol-amid-south-china-sea-disputes/ (accessed on 22.03.2016)
53. 'Pacific Navy Agree on Code of Conduct for Unplanned Encounters', *The Wall Street Journal*, April 22, 2014, http://www.wsj.com/articles/SB10001424052702304049904579517342779110078 (accessed on 22.03.2016)
54. 'Malaysia seeks Australian support in South China Sea dispute', *The Guardian*, March 16, 2016, http://www.theguardian.com/world/2016/mar/15/malaysia-seeks-australian-support south-china-sea-dispute (accessed on 22.03.2016)
55. Ibid
56. Allan Collins, op cit, p.171
57. 'Philippines, China close ranks. 13 pacts pave way for calm on seas', *The Statesman*, 21st October, 2016, p.10
58. 'Duterte wants U troops out in 2 years', *The Statesman*, 27th October, 2016, p.9
59. 'New Fire in Duterte crime war', *The Statesman*, 15th October, 2016, p.9
60. *The Statesman*, 21st October, 2016, op cit, p.10
61. Even in case of European Union, US-led NATO has been its main physical security provider a system that ASEAN lacks. However, the supra-national character of the EU got a massive jolt with the British decision for withdrawal following referendum in June 2016.

Bibliography

Books

Alagappa, Muthiah (ed), *Asian Security Practice*, Stanford, Stanford University Press, 1998

Banerji, Arun Kumar and Purushottam Bhattacharya (eds), *People's Republic of China at Fifty: Politics, Economy and Foreign Relations*, New Delhi, Lancer Books, 2001

Beri, K., *History and Culture of Southeast Asia: Modern*, Sterling Publishers Pvt Ltd, 1994

Betts, Richard K. (ed), *Conflict After the Cold War: Arguments on Causes of War and Peace*, New York, Pearson Longman, 2008

Bhattacharya, Subhadeep, Looking *East Since 1947: India's Southeast Asia Policy*, New Delhi, Knowledge World, 2016

Buszynski, Leszek (ed), *Asia Pacific Security*, Volume I, II, III, IV, London and New York, Routledge, 2014

Buszynski, Leszek and Christopher B. Roberts (eds), *The South China Sea Maritime Dispute: political, legal and regional perspectives*, London and New York, Routledge, 2015

Brook, Timothy, *The Troubled Empire,: China in the Yuan and Ming Dynasties*, The Belknap Press of Harvard University Press, 2010

Caceres, Sigfrido Burgos, *China's Strategic Interests in the South China Sea: Power and Resources*, London and New York, Routledge, 2014

Calvocoressi, Peter and Guy Wint, *Total War, Volume I: The War in Asia*, New York, Ballantine Books, 1972.

____*Total War, Volume II: The War in the West*, New York, Ballantine Books, 1972

Chachavalpongpun, Pavin (ed), *Entering Uncharted Waters: ASEAN and the South China Sea*, Singapore, Institute of South East Asian Studies, 2014

Collins, Allan, *Security and Southeast Asia: Domestic, Regional and Global Issue*, Singapore, Viva Books Pvt. Ltd., 2005

Chomsky, Noam, *American Power & the New Mandarins*, Gurgaon (Haryana, India), Penguin Books, 2002

Christie, Clive, *Ideology and Revolution in Southeast Asia, 1900-1980*, Richmond, Curzon, 2001

Deal, William E., *Handbook to Life in Medieval and Early Modern Japan*, Oxford University Press, Oxford, 2006

Feener, R. Michael and Terenjit Seuea (ed), *Islamic Connections: Muslim Societies in South and Southeast Asia*, Singapore, Institute of Southeast Asian Studies, 2009

Feis, Herbert, *Japan Subdued: The Atomic Bomb and the End of the War in the Pacific*, New Jersey, Princeton University Press, 1961

Fisher, Charles A., *Southeast Asia: A Social, Economic and Political Geography*, Methuen & Co. Ltd, London, 1964

Fisher, Richard D. Jr., *China's Military Modernization: Building for Regional and Global Reach*, Stanford, California, Stanford University Press, 2010

Frankam, Ronald Bruce, *Operation Passage to Freedom : United States Navy in Vietnam, 1954-1955*, Lubbock, Texas, Texas Tech University Press, 2007

Fuller, Maj. Gen. J.F.C., *The Second World War, 1939-45: A Strategical and Tactical History*, London, Eyre and Spottiswoode, 1968

Glover, Ian and Peter Bellwood (eds), *Southeast Asia: From prehistory to history*, London and New York, Routledge Curzon, 2004

Goldrick, James and Jack McCaffrie, *Navies of South-East Asia: A Comparative Study*, London and New York, Routledge, 2013

Gordon, Sandy, *India's Rise to power in the Twentieth Century and Beyond*, London, Macmillan Press Ltd, 1995 and New York, St. Martin's Press, Inc, 1995

Gupta, Rakesh (ed), *India's Security Problems in the Nineties*, New Delhi, Patriot Publishers, 1989

Hall, D.G.E., *A History of Southeast Asia*, Palgrave McMillan, 1981

Hall, Kenneth, *Maritime Trade and State Development in Southeast Asia*, University of Hawaii Press, Honolulu, 1985,

____ *A History of Early Southeast Asia: Maritime Trade and Societal Development, 100-1500*, Plymouth, UK, Roman and Littlefield Publishers Inc, 2011

Hall, Kenneth R. and John K. Whitemore (eds), *Explorations in Early South East Asian Statecraft*, Ann Arbor Centre for South and South East Asian Studies, the University of Michigan, Michigan Papers on South and South East Asia, 1976

Hammerston, Sir John and Major General Sir Charles Gwynn (eds), *The Second World War: A Standard History*, London, The Amalgamated Press Ltd, 1946

Hara, Kimie, *Cold War Frontier in the Asia-Pacific: Divided Territories in the San Francisco System*, Oxon, Routledge, 2007

Hayton, Bill, *The South China Sea: The Struggle for Power in Asia*, New Haven and London, Yale University Press, 2014

Herbert, Murry Phuong Nguyen and Gregory B. Poling, *A New Era in US-Vietnam Relations: Deepening Ties Two Decades after Normalization*, Center for Strategic and International Studies, 2014

Higham, Charles, *The Civilization of Angkor*, University of California Press, Berkley and Los Angeles, 2001

Ho, Joshua H. Ho and Sam Bateman (eds), *Maritime Challenges and Priorities in Asia: Implications for regional security*, London and New York, Routledge, 2012

Huang, Jing and Andrew Billo (eds), *Territorial Disputes in the South China Sea: Navigating Rough Waters*, New York, Palgrave McMillan, 2015

Hussin, Nordin, *Trade and Society in the Straits of Maleka: Dutch Maleka and English Penang 1780-1830*, Singapore, NUS Press, 2007

Joo-Jock, Lim, *Geostrategy and South China Sea Basin: Regional balance, Maritime Issues, Future Patterns*, Singapore, Singapore University Press, 1979

Jonston, Alastair Iain and Robert Ross (eds), *Engaging China: The Management of Emerging Power*, London and New York, Routledge, 1999

Kaplan, Robert D., *Asia's Cauldron: The South China Sea and the End of a Stable Pacific*, New York, Random House, 2014

____ *Monsoon: The Indian Ocean and the Future of American Power*, New York, Random House Trade Paperback Edition, 2011

Kennedy, Andrew Bingham, *The International Ambitions of Mao and Nehru: National Efficacy Beliefs and the Making of Foreign Policy*, New York, Cambridge University Press, 2012

Kivimäki, Tomo (ed), *War or Peace in the South China Sea*, Copenhagen, Nias Press, 2002

Kwa, Chong Guan and John K. Skogan (eds), *Maritime Security in Southeast Asia*, London and New York, Routledge, 2007

Langsam, Walter Consuelo, *Historic Document of World War II*, New York, D Van Nostrand Company Inc, 1958

Latourette, Kenneth Scott, *The American Record in the Far East, 1945-1951*, New York, The Macmillan Company, 1952

Leonard, Jane Kate, *Wei Yuan and China's Rediscovery of the Maritime World*, Harvard East Asian Monographs, Council on east Asian Studies, 1984

Mahbubani, Kishore, *The New Asian Hemisphere: The Irresistible Shift of Global Power to the East*, New York, Public Affairs, 2008

Medeiros, Evan S., *China's International Behavior : Activism, Opportunism and Diversification*, Santa Monica, Rand Corporation, 2009

McGrew, Anthony and Christopher Brook (eds), *Asia-Pacific in the New World Order*, London and New York, Routledge, 1998

Matsuo, Kinoaki, *How Japan Plans to Win* (translated by Kilsoo K. Haan), London, George Harrap & Co. Ltd., 1942

Morrison, Ian, *The War Against Japan: Thoughts on the Present Conflict in the Far East*, London, Faber And Faber Ltd., 1943

Percival, Bronson, *The Dragon looks South: China and Southeast Asia in the New Century*, Connecticut and London, Praeger Security International, 2007

Polomka, Peter, *Ocean Politics in South East Asia*, Singapore, Institute of South East Asian Studies, 1978

Preston, Diana and Michael Preston, *A Pirate of Exquisite Mind: The Life of William Dampier, Explorer, Naturalist and Buccaneer*, UK, Doubleday, 2004

Qingxin, Li, *British Maritime Silk Road*, China Intercontinental Press, 2006

Raja Mohan, C., *Samudra Manthan: Sino-Indian Rivalry in the Indo-Pacific*, Washington D.C., Carnegie Endowment for International Peace, 2012

Reid, Anthony, *Southeast Asia in the Age of Commerce, 1450-1680: Expansion and Crisis*, Vol 2, Yale University Press, New Haven and London, 1993

Rowe, William T., *China's Last Empire: The Great Qing*, The Belknap Press of Harvard University Press, 2009

Roy, Arpita Basu and Subhadeep Bhattacharya (eds), *India and South East Asia: States, Borders and Culture*, Delhi, Shipra Publications, 2015

Roy, Denny, *Taiwan: A Political History*, Ithaca, New York, Cornell University Press, 2003

Rozman, Gilbert, *Chinese Strategic Thought towards Asia*, New York, Palgrave Macmillan, 2010

Sakhuja, Vijay, *Asian Maritime Power in the 21st Century: Strategic Transactions, China, India and Southeast Asia*, Singapore, Institute of South East Asian Studies, 2011

Samuels, Marwyn, *Contest for South China Sea*, Methuen, New York, London, 1982

Sardesai,, D.R., *British Trade & Expansion in Southeast Asia, 1830-1914*, Bombay, Allied Publishers Pvt. Ltd, 1977

Saunders, Phillip C. Christopher Yung, Michael Swaine, Andre Nien-Dzu Yang (eds), *The Chinese Navy: Expanding Capabilities, Evolving Roles*, Washington D.C., National Defense University Press, 2011

Scott, David, *China Stands Up: The PRC and the international system*, London and New York, Routledge, 2007

Singh, K.R., *The Indian ocean: Big Power presence and Local Response*, New Delhi, South Asia Books, 1978

Souza, George Bryan, *The Survival of Empire: Portuguese Trade and Society in China and the Trade in South China Sea, 1630-1754*, Cambridge University Press, New York, 1986

Srivastava, Renu, *India and the Nonaligned Summits: Belgrade to Jakarta*, New Delhi, Northern Book Centre, 1995

Tarling, Nicholas (ed), *Cambridge History of Southeast Asia, From Early Times to c.1500*, Vol. 1, part 1, Cambridge University Press, 1999

Testa, David W. Del (ed), *Global History: Cultural Encounters from Antiquity to the Present*, Volume 1, Sharpe Reference, New York, 2004

Thien, Ton That, *India and Southeast Asia 1947-1960: A Study of India's Foreign Policy towards the South East Asian Countries in the Period 1947-1960* Geneve, Librairie Droz, 1963

Till, Geoffrey and Patrick C. Bratton (eds), *Sea Power and the Asia Pacific: The Triumph of Neptune?*, London and New York, Routledge, 2012

Tomohiko, Uyama (ed), *Empire and After: Essays in Comparative Imperial and Decolonization Studies*, Hokkaido, Slavic Research Centre, Hokkaido University, 2012

Valencia, Mark J. and Jon M. Van Dyke, Noel A. Ludwig, *Sharing the Resources of the South China Sea*, Honolulu, University of Hawaii Press, 1999

Womack, Brantly, *China and Vietnam: The Politics of Asymmetry*, New York, Cambridge University Press, 2006

Watson, Bruce W., *Red Navy at Sea: Soviet naval Operations on the High Seas, 1956-1980*, Colorado, Westview Press, 1982

____ *The Changing Face of the World's Navies: 1945 to the Present*, London, Arms and Armor Press, 1991

Wolters, O.W., *Early Southeast Asia: Selected Essays*, Southeast Asia Program Publications, Cornwall University, New York, 2008

Yoshihara, Toshi and James R. Holmes (eds), *Asia Looks Seaward: Power and Maritime Strategy*, Westport, Connecticut, Praeger Security International, 2008

Zhu, Zhiqun, *US-China Relations in the 21st Century: Power transition and peace*, London and New York, 2006

Articles

Amitav Acharya, 'Will Asia's Past be Its Future', *International Security*, Vol. 28, No.3, Winter 2003-04

Atsushi, Ota, *The Dutch East India Company and the Rise of Intra Asian Commerce*

Baruah, Darshana M., 'Asia's Nightmare: Could India and China Clash over South China Sea?', *The National Interest*, July 14, 2015

Batongbakal, Jay J., 'Arbitration 101: Philippines V China', *Asia Maritime Transparency Initiative*, January 21, 2015

Bosco, Joseph A., 'Taiwan and Strategic Security', *The Diplomat*, May, 15, 2015

Buzan, Barry and Gerald Segal, 'Rethinking East Asian Security', *Survival*, vol. no. 36, Summer 1994

Chakraborti, Tridib and Subhadeep Bhattacharya, 'South China Sea Imbroglio: Problems, Outcome and India's Stand', Institute of Foreign Policy Studies, *Policy Brief*, No.5, December 2012

Chellaney, Brahma, 'Japan and India need to deal with South China Sea dispute', *Hindustan Times*, Jan 20, 2016

Christian, John L. 'Anglo-French Rivalry in Southeast Asia: Its Historical Geography and Diplomatic Climate', *Geographical Review*, Vol. 31, No. 2 (Apr., 1941)

Copper, John F., 'Why We Need Taiwan', *The National Interests*, August 29, 2011

Darling, Frank C., 'United States Policy in Southeast Asia: Permanency and Change', *Asian Survey, Vol14, No.7* (July, 1974), University of California Press

Dower, John D., The San Francisco System: Past, Present, Future in U.S.-Japan-China Relations, *The Asia-Pacific Journal*, Vol 12, Issue 8, February 28, 2014

Erikson, Andrew S. Walter C. Ladwig III, Justin D. Mikolay, 'Diego Garcia and the United States: Emerging Indian Ocean Strategy', *Asian Security*, vol.6, no.3, 2010

Fisher, Richard D., 'Moscow's Growing Muscle in Southeast Asia', *Asian Backgrounder*, Asian Studies Center, April 4, 1984

Friedberg, Aaron, 'Ripe for Rivalry: Prospects for Peace in Multipolar Asia', *International Security*, Vol.18, No.3, 1994

____ 'Will Europe's Past Be Asia's Future?', *Survival*, vol.42, no.3, 2000

Gang, Ding, 'Colonial legacy buried seeds of territorial row', *Global Times*

Godwin, Paul H.B., 'From Continent to Periphery: PLA Doctrine, Strategy and Capabilities towards 2000', *The China Quarterly*, No.146, Special Issue: China's Military Transition, Jun, 1996

Goh, Evelyn, 'Great power and Hierarchical Order in Southeast Asia: Analyzing Regional Security Strategies', *International Security*, Vol.32, No.3, Winter 2007/2008

Guan, Ang Cheng, 'The South China Sea Dispute Re-visited', *Institute of Defence and Strategic Studies (IDSS)*, Singapore, Rajaratnam School of International Studies, August, 1999

Gurtov, Melvin, Sino-Soviet Relations and Southeast Asia: Recent Developments and Future Possibilities, *Pacific Affairs*, Vol.43, No.4, Winter, 1970-1971

Granados, Ulises, 'As China Meets the Southern Sea Frontier: Ocean Identity in the Making, 1902-1937,'*Pacific Affairs, Vol.78*, University of British Columbia, 2005

Hagan, Charles B., 'Geopolitics', *The Journal of Politics*, Vol.4, No.4, Nov, 1942

Hamashita, Takeshi, *A History of Maritime Asia and East Asian Regional Dynamism 1600-1900: Maritime Asia from the Ryukyu-Okinawa to the Hong Kong Networks*, Institute of Oriental Culture, the University of Tokyo

Hawkins, David C., 'Britain and Malaysia- Another View: Was the Decision to Withdraw Entirely Voluntary was Britain Pushed a Little?, *Asian Survey*, Vol.9, No.7, July 1969, University of California Press

Hayton, Bill, *Calm and Storm: The South China Sea after the Second World War*, Asia Maritime Transparency Initiative, August 13, 2015

Herbert, Murry Phuong Nguyen and Gregory B. Poling, 'A New Era in US-Vietnam Relations: Deepening Ties Two Decades after Normalization', *Center for Strategic and International Studies*, 2014

Holmes, James R. and Toshi Yoshihara, 'China's Caribbean in South China Sea', *SAIS Review of International Affairs*, Volume 26, No.1, John Hopkins University Press,2006

Ladwig III, Walter C., 'Delhi's Pacific Ambition: Naval Power, "Look East" and India's Emerging Influence in the Asia-Pacific", *Asian Security*, Vol.5, No.2, 2009

Islam, Dr. Arshad, 'Arab Navigation in the Indian Ocean Before European Dominance in South And Southeast Asia: A Historical Study', *Journal of the Pakistan Historical Society*

Kang, David, 'Getting Asia Wrong: The Need for New Analytical Frameworks', *International Security*, Vol.27, No.4, MIT Press

Kennedy, Paul, 'The rise and fall of navies', *The New York Times*, April 5, 2007

Levi, Warner, 'The Future of Southeast Asia', *Asian Survey*, Vol.10, No.4, 1970

Marolda, Edward J., 'The US Navy in the Cold War Era, 1945-1991', *Naval History and Heritage Command*

Mauzy, Diane K. and Brian L. Job, 'U.S Policy in Southeast Asia: Limited Reengagement after years of benign neglect', *Asian Survey*, Vol.XLVII, No.4, July/August, 2007,

MccGwire, Michael, Naval power and Soviet Global Strategy, *International Security* Volume 3, Number 4, Spring 1979

Muni, S.D., 'The Turbulent South China Sea Waters: India, Vietnam and China', Singapore, ISAS Insight, No.40, 11 October, 2011, *Institute of South Asian Studies*,

Naskar, Ishani, 'The South China Sea Issue: India's Interests and Approach', *Policy Brief* No.1, Institute of Foreign Policy Studies, University of Calcutta, December 2012

Ovendale, Richie, 'Britain, United States and the Cold War in South-East Asia, 1949-1950', Royal Institute of *International Affairs*, Vol.53, No.8, (summer 1982)

Pant, Harsh V., 'India-Vietnam Axis', *The Wall Street Journal*, September 22, 2011

Parameswaran, Prashanth, 'Playing it Safe: Malaysia's Approach to the South China Sea and Implications for the United States', *Maritime Strategy Series*, Center for a New American Society, February 2015

Porter, Gareth, 'The Decline of U.S. Diplomacy in Southeast Asia', *SAIAS Review*, No. 1, Winter 1981, John Hopkins University Press

Qimao, Chen, 'The Taiwan Strait Crisis: Its Crux and Solutions', *Asian Survey*, Vol.36, No.11, Nov.1996

Ross, Robert, 'Geography of the Peace: East Asia in the Twenty-first Century', *International Survey*, Vol.23, No.4, Spring 1999

Sajima, Naoko and Kyoichi Tachikawa, *Japanese Sea Power: A Maritime Nation's Struggle for Identity*, Australia, Sea Power center

Sharma, Rajeev, 'China and India jostle in Indian Ocean', *Global Times*, 2012

Segal, Gerald, 'East Asia and the "Constrainment" of China', *International Security*, Vol. 20, No.4, 1996

Shen, Jianming, 'China's Sovereignty over South China Sea Islands: A Historical Perspective', *Chinese Journal of International Law* (CJI) 1 (1), 2002

Tanham, George K., *Indian Strategic Thought: Am Interpretive Essay*, Santa Monica, C.A., Rand Corporation, National Defense Research Institute, 1992

Thayer, Carl, 'India and Vietnam Advance their Strategic Partnership', *The Diplomat*, December 11, 2014

Thien, Ton That, 'South East Asia Post Cold War Geopolitics', *Global Affairs: The American Journal of Geopolitics*, Vol.VIII, No.1, Winter, 1993

To, Lee Lao, 'East Asian Assessments of China's Security Policy', *International Affairs*, Vol.73, No.2, Asia and the Pacific, Apr.1997

Tønnesson, Stein, 'An International History of the Dispute of the South China Sea', *EAI Working Paper No. 71*, 2001

____ 'The South China Sea in the Age of European Decline', *Modern Asian Studies*, Vol.40, No.1, Cambridge University Press, Feb, 2006

Thanh, Ngyuen Thi Ha, *European Trade on the Far East and the Mercantile Relationship with Vietnam from the 16th to 19th Century*

Vinh, Vo Xuan, 'India's Stand on the East Sea Disputes and its Impacts on Vietnam-India Relations', *Southeast Asian Studies*, Institute of Southeast Asian Studies, Vietnam Academy of Social Sciences, 2013

Wade, Geoff, 'An Early Age of Commerce in Southeast Asia, 900–1300 CE', *Journal of Southeast Asian Studies*, 40(2), June 2009

Williams, Michael C., 'New Soviet Policy Toward Southeast Asia: Reorientation and Change', *Asian Survey*, Vol.31, No.4, April 1991

Wolfe, Thomas W., *The Soviet Quest for More Globally Mobile Military Power*, Memorandum RM5554-PR, December, 1967

Winterford, David, 'Assessing the Soviet Naval Build-up in Southeast Asia: Threats to Regional Security', Naval Postgraduate School

Yee, Andy, 'Maritime Territorial Disputes in East Asia: A Comparative Analysis of the South China Sea and East China Sea', *Journal of Current Chinese Affairs*, 2011

Zagoria, Donald S., 'The End of the Cold War in Asia: Its Impact on China', *Proceedings of Academy of Political Science*, Vol.38, No.2, The China Challenge: American Policies in East Asia, 1991

Primary Sources

Documents, Ministry of Foreign Affairs, Socialist Republic of Vietnam, April, 1988, file:///C:/Users/User%20Account/Downloads/42905-bngvietnam88.pdf

Documents, Ministry of Foreign Affairs, Republic of Vietnam, 1975 file:///C:/Users/User%20Account/Downloads/lpbcta_1975_vietnam%20claims%20of%20spratlys%20part%201_002.pdf

United States-Vietnam Relations, 1945-1967, Vietnam Task Force, Office of the Secretary of Defense, I, (Pentagon papers, declassified), https://www.archives.gov/research/pentagon-papers/

Declassified National Security Agency report https://www.nsa.gov/public_info/_files/gulf_of_tonkin/articles/rel2_gulf_tonkin_incident_desoto.pdf

Address to the Nation on the War in Vietnam, November 3, 1969, p-691101, 11/3/1969 www.nixonlibrary.gov/forkids/speechesforkids/silentmajority/silentmajority_transcript.pdf

Declassified secret report, Studies in Intelligence, Central Intelligence Agency, Volume 30, 1986, www.foia.cia.gov/sites/default/files/DOC_0000620600.pdf

The People's Liberation Army Navy, August 2009, pp.5,6, http://fas.org/irp/agency/oni/pla-navy.pdf

The Law on the Territorial Sea and the Contiguous Zone on 25th February 1992, *UN* http://www.un.org/depts/los/LEGISLATIONANDTREATIES/PDFFILES/CHN_1992_Law.pdf

Territorial Sea and Contiguous Zone', Section 1: General provisions, *United Nations Convention on the Law of the Sea*, http://www.un.org/depts/los/convention_agreements/texts/unclos/unclos_e.pdf

National Defense policy', China's National Defense in 2004, http://www.china.org.cn/e-white/20041227/

Executive Summary, 'Joint Submission to the Commission on the Limits of the Continental Shelf pursuant to the Article 76, Paragraph 8 of the United Nations Convention on the Law of the Sea 1982 in respect of the southern part of the South China Sea', Malaysia, Socialist Republic of Vietnam, May, 2009, http://www.un.org/depts/los/clcs_new/submissions_files/mysvnm33_09/mys_vnm2009excutivesummary.pdf

Permanent Missions of the Socialist Republic of Viet Nam to the United Nations, No.86/HC-2009, 8th May, 2009, http://www.un.org/depts/los/clcs_new/submissions_files/mysvnm33_09/vnm_chn_2009re_

mys_vnm_e.pdf
'Vietnam National Defence', Socialist republic of Vietnam, Ministry of Defence, Hanoi
Defence Intelligence Organisation, Govt. of Australia
Bureau of Public Affairs, U.S. Department of State, December 16, 2013, http://www.state.gov/r/pa/pl/2013/218776.htm
US Pacific Command' (USPACOM) website, http://www.pacom.mil/AboutUSPACOM.aspx
Department of Defense, United States of America, http://www.defense.gov/Portals/1/Documents/pubs/NDAA%20A-P_Maritime_SecuritY_Strategy-08142015-1300-FINALFORMAT.PDF
Indian Navy website
Annual Reports, Ministry of External Affairs, Government of India
White Papers, Department of Defence, Australian Government, http://www.defence.gov.au/WhitePaper/Docs/2016-Defence-White-Paper.pdf
Documents U.S Department of State, http://www.state.gov/p/io/potusunga/207375.htm
Interviews with scholars

Web Sources

www.jstor.org/
http://www.sipri.org/
http://www.globaltimes.cn/content/925267.shtml
http://chinesejil.oxfordjournals.org/content/1/1/94.full.pdf
http://www.navy.gov.au/sites/default/files/documents/IntSP_2_JapaneseSP.pdf
https://www.archives.gov/research/pentagon-papers/
http://www.rand.org/content/dam/rand/pubs/research_memoranda
http://www.heritage.org/research/reports
http://calhoun.nps.edu/bitstream/handle/10945/28864/assessingsovietn00wint.pdf?sequence=1
http://www.nytimes.com
http://www.history.navy.mil/research/library/online-reading-room
https://www.nsa.gov/public_info/_files
www.nixonlibrary.gov
www.foia.cia.gov/sites/default/files
http://www.tonthatthien.com
http://fas.org/irp/agency/oni/pla-navy.pdf
http://www.ait.org.tw/en/taiwan-relations-act.html
http://nationalinterest.org/commentary/
http://thediplomat.com/

http://www.un.org/depts/los
http://www.un.org/depts/los/convention_agreements/texts/unclos/unclos_e.pdf
http://www.chinaembassy.ee/eng/ztlm/zfbps/t112926.htm
http://www.china.org.cn/e-white/20041227/
http://www.un.org/depts/los/clcs_new/submissions_files/mysvnm33_09/mys_vnm2009excutivesummary.pdf
http://www.washingtonpost.com
http://www.bbc.com/news/world-asia-
http://www.economist.com/blogs/
http://en.hainan.gov.cn/englishgov/Government/201001/t20100107_40311.html
http://www.telegraph.co.uk/news/worldnews/asia/
http://www.defence.gov.au/dio/documents/det_10.pdf
http://news.xinhuanet.com/english/china/
http://www.theguardian.com/world/
https://www.rt.com/news/
http://www.chinadaily.com.cn/world
http://www.scmp.com/news/china/article
http://www.voanews.com
http://zeenews.india.com/news/world
http://www.ibtimes.com
http://amti.csis.org/
http://manilastandardtoday.com/news/
http://uk.reuters.com/article/
http://www.thejakartapost.com/news
http://www.wsj.com/articles/
http://www.philstar.com/headlines
http://www.state.gov/
http://www.foxnews.com/world/
https://www.washingtonpost.com/world
https://ifr16.indiannavy.gov.in/writereaddata/images/pdf/maritime_strat.pdf
http://articles.economictimes.indiatimes.com
http://indianexpress.com/article/
http://www.business-standard.com/article
http://www.thehindu.com
http://www.mea.gov.in/
http://foreignpolicy.com
http://www.japantimes.co.jp/news
http://csis.org/publication/
http://jakartaglobe.beritasatu.com/news
http://www.hindustantimes.com

http://www.themua.org/vietnam/prt.php?content=prt4
http://www.oslo2000.uio.no/program/papers/m1b/m1b-hamashita.pdf,
http://www.silk-road.com/artl/marcopolo.shtml

Newspaper

The Statesman
The Hindu
The Telegraph
The Times of India

Journals

Foreign Affairs
Frontline
International Affairs
India Quarterly
India Today
Journal of Southeast Asian Studies
Review of International Studies
Economic and Political Weekly

Index